What to Do Until the Grownup Arrives

The Art and Science of Raising Teenagers

Also by Joseph R. Novello

❏ *Bringing Up Kids American Style*, Dr. Novello's basic formula for parents: Establishing family values, How to communicate with children, A 6-Step approach to discipline without hassles, How to work yourself out of a job. A practical, everyday guide to raising children. A&W Publishers [1981, 212 pp] $10.95

❏ *How To Survive Your Kids*, Dr Novello's answers to the questions most often asked by parents. Based upon developmental stages from pregnancy through age 10. This book is based upon Dr. Novello's column, "You and Your Child," which appears weekly in *Woman's World* magazine. McGraw-Hill [1988, 348 pp] $12.95

❏ *The Four Stages of Teenage Drug Abuse.* [Single page article.] How to spot the warning signs and what to do about them. $0.75

❏ *Discipline Is Not a Dirty Word.* [Single page article.] A summary of Dr. Novello's successful discipline formula. The most effective techniques, including: parent example, positive reinforcement, logical consequences, contracts, and punishment that teaches. $0.75

These items are available for purchase, via a nonprofit foundation in Washington DC. Please add $2.50 for postage and handling, make checks or money orders payable to Lifeline, Inc and send to Lifeline, Inc, Box 25694, Washington DC 20007. Please allow several weeks for mailing.

What to Do Until the Grownup Arrives

The Art and Science of Raising Teenagers

Joseph R. Novello, M.D.

Hogrefe & Huber Publishers
Seattle • Toronto • Bern • Göttingen

Library of Congress Cataloging-in-Publication Data

Novello, Joseph R.
    What to do until the grownup arrives : the art and science of raising
teenagers / by Joseph R. Novello.
    p.   cm.
    Includes index.
    ISBN 0-88937-040-0 : $24.50
    1. Parent and teenager—United States. I. Title
HQ799.15.N68   1992
649'.125—dc20

91-18659
CIP

Canadian Cataloguing in Publication Data

Novello, Joseph R.
    What to do until the grownup arrives

ISBN 0-88937-040-0

    1. Teenagers.   2. Child rearing.   3. Parent and child.
    4. Adolescent psychology.   I. Title.

HQ799.15.N68   1992   649'.125   C91-094277-3

P.O. Box 2487, Kirkland, WA 98083-2487
12-14 Bruce Park Ave., Toronto, Ontario M4P 2S3

Printed in the U.S.A.

ISBN 0-88037-042-0
Hogrefe & Huber Publishers, Seattle • Toronto
ISBN 3-456-81871-8
Verlag Hans Huber, Bern • Göttingen

Contents

Acknowledgements

In some ways this book wrote itself over a period of years.

My special interest in adolescent psychiatry dates from my residency training at the University of Michigan, where I was blessed with exciting and stimulating mentors such as Will Hendrickson and Derek Miller. It was later nurtured in my early years of practice in Washington, D.C. by colleagues such as John Meeks and the late Reg Lourie.

By the time I became a teacher myself it was a given that I would be asked to lecture the students and residents of Georgetown University on the subject of adolescence. Many of those lectures have, in one way or another, found themselves into these pages. I am grateful to my colleagues and students at Georgetown for their contributions to this book.

Similarly, my call-in radio programs on WMAL and WRC and my segments on WJLA-TV often focused upon teenagers and have provided a good sounding board for the advice within.

Most of the questions and answers in *What to Do Until the Grownup Arrives* have been adapted from my weekly column in *Woman's World Magazine.* Appreciation is due to my Editors-in-Chief Dennis Neeld and Dena Vane, to Executive Director Stephanie Saible, and to Features Editor Esther Davidowitz. Special thanks to the column's on-line editors over the past nine years: Maris Cakers, Norm Zeitchik, Joan Klein, Karen Kreps, Joe Gustaitus, and Kathy Fitzpatrick.

Although they must remain anonymous, my adolescent patients and their families have left their mark throughout. While it may be true that the only thing tougher than being a teenager is to be the parent of a teenager, perhaps even tougher than being the parent of an adolescent is to be an adolescent psychiatrist. But I wouldn't trade it. The therapist who shares the burden of struggle with an angry 13-year-old or a depressed 17-year-old shares a journey of hope and is given much along the way. This book, I hope, begins to repay that debt.

Susan Barrows was the editor of one of my earlier books, *The Short Course in Adolescent Psychiatry.* It was pure serendipity when, at a recent annual meeting of the American Psychiatric Association, she introduced me to Tom Tabasz of Hogrefe & Huber Publishers. Thanks to Susan for the intro and to Tom for his invaluable help.

Lo Ann Ward has been my administrative assistant and right hand for ten years. Our books in common have spanned the technological advances from manual typewriter to Selectric to word processor. Like the equipment, Lo Ann only gets better with time.

My wife Toni, as a pediatrician, has always made substantive contributions to my literary efforts, but this time there is a difference. While she is still spouse of the author, her husband is now spouse of the U.S. Surgeon General — and proud of it.

Introduction

"It was the best of times, it was the worst of times, it was the age of wisdom, it was the age of foolishness...it was the season of Light, it was the season of Darkness, it was the spring of hope, it was the winter of despair."

Charles Dickens,
A Tale of Two Cities

In describing the mood of the times for his epic about the French Revolution, Dickens has also beautifully and unwittingly captured, as perhaps only a great novelist can, something of the paradoxical joys and sorrows of that stage of life called adolescence.

Adolescence. Nothing matters in our lives quite as much as it matters in adolescence. That's why it is tough to be a teenager, almost as tough as being the parent of one.

This is a book written to help parents help their kids. It is based on the questions that parents around the country have most commonly asked me about raising teenagers. It is drawn from my clinical practice of psychiatry, my lectures, my magazine column, my radio and television programs, and my review of the literature.

What to Do Until the Grownup Arrives describes a different world than we knew as adolescents. Simply doing things the way our parents did (or opposite of how our parents did things) will not work. Today's teen scene requires that mothers and fathers *get informed* about the world their youngsters inhabit, *get involved* in the lives of their sons and daughters as never before, and *get in*

charge of their adolescents, while at the same time gently working themselves out of a job.

In Chapter 1, "The Principles of Parentcraft," I've attempted to distill the essence: the basic building blocks for successfully steering your teenagers through the years 'twixt twelve and twenty.

The remainder of the book is designed along developmental lines: pre-adolescence (11–12), early adolescence (13–14), middle adolescence (15–16), and late adolescence (17+). The terrain shifts rapidly through these stages and with it your teenagers' strengths and vulnerabilities, challenges and opportunities. You must change too as you ride that developmental roller coaster with your sons and daughters. The ride can be fun — and it can be perilous. I hope my practical responses to the practical questions posed by parents like yourself will ease the perils and restore the fun.

As I stress in the first chapter, good parents are made, not born. You have to work at it. That's why I've written this book in the form of a study course: principles, questions and answers, quizzes. You'll learn a lot about yourself too.

Apply the knowledge in this book. Make it work. Your sons and daughters may not thank you for it now, but I hope that in future years, whatever life has in store for them, they'll look back and feel satisfied, on balance, with themselves, and how they were raised. That, in the face of the world's uncertainties and our own human limitations, spells success — for them and for you.

Joseph R. Novello
Washington, DC

1

Principles of Parentcraft

Perhaps psychiatrists should not be surprised by their patients' requests, but I must admit I was caught a bit off guard when one day, a few years ago, I was asked for an unusual favor. I had been seeing this particular man, his wife, and their two teenagers in family therapy for several months. Although the treatment initially had involved some bumpy going, things were going well now: the 15-year-old son, once a cauldron of rage, was no longer threatening to run away; the 13-year-old daughter was no longer lonely and depressed; Mom was no longer threatening divorce; and Dad was grateful for having his family back again. However, the treatment was about to end because the family was leaving Washington, D.C. to move to Florida. Since there still remained some unfinished business, I had urged continued therapy and had even given them the name of a respected colleague in their new city. But, in their last session with me, the father, an attorney, made a strong case for trying it on their own without the recommended treatment.

"We've come a long way," said Dad, "and we just need some time to put into practice all the things we've learned." Mom and the kids agreed. But there was a catch. "What we'd like you to do," Dad continued, "is to write out a list

of principles that will help us. Kind of a checklist to keep us on target."

An intriguing proposition, but I was cautious. "There's no way I can prescribe for you how to lead your lives," I answered.

"Oh no, we know you too well to ask that," responded the son, chuckling as he recalled my many disclaimers and admonitions from previous sessions.

Dad picked up the ball. "Just give us the basic guidelines, something we can refer to when we need it. We'll make our own modifications as we go along. We have the confidence now." And, knowing what I must have been thinking, he added cleverly, "You can keep it brief. Just a couple of pages."

Now it was my turn to chuckle. "So you want the *One-Minute Parent*, eh?"

I wish I could report to you that, stimulated by this surprise, I quickly agreed and that the family, armed with my guidelines, is now living happily in the Sunshine State. But I passed up their request. Instead, I reviewed with them the history of their conflicts, and how we had resolved most of them. It was a good exercise, and they were pleased, if not entirely satisfied. However, I'm the one who was not content. From time to time, the family's unique but reasonable request would float back up into my

1

conscious awareness. A list of principles. A checklist. Guidelines to staying on target. Well, the family is living happily in the Sunshine State now and I've finally accepted their challenge.

My "Principles of Parentcraft" is a distillation of the concepts and techniques that I have found most successful in helping adolescents and their parents. It is founded in the three gets:

- Get Informed
- Get Involved
- Get in Charge

This book is not intended to be an exhaustive, everything-you-ever-wanted-to-know-about-raising-teenagers tome, even though it has grown well beyond the "couple of pages" originally requested. Parenting is far too complex to be captured in the pages of one chapter, or even one book. Although the general approach is explained and illustrated extensively with the help of some 500 specific, but brief, case examples, I urge you to also study the overall principles carefully, and to make your own modifications with increasing confidence.

This brief summary chapter, and the book which has grown up around it, may be too late for the family that got this project started, but I'm comforted to know they no longer need it. And so it is with gratitude to them that I now offer it to you and your family.

Get Informed

Good parents, like good managers, really are made, not born. If you want to be a good parent, you have to work at it.

But there's so much to learn. Where to start? Do you read books? Take courses? Talk to other parents? All of the above will help build the knowledge and skill you will need to raise adolescents, and I encourage you to make a serious study of parenting — the most important management job you will ever have. Getting informed, however, also means learning

about yourself. After all, you are the most powerful influence in your youngster's life, and although you will discover many practical techniques in this book for bringing up teenagers, techniques, when all is said and done, are simply artificial devices to help you develop your full potential as a parent until the grownup arrives.

Know Your Own Values. Unfortunately, few parents take the time to stop and ask themselves just what it is they believe in. Fewer take the time to accurately communicate these values to their teenagers. But, your personal belief system is the most powerful force of all when it comes to creating the kind of person your youngster will be — whether you know it or not, your belief system is being transmitted to your son or daughter through your daily behavior. Values, after all, are caught more often than taught.

So, as a first step, I urge you to take your own personal moral inventory. To help get you started, I'll list a number of values that I believe American teenagers need to succeed in today's world. Please don't take my list as gospel — delete, add, personalize. Then, communicate your beliefs to your youngsters through word and action.

Religion, Philosophy. Without religious and philosophical beliefs, life is empty and meaningless. Without a moral code that is put into action in your daily life, there is no integrity.

Love. Love, according to Harry Stack Sullivan, is when the happiness and security of the other person means as much to you as your own happiness and security. A golden rule of family life.

Empathy. The ability to see with another person's eyes, to hear with another person's ears, to feel with another person's heart.

Self-Esteem. The youngster who is loved for who he is, rather than for what he does, can learn to love himself. A cliché? No way. It's a fundamental fact of life.

Trust. Can you be trusted? Are you reliable, honest, consistent? These are the elements of trust. The teenager who can trust her parents learns to trust others and to become trustworthy herself.

The Courage To Do Your Best. Happy teenagers, like happy adults, find joy in performing at their full potential. They reap the harvest of perseverance. Happy teenagers are kids who are good at something. When everything else seems to be going wrong (as it often does in adolescence), they can say: "Hold it. I'm OK. I'm not perfect — I have my faults. But I am good at some things too!" Good results create good feelings. But good feelings can also result from failure. The courage to do your best also means that youngsters must dare to reach beyond themselves on occasion. After all, limited goals yield only limited results. One thing is for sure: the youngster who sometimes dares to reach for the stars will not come up grasping a handful of mud.

Respect for Law and for What Is Right. Teenagers must learn respect not only for the law, but also for human rights. Tolerance for others' beliefs and differences is a rock upon which America is built. And let's not forget another quality that distinguishes free people: a healthy skepticism of the status quo. To paraphrase Thoreau: while it is desirable to cultivate a respect for the law, it is even more desirable to cultivate a respect for what is right.

The Loyal Opposition. One must agree to disagree and to do it within the framework of existing rules, procedures, and conventions. Learning how to be a tough, but law-abiding, opponent is a lesson that should be learned in adolescence. It is a quality that distinguishes citizens of a well-functioning democracy.

Grace in Victory and in Defeat. Teens can learn it in the classroom, on the playing field, and in the home. It is an important lesson for them to carry forward into their adult lives.

With Privilege Comes Responsibility. The battle cry of every 13-year-old is "I Want To Be Free." Teens want more and more privileges. It goes with the territory. Your job is to allow them more and more choices as they mature. But it comes as a rude shock to many youngsters that freedom has a price: responsibility.

Discipline. The purpose of parental discipline is not to oppress, but to teach. The goal of discipline is to raise a youngster who learns self-discipline. Without it he won't get very far.

Stand Up for Your Beliefs. Drugs? Sex? Social injustice? It's tough for most early adolescents to "just say no," but if they don't learn from you how to stand up for their beliefs, where will they learn? Teenagers (and adults) with such integrity are what stand between us and the abyss.

Charity and Social Interest. Giving something back to society — that's what this value is all about. Giving without asking, "What's in it for me?"

Laughter and Good Humor. What is the prevailing mood in your family? Irritation, anger, sadness? I hope not. In my clinical experience, I have found that the family that values good humor, the family that laughs together, is likely to be a healthy family. Yes, you might argue that it is a circular argument, i.e., they laugh because they're healthy, not vice versa, but I encourage you to try it. Laughter, scientists have discovered, is good medicine. Share jokes, poke some good-natured fun at each other, and above all, dare to laugh at yourself.

Tradition. The sum of your values defines you as a person, but to give your teenagers life, you must celebrate them as a tradition. How? Keep it simple. A mother and father in the Washington area gave their children what they called "honor pebbles" — stones collected from summertime strolls along the Delaware beaches, to mark special achievements and family events. The cherished pebbles were displayed atop dressers and desk tops as potent reminders of what mattered most. The children, now grown and married, still display these time-worn pebbles and have passed the tradition on to their own sons and daughters.

Tradition is like a psychological gyroscope maintaining the family steadfastly on course from one generation to the next: a celebration of what we believe, who we are.

Know the Parents of Your Teenager's Friends. Can you name your teenager's five closest friends? Do you know their parents? I hope so, and I hope you're in touch with them too. Teens compare notes — so should parents.

Wants vs Needs. Most teenagers have a long list of wants. The savvy parent, however, knows that the surest way to raise a spoiled child is to simply give her everything she wants. Your job is not only to respond judiciously to appropriate wants, but to make sure your adolescent gets what she needs. A sometime source of conflict? You bet. Bridging the gap between a youngster's wants and needs is the essence of being a good mother or father.

Today's Teen Scene. Getting informed means knowing something about the three stages of adolescence and the four tasks of adolescent development. It also means knowing something about the world your teenager has inherited. Things like drugs, sex, and rock 'n roll, to name a few. It's a different world from the one we knew as kids. Get informed. Of course, I hope you'll study these issues carefully in this book. But don't stop here — read what other experts are saying. Enroll in a parenting class. Who knows? You may discover a thing or two about yourself in the bargain.

Get Involved

Being informed is not enough. Being informed without being involved in your teenager's life is like knowing everything there is to know about growing roses, only to see them wither and fail because you neglect to water them. Adolescents, like roses, need plenty of nurturing. They need you.

Your Priorities. Are your children the top priority in your life? I hope not. A contradiction? Heresy from an author of a book about raising teenagers? Not at all. I believe your marriage should come first. After all, it predated the kids and you hope it will still be flourishing when the youngsters have grown and left you. But there are even stronger reasons for my position. I have found, as a child/adolescent psychiatrist, that happy marriages make for happy children. So, after your spouse, make sure your children come next in your scheme of things — before work, before friends, before everything. They didn't ask to be brought into the world. You did it. They need you, and they're the most important responsibility you'll ever have.

The Myth of Quality Time. There are no shortcuts to raising teenagers. While the quality of your involvement certainly counts, there is no substitute for quantity regardless of the prevailing paperback wisdom or the rationalizations of some busy, busy parents. The wholesale emphasis on so-called parental quality time is a leftover of a self-indulgent decade and the lingering whisper of the You-Can-Have-It-All shills. Simply put, raising children takes time, lots of time — your time.

Successful Teens. Studies have shown that teenagers who have achieved remarkable success in academics, sports, music, and the arts share one thing in common. Interestingly, it isn't a first-class genetic pedigree, an astronomical IQ, family wealth, or physical endowment. It is parents who have actively supported and participated in their interests. Parents of successful teenagers show that they care by being there: by chauffeuring their teenagers to early morning swimming practice, by staying up with them for late night study sessions.

Involvement Yes, Intrusion No. Is it possible for a parent to be too involved? You bet. Some parents view their child as narcissistic extensions of themselves. They drive their youngsters to over-achieve in order to fulfill their own private dreams. Kids usually resent this kind of intrusion, as they well should. Teens must be allowed the freedom to define their own interests. Your job, as a parent, is to facilitate those interests with your own active support and involvement.

Be a Parent, Not a Best Friend. It may be tempting, as your teenager matures, for you to want to be her best friend. I hope you resist that temptation. The parent who attempts to out-adolescent her adolescent may end up without a friend or a daughter. The roles of best friend and parent are not compatible. Having a peer as confidant and best friend is an important part of growing up. Don't rob your adolescent of that developmental opportunity. Be friendly, but not a best friend. You don't have to be a boss and you need not be a buddy.

Get in Charge

Someone has to be in charge of the family. That someone should be you, not your adolescent. Now I don't believe that teenagers get up in the morning plotting how they're going to make your life miserable, and I don't suggest that you have to rule with a heavy hand. The best formula: be firm, but gentle.

Your Parenting Style. Parents sometimes ask: is it better to be authoritarian or permissive? Let's take a look. Teenagers raised by no-nonsense authoritarian parents may be outwardly compliant, but they tend to keep their problems inside: anger, resentment, and tension headaches among other symptoms. Teenagers raised by laissez-faire, permissive parents tend to wear their problems on the outside: forever seeking the limits of self-indulgence. They end up in conflict with society. That's why I recommend a middle course. I call it Participatory Parenting. The wise parent, while remaining in charge, allows his teenager to grow in responsibility and self-reliance through active participation in family decision-

making. I urge a game plan that ever so gently turns over the reins to the kids as they demonstrate their ability to handle more and more responsibility. After all, parenthood is all about raising a person. You want that person to eventually leave you as a mature, independent individual. So, hang in there, but don't hang on. Call it working yourself out of a job.

Communication. Communication, the cornerstone of successful parenting, is how you establish family values, how you stay involved, and how you remain in charge. That's why I've included so many tips on communication in this book. A few highlights:

Listen. The first and most important quality of a good communicator is the ability to listen. You can listen your way into a better relationship with your teenager, but you won't often be able to talk your way in.

Make It Positive. Try keeping a log of how you address your youngsters. Do you tend to order, warn, threaten, moralize, compare, belittle, criticize, shame, psychoanalyze? Instead, try encouragement, support, understanding, acceptance, and above all, empathy.

Facts vs Feelings. We adults live in a world of facts and we learn to communicate them well. Adolescents live largely in a world of feelings. We must learn how to communicate feelings too.

Say What You Mean. Be clear. Be concise. Avoid veiled threats, vague promises, innuendo, and mixed messages. Say what you really mean.

Mean What You Say. The clarity of what you communicate is only half of the equation. You must mean what you say, and be prepared to follow through consistently with rewards and punishments if they are warranted.

Praise. There's nothing like effective praise to encourage a teenager to do what you'd like him to do. But puffery and flattery will not work. Limit your praise to an observable event.

Criticism. That old standby, constructive criticism, is a crucial tool in communication.

Preserve your youngster's self-esteem by first telling him what he did correctly. Next, tell him what he did wrong. Then, invite his response and invite possible alternatives. Allow criticism to teach, not humiliate. Finally — keep it private.

Where To Draw the Line — Conflict Resolution. Conflict goes with the territory when you're raising a teenager, but you can make it manageable if you know where to draw the line. Certain things must be non-negotiable: your core family values, your adolescent's health and safety.

So many other conflicts are really about peripheral, negotiable items. Instead of making new rules on the spot whenever a difference develops, why not invite your son or daughter into the decision-making process. Given a chance, they'll often surprise you, pleasantly.

How To Draw the Line — Discipline. Discipline is not a dirty word. It is derived from the Latin word meaning "to teach." The goal of parental discipline, therefore, is to teach an adolescent to be self-disciplined. But, how do you do this?

Parental Example. The most effective teacher of discipline is you and your own behavior. Disciplined parents raise disciplined teenagers. You may have gotten away with some contradiction and hypocrisy in their earliest years, but now that they're adolescents, they'll call you on it. Teens learn more from what you do than from what you say.

Accentuate the Positive. Do you remember your own high school or college basic psychology course? If you want to teach a desired behavior, the most successful technique is to reward that behavior. In other words, catch 'em being good and let them know how proud you are of their actions.

Ignore the Negative. It's a well-known paradox that punishment often results in more, not less, misbehavior. While punishment is necessary, save it for those important non-negotiable family values. So much adolescent

misbehavior and limit-testing, if simply ignored, will disappear through its own inertia.

Chores. Chores teach self-discipline too. I believe that all teenagers should have assigned chores. It's their personal contribution to family life and it's not something they should be paid for, either. Believe it or not, adolescents like to feel needed; they like to contribute. Give them a chance.

Allowance. Even that time-honored American institution, the weekly allowance, can be used to teach self-discipline. After all, learning how to manage money is a necessary lesson for life. Deficit spending? Borrowing against the future because you've spent it all? You've seen where it's gotten the federal government. Instead, teach them how to spend wisely, to plan ahead, to save. Offer a few incentives along the way: if they want a bigger piece of the pie, let them do more of the baking.

Logical Consequences. Whenever possible, allow your teenager to learn from his own mistakes. What is the logical consequence of his action? There does not have to be a punitive parental solution to all adolescent misbehavior. Keep your powder dry for the things that really matter.

Contracts. Persistent misbehavior of a specific sort may call for a contract — the family version of "Let's Make A Deal." Identify the problem. Allow your teen to suggest solutions. Select one and try it out. Be clear about what the consequence will be if the misbehavior continues. In this way, if your son or daughter fails to live by the solution, he or she will have chosen to suffer the consequence. Contracts teach negotiating skills, problem-solving, and responsibility, and they keep you out of the punishment role.

Punishment. Punishment is last on the list because, while necessary, it is a less effective teacher of discipline than the other techniques. Yet you can increase the effectiveness (teaching power) of your punishment by: punishing a specific misbehavior rather than humiliating your youngster, making it immediate, applying it without anger or malice, making it consistent, doing it in private, having a hierarchy of options from simple scolding to various restrictions of privileges. Remember: over-reaction is ultimately as self-defeating as under-reaction. And remember also that after the punishment is delivered, the slate is wiped clean. Welcome your teen back quickly into your good graces.

Going for Help. Do not hesitate to seek professional help. As a child/adolescent psychiatrist it troubles me that too many parents delay or avoid professional consultation. On the other hand, I understand. There are any number of barriers: shame, guilt, stigma, denial, the hope that "it's only a phase," financial constraints, and, of course, a teenager's own reluctance. Some parents rationalize the delay by leaving it up to the kids: "When's she's ready, she'll ask for help." Don't wait for them to hit bottom. Teenagers don't want to visit the pediatrician or the dentist either, but you can still manage to get them there. My experience is that if an adolescent looks like she's in psychological trouble, she's probably in a lot more trouble than you think. And while time may be running out in some respects, time is also on a teenager's side. Physicians like me are drawn to adolescent psychiatry because our young patients are so workable. They offer a therapist the best of both worlds: the plasticity of childhood and the power of self-observation of adulthood. They may not be thrilled about coming to see us. That's our problem. But you have to get them to us first.

Letting Go. When the grownup finally arrives, what then? What about the helpless infant you cuddled in your arms, that sassy toddler who wouldn't accept "No" for an answer, the 7-year-old you nursed through a long feverish night, the awkward adolescent you coached through her first date, the beaming 18-year-old standing on stage clutching his high school diploma? Are those days really gone forever? Of course. Does your son or daughter no longer need you? Of course not. He still needs you but he needs you in new ways. And, believe it or not, one day soon you will need him, but that's another chapter for another book.

So for now, Mom and Dad, you can breathe a sigh of longing, but also of relief. For you it is also a time to get on with life, an exciting time of new beginnings, a time to recall the wisdom of Gibran:

> *"You are the bows from which your children as living arrows are sent forth. The archer sees the mark upon the path of the infinite and He bends you with His might that His arrows may go swift and far. Let your bending in the archer's hand be for gladness. For even as He loves the arrow that flies, so He loves also the bow that is stable."*[1]

---

1. Gibran, K. (1965). *The Prophet*, p. 17. New York: Alfred Knopf.

2

Pre-Teens (11-12)

Things start to get a little tricky here.

While most 9- or 10-year-olds are pretty much alike from a developmental standpoint, youngsters begin moving at a more individualized pace at 11 and 12. It's as though children break out of the lockstep of the latency stage (5-10), and begin parading and dancing to their own drumbeats.

Even the designation "teen" is not an entirely satisfactory description of all these youngsters. Early-developing girls, for example, may well experience their first menstrual period at age 11 and be launched into puberty. Some of these girls can be considered "adolescent," some can't, because their emotional maturity lags behind their physical maturity.

A major result of this uneven development is that youngsters may lose touch with their age group, their natural peers. This sets in motion a phenomenon that will accelerate in the next few years, and which can result in a lot of tension for kids — and their parents.

Parents notice that something is changing. That docile, orderly latency-stage child is becoming a little difficult. Study the questions and answers in this chapter carefully. They should help you understand your pre-adolescent and they could form the basis of your own preparation for the next stage of your child's life: early adolescence. You might consider, therefore, pre-adolescence as a preview of coming attractions.

Stay tuned.

Discipline

Six Steps to Discipline

Discipline can be relatively hassle-free. Try this proven six-step formula:
1) parental example,
2) accentuate the positive,
3) ignore the negative,
4) logical consequences,
5) behavior contracts,
6) punishment.

Q: My children, 11 and 14, are getting out of control. They just will not accept any discipline at all. I've tried just about every punishment in the book, but nothing seems to work. SOS.

A: Punishment ranks very low as a teacher of discipline. You are probably missing many opportunities to teach real discipline to the children because you are jumping immediately to the punishment solution instead of using other, more effective techniques.

Try my six-step formula for achieving discipline without hassles:

1) *Parental example.* The most effective tool of discipline, by far, is for you to set a good parental example of self-discipline. I don't mean you have to be perfect — none of us is perfect, but try your best to set the right tone in your own home.

2) *Accentuate the positive.* Miss no opportunity to praise your children when they do things right. This is also called the art of catching 'em when they're good. Praise and reward are better than punishment any day.

3) *Ignore the negative.* That's right. Stop and think about it. Most misbehavior of children can be safely ignored. This theory works. When negative behavior is ignored, it dies a quiet death. (But do not ignore behavior that jeopardizes health and safety, or behavior that violates important family values.)

4) *Logical consequences.* Let your children learn from their own mistakes whenever possible. Remember, there does not have to be a parental solution to every problem.

5) *Contract.* If you have identified a specific pattern of misbehavior, talk it over with your child. Explain your position. Ask for his ideas. Try to make him part of the solution. Finally, be very clear about what he can expect if the misbehavior continues. In this way you're putting the decision up to him. If he chooses to misbehave, he chooses to lose a privilege. You are removed from the hassle.

6) *Punishment.* Yes, there is a place for punishment, but it comes last because it is simply not as effective as the other five methods. Punishment should be consistent and "fit the crime," and you should have a graduated response plan that ranges from scolding, through timeouts, to restriction of privileges.

Spanking comes last. It's effectiveness is mostly limited to pre-verbal children. It should be used sparingly.

Remember, the word "discipline" derives from the Latin meaning "to teach." Discipline, therefore, is not a dirty word. The goal of parental discipline is to teach youngsters self-discipline, without which they will not be able to grow into independent, productive adults who will utilize their full potential in life.

Rewards Yes, Bribes No

Q: My 11-year-old son, Erik, has a mind of his own. Lately, he won't do a thing we ask. I've tried to reason with him. My husband has tried punishment. Nothing has worked, until last night, when my husband offered Rick $5 if he would come with us for a visit to his aunt and uncle. Erik took the money and came with us, but I don't like it. I told my husband that it's bribery, but he's so frustrated that he says he'll do anything that works. What do you say?

Rewards (positive reinforcement) are powerful motivators. Bribes will backfire.

A: Bribery, for the short term, will work, but you will end up paying a greater price both financially and emotionally. Furthermore, Erik will not learn much about discipline or family life; he'll learn how to be a good huckster.

There is a tremendous difference between rewarding a youngster when he does something especially praiseworthy and paying him a fee to do something that is expected of him. The first response is called "reward," the second is a form of "bribery."

Bribery not only robs you of money, it robs you of your parental role. It also robs Erik himself. It robs him of learning the value of cooperation and self-discipline.

So, reward Erik, but do not bribe him.

Don't Complete His Work

Q: Our middle child, Barry, 11, never seems to complete his chores or his schoolwork. It infuriates us, but it doesn't bother him at all. Is this simple procrastination? What should we do?

All behavior has a reason. Try to identify the goals of procrastination and remove them. When the behavior no longer results in the desired goals, it will change.

A: No. The typical procrastinator puts things off to the last minute, then he wraps up the job. Barry just isn't getting the job done at all.

Why? It's difficult to say, but you can try this test: Why is Barry a non-performer? What are his hidden goals of misbehavior? Remember this behavior makes sense to your son.

For example, if he's secretly seeking attention, he's sure getting it. If he fears success, he's avoiding it. If he's out to frustrate Mom and Dad, he's doing a good job of it.

The plan? Deny Barry what you estimate to be the hidden goal of his behavior. When you hit on the answer, he'll have to change because the behavior is no longer working for him.

Before you start, have a talk with Barry. Show concern and be helpful, but make it his problem, not yours. For example, if he's simply overwhelmed by some tasks, show him how he can break the job into smaller parts and make it more manageable.

Aim to reward Barry for a job well done, but try to avoid punishment, if possible, for incomplete work. Keep it positive.

What Price Obedience?

Youngsters raised in overly strict, authoritarian homes may be obedient, but may pay a price for it in apathy and passivity. Steer a middle course between authoritarian and permissive parenting.

Q: My husband runs the family like a drill instructor. He's obsessed with obedience. "You have to train the kids to obey, obey, obey," he says. Well, our children, 11 and 13, obey, but I'm not sure it's so good for them. They're like little robots. They can't think for themselves. They bring everything to Dad to decide. What do you think about this?

A: You can force children into blind obedience, but, as you suggest, you (and they) pay a price for it.

Researchers at the University of North Carolina, after studying over 100 youngsters, concluded that children who are raised by do-it-because-I-say-so parents tend to be easily distracted and uncreative; they have little intellectual curiosity and tend to be passive and apathetic.

Children, of course, must be taught to respect the core values of the family, to keep the basic rules. At the same time, however, it's important to instill in them a healthy skepticism. Kids should be encouraged to ask questions, to express their ideas and their feelings.

Steer a middle course between being authoritarian and permissive. That's your best bet to raise children who have a healthy respect for authority, but who can, and will, think for themselves.

Southern Exposure?

Q: We've just moved to the Deep South from the Boston area with our two children, 11 and 12½. The kids were amazed (and scared) that so many of their new friends regularly get "whooped" (whipped) by their parents. Any comments?

There is no place for spanking and physical punishment in the teaching of discipline to pre-teens and teens.

A: Child discipline practices do follow regional biases.

For example, a national poll by the Gordon S. Block Corp. asked parents if they thought it was child abuse when a parent hits a youngster with a belt or switch without leaving marks.

In the Northeast U.S., 52% of respondents answered "Yes." But in the South, only 18% said "Yes." Other results: Great Lakes, 35%; Central, 27%; West, 32%.

Be sure to reassure your children that you do not plan to change your discipline practices. What worked in Boston will work in Biloxi, so to speak.

Me? I do not believe that physical punishment has a place in child discipline. It's potentially abusive and less effective than other forms of punishment. It's based on power, and one thing is for sure: you may have the power now, but just wait another year or two!

She Wants To Be Spanked

Q: Believe it or not, Karin, our 11-year-old, wants to be spanked. She's been acting up lately and when we threaten to punish her, she says, "OK, aren't you going to spank me?" We haven't spanked her in years, so we've been confused. Finally, my husband gave in. He put her over his knee and spanked her. Now, of course, Karin wants more! What's going on here? Should we spank her or not?

The youngster who appears to seek punishment may do so because of underlying guilt or poor self-esteem. For some pre-teens it may even have sexual overtones.

A: No. Spanking is not the answer to this problem. The first step is to understand Karin's puzzling behavior. There are several possibilities. Karin may be feeling guilty about something and is, therefore, seeking punishment. But why spanking? She may be regressing to an earlier childlike behavior because her guilt involves some new adolescent-flavored issues such as worries about sexuality. Her return to spanking, then, is part of her psychological avoidance.

And the plot thickens. I notice that Karin was spanked by her father. This increases my suspicion that Karin may unconsciously equate spanking with sexual arousal. It goes something like this: Karin has sexual thoughts or feelings (natural for early-developing 11-year-old girls). She feels guilty and seeks a punishment that curiously may symbolically satisfy her sexual impulses at the same time. Hence her "punishment" serves a dual purpose: atonement and satisfaction.

I realize that my interpretation may sound a bit far-fetched. And I don't mean to imply that all spanking has sexual over-tones. But, given the information you've provided, it is a strong possibility in this case.

How to respond? No spanking. At best, it's simply not necessary. At worst, Dad could be an unwitting participant in Karin's unconscious drama. I suggest that you have a good talk with her. Keep it general. How's she feeling about herself — that sort of thing. Be sure, however, to use the talk as an opportunity to discuss sexuality. At 11, Karin needs such a frank discussion anyway.

Put a Contract out on Your Own Son?

A written behavioral contract is an effective device to deal with chronic misbehavior.

Q: When my son Petey, 11, first started telling me about the new neighbors, I thought they might be gangsters or something. I mean they punish their son by "putting a contract on him" or something. Now that I know a little bit more about it, I think I get the picture. Can you tell me more about "contracts" for children?

A: You must be talking about a behavioral contract. It's a good device, especially when a youngster has a chronic problem in a specific area such as lateness, not doing chores, and so forth.

It works like this: You talk the problem over first, then you write out a "contract" that contains a description of the desired behavior, the consequences (punishment) for failing, and the rewards (if any) for succeeding. The contract should be discussed thoroughly and agreed to, preferably in writing.

The beauty of it is that it leaves very little to the imagination. The child knows exactly what to expect. In essence, he "decides" to accept the consequence if he fails to perform. It's automatic. Mom and Dad are not the bad guys of the piece — and you don't have to come up with a new response in the face of every misbehavior.

Ignore the Negative

Punishment has a definite place in teaching discipline, but it can sometimes lead, paradoxically, to more, not less, misbehavior. Sometimes it's best to simply ignore misbehavior.

Q: Our 12-year-old daughter, Erin, has become very negative. She opposes almost everything we say. My husband says we should "tough it out" and punish her whenever she breaks a rule. We've been following this principle, but Erin is winning. We're exhausted. Any ideas?

A: You husband is correct in wanting to remain "in charge" in the face of Erin's testing of your limits, but his efforts seem to be self-defeating. What is the goal of Erin's misbehavior? It may be simply to get your attention. If so, she has certainly succeeded, even if the "attention" that she's getting (punishment) is negative. Paradoxically, if a child's goal is attention, punishment can actually cause more, not less, misbehavior. Many youngsters go through such a stage at 12 or 13. It goes with the territory.

Some youngsters seek not attention, but revenge. For them, getting punished is a way of getting Mom and Dad shook up — a way of getting back at them. This is more serious and may indicate real hostility.

Most misbehavior can actually be ignored. That's right. Try ignoring Erin's actions unless they violate core family values or they threaten her health or safety. At the same time try to find opportunities to praise her positive behavior. Turn the tables on her. Get her back in the habit of getting attention on the positive side of life. The attention-seeking youngster will generally respond to this approach. The child who seeks revenge, or who is so despondent that she is locked into misbehavior, may require consultation. But first try to "eliminate the negative and accentuate the positive." If Erin latches on to the affirmative, you won't have to go any further.

How To Praise Your Child

Q: It seems strange to my husband and me, but our 11-year-old daughter just cannot handle praise. Whenever we compliment her, or try to give her a little boost, she gets very turned off and irritated. Do you have any suggestions?

Praise, like punishment, must be properly administered if you wish your pre-teen to learn from it. Try these steps: 1) praise, do not flatter, 2) praise the event, not the child, 3) beware praise that handcuffs your youngster.

A: I have found that some parents have difficulty when it comes to praising their children. Their boys and girls, in turn, become uncomfortable when they are on the receiving end of these well-intentioned compliments from Mom and Dad.

Try the following guidelines:

1) *Praise, not puffery.* There is nothing like flattery or puffery to really turn off kids. Therefore, try to avoid superlatives ("best," "greatest," etc.) when praising children. Since youngsters know they're not the greatest thing to hit the streets since steel-belted radials, flattery and puffery will get you

nowhere. In fact, most youngsters get suspicious of this dishonest tactic. "What's Mom after?" they'll ask. Or, "I must really be a miserable creature if Mom has to go to such great lengths to find something good to say about me." Kids know instinctively that flattery is an empty gesture; it is easier to flatter than to praise. Flattery is aimed at artificially puffing up a child's self-esteem, e.g., "You must be one of the fastest runners in all of New England," while effective praise is a realistic statement about a specific accomplishment, e.g., "You ran a great race." Effective praise does more than just create good feelings between parent and child; it gives the youngster some realistic feedback about herself and assists her in finding her honest place in the world. Hype jobs may work on TV for laundry detergents, but they won't cut it with children.

2) *Praise the event, not the child.* Most children struggle against self-doubts and secrets about their imperfect inner worlds. Telling a youngster that he's a "wonderful boy" because he was so nice to the minister when he visited the house may make the boy cringe. He probably doesn't feel "wonderful" and may have secretly resented the minister's presence since it kept him from watching Monday Night Football. But expressing pride in the way he helped to serve the carrot cake will accomplish your purpose: to reward his positive behavior with a kind word.

Another reason, of course, to limit your praise to an observable event is that youngsters will learn to distrust parental judgement entirely if you get too lavish and inaccurate in your comments.

3) *Beware the golden handcuffs.* Praise can be a weapon that ensnares and traps. Youngsters who are continually overpraised for accomplishments learn instinctively to resent it because it implies that they are expected to do better and better, perhaps to be perfect. This can be frightening to children. It also implies that love and good feelings from Mom and Dad are contingent on what children do, not on who they are. Such tactics trap kids into a tight set of parental expectations. It's like locking them into golden handcuffs. Children start wondering if Mom and Dad can ever really be satisfied. They begin to worry about failing for fear that they will lose the parental praise that they come to equate with love. Such youngsters may be driven to continuous accomplishment which empties of meaning as soon as it is attained, for once they have received their parents' praise, they must go right back to work and make more A's, or win another race. These poor kids are always clutching emptiness in search of parental love. Some youngsters, on the other hand, feel so pressured to succeed that they simply stop

trying; they take revenge on their parents, not through success, but through failures. Beware the golden handcuffs.

Praise the Producers

Q: Our son, Freddy, is 12. My husband doesn't believe in praise. He says it will only give Freddy a big head. I try to make it up to Freddy and praise him every chance I get, but I realize it's probably not the right thing to do. Any suggestions?

A: Yes. Both you and your husband are erring to the extreme. Ask you husband how he would like it if he never received praise for a job well done. He'd feel resentful and unsure of himself. Now magnify those hurts by 100: that's how Freddy must feel.

On the other hand, your efforts to compensate also leave Freddy confused. He knows he's not the greatest. There are some things he does well (praise these accomplishments) and some things he doesn't do well (give realistic feedback and encouragement).

Both of you should use praise to teach, to encourage, and to produce more of the same positive behavior. Next time Freddy, for example, cleans his room, you can say: "I'm proud of the way you did that chore. When you do good work like that it gives me more time to spend with you doing fun things."

Praise, properly applied, is a powerful motivation. Make it realistic. Praise the event, not your child's personality.

Eat It All?

Q: It's a battle. My husband insists that our children, 12, 9, and 7, eat everything that they put on their plates. If they don't, he puts their plates into the refrigerator and they have to eat the food in the morning before they can eat breakfast. Imagine cold meatloaf and string beans at seven o'clock in the morning. The kids fight it, and I sneak them food at night, but then my husband accuses me of "sabotaging" him. What can I do?

A: It's a losing battle for everyone. First of all, your husband's plan is unreasonable. Children, like adults, sometimes take more food onto their plates than they can eat. It doesn't warrant punishment. Secondly, it's not a good idea to turn the family dinner hour into a test of wills. Finally, although I appreciate your sympathy for the children, your efforts are sure to create a split between you and Dad, and in the long haul, this could be the worst result of all.

You need a new plan. No more forced feeding. Insist only that the youngsters try not to take more than they can eat, and

Don't turn the dinner table into a battleground by insisting that your youngster eats absolutely everything on his plate. It's a battle you can't win.

they remain at the dinner table for a friendly family chat every night. Bon appétit.

Inconsistent Parent

Youngsters learn more from what you do than from what you say.

Q: My husband has always been inconsistent and it bothers him. It wasn't much of a problem when the children were younger, but now they're able to observe his behavior and they call him on it. For example, he warns our 12-year-old not to smoke, but he smokes. He tells our 8-year-old not to have temper tantrums, but he rants and raves worse than the kids. He excuses this behavior by saying: "I'm not perfect. Do as I say, not as I do." My problem is that I don't think children make the distinction. Do they?

A: Not usually. Children, as you suggest, learn from what their parents do, not from what they say.

You might be interested to know that research in Sweden on the subject of child discipline has revealed some telling facts. Good discipline was found to be largely unrelated to socioeconomic factors, religious factors, or philosophical factors. The key to good discipline is having parents who actually practice what they preach. When children experience inconsistency from parents, they either choose to identify with this parental behavior or they search for other models of behavior, sometimes in the form of "wrong friends."

Your husband, of course, is correct when he says that he's not perfect. No one is. But he may be using this axiom as a cop-out. His behavior bothers him. Good. His discomfort and self-observation can be the first steps to positive change.

Seen and Not Heard?

It's unreasonable to expect today's pre-teens to be seen and not heard. Include them in family conversations, but keep private adult matters just that — private.

Q: My husband and I were taught as children that we should stay out of adult conversations. We learned that children should be seen, but not heard. Our 12-year-old, Johnny, has other ideas: he constantly butts into our discussions. Worse yet, he blabs our family business all over town. And we live in a small town. Nothing works — not even spanking. What can we do?

A: I don't like the sound of this. Spanking should not be necessary to deal with this situation. Johnny is obviously pushing a sensitive button and he knows it. He seems to be out for revenge. Why?

Although children should not butt in on conversations, it's a little unreasonable to expect them to "be seen and not heard" these days. Maybe Johnny feels excluded and his actions are designed to get himself back into the picture.

Try including him in some of your discussions — especially at the dinner table. It's good training for him. If there's something sensitive or confidential you have to discuss with your husband, let it wait until the two of you are alone.

Punishment — Wiping the Slate Clean

Q: Once I've punished our son Ronald, 12, I figure it's over. For example, if I take away his TV viewing for a day, that's it. When the day is up, I don't say another word about it. Everything's forgiven.

But not my husband. He just keeps hammering away at Ronnie, reminding him of what he did wrong. "Driving home the point," he calls it. Sometimes he even extends the punishment if Ronnie doesn't respond to his liking. What's your opinion of this approach?

A: It's not good. Effective punishment should be exact and time-limited. No loose ends. When Ronnie has gone without TV for a full day, for example, he has accepted his punishment. It should be made clear to him that he has been forgiven and that things will be "business as usual." In essence, you're wiping his slate clean.

Effective punishment, you see, should absolve a child's wrongdoing. He should feel better when it's over. But if your husband's technique never really ends, Ronnie is apt to feel uneasy and resentful.

Punishment should be immediate, related to the offense, and time-limited. It should wipe the slate clean. Paddling and spanking have no place in the disciplining of children.

Divorce

Divorce Pitfalls

Q: I'm divorcing my husband. I have three children, ages 11, 9, and 6. I don't want them to suffer. What are the things that usually cause kids to have problems?

A: The list is long and each child's vulnerabilities are unique. But in my experience, here are some of the major causes of problems:

Among the pitfalls to avoid: leaving kids in the dark, telling them too much, forcing them to take sides, over-compensation through spoiling. Read on. There's more.

1) When children are left completely in the dark.

2) When they're led to think that it's their fault.

3) When they're told too much — especially intimate marital details.

4) When they're forced to take sides or to spy on the other spouse.

5) When Dad fails to visit or support the children.

6) When Mom uses visitation as a lever to get revenge on Dad, and when children are exposed to parental arguments or violence.

7) When one child is favored.

8) When the children are spoiled in an effort to "make it up to them," or to gain favor against the other parent.

9) When one child is identified with the hated spouse, i.e., "you're just like your mother/father."

10) When children are asked too soon to accept a parent's new boyfriend or girlfriend.

Does Joint Custody Work?

Joint custody has been oversold. It's an ideal solution, but when hostilities continue between ex-spouses (the majority of divorces), it is doomed to fail.

Q: My husband and I are in the midst of working out a very tough divorce settlement. His attorney has just suggested joint custody. I'm leery of it, but I do think it would be good for the children, ages 11 and 12, to have both parents remain in their lives. What do you think?

A: Joint custody has received a lot of favorable press lately. But I'd suggest that you read these articles carefully. Most of them are written on a theoretical basis, i.e., theoretically joint custody might well be the best arrangement for children of divorce. But, since we live in the real world, we are faced with stark realities: joint custody is virtually doomed to failure when there remains a great deal of hostility between former spouses. In such cases the children remain "caught in the middle"; they remain as pawns in the ongoing conflict between Mom and Dad. In such cases, joint custody can be disastrous for children. It can make children feel, ultimately, that it's all their fault.

And remember that joint custody may work temporarily, only to become unglued when either spouse remarries and/or moves out of the area. Inevitable conflicts involving the stepparent are made much more difficult by such arrangements.

Yes, your children will always need each of you as a parent. But they also need a conflict-free "home base," a sense of security. You describe your divorce settlement as "tough." Joint custody has worked well for some divorced couples, but they have generally managed "good" rather than "tough" settlements. Be careful.

Joint Custody or Court Battle?

Q: I have been separated from my husband for six months. We have three children, 12½, 9½, and 6. Things are horrible between Bob and me. We fight over everything. Now he's offered me a deal through his attorney: he'll "go easy" on me if I agree to joint legal custody of the children. If I don't agree, he promises to "fight for full custody." I know a court battle would hurt the kids, even though my attorney says I would probably win. Is it worth it? Should I give in to my husband?

A: There are no winners in bitter custody fights. But you've got to take a long-term view of the problem. Joint custody is an ideal arrangement — for about 10% of divorcing parents. It works when two people part as friends or are mature enough to cooperate when it comes to raising the children. It's kind of like running a business — you don't have to love each other, but you have to be able to work together, to trust each other.

A bad marriage, a nasty separation, and threats during the pre-divorce negotiations do not sound like the makings of a viable joint custody.

Based upon what you've told me, I'd recommend that you go for sole custody, with liberal visitation for your husband, assuming he's been a fit father for the children. I also recommend some counselling for the children now. It will help them cope with what could be some rough days ahead.

Your ex-spouse will be the only father or mother your youngster will ever have. You may have divorced, but the children have not been divorced. Even if the relationship between the two of you is strained, try to maintain a cooperative attitude where the youngsters are concerned. They'll need both of you.

Talk Radio Divorce

Q: I was flabbergasted. It happened yesterday. I was driving home from work listening to one of these call-in radio programs — you know, where you call the host and tell him whatever's on your mind. Well, I'm driving along and all of a sudden I heard the anonymous, but unmistakable, voice of my 12-year-old daughter, Sally. I almost crashed into the car in front of me. She was calling to say that "divorce is better for kids than living in a sick family." I almost got sick. I thought my husband and I have kept our problems hidden from her, but obviously we haven't. But here's my question: now what do I do?

A: As the host of a call-in radio program, I'm not surprised. I've had several children call me, using the anonymity of the

Pre-teens are very perceptive. It's better to let them know if you're having marital problems. They'll know anyway — and assume the worst.

telephone and radio, to ask questions or say things that they can't address with their parents. I always listen carefully, give some practical advice, then encourage them to bring it up with Mom and Dad.

Whether your daughter knew you'd be listening or not is immaterial. She has something on her mind. She's very much aware of trouble in your marriage and she's hurting. My best advice is the same I'd give to the youngsters who call me on the radio: continue the conversation at home. By the way, you don't have to mention you heard Sally on the radio — just be sure to tune her in to the program that's airing at home.

Oldest Kids and Divorce

Oldest children (and only children) tend to be at highest emotional risk in divorce. Understand their special vulnerabilities and needs.

Q: My girlfriend and I are both divorced. It's hurt all of the children in various ways, but in each family it's been the oldest child, 11 and 9½, who has seemed to suffer most. Is this a general trend?

A: Yes. Psychologists at the Center for the Family in Transition in California have found that oldest children are at highest risk in divorce. Several reasons are suggested: 1) The oldest may be under more pressure to take care of siblings and be a confidant for the custodial parent, 2) Younger children may naturally get more caring from a stressed mother, 3) The oldest may be more tightly drawn into the ongoing post-divorce skirmishes between the parents.

The best adjusted youngsters in the study were those who had a good relationship with Mom before the divorce and were kept out of the parental battles.

Surrogate Spouse Syndrome

In divorce, the oldest (or only) child is in danger of becoming a best friend and confidant (surrogate spouse) of the one parent. When the customary boundary between parent and youngster is blurred, the child is robbed of part of his childhood.

Q: My girlfriend Jackie has been divorced for two years. She's over the rough spots now but I don't like what's happening in her family. She gives far too much responsibility to her 11-year-old son, Joey. She sends him to the supermarket, confides in him, asks him advice about money matters, even lets him decide how to discipline his sister, 5. What do you think?

A: Sounds like Jackie is slipping into the surrogate spouse syndrome. Joey is becoming a kind of substitute for the husband she lacks. This is a fairly common phenomenon, particularly between custodial mothers and oldest sons, but it can also happen between mothers and daughters, and also between fathers and both sons and daughters.

The natural post-divorce closeness that develops between a custodial parent and a child can, of course, be very positive. It can become a problem, however, when the clear line separating parent from child is blurred. The mother, for example, who leans on a son for emotional or practical support may be robbing him of developmental opportunities. Joey, at age 11, should be turning his attention to the world of peers. If Mom is forcing him (consciously or unconsciously) to turn inward to herself and the family, she is beating against the natural flow of pre-adolescent growth.

Your friend Jackie may be over the rough spots, but she still has needs for support and intimacy. Better for her and Joey that she gets them met outside the family.

Ex-Husband Blocks Move

Q: I have full custody of my children, ages 11, 9, and 7. We have resided one mile away from my former husband since the divorce three years ago, and he has seen the children weekly. My new husband, however, has been transferred to another city and we are planning to move — or thought we were. My former husband is going to court to block the move. He claims that the children will be "psychologically damaged," first, by changing residences, and second, if they are denied frequent visits with him. My lawyer says we need a psychiatric expert to testify for us. I'm confused. Any advice?

A: When your husband gave up legal custody of the children (either voluntarily or via a legal custody case), he forfeited his right to stop you and the children from moving. I'm pleased that he's remained a father to the youngsters, and obviously he's going to miss that close association, but he should have foreseen this possibility. After all, people move.

His only legal option is to prove to the court that it would be harmful for the children to be moved. In essence, he's asking the court to find you an unfit parent.

A psychiatrist could help by conducting an evaluation in the best interests of the children. If they are doing well emotionally, physically, academically, etc., and have always been with you, the psychiatrist would recommend, in all probability, that they continue to reside with you. Then, of course, it's up to the judge. Be prepared, however, to adjust visitation in view of your new living arrangements.

Ex-spouses, even if they don't have custody, can make problems. Any way you cut it, they're going to be part of your life for years. Best to learn cooperation, at least where the children are concerned.

Should Children Vote on Remarriage?

The decision to remarry is obviously yours, not your youngsters', but it can be quite a trauma for them. Listen to them. Both you and your spouse-to-be should have frank discussions with them. Make them feel a part of the team from the very start.

Q: I have been divorced for several years and have two sons, 12 and 14. I've been dating Jack for three years and we have recently decided to marry. His own son, 17, is all for the idea. My boys are against it. They say we should put it to a vote. I know it sounds silly, but I'm stymied. I love Jack and I love my boys. Any advice?

A: Democracy is wonderful for nations, but has very limited usefulness in family life. The participation of children in decision-making when "negotiable" issues are being resolved (such as which movie to see on a Friday evening) can be healthy, but your decision to marry Jack should not be "negotiated" by the children. The boys should not be led to think that they have such power and control over you.

The reaction of your sons is somewhat predictable based on their developmental stage. They are in the throes of a "romance" with you and may resent Jack as an unwelcome intruder. Jack's son, on the other hand, is not threatened by you. Listen to your boys. Have a frank and private chat, just the three of you. Let them pour out their feelings. You may learn more about their opposition to your remarriage. Chances are that their resentment has less to do with Jack as a person and more to do with other things: "Will we have to move?" "Will I keep my own room?" "Will the rules change?"

When some of the major conflicts have surfaced and, hopefully, been resolved, bring Jack into the picture for another chat. Give him a chance to answer questions directly. Try to anticipate problems and plan ahead. But, by all means, proceed with those wedding plans.

It's Either My Stepdaughter or Me

The best medicine for all concerned is to make your marriage your first priority.

Q: My stepdaughter, Denise, is 11 years old. I've tried my darndest for the past three years, but I'm ready to throw in the towel. One of us has to go. She hates me, and now she's driving a wedge between her father and me because, in his eyes, she can do no wrong. He feels he has to protect her, to make up for his divorce. I'm afraid there's going to be another divorce soon.

A: The key to situations like this is not the child, but the marriage. Just how are things between you and your husband? Is there trust? Love? Is there a spirit of oneness, a marital and parental coalition?

Many youngsters, like Denise, will attempt to divide and conquer. Kids, after all, will be kids. But in this case, it sounds like your husband is paving the way for a splitting of alliances and, yes, jeopardizing your marriage.

If your husband feels guilty about his divorce, he is not doing Denise any favors by pampering her and allowing her to pit you against him in a classic Good Guy vs Bad Guy stand-off.

Go back to square one. Talk to your husband not about Denise, but about the marriage. If you put your marriage first, the rest will take care of itself.

Blended Family

Q: My husband and I have been married for a year. Things are going well for us, but not for our children. Jack, my husband, has two daughters, 11 and 7. I have two boys, 10 and 7, and a daughter, 6. We really hoped that they would all merge into one big, happy family, but it isn't working that way. Jack and I don't play favorites. We try to be reasonable with all of the kids. But it's fight, fight, fight. What's happening?

A: Blended families are not that unusual these days, but they do present challenges. It's unrealistic, for example, to assume that you will magically become one big, happy family. Look at the facts.

Blended families, first of all, are born of loss — either death or divorce. There are two biological parents who loom over your family in some way or other.

Then there's the tremendous disruption in the ordinal position of the children. Your oldest son, 10, for example, is no longer the oldest in the family. He's been displaced by Jack's 11-year-old daughter. But Jack's 7-year-old daughter has also been displaced. She's given up the "youngest child" slot to your 6-year-old daughter.

"Who's who" is the name of the game here. Where does everyone fit? You've got to expect a period of jockeying for position, for re-alignment. Be patient. Be firm. Be clear. And don't hesitate to seek help if things get out of hand.

New Summer Visitor

Q: Jack and I were recently married. We are expecting his 11-year-old daughter, Christie, whom I've never met, to visit us this summer. I really want it to go well. Any suggestions?

The blended family (the so-called his-hers-and-ours family) is made, not born. It takes time, understanding, and patience.

Love from your stepchildren is not a given. It has to be earned.

A: If possible, get ahead of things by writing some letters now to Christie. Tell her a little about yourself, send pictures. Ask her about herself and her interests. It would also be wise to let Christie's mother know what you're doing, so you don't antagonize her.

When Christie arrives, don't be too pushy. Give her time to get to know you. Try to be a friend to her, or something like a "good aunt," but don't try to be a mother. Let your husband do the disciplining, but support him in his decisions. And, by all means, allow Jack sufficient private time with Christie. They have a lot to discuss. There is no need to feel left out. After all, Jack and Christie had an established history together long before you came on the scene.

Don't expect love at first sight from your visitor. You'll have to earn it one day at a time. If things don't go well on this visit, don't despair. You'll have other chances.

Finally, be supportive of Jack. This visit may be tough on him too. Make Jack, not Christie, your first priority.

Stepmother's Day?

Stepparents are often forgotten on holidays. They deserve special recognition. Why not a Stepmother's Day and Stepfather's Day?

Q: Paul and I were married 6 months ago. Paul has custody of his 12-year-old daughter, Claire. Paul's former wife lives in town, but Claire rarely sees her because their relationship is very poor. Here's my problem: Mother's Day is approaching. Paul wants Claire to spend the day with her mother. He also suggests that we make the following Sunday our own Stepmother's Day so Claire and he can honor me with a special occasion. What do you think?

A: This is a sign of the times. Approximately one of every 7 children is a stepchild. One of every 5 adults is a stepparent or will become one. Yet, the question of where a stepmother fits on Mother's Day is still left to trial and error.

I think I understand Paul's logic. Claire's mother, good relationship or bad, will always be her mother. He correctly senses that any effort to formally displace her on Mother's Day could backfire on all of you.

Paul also wants to honor you with special recognition — to solidify your new role. What to do?

I'd ask first if you understand your role. What is it? What does Claire call you? What does she want from you? Need from you?

You should bring Claire into the decision. She's old enough. She may not want to spend the entire day with her mother. And what about Claire's mother herself? Why not check with her too?

I really like Paul's idea for Stepmother's Day. You just have a few details to work out yet.

Should New Stepfather Meet Ex?

Q: I'm the divorced mother of three, ages 12, 10, and 7. My former husband and I have joint custody of the children and it seems to be working pretty well. Our relationship is strained, but cooperative where the kids are concerned. The kids see their father every other weekend. I'm going to remarry in a few months. My husband-to-be thinks it would be a good idea for him to meet my ex-husband "to discuss the children." I'm wary. What do you say?

A: I think it's an excellent idea. Why? However you cut it, these two men are going to be part of the children's lives (and of each other's lives) for many years to come.

I hope your fiancee uses the opportunity to reassure your Ex that he does not plan to supplant him as the children's father. At the same time, however, he should ask for support and respect in his new role as stepfather. Finally, I hope you can all agree to talk, or meet periodically as the need arises.

Whatever your own differences with your former husband, it is important to be able to put them aside where the best interests of the youngsters are concerned.

When an ex-spouse has remained a steady and positive factor in the youngsters' lives, it is a good idea for him or her to meet your new spouse. After all, they will now be part of each other's lives. The children will benefit from their cooperation.

Stepfathers and Incest

Q: An 11-year-old girl in our neighborhood just reported that she was sexually abused by her stepfather. You hear a lot about incest these days. Isn't the problem really the high divorce rate — and stepfathers?

A: No. You might be surprised to learn that stepfathers are not the prime culprits. Based on a study by Russell in California, here's the breakdown:

Uncles were responsible for 25% of incest cases; fathers, 15%; brothers, 12%; stepfathers, 8%; sisters, 2%; and mothers, 1%.

Incest is a scourge that has been with us throughout history. To blame it on divorce or on stepfathers is simply not realistic. You hear a lot about it these days mostly because the societal climate is finally allowing it to be reported more often.

Stepfathers, contrary to popular belief, are not the prime offenders in incest.

The vast majority of stepfathers love their stepchildren and work hard to play a healthy, constructive role in their lives.

One final note: your young neighbor needs your support and understanding. Treat her naturally. She will have some emotional scars from the experience, but she can go on to live a happy and normal life.

Stepfamilies and Holidays

Rituals and traditions, such as the way various holidays are celebrated, are important organizers of family life. Preserve them, even if our pre-teen has other ideas.

Q: I have recently remarried. I have two children, 12 and 14, from my previous marriage. My husband would like all of us to spend New Year's Eve with his family this year. I'm not so sure. You see, his family has a very morbid "tradition": they name all the deceased members of the family, make a speech about each, and end up sobbing the night away. It's touching in a way, but my children don't know anything about these people. It wouldn't make any sense for them. I'm afraid they'd just get depressed. What do you think?

A: I see your point. The tradition is touching. It certainly keeps your husband's family in touch with its history, its roots. On the other hand, it could make for a depressing night — especially for outsiders.

Your children, at ages 12 and 14, are old enough to understand the situation. Have you discussed it with them? I'm not suggesting that you merely put the decision to them, but that you take their feelings into account in arriving at your decision.

How strongly does your husband feel about this? You'll also have to consider his feelings.

On balance, it's not the worst thing that could happen on New Year's Eve. Your husband wants to make the children part of his family. Are you ready for it?

Dress Code

No Shoelaces

Dressing like your peers says you belong, which is so important to pre-teens. If it's not too outrageous, go with the flow.

Q: Our Nancy is 11. She insists on going to school wearing tennis shoes without shoelaces. She says all the other kids are doing it. What should we do?

A: Nancy's 11-year-old world is a world of peers — my peer group, right or wrong. She has a desperate need to belong, to be like all the rest. Hence, the absence of shoelaces.

What to do? Check with the parents of some of Nancy's best friends (you should know who they are, of course). Then, discuss it with your husband.

I wouldn't make a big deal out of it. After all, no core family value is at stake. Nancy's choice is one of many she will make on the road to her own adult independence. But seize the opportunity to talk to her about values, peer pressure, and independent thinking. Explain that while you think laceless shoes are silly, you know she doesn't and you'll go along with the plan, but on important issues of values she should not expect you to cave in to peer pressure. And you hope she won't either.

Dress Sisters Alike?

Q: My cousin has two daughters, ages 11 and 8. She has always dressed them alike. Most of us considered it cute, but now I wonder. The oldest, Shaina, is almost pubertal. She's starting to look silly in her "little girl" dresses. Comments?

A: Generally, I don't agree with this practice for girls or boys. It forces an unnatural and unnecessary "togetherness" on siblings and potentially robs each of some individuality. Remember, pre-teens and teens, desperately in search of individuality, often express it in their style of dress. Forced sameness for siblings usually results out of some parental need to project a special identification on the children. This is not necessarily a bad idea, but should be limited to abstractions like family values.

Your point about Shaina being "dressed down" to the level of her younger sister raises another problem from a developmental perspective. What's going to happen here? Sooner or later Shaina will rebel, perhaps at the expense of alienating her parents, or Mom and Dad will correct their dress code.

So, Shaina should be allowed some individuality, but the line should be crossed at the point that allows her parents to be comfortable too.

Pre-teens are caught between two worlds. It's not a good idea to let them dress up to the level of adolescent siblings, and a poor idea to dress them down to the level of younger brothers or sisters.

29

Friends and Dating

They Call My Son Names

Pre-teens are especially sensitive to being called names. You can help. Be supportive, help them analyze the problem, and chart a course of action. Resist the urge to take matters immediately into your own hands.

Q: My son Geoffrey is 12 years old. He comes home from school in tears almost every day because the other kids are calling him names. I'm heartbroken, but I feel powerless to do anything. Do you have any suggestions?

A: Yes. You've apparently already accomplished the first step: to maintain a supportive emotional climate at home for Geoffrey. He's got to know, in no uncertain terms, that Mom is on his side.

The second step is to help him analyze the problem. What kind of names are the kids using? Why would they specifically call him those things? Is it a matter of blind prejudice or has Geoffrey in any way "victimized" himself? In other words, does he feed into it somehow? And how does he react when he's the target of name-calling? As you know, 12-year-old peers can be cruel at times and tend to intensify their taunts if their victim breaks into sobs or tantrums.

The third step is to help Geoffrey chart a course of action. How can he solve this problem? He can't control the other kids, but he can control himself. Is there anything he can personally change that would help? Careful here. You're not implying that the bullies are right — that it's all Geoffrey's fault and he's the one that has to change. But you are plotting with Geoffrey to take some positive action, to take the bullies by the horns, to turn the tables on his tormentors through positive, but non-aggressive, action. How can he win their friendship? That's the key.

By the way, advising him to "ignore" the name calling is OK, but it usually doesn't work too well. If Geoffrey had been able to ignore it in the beginning, it probably would not have continued to this point.

Stay close to the situation. Geoffrey's first attempts at solving the problem will be cautious and timid. The original plan may not work. Be ready to go back to the drawing board if necessary — all the while maintaining a supportive, optimistic posture.

Your ace in the hole, of course, is to go directly to Geoffrey's teacher or the parents of the name-callers. While it might be helpful to let your son know that you care enough to walk this last mile with him, don't do it unless the plan has his blessing.

Many kids are humiliated by this kind of maneuver because they fear backlash. It's bad enough to be called "Stinky," but "Mama's Boy" or "Teacher's Pet" is even worse. Better that your initial efforts go into helping Geoffrey solve the problem himself. But don't hesitate to get directly involved if things don't improve. If things get really bad, you may even have to do it over Geoffrey's protests. It's a judgement call — one of those things that makes being a parent a tough job at times.

Clique Counterattack

Q: Our Kelly, 11½, is stunned and hurt. Her girlfriends have been ignoring her for an entire week. She can't understand it. Nothing has happened that could explain it. I've told her to ignore them and get some new friends, but my advice just brings more tears. Please help.

A: Cliques are an important developmental way station on the path to personal independence, autonomy, and self-esteem for most youngsters. By banding together, pre-teens and early teens feel the strength and security that they lack as individuals. Acceptance by the group, therefore, signifies that all is right with you.

Unfortunately, when an insecure clique member wishes to reaffirm her own shaky self-worth she often does it by putting someone else down. My hunch is that Kelly is being blamed by one of the other girls for a shortcoming that she cannot accept in herself. So much for the theory. How to help Kelly?

1) *Listen to feelings.* Absorb Kelly's feelings — non-judgementally.

2) *Explain.* Describe the clique phenomenon to Kelly. It may be a bit abstract, but it's worth a try.

3) *Fact-finding.* Encourage Kelly to examine herself. Is there anything she's doing to encourage the clique's response? Has she fallen into a pattern of some type?

4) *Counter-attack.* Kelly needs a plan. I suggest some 1:1 talks with members of the group. Divide and conquer, if possible.

5) *Encouragement.* Make an inventory of Kelly's assets. She's still the same girl she's always been. Whatever she does, she shouldn't let the clique rob her of that.

Cliques are a way station on the path to independence, autonomy, and self-esteem for most pre-teens. Parents may not like them, and they may cause your youngster occasional pain, but they won't go away. Help your pre-teen understand their significance.

Pajama Party

Pre-teen parties should be supervised.

Q: Our 11-year-old daughter, Michelle, tells us that some of her classmates are beginning to have pajama parties. It seems a little early to my husband and me. For example, I wasn't allowed to attend pajama parties until I was 16. What do you think?

A: It is not unusual for 11-year-olds to attend pajama parties today. It can be part and parcel of their transition from the world of family to the world of friends. The closeness and intimacy that develops through such social contacts can be a healthy bridge to adolescence.

These pre-adolescent slumber parties that I'm describing should be well-supervised. If you have any doubts about the supervision, by all means contact the mothers of Michelle's friends. It would also be a fine idea to share your concerns with Michelle herself.

The pajama parties of 16-year-olds are usually much different affairs than the parties of barely pubescent youngsters — just as they were, I bet, when you and I were teenagers.

Boy-Girl Parties

Another rite of passage for many pre-teens. No, they're not ready for unchaperoned parties. Know the host and talk to his or her parents. Apply reasonable guidelines.

Q: We knew it was coming. It had to happen sooner or later. Our son Ricky, 12, has been invited to his first boy-girl party. It seems to be "the thing" at his school. He came home yesterday and casually told us that he was going to a party at Lucy's house next week. He dropped his books on the kitchen table and went to his room. Nothing more was said. But what should we say? Should we ask questions? Should we call Lucy's mother (whoever Lucy is)? We need some guidelines.

A: Ricky is the one who needs guidance and I bet he knows it.
Here are some rules to consider:

1) *Permission.* Children shouldn't announce invitations, they should ask your permission.

2) *Call the host.* Yes, call Lucy's parents. Inquire not only about supervision, but about what the kids will be doing.

3) *Don't be embarrassed.* Don't worry about the reaction of the host parents. If you voice reasonable parental concern, they'll respect you for it. They may even be relieved. It gives them "permission" to call you when Lucy gets invited to your house someday.

4) *Handling complaints.* Be sure to tell Ricky in advance that you're going to call Lucy's parents. Yes, he may complain. He'll probably claim that no one else's mother calls about parties and that you don't trust him. Gently turn these complaints aside. What other parents do is not the issue. You have a responsibility to him as a parent. You're exercising that responsibility.

Finally, there's one more piece of advice you might consider. You're not alone in your dilemma. If mixed parties are "the thing" for Ricky's classmates, you can bet that a number of the other parents would also like some guidelines. Why not get in touch with them? I bet that almost no one will think you're a busybody. They'll probably be relieved.

Sharing the Family Turkey

Q: This Thanksgiving will be the first holiday for me and the children since my divorce last summer. My middle daughter Brenda, 12, would like to invite an exchange student from her school to join us for a traditional turkey dinner. It's a beautiful gesture, but is it Brenda's way of covering up and avoiding the absence of her father?

Pre-teens, peer-oriented as they are, may want to invite friends to share in family traditions, such as holiday dinners. Rather than fight it, why not absorb the friends creatively?

A: Could be, but I wonder if you're not stretching the analysis a bit. I hope you've encouraged Brenda and your other children to freely express their thoughts and feelings about the divorce. The same goes for Mom. If Thanksgiving stirs up some strong emotions, I hope there's someone to whom you can talk.

If you're concerned about having a guest, why not discuss it with all of the children as a group? If everyone agrees, you could make it a truly American family event. Some tips: 1) Have one of the children study the history of Thanksgiving and recite it before dinner. 2) Another child could write a special "Grace" for the event. 3) Everyone should learn something about your guest's own country and even try to learn a few words in her native language.

Ritual and tradition are important organizers of family life. They're worth preserving through bad times and good.

Death of a Classmate

Q: A classmate and good friend of our 12-year-old, Billy, died recently in an accidental fall at a construction site. Billy is still broken-up about it. How can we help him?

Pre-teens, like adults, must be allowed to grieve the loss of a loved one. The steps include grieving through the expression of feelings, helping your youngster understand the event in perspective, commemorating the memory of the loved one, and going on with life.

A: Grief is a process that must be felt and experienced in order to be resolved.

Here are some tips based on the concepts developed at a children's counseling center in Boston:

1) *Grieving.* Allow Billy to express his feelings. Remember, he may feel sad, but he may feel angry or even guilty too because he's alive and his friend is dead.

2) *Understanding.* Help Billy achieve some intellectual understanding of the meaning of his friend's passing.

3) *Commemorating.* It's a good idea to let youngsters honor the memory of a deceased peer by some type of commemoration such as a memorial service, a plaque at school, and so forth.

4) *Going on.* At some point children must be given the tacit permission that it's OK to get on with life. After all, their friend would have wanted it that way.

Hobbies, Sports, and Other Interests

Dungeons and Dragons

Q: My 11-year-old son, Eric, is absolutely fascinated by the game Dungeons and Dragons. He spends hours playing it with his best friends. Is it harmful?

Pre-teens love fantasy games. They're not harmful as long as youngsters have a healthy life that includes family, school, friends, hobbies, and other interests.

A: Dungeons and Dragons is indeed a fascinating game. In it, youngsters develop their own characters and engage in make-believe plots, which sometimes take hours and hours to unfold. The game provides a marvelous opportunity for teens and pre-teens to indulge in creative fantasy. The only youngster potentially harmed by such games is one who has a strong tendency toward isolation, daydreaming, or blurring of reality. Other youngsters can actually benefit from this kind of play, as long as it is kept in balance. Any pastime that absorbs so much of a boy's or girl's time that it is used as an "escape" can be harmful from a developmental standpoint. Therefore, be sure that Eric is not spending so much time in that fantasy world of "D and D" that he neglects real-world, "bread-and-butter" items like family life, chores, school work, friends, hobbies, and athletics. As long as Eric has both feet firmly planted in reality and leaves plenty of room in his life for these other important things, there is no danger in Dungeons and Dragons.

Future TV News Anchor?

Q: Barbara Jo, our 11-year-old, has a dream. She wants to be a TV news anchor. She's visited all of the stations in town, and even writes to one of the local reporters who has been nice to her.

We have no problem with this, except that "BJ" has a cockeyed notion of what it's all about. She thinks the major requirement is to be beautiful. That's why, I guess, she cuts her hair like one of the network stars. She practices "anchoring" in front of the mirror, i.e., facial and hand gestures, but we never hear her talk about what's news!

What's happening? Is it a phase? Why is she just interested in the superficial aspects of what is probably a complicated job?

A: Yes, it's probably a phase, but you have an opportunity here to teach some important values to your daughter. You can start by telling her that most women who make it to the top of TV news are bright and educated people. She's selling them short if she assumes that it's a simple case of beauty over brains.

More importantly, BJ is selling herself short if she assumes that looking good is the best she can do. Why not sit down with her and watch a news cast? Point out how much the anchors have to know about current events and history, interviewing, and communicating.

Ask BJ to "anchor" a mini newscast for you in the living room. When she does, praise her for her brains. Beauty won't hurt, of course, but it'll never win her an Emmy.

Pre-teens like to toy with the future. Their musings about "what I'm going to be when I grow up" are subject to almost daily change. But there's something to be learned.

Autograph Hound

Q: My Michael, 12, is an autograph hound. He's collected several signatures of local and national sports stars and celebrities. Sometimes he'll wait outside a TV studio for hours if he knows a "personality" is inside. Do you see any potential harm in his unusual hobby?

A: No, as long as he doesn't go overboard. There are many things more important in life than chatting up celebrities. Make sure Michael keeps his priorities straight.

Don't let Michael mistake celebrity for substance, i.e., I don't like the notion of a "personality" being inside. Everyone has a personality.

Some people become celebrities because of hard work, some by accident; some are famous, some infamous. They're

Pre-teens may wish to shed hobbies, including music lessons, left over from earlier years. Try to be understanding, but encourage their active involvement in some wholesome alternative activity of their choice. Hobbies build self-esteem and may lead to later career choices.

different from, not better than, the "personality" who lives next door. Celebrity is also temporary in most cases. If Michael's hobby helps him learn important lessons, it will reward him with a lot more than a few scribbled signatures on crumpled paper.

Pre-teens' hobbies are healthy if kept on the positive side of life. They can stimulate self-esteem and even lead to later career choices. Who knows? Michael could end up as an autograph dealer or even a talk-show host.

Daughter Sacks Saxophone

Pre-teen musicians are well-known for dropping their music lessons; the instrument may represent their childhood. Interestingly, most youngsters later regret the decision. Be flexible and creative. Maybe changing to a different instrument would help.

Q: Our Carolyn, 12, has played the saxophone for the past two years. Her teacher says she's one of the best young students he's ever had. The problem is that she wants to drop it. We think it's because she's getting interested in boys and she doesn't think it's "cool" to be seen lugging her instruments onto the school bus. We know she'll regret it later, but our hands are tied. She won't practice. What can we do?

A: Some positive peer pressure would sure help. If she's not in the band, I suggest looking into that possibility. If the problem is simply the bus issue, perhaps there's some way to solve it.

On the other hand, maybe the instrument itself is the culprit. Maybe Carolyn would be more comfortable at this stage in her life with a more popular instrument such as a guitar. If that's the case, she could always return to the sax in later years.

You're right, by the way, when you suggest that your daughter will probably regret a decision to drop her music lessons. A survey of 1,313 teenagers by the American Music Conference found that 55% of former music students regretted their decision, and that 32% of them felt better about themselves when they played music.

Talk it over with Carolyn. Give her some options. Let's hope she keeps making music.

Sports Aggression

Good aggression, which is used for socially appropriate goals and applied within the rules, should be encouraged. Bad aggression should not be allowed.

Q: Our 12-year-old son, Timmy, plays Little League baseball. My husband is always after him to "be more aggressive." I think it's wrong. What do you say?

A: Aggression does not have to be a dirty word. Kids, in fact, should be aggressive, but there are limits.

Good aggression is the type of drive that allows youngsters to maximize their performance within the rules of the game. This might mean attacking the ball when you're at bat, stretching a single into a double when you're running the bases, and so forth.

Bad aggression, however, is what happens when that drive activity is used outside the rules. Deliberately harming another player, for example, is bad aggression.

So maybe you and your husband are simply disagreeing about the definition or spirit of the word. I hope that Timmy is aggressive on the field (and in all of his pursuits), but that it stays on the positive side.

She Wants to Baby-Sit

Q: Our 12-year-old Wendy is mature for her age. She's really been a big help to me in caring for her 5-year-old brother. Now she wants to put her child-care experience to work. She wants to baby-sit. When I tell her she's too young, she reminds me that she's old enough to take care of her own brother. Any suggestions?

A: Wendy may be telling you that she feels burdened by taking care of her brother. Is it so? Is she perhaps being "used"? I suggest that you first examine this question.

As a 12-year-old Wendy is entering the world of peers. Do her home chores keep her from enjoying the company of her friends? A year or two ago it wouldn't have mattered as much.

Of course, Wendy should be expected to help you. Every child should have assigned chores that contribute to the welfare of the family, but parents should balance these obligations with ample amounts of freedom and leisure time.

Wendy might also be obliquely suggesting that you should pay her for watching her brother. She realizes, after all, that she could be compensated for doing the same thing for the neighbor's 5-year-old. Be careful. While you might want to pay her something for taking on special tasks, it is not a good idea to pay youngsters for doing reasonable, expected chores.

My solution: keep Wendy's work load reasonable and give her a chance to baby-sit in the neighborhood, but be sure she has help available, such as yourself, if there's a problem.

Baby-sitting for pay is another rite of passage for pre-teen girls, and some boys too. Encourage it, but prepare them for the responsibility that goes along with it.

Money and Allowance

Allowance

Pre-teens should receive an allowance. Talk it over with them. Negotiate. It's a good lesson in money management.

Q: Kerry, our oldest, is 11. She wants an allowance. Should we give her one? How much? Should we withhold it if she doesn't do her chores?

A: Pre-teens should receive an allowance. It's an important teacher of money management.

How much? It depends on Kerry's legitimate needs. Sit down with her and review the numbers. Start with her fixed expenses: Does she buy a lunch at school? Buy bus tokens? Then, consider how much she should have for incidentals and fun. Don't be overly generous. Too much money in the hands of a youngster is not a good idea. But, by all means, listen to her requests. Negotiate with her. It's a good experience.

Withhold allowance? I'm not in favor of it. No strings attached. There are other ways, such as the loss of privileges, to deal with misbehavior.

He Wants an Advance

If you make it a habit of giving your pre-teen an advance because he has overspent his allowance, you're teaching the joys of deficit spending. And we all know where that leads.

Q: My 12-year-old son, Kenny, receives a weekly allowance every Monday morning. The trouble is that he spends it as fast as he gets it. By Friday he's broke. Then, he comes around to me and asks for an "advance" on next week's allowance. I guess I shouldn't, but I generally give it to him. Of course, he "forgets" about the advance and expects his full allowance again on Monday — which, again, I usually give him. My sister-in-law says this is wrong. What do you suggest?

A: You are instructing Kenny in the ways of deficit spending. I'm concerned that he'll never learn how to handle money as long as he knows that Mom is standing by to bail him out. Why not practice the principle of Logical Consequences? The consequence of spending your allowance by Friday is that you wait until Monday to refill the coffers. The choice is Kenny's: budget or bust.

Hold Back Allowance?

No strings attached, for the most part. But you may want to find some special for-pay projects for your pre-teen to tackle.

Q: Tommy, our 12-year-old, gets an allowance of $5 per week. We're happy to give it to him, but we're quick to withhold it if he misbehaves or if he doesn't do his chores. Tommy thinks he should get it without any strings attached. What do you think?

A: I agree with Tommy — up to a point. Let me explain. Most 12-year-olds have certain legitimate expenses such as school supplies, bus fare, and so forth. I believe a basic allowance, or expense account, should cover these items and should be paid regularly each week — with no strings attached.

This practice is designed to teach money management. But I'm against advances and other forms of deficit spending.

I don't believe that youngsters should be paid to perform routine chores. These are responsibilities that children have to the family. If a youngster fails to perform (or breaks a family rule), there are other ways to apply punishment, such as loss of privileges.

If you want to provide Tommy with some financial incentives, you could give him some opportunities to perform specific tasks, above and beyond his routine chores, at a fixed fee. These must be tasks that you would otherwise hire someone to do. In this way, everybody's happy, and Tommy will have a legitimate sense of importance.

Hire Our Son?

Q: Our son, Joey, is 12. He's a good boy. We're planning to paint the basement and when my husband suggested hiring a couple of neighborhood teenagers to do it, Joey suggested he could do it. My husband hesitated because he's reluctant to pay Joey to do the work in our own house. For example, Joey does his chores without pay. Wouldn't we be setting a bad precedent if we begin paying him now?

A: No. Joey is old enough to know the difference between basic chores and special projects. Why not make this a real learning experience for Joey? Let him bid on the project. How much paint will be used? How many hours will the job require? How much is his time worth? How much should he charge? What's the estimated date of completion?

The precedent is a good one. You'll be launching Joey into a new phase. But don't let him forget those chores. After all, even big-time business executives put away their own clean socks!

All youngsters should have assigned chores. It's part of their responsibility of being a family member. Basic chores should be done free of charge, but there is nothing wrong with contracting specific jobs for pay. Let them learn from the experience.

The Money Taboo

Pre-teens should learn money management. They should have some general idea about family finances. Money talk should not be a taboo subject.

Q: My husband is wonderfully open with the children on almost any subject: sex, feelings, religion, you name it. The only subject he won't discuss with them is money. I believe the children, 11 and 12, should know something about the family finances. What is your opinion?

A: I tend to agree with you. Yet, I'm not surprised at all about your husband's attitude. It is quite typical of our culture. As a psychiatrist, I can tell you that adults would rather talk about almost anything, even the darkest secrets of their souls, before they talk about how much they spend and earn. The money taboo may be the last frontier of personal intimacy.

I do believe, however, that part of a parent's obligation to teach children about proper money management is to give them a realistic glimpse into how the family financial system works. Without a few guideposts, some youngsters tend to grossly exaggerate the family's fiscal position, and behave accordingly. Other children underestimate family money matters and worry unnecessarily.

Your children are old enough to grasp the basics. It is not necessary for you to divulge all the details, but some general instruction in the family budget would be a good idea.

Money Miser

A pre-teen's preoccupation with money or material possessions may signal problems with popularity, physical attractiveness, and self-esteem.

Q: My husband, George, worries excessively about money — how to make it, how to save it, will we make it, what then? Now our son, Carl, 11, seems to be catching the bug. He's becoming a real miser. We're actually pretty well off. Why are they so obsessed with money?

A: Money means different things to different people. For some it's nurturance or security, for others it's control or power over things and people, for some it's self-esteem, for others it equates to sex appeal. The list goes on.

Your husband's own personal history may, of course, provide some answers too. What were his parents' attitudes toward money? What has been his own financial history?

Money, as a preoccupation, can also serve defensive purposes for people who have obsessive-compulsive traits. Most of these people would be described as "miserly"; they spend endless hours counting it, but part with it only grudgingly. Carl, from your description, may fit into this category, but of course, his natural identification with his father is an obvious factor as well.

Excessive, unrealistic worries of any type are not healthy. That's how I'd approach this problem. Start with your husband. Tell him you'd like to help him understand his worries. Self-knowledge is the first step toward change and self-improvement.

Yuletide Recession

Q: We've always celebrated Christmas with a lot of gift giving. This year, however, has been tough on us financially. My husband wants to borrow money so the children, 11 and 12, can have their usual holiday. He doesn't want to disappoint them. He says they'll be worried about our financial situation if they don't see a lot of boxes under the tree. What do you think?

A: A little worry of this kind is not a bad thing. In fact, it can be a growth experience for your children. Family life has its ups and downs. Why hide what must be obvious to them? Maybe your husband needs some help. His financial worries may be highlighted at Christmas — a time of gifts and good cheer in years past. Let him know that there is love and strength in the family. His value as a father is not measured by the number of gifts under the tree.

Children must be taught to love their parents for who they are — not for what they buy.

He Loves Money

Q: Danny, our 12-year-old, has a dream. He plans to become a self-made millionaire by the time he's 21. Sounds fantastic, I know, but he could do it. Everything he touches seems to make money. Last week, for example, he contracted with a video rental store to provide delivery of tapes. Then he went out and "hired" five of his friends to do the job, said he couldn't tie himself down with "details." Danny is a good boy, but frankly, we're concerned about his love affair with money. We want him to be a happy person. Won't his pursuit of wealth hinder his happiness?

A: Not necessarily — but money obviously won't buy him the happiness you want for him. The key is to help him build balance into his life. He'll need physical, emotional, and spiritual health if he's to grow into a well-balanced, happy adult. The child who loves money may be compensating for a lack of something else, such as self-esteem. Think it over. Talk it over.

Pre-teens often equate making money with growing up. Some develop into genuine mini-entrepreneurs. No problem, as long as the quest for cash is balanced with other important values such as doing good — while you're doing well.

Then, devise a plan to help your son become a whole person. Danny is developing into a real entrepreneur. No problem. Some could say it's the American way. But don't let him lose sight of other values. Doing well is fine, but it's more important to do good.

Debts and Lies

A pre-teen's debts to friends may well be innocent, but you have a right and responsibility to know the facts. Where's the money going? Every parent's fear: drugs. Get involved, stay informed, be in charge.

Q: Last week Leonard, our 12-year-old, told us that he had lost his new Walkman radio. Last night I overhead him on the telephone talking about some money that he still owed a boy at school. I was curious. Later I asked him again about the radio. This time he said he sold it to someone. I asked to see the money. He said he spent it. On what? "Things," he answered. Doctor, I don't like the sound of this at all. I think he's lying. Any suggestions?

A: Sounds to me like Leonard is in trouble and he's digging himself in deeper every day. This is what usually happens with lies and cover-ups.

Leonard obviously didn't lose the radio. He probably gave it to someone to partially satisfy a debt. What kind of debt? Today's parents of pre-teens know that drug use is not unheard of at 12. Whatever is going on, you need to know about it. You may feel angry at this point. You may feel like punishing Leonard for lying to you and then trying to cover his tracks. While I agree that lying and cover-ups should be dealt with seriously, the first order of business is to find out what's going on here. Leonard may be in trouble of some kind. Approach him openly and non-punitively. Create an environment in which he can open up to you. He may need understanding, advice, help. After the air is cleared, you can decide on the proper consequence for Leonard's lies to you.

Mothers and Fathers

Mom vs Dad

Most youngsters tend to go to Mom with their problems. Don't let Dad be written out of the script.

Q: My husband gets upset because our sons, 11 and 12, tend to come to me rather than to him for advice. He says that they needed me more in their younger years, now they should start coming to him for "man to man" kinds of things. I try to tell him that it's natural; most children go to their mothers first. Right?

A: Right, but I applaud your husband for wanting to be a complete father to his children. Most studies show that 70-80% of children of all ages, boys as well as girls, will go to Mom first with worries, problems, requests, and all the other things, big and small, on their minds. It's interesting, by the way, that even teenage boys tend to go to Mom, rather than Dad, about sexual matters.

Why? Fathers in our society tend to shy away from intimacy with their children, even from an early age. If they wake up and try to recapture it in later years, it may be too late.

What's the answer? Support your husband's efforts. Help him and the boys re-establish communication. But don't take yourself out of the picture. The boys need both of you.

Parents Too Involved?

Q: I love my grandchildren, Crystal, 11, and John Edward, 12, but I'm concerned. Their parents, in my opinion, are just too involved with them. I mean they can't do enough for their children. The whole household revolves around school, music lessons, soccer games, etc. My daughter and son-in-law have almost no life of their own. This isn't good, is it?

Try to draw the line between being uninvolved and over-involved in your child's life.

A: No. In some cases it can almost be as bad as out-and-out neglect. A couple's first responsibility should be to each other. If the marriage is in good shape, the child-raising will go well, but the opposite is not necessarily true.

Why should children dominate this marriage? There are many possible explanations. Maybe Mom and Dad have very little in common except the children. If so, Crystal and John Edward are being used as the "glue" to keep things together. Not only is the over-indulgence bad for the children, but what happens after they've grown up and left home?

There are, of course, other possibilities too. Some parents, unsatisfied with their own lives, throw everything into raising their children in order to accomplish through them what they have not been able to accomplish for themselves. Whatever the reason, all four members of the family would be better off with more balance and perspective in their lives.

Dad Covers His Mistakes

Q: My husband is like Watergate. Instead of admitting his mistakes to our children, Wendy, 11, William, 9, and Walker, 7, he goes to elaborate lengths to cover up. For example, yesterday

Youngsters are forgiving creatures. Admit your mistakes.

he forgot that he promised to take them shopping. Instead of saying, "Sorry, I forgot," he cooked up a story about a special meeting at his office. The kids aren't dumb. They know he's lying. What will this do to them?

A: Children are marvelously forgiving creatures if you communicate your love, admit your mistakes, and try to do better next time. They don't expect perfection, but they do expect honesty and consistency.

There's nothing wrong with changing your mind about a plan, or even forgetting it altogether — as long as it isn't a pattern, and as long as you admit the truth.

Cover-ups, however, breed distrust and erode parental credibility. The nation doesn't like Watergates — and kids don't either.

Mom Returns from Hospital

Children, paradoxically, are often at their best in the midst of a family crisis. Set your expectations high, but give them a little slack when things settle down. After all, pre-teens are still kids at heart.

Q: My wife was recently hospitalized for gall bladder surgery. I took off work and took care of the kids, ages 11, 7, and 5. They were marvelous: helped with the chores, no fuss at all. But now that Mom's home, it's a different story. They're impossible. What goes?

A: Kids will be kids. They demonstrated cooperation and maturity in the face of a crisis — score one for them. Now that Mom is home, they're relieved. The fears and anxieties that were previously repressed can now be expressed in their behavior. But it's not such a bad thing at all: they feel comfortable enough to return to business as usual.

What to do? Talk it over with them. Help them understand the process. Let them know how proud you were of them earlier, and let them know that your expectations will still be a little bit higher than usual while Mom is recuperating. But don't be too hard on them.

Monarchy vs Democracy

Someone has to be in charge of the family; that someone should be the parents, not the children. But being in charge doesn't mean heavy-handedness. Rule lightly and in good humor, turning over responsibility gradually to your children. The goal is to work yourself out of a job.

Q: We have three children, ages 11, 8½, and 5. My husband wants our family to be a monarchy with the two of us as King and Queen. I say, let's have a democracy. After all, we live in one, right?

A: Actually, you probably need a mixture of both. Let me explain. A family is not quite like a nation. Someone has to be

44

firmly (but lovingly) in charge of children. This "someone" should be parents. Yet, to raise children properly in this society we have to turn power and responsibility over to them gradually, so they will know how to make the right decisions when they grow up and leave us.

A family, however, can never be a "pure" democracy. If you really intend to operate on the premises of one man, one vote, you and "the King" had better be prepared to be voted out of office.

Eavesdropping

Q: My 12-year-old son, George, will soon be going to summer camp. It's his first camp experience. Last night he overheard me talking on the telephone to my girlfriend. I was telling her how happy I'll be when he's away. I didn't mean it in the way I know he heard it. I was thinking about the freedom, the change of pace. I'll miss him too, but I didn't say that on the phone. He hasn't said anything to me. I feel horrible. I feel guilty. Should I bring it up or let it go?

Parents enjoy a break now and then. Admit it and enjoy.

A: Bring it up. Don't jump immediately into a gushy apology, though. Tell him that you're aware he overheard your conversation. Ask him about his interpretation of what you said. In this way you'll be able to respond not to what you think he feels, but to what's really on his mind. If he clams up, as he might, suggest how he may be feeling. Try to coax him into an open conversation. If that fails, launch into a gentle explanation.

Above all, do not feel guilty. I think I know what you meant. All parents say these things. All children have heard these comments. Parents need some vacation from children too. It's nothing to be ashamed about.

Mommy Track

Q: Christy, my 12-year-old, saw a TV talk show where a woman apparently was promoting something called a "Mommy Track" for career women who have children. This would be the slow track, of course, with the fast track reserved for childless women who supposedly are more committed to the corporation and more deserving of promotion in the ranks. I think I've done a good job of balancing career and family, but now Christy is confused. Any thoughts?

All mothers are working mothers. Some, in addition to having household responsibilities, are employed outside of the home. For them, it's tough to have it all, but with support and teamwork on the home front, they can strive to have the best of both worlds.

A: I'm not in favor of the so-called Mommy Track. Such a plan might allow some companies to penalize women with dead-end jobs, and it certainly reinforces the perception that only a man's work is vital. I'd like to see more flexibility for all career women (and men) in terms of scheduling, duties, and promotion. While it is undeniably tough for a career-oriented mother to "have it all," you can manage nicely with well-established priorities, a long-term game plan, the cooperation of spouse and children, and a supportive employer. Talk it over with Christy. You have an opportunity here to provide her with a solid model for her own future.

Best of Both Worlds

Most bicultural pre-teens turn away from their parents' culture because of peer pressure. Back off, but don't back out of your interest in preserving their root identity. They'll thank you for it in a few years.

Q: My husband and I are from Latin America. We are living here temporarily. We have a boy, 11, and a girl, 9. The children are adapting to life in the U.S. better and faster than we are. In fact, that's the problem. They want to be "American." They won't speak Spanish in front of their friends, and they say that their father and I are "old-fashioned and old country." Should we just give in and let them be American? What do you suggest?

A: The problem of the bilingual-bicultural child is not at all uncommon in our society. No child wants to be different from his peers. Hence, it is natural for your son and daughter to wish to be perceived as "American" by their new American friends. This is less a problem for younger children who are less peer-influenced, and interestingly, less a problem for adolescents over the age of eighteen, as young adults generally appreciate their uniqueness and accommodate to bicultural status.

But right now you've got a problem. How to deal with it? First of all, I notice that you are here temporarily. This is very important. You can't afford to let your youngsters lose touch with your culture's traditions, family rules, and values. If you do, they'll be in real trouble when you return home. The children will be in danger of belonging nowhere. So, maintain your most important traditions. At the same time, it would be useful to talk to other American parents. Learn from them about their own home rules, behavioral expectations, and so forth. In this way you may be able to give your children the best of both worlds.

Moving to Another City

Q: My husband is being transferred in his job and we will soon be moving to another area of the country. Our 12-year-old son is having a tough time. He doesn't want to leave his friends and his school. Is there anything we can do to help him?

A: Moving to a new city is stressful for children and for parents too. Yet your son's dilemma is common: the average American family moves once every 3 years.

The major losses for a 12-year-old, of course, are peer related. You can help him by allowing him to talk about his friends and how much he will miss them. Try to resist the temptation to give him a pep talk or a hype job about the new city and how great it's going to be for him. Instead, empathize with him: "Yes, you're going to miss Peter," and "Yes, you sure have had some good times at Jackson School."

Your son will appreciate your sensitivity and your understanding.

Next, help him plan ways to say good-bye to his friends and to keep in touch with them after you've moved. It will be a big boost to his psychological development if you help him to develop depth and permanence in these relationships. Depth comes from sharing and commitment and learning how to express feeling when you say "good-bye." Permanence comes from sustaining relationships by letter, by phone, or by visiting after having moved away. Some suggestions:

1) Have your son make a list of people to whom he will personally say "good-bye." He should see each of them individually and tell them how much they've meant to him.

2) He might give each of them something of his own as a memento.

3) He may want to make a photo album of his friends, his school, his room, his "favorite places."

4) He should also plan to write regularly to a few friends. Some kids even like to make cassette tapes for their friends.

5) When you actually make the move, be sure that he packs a number of familiar objects (posters, records, etc.) so that his "new room" will feel at least a little bit like "home."

Of course, your son, as a 12-year-old, is also anxious about what the kids will be like in the next school. Will he be accepted? Encourage him to talk this out with you. Help him plan some strategies for taking the initiative in making new friends. One youngster I know has it down to a science. She embarks on a vigorous "Friend Hunt" as soon as she starts at a new school.

Moves, even to another neighborhood in the same city, can be very traumatic for pre-teens. After all, they're searching for permanence, since so much of their lives is about to change so dramatically. Develop a sensitive plan to ease the transition.

47

One final word: your youngster will pick up many of his cues from you and your husband. If you are positive and optimistic about the move, it's bound to rub off on him — at least a little bit. And that can help a lot if you're a 12-year-old and unhappy.

Assertiveness Training for Parents

Assertiveness training teaches how to be authoritative without being authoritarian. Good for kids — and parents too.

Q: My husband and I are very easygoing. Over the years, our children, 12, 10, and 7, have learned to take advantage of us. When we say "no," for example, they realize they can go right ahead and do whatever they want. We're finally starting to wake up. My neighbor has recommended something called Assertiveness Training for us. What is it? Does it work?

A: Assertiveness Training teaches parents how to regain control of their children. Taught properly, it teaches parents how to set limits, to enforce rules, and to teach discipline. Taught properly, it teaches that assertiveness is not the same as aggressiveness; that you can be authoritative without being authoritarian.

In one study of parents in San Diego who took such a course, the researchers found that behavior problems of children decreased 29% to 42%.

The first step in raising children to be self-disciplined is to be disciplined yourself. You can't control a child's misbehavior unless you control your own actions. You also have needs and rights. Parents should be in charge of their own families. That's what AT is all about.

Psychiatric and Behavioral Concerns

Kids on the Couch

Don't be stonewalled by therapists. You have every right to know your youngster's diagnosis, how it got to be a problem, what treatment will be used, and the estimated cost. Also, ask what you can do to help. Be a partner with the therapist in your child's treatment.

Q: Arthur, our 11-year-old, has just started seeing a psychiatrist. When we asked how long it would take, the doctor made us feel we were asking an impossible question. Shouldn't we be able to get this information?

A: Yes — and no. You should certainly work with the psychiatrist in determining the specific goals of the treatment. The doctor should then explain what techniques he will use. He or she should also give you an overall diagnosis and explain it to you. This basic information is the "road map" of therapy, i.e., "Where are we going?"

Your question "How long will it take to get there?" is tougher to answer. Length of treatment depends on several factors, including the severity of the problem, the child's relative resistance to treatment, the effectiveness of family responses, unforeseen external influences, and of course, the skill of the psychiatrist. Nevertheless, the doctor, experienced with similar cases, should be able to give you a good ballpark estimate. Be sure to ask again.

Our Daughter Wants Family Therapy

Q: Merrie, our 12-year-old, is seeing a psychiatrist. She's had weekly individual sessions for the past two months and they seem to be helping. But now there's a twist. She wants her father and me and her two brothers to join her for her appointments. She wants to switch to family therapy. I called her doctor, of course, but she said that "it's up to Merrie." I'm confused. We know that Merrie has a problem, but we didn't know it was a family problem. What should we do?

Family therapy is often the preferred treatment for pre-teens. It's not necessarily that the family is causing their problems, but that family life is the stage upon which they act out their problems.

A: You need more clarification. Start with Merrie herself. Why does she want family therapy? I can guess at some possibilities.

1) She may feel scapegoated, i.e., she may think that she's been singled out as having a problem while there are other members of the family who need help too. 2) She may simply want more support. 3) She may be at a phase in her treatment where she is dealing with some issues that specifically involve other family members, and can best be dealt with in a family therapy setting.

Next, schedule a meeting for yourself and your husband with Merrie's doctor. She may be able to give you a better rationale than, "It's up to Merrie."

You should know that family therapy, or a combination of individual and family sessions, is the customary treatment for pre-teens. The reason? Their problems tend to be played out in family life. Because the family is the arena for much of their difficulty (conflict with their parents and siblings, etc.), the family must ultimately be part of the solution.

Male vs Female Therapist

The gender of a youngster's therapist may be an important factor in some cases, but more important is the therapist's experience and skill.

Q: We recently took our daughter Colleen, 12, to a clinic for a psychiatric evaluation. She's been very depressed lately and her grades have fallen drastically. We weren't really surprised when the doctor recommended therapy. We were surprised, though, that he stressed Colleen should have a female therapist. I should have asked questions, but I didn't. Is it because Colleen's a girl? Is it because I'm the cause of her problem and she needs a substitute mother? Or what?

A: The proper selection of a therapist is very important. The most crucial factors are the skill and the training of the therapist to deal with Colleen's particular problem; a child psychiatrist or a non-medical therapist who has specific training in child therapy would be a must. Next come the personal attributes of the therapist: warmth, interest, empathy. Then there are a host of other factors; one of them is sex.

The therapist's sex can be an important factor in some cases. For example, a girl who has been sexually abused and fears men may do better with a sympathetic female therapist. But wait. It's not that simple. It might be argued, in a specific case, that the girl should have a male therapist — since he can provide her with a corrective emotional experience, his respectful caring for her can lead her more quickly to a trust of other males. My overall opinion is that selection of a therapist by sex alone is usually unwise. Good therapists, male and female, tend to work well with both sexes.

What about Colleen? Why the recommendation for a female therapist? Don't jump to conclusions. Your best bet is to call the doctor who performed the initial evaluation and ask him. He should be willing to answer your question.

Daughter Won't Go for Help

If your child, needing help, refuses it — go yourself.

Q: My daughter, Heather, is 11. She's been a difficult child ever since her father and I divorced four years ago. She's testy, defiant, calls me names, sasses her teachers. I know she needs help, and I made an appointment with a psychologist last week, but she refuses to go. What should I do ?

A: Go yourself. Start the ball rolling: I agree that Heather needs help — and so do you.

Most kids can think of three dozen things they'd rather do than see a psychiatrist. In Heather's case, her defiance is undoubtedly a factor. I have found that a youngster's initial refusal of therapy is a test: How serious are you? To what extent are you willing to go ?

Look at it another way. If, instead of a behavior problem, Heather had a serious medical problem and refused to see the doctor, you'd find some way to get her there, wouldn't you?

Talk it over with the psychologist. The two of you should be able to come up with a workable strategy. Once you have this, it's the psychologist's job to keep her coming back — with your cooperation and, ultimately, Heather's too.

Confidentiality in Child Therapy

Q: Our 11-year-old, Julie, sees a doctor for therapy. No problem. She needs it. The problem is that the doctor won't tell us what's going on. He says it's "confidential." Don't we have a right, as parents, to know what's happening?

A: You certainly have a right to know "how it's going," but you should not necessarily expect to be told "what's being said." The difference is crucial. Like an adult patient, Julie must be able to trust in the confidential relationship with her doctor. If she feels he is reporting everything right back to you, she'll feel cheated: She'll assume that the doctor is acting, not as her special helper, but as the hired hand of Mom and Dad.

On the other hand, it's my opinion that some child therapists carry confidentiality too far, and even hide behind it in an effort to exclude parents. You should know what the problem is, how it got to be a problem, and what's being done about it. You should also expect the doctor to break Julie's confidentiality if he learns of anything that urgently threatens her health or safety. Get these assurances, then relax. Therapy usually takes time.

Parents should expect to know from the therapist how things are going, but not what is being said.

Do Teenagers Outgrow Hyperactivity?

Q: Our son Lawrence, 12, is hyperactive. He's been treated with medication and counseling for about five years. When he was initially diagnosed we were told that he would "outgrow" it when he hit puberty. His current psychiatrist says that many kids need some type of treatment throughout their adolescence. Lawrence has always assumed he could "quit therapy" at 13. He's really pushing for it. Should we go along, at least on a trial basis?

Attention Deficit Hyperactivity Disorder (ADHD), contrary to earlier belief, may extend through adolescence. Continued treatment with medication and/or counseling may be necessary.

A: An early theory was that Attention Deficit Hyperactivity Disorder (ADHD) was due to a developmental lag and that youngsters would indeed "outgrow" it — most likely in adolescence. More recent studies, however, suggest that many youngsters do not.

These studies, I must point out, are somewhat mixed and contradictory. One reason is the variable design method of the studies, i.e., ages of subjects, length of follow-up, retrospective, prospective use of controls, etc. Dr. Lilly Hechman of Montreal Children's Hospital reports in Psychiatric Annals, November 1989, that generally 70% of adolescents who have had ADHD as children continue to have symptoms such as overactivity, poor concentration, academic difficulties, and emotional or behavioral problems.

What to do about Lawrence? Talk it over with his doctor. You might even get a second opinion as part of a comprehensive re-evaluation. Then share the information with your son. Make him part of the decision-making process.

Hyperactivity and Delinquency

Hyperactive boys who do not receive appropriate treatment (medication plus therapy) are twice as likely to be delinquent.

Q: Our hyperactive 12-year-old, Scott, is taking medication. It seems to work. Scott isn't so restless and his concentration is better. Our pediatrician says that Scott should have psychiatric counseling, but we don't see the need for it. What do you think?

A: In general, the treatment of choice for hyperactivity (or Attention Deficit Hyperactivity Disorder, its new name) is a combination of medication, counseling, family education, and special academic approaches in the classroom.

A study conducted by the National Center for Hyperactive Children shows that medication plus psychotherapy is a far superior treatment than medication alone. Nine years after treatment, hyperactive boys who received only medication, for example, were twice as likely to be multiple felony offenders (robbery, grand theft, assault, etc.), and three times more likely to have been institutionalized. I think that your pediatrician is giving you some good advice.

Ritalin: Good or Bad?

Ritalin and other medications, properly indicated and supervised, can be extremely valuable in the treatment of Attention Deficit Hyperactivity Disorder.

Q: On several morning talk shows lately I've seen discussions on the drug Ritalin. The psychiatrists say it's good. Parents of some kids who have been on it say that it is bad. With so many side effects, why do doctors use it? Is it good or bad?

P.S. My 11-year-old nephew is on it.

A: No approved medication is inherently good or bad. Medication, however, can be misused. There is no doubt, for example, that Ritalin, a drug used to treat hyperactivity, has been misused by some practitioners. When a youngster is properly diagnosed, Ritalin can have some dramatically positive effects. Close follow-up is also necessary to guard against side effects. Finally, it's important to add that proper treatment of hyperactivity (or Attention Deficit Disorder) should also include counseling for the young patient and his parents.

Stimulant Rebound

Q: Stephen, our 11-year-old, has been diagnosed as having Attention Deficit Disorder with Hyperactivity. The medication, amphetamine, has been almost miraculous. For the first time he can sit still in school, concentrate, follow directions. He's no longer the class "bad actor" and he feels good about himself. The trouble occurs when he gets home: he's more hyper than ever. Is this the medication or something else?

Medication must be carefully monitored by a physician. A youngster's needs change over time. Modification of dosage and frequency is often necessary.

A: Some children appear to suffer a so-called "rebound effect" about 5 hours after the administration of a single dose of dextro-amphetamine.

There are studies suggesting that this is frequently the case, but there are other studies, using placebo double blinds, suggesting that the effects are neither great nor clinically significant.

Your own case, however, is what we have to deal with here. There are several steps:

1) Review the medication with a child psychiatrist. A modification in dosage and/or timing may be all that's needed.

2) Consider a change to Ritalin or Cylert, both psychostimulants to which Stephen may have better response.

3) Closely examine Stephen's routine at home. Are there behavioral modifications that can be made, such as more structure?

It's still early in Stephen's treatment. Hang in there. You'll find the answers.

Tics and Hyperactivity

Q: Our son, Joseph, is 12. He has facial tics because of Tourette's Syndrome (TS). Recently his pediatrician, working

Psychiatrists have several alternatives if medication side effects develop.

closely with his classroom teacher, diagnosed hyperactivity. The doctor, however, says that he's reluctant to treat the hyperactivity because the medication will probably make the tics worse. Is there a solution?

A: Yes. Your pediatrician is following an understandable, conservative path. He knows that about 30% of TS patients treated with methylphenidate or amphetamines, the two most commonly used medications in the treatment of hyperactivity, develop worse tics. For this reason, many clinicians have avoided such treatment — even when there is a family history of TS.

A recent study, however, from the Yale University School of Medicine holds out some hope. Research child psychiatrists used desipramine, an antidepressant, to treat hyperactivity in seven boys who also had TS. The treatment was successful in five cases. Only one boy suffered increased tics — an intermittent eye blink.

Why not talk it over with the pediatrician? I'm sure that you and he don't want to leave any stones unturned.

Shoplifting

Whenever possible, allow your child to learn from his own mistakes (logical consequences). There does not have to be a parental solution (punishment) to all episodes of misbehavior.

Q: My wife and I are humiliated. Our 11-year-old son was just caught for shoplifting. He's never been in trouble before. What should we do?

A: I'm glad that you're concerned. This could be serious. But, before jumping to conclusions, let's review the situation.

The first reaction of most parents is similar to your own: humiliation, anger, confusion. Rule Number 1: there is no reason to hide your feelings. They are bound to show anyway. Let your son know exactly how you feel — without calling him names, jumping to conclusions, or making threats.

The next step is to listen to your boy. Really listen. What does his behavior mean? Is he sending a signal to you that he feels deprived or that he needs attention? Was he pressured by peers? Was he trying to "look big" for some of his friends?

It is important to listen and to understand. Many children try shoplifting once or twice, usually on impulse or on a dare from friends. While such behavior is serious and calls for effective parental response, it is not as serious as when shoplifting is a symptom of underlying depression or loneliness or when shoplifting has become a habit. Listen and learn.

Whatever the underlying cause of your son's behavior, he should definitely be given a chance to learn something from this experience. Many parents would be tempted to take this matter into their own hands by apologizing to the store owner, and even paying for the stolen merchandise. Please resist this temptation. Let your son do it. The consequence of shoplifting is that he should face the music.

Since, however, this seems to be your son's first such episode, I would suggest that you have a private talk with the store owner first so that you can be sure that he'll be reasonable with your son: not too lenient, not too tough. One good solution, for example, is for your son to pay back the store owner by stocking shelves on Saturdays for a couple of weeks.

She's Pulling Her Hair Out

Q: My 11-year-old daughter, Stephanie, is pulling her hair out. She's been at it for about 6 months and we can't stop her. It's an irresistible urge. One doctor suggested putting mittens on her hands, but even that plan flopped. What do you suggest?

A: Your daughter's symptom is trichotillomania. It's not as rare as you might think. It's a habit disorder of childhood, like nail biting or thumb sucking. The symptom usually begins as a child's preoccupation with stroking, brushing, or twirling her hair excessively. This can lead to the uncontrollable habit of pulling out individual follicles or yanking out hair in small patches.

Stephanie's hair-pulling may be symptomatic of underlying emotional conflict. Her symptom can be viewed as "body language," i.e., to "pull your hair out" usually signifies tension or frustration. Furthermore, the research on trichotillomania suggests that many of these youngsters suffer from hidden depression.

Because Stephanie's symptom has not responded to earlier treatment, she should certainly be evaluated by a child psychiatrist. A combination of talking therapy and behavior modification is successful in most cases. In others, newer treatments using medications commonly used to treat anxiety disorders and obsessive-compulsive disorders may be helpful.

Accidents as Suicide Attempts

Q: Our nephew is 11 and we're worried. He keeps having serious accidents. In the past year he has fallen off the garage

It's called trichotillomania, a real mouthful that describes the chronic habit of pulling hair out of one's own scalp. Treatment with behavior modification and medication is effective.

Accident proneness can signal serious depression and even suicidal tendency.

roof, had his clothes set on fire, and "accidently" cut himself with a very sharp knife. He's having trouble in school, and he's angry at his parents most of the time. Bob and Louisa, his parents, don't think there's a problem. "It's a phase," they say. They won't take him for help. What do you think?

A: I think your nephew is not the only one playing with fire. Bob and Louisa are wearing psychological blinders. Their son is at serious risk. In fact, he may be suicidal.

Why? Repeated accidents of this magnitude in an unhappy boy with school performance problems and serious conflicts with his parents define the profile of possible childhood suicide. These "accidents" may be disguised episodes of self-inflicted injury. They could be the prelude to something even more serious.

Don't wait for tragedy to strike. Do whatever you can to help. Don't delay.

Fear of Success

The pre-teen whose major success is failure is struggling with unconscious conflicts. Seek help before the pattern becomes a well-defined lifestyle.

Q: Anthony, our 11-year-old, just can't seem to do anything right. The poor little guy struggles in school, he struggles in sports, he struggles in Scouts, he can't even do the dishes without creating havoc. The funny thing about it, though, is that he doesn't really seem unhappy. That's why we were a little surprised when a school counselor suggested that maybe he was suffering from something called "Fear of Success." I've never heard of it. What is it?

A: You won't find "Fear of Success" listed in the diagnostic nomenclature of psychiatric textbooks, yet it's not an uncommon problem.

The child who unconsciously is afraid to succeed at things will somehow manage to always mess things up — since, if he succeeds, he will become very anxious. Why? There are several possibilities. Some boys, for example, equate success to competition with their fathers and they are afraid to win, as the classic Freudian explanation goes, lest Dad retaliate against them. Other youngsters simply feel unworthy of success. Still other children shy away from success, because they fear that Mom and Dad will simply demand more and greater accomplishments from them; they view success as a tiresome treadmill.

Is Anthony's problem really a fear of success? Hard to say. One tip-off, though, is that he isn't upset by it. This leads me to suspect that his failures have become acceptable to him. It could be, therefore, that his lack of success serves to defend him psychologically against something that he unconsciously dreads even more than failure.

My advice is to have him evaluated by a child psychiatrist. Let's get to the bottom of this. He'll soon be entering adolescence. Now's the time to take action.

Obsessive-Compulsive?

Q: I think my 11-year-old, Jeff, is classified or something. Every time he encounters something he wants to "put it into a classification." For example, a car might be: "1) Sedan, 2) Buick, 3) General Motors, 4) Automobile, 5) Type of ground transportation." He's like a broken record. Is this good or bad? Is he obsessive-compulsive?

A: Good or bad? If you mean "healthy/normal" or "unhealthy/abnormal," it's not easy to tell.

Children of 8-11 usually have a fascination with order, organization, and classification. It's one way they strive to bring order to their world. It's also healthy evidence of their expanding intellectual capacities.

If Jeff, on the other hand, is absolutely obsessed with his classification schemes, it may signal abnormal behavior. Does he have any rituals? Magic words? Does he become very anxious if he's stopped from "classifying"? If so, and if the behavior is truly excessive, it may be symptomatic of Obsessive-Compulsive Disorder. In this case a consultation with a child psychiatrist would be in order.

Pre-teen collections in the form of hobbies are healthy and should be encouraged. Excessive preoccupation, however, with order and classification may signal a problem such as Obsessive-Compulsive Disorder, especially if the youngster becomes very upset if her activity is interrupted.

Temper Tantrums

Q: Our 11-year-old, Martin, is seeing a child psychiatrist because of temper tantrums. He's fine at school and in the neighborhood. His explosions (kicking, screaming, hitting) only happen at home. I think I know why he's got the problem, but I've been afraid to tell the doctor. My husband, who always appears reasonable and in control at the psychiatrist's office, is just like Marty at home. My question is: Can Marty really be helped if I don't come clean about his father?

A: No. Everyone will suffer from the cover-up. Marty's trust in you, by the way, will suffer too.

Temper tantrums are not unusual among pre-teens, especially if there is poor modeling of frustration tolerance in the home.

Sounds like you're afraid of your husband. Sounds like you need some help. I suggest a private chat first with the doctor, either by phone or in person. Level with him or her and ask for advice on how to proceed.

Unless Dad's behavior is modified, Marty is in trouble and so are you. I think you know this, and your getting Marty into treatment was simply a first step toward getting help for your husband and your marriage. It's not a bad plan — pursue it all the way. The whole family may be at stake.

Cruelty to Pets

Cruelty to pets is a strong predictor of future violence toward people.

Q: My nephew, Brandon, is 11. He has a bad temper and has a tough time keeping friends. The thing that really bothers me though is that he abuses his pet dog and cat. He beats them with sticks and throws them off the porch. He even makes a game out of it that he calls "Dead or Alive." Does he need help or is this just a stage?

A: I'm very concerned about this behavior. Psychiatrists have long known that cruelty to animals, especially pets, is a marker for future violent behavior, including aggression toward people.

In one recent study reported by researchers from Yale and the University of Texas, for example, it was found that 25% of 150 prisoners in two federal penitentiaries had tortured animals during their childhoods.

Brandon's behavior, including his problems with peers, suggests that he is a very angry boy. Yes, he's at risk. It's not a stage. He needs help. See a child psychiatrist now to avoid bigger problems later.

Shyness

Pre-teens, like early adolescents, are often unsure of themselves. That's why they may be overly sensitive to criticism. The old ounce of honey vs a gallon of vinegar aphorism applies here.

Q: Michael, my 12-year-old, has always been a little shy, but lately he's been overly sensitive to criticism. He breaks down in tears at the slightest negative comment. Is it a phase?

A: Yes and no. Twelve-year-olds are vulnerable to criticism because they harbor so many secret doubts about themselves. They feel awkward. Everything seems out of control: their thoughts, their feelings, their bodies — everything. Criticism of any kind, therefore, can tap this wellspring of self-centered preoccupation.

On the other hand, Michael's sensitivity may well be related to his longtime shyness and a basic sense of poor self-esteem.

If so, he could be headed for trouble. You ought to consider professional help.

Shy or Withdrawn?

Q: Taylor is 12. We've always considered him to be shy. He gets very nervous in front of strangers, but he struggles to make and keep friends. His teacher recently said he's "withdrawn" and should see the school counselor. What's the difference? What should we do?

A: I can tell you the distinctions I make. A withdrawn child is often depressed and discouraged. He pulls away from other youngsters because he doesn't feel good about himself. He lacks self-esteem and is convinced that no one else likes him either. He's a pessimist. If things are bad, they're going to get worse. These feelings are fixed and painful.

The shy youngster may also lack self-esteem, but his shyness is more often linked to new experiences, strangers, or group phenomena. Often, like Taylor, the shy child fights against his shyness, while the chronically withdrawn youngster tends to surrender to his depression. The pain of shyness, by the way, is typically anxiety rather than depression, while the pain of withdrawal is usually depression. On the other hand, some shy youngsters suffer a secondary or reactive depression if their efforts to overcome their problem meet with continued failure.

Those are my distinctions. Why not review them with Taylor's teacher? The most important issue is Taylor's current level of discomfort and functioning. Shy or withdrawn? If Taylor needs help, the distinction doesn't amount to much more than a word game.

It's sometimes hard to tell them apart, but the shy youngster is usually anxious, the withdrawn youngster, depressed.

Shyness and Behavior Therapy

Q: Our son Scott, 11, is very shy. He cries and shakes when he has to recite in front of the class. A psychologist has recommended behavior therapy. What is it? Will it work?

A: Behavior therapy is based upon learning theory. It assumes that symptoms, such as shyness, are learned responses to specific stimuli, such as reciting in front of a class. Using techniques such as positive reinforcement (rewards), it attacks the symptom itself rather than searching for hidden meanings for the problem. Generally speaking, behavior modification

Shyness can be seriously disabling. Untreated, it does not tend to go away. Treatment, especially after behavior modification, is effective.

treatment is more focused and shorter than talking therapies that seek to uncover unconscious causes.

Does it work? Yes, in many cases it does. Will it work for Scott? Time will tell. Keep in touch with the therapist. Watch Scott's progress. If you don't see results in three or four months of weekly sessions, consult with the psychologist about a switch to another form of treatment.

The goal of treatment? Less performance anxiety. More comfort in front of groups. No, treatment may not eliminate the butterflies completely, but it should get them to fly in formation.

Over-Sensitive to Smells

A youngster who is overly sensitive to smells may suffer from other perceptual problems and even learning disabilities.

Q: Our James, 11, has always been touchy and over-reactive. Noise distracts him. Tight clothes bother him. But the thing that really bugs us is that he often complains that things smell bad. The problem is that it's usually me — especially my hair spray, or my cologne. I tell him to ignore it, but he says he can't. Is he just angry at me? Why does he take it out on me like this?

A: I need a lot more for a diagnosis, but it is possible that James suffers from a general disorder of perception. You've already identified three intensified senses: sound, touch, and smell. Is he bothered by bright light? By unusual tastes?

Children with such perceptual problems often have learning disabilities as well. They may have trouble with fine motor coordination. For example, was it tough for James to learn to tie his shoes? Is he still clumsy?

To arrive at an accurate diagnosis, James will have to be seen by a child psychiatrist. Treatment would be aimed at identified symptoms. Although there is no specific treatment for his disorder of smell, it may respond to the overall treatment, which may include medication.

Video Game Addiction

Video games are neither good nor bad, but preoccupation with them is unhealthy. Studies suggest that they can be habituating because of the way in which they are designed to induce reinforcement.

Q: I think my nephew, 11, is addicted to video games. He sits there almost in a trance day and night. He even skips school to play video games. Unfortunately, his parents don't do anything about it. His father is an alcoholic and his mother is just too harried with the other three children. Could my nephew be addicted to video games?

A: I don't like the sound of it. Video games, per se, are neither good nor bad, but preoccupation with any escapist activity is not healthy. Your nephew's obsession with video games may be his way of coping with the turmoil in his family.

Addiction to video games, of course, is not based on physiological dependence as is drug and alcohol abuse, but there is some evidence that video game programmers seek to create a psychological habituation in the players. Dr. George Keepers reports in the *Journal of American Academy of Child and Adolescent Psychiatry*, January 1990, that factors which induce players to continue to play have been scientifically studied and have been incorporated into the games.

Your nephew? I view his video gaming as an unhealthy and unsuccessful attempt to defend against his hurt. He needs help, and so does his entire family.

Stuttering

Q: Tommy, our 12-year-old, stutters. He sees a speech therapist and it helps. But he's so miserable. He thinks he's "dumb." He gets so frustrated. And my husband doesn't help either. He refuses to respond to Tommy unless the boy "says it right." Is this right? Should we see a child psychiatrist or what?

Stuttering is a disorder of speech, not a psychiatric problem in most cases. Get your child to a speech therapist. The psychiatrist can usually wait.

A: Stutterers are not dumb. Tommy is in good company. Isaac Newton and Winston Churchill, for example, were both stutterers.

Stuttering (or stammering, as some call it) results when the normal free flow of speech is broken by repetitions or prolongations of sounds or syllables. It is not considered a mental or psychiatric disorder.

Causes? We're not sure. There are probably a variety of causes: neurological, muscular, stress, family history, and even improper learning of normal speech patterns.

Perhaps your husband believes his approach is what Tommy needs, but it's not. Tommy does not need punishment or negative reinforcement. Such approaches often just add fuel to the fire. They can lead to shame, frustration, poor self-esteem, and even depression. That's when you have to call in the child psychiatrist.

I would urge both of you to approach Tommy naturally. Look at him when he speaks. Be patient. Don't hurry him. Don't finish his sentences for him. Consult with the speech therapist for other suggestions.

Does Stress = Success?

High stress pre-teens tend to develop physical symptoms, body language at its worst.

Q: My husband and I are both high-achievers, your classic Type-A personalities. It may sound bad, but it isn't. We thrive on pressure and stress. We're happy in our careers. But our 12-year-old, Sherri, isn't so happy with herself. She doesn't handle stress very well. Any advice?

A: Stress exacts a price. You and your husband apparently are willing to pay it. Sherri is struggling.

In one study of 7th graders, a Stanford University researcher found that not only do high-stress youngsters tend to develop physical symptoms (headaches, upset stomachs, day-time fatigue), but they don't do any better academically than low-stress children.

This is a most interesting finding since many Type-A parents tend to rationalize their stressful lifestyles by saying something like: "Oh well, it's the price I pay for success." Their children, then, identify with their driven aggressive behavior in an effort to duplicate parental achievements. But if, perhaps like Sherri, they're just built differently from Mom and Dad, if they lack their parents' intellectual, emotional, and physical drive, they fail to complete the formula. For them stress does not create success. It creates frustration, shame, and anger.

Help Sherri find her own equation for success. Encourage her to slow down — even if you can't.

Stressbusters

Pre-teens may start to feel out of control, which leads to stress. Getting them organized and in control of things is a great stressbuster.

Q: Tammy, 12, is a gifted child, so we've given her a lot of special opportunities. Last year, however, she was so stressed out by her schedule of school, homework, ballet, computer tutoring, etc. that we insisted that she cut back a bit. It helped but she's still overwhelmed much of the time. We're afraid to eliminate more of her activities for fear that she'll lose confidence in herself. What can we do?

A: I believe that all children should be required to do their very best according to their individual abilities. The key, of course, is to neither underload nor overload a child with "opportunities."

The first step, then, is a realistic assessment of Tammy's capabilities.

Once you've decided on a workable schedule for her, put the emphasis on teaching her to control her life. Learning how to set priorities (such as making a list of "Things To Do" each day) is a start. Next comes a network of support in the family. Finally, encourage her to be flexible and optimistic and not to demand perfection from herself.

Lateness

Q: David, our 11-year-old, is always late. It used to be cute, but now it gets on our nerves. I sometimes think he does it for attention, but maybe there's a deeper meaning. Any ideas?

A: Yes. All behavior has meaning and purpose. Lateness is behavior. Therefore, David's lateness has meaning and purpose. Let's examine some of the most common causes of lateness:

1) *Disorganization.* No deep psychological motives here. Some youngsters are just too disorganized to get to places on time.

2) *Attention-getting.* Yes, some children crave the attention of being fussed over and scolded. Negative attention is better than no attention at all.

3) *Avoidance.* Some youngsters secretly aim to avoid certain people or situations by being late.

4) *Resentment and hostility.* This is the classic Freudian explanation. Lateness can be the passive expression of anger.

5) *Revenge.* If Mom and Dad value punctuality and a child wants to retaliate, he may take his revenge through lateness.

6) *Autonomy.* Some boys and girls are engaged in a struggle to be independent. They march to their own drummer. Being late symbolizes their autonomy.

7) *Power trip.* The child who needs to show that he's boss may be habitually late in making his less-than-subtle point.

Please look this list over. Try to understand David's motives. Then, help him change. After all, better late than never.

Chronic, habitual lateness or procrastination has many psychological meanings. Before confronting your child, understand his hidden meanings.

Cuss Words Are Cop-Outs

Q: Our 11-year-old, Alex, is picking up quite a vocabulary of foul, four-letter words and it is causing a big conflict in our home.

My husband believes that it is good for Alex to "express his feelings" and, therefore, condones the cussing. I'm shocked and don't like that kind of language one bit. What is your opinion?

A: I definitely side with you in this conflict, but not because I am shocked. While your husband is quite correct in wanting

The verbal expression of feelings is good, but don't allow profanity. It's inflammatory.

63

Alex to freely express his feelings, he is doing your son a disservice by allowing cuss words. These expletives do not allow Alex to express his feelings one bit. To the contrary, cuss words are cop-outs. They are inexact, meaning everything and nothing. Most of the time they actually obscure the true underlying feelings. Better you insist that Alex takes the time to find the correct words that accurately express his feelings. Allowing him to "shoot from the lip" is hardly good practice for thoughtful expression.

There are other good reasons, of course, to forbid such language: it can be abusive, and it creates a nasty, negative conversational environment. Such language can be inflammatory and turn a would-be listener into a defensive counter-attacker.

Alcohol and Drug Abuse

Early Drug Abuse Prevention

While there's no guaranteed formula, wise parents will set a good example, get informed, stay involved, and go for help if necessary.

Q: Our daughter, Robin, is 11. Like all parents of pre-teens, we're concerned about what lies ahead in adolescence — especially the drug scene. My husband and I have read a lot about teen drug use and we've even attended some meetings. What advice would you give us to help ensure that Robin does not get into drugs?

A: There is, of course, no foolproof formula, but I will pass along some ideas.

1) *Parental example.* Mothers and fathers who abuse alcohol or drugs are inviting their children to do the same — no matter how much they may preach against it. You don't have to be a teetotaler, by the way; that's not what I mean. But if you usually turn to alcohol to change your mood, if you use illegal substances, if your life becomes unmanageable as a result of substance abuse — you're setting a dangerous example.

2) *Early influence.* A parent's biggest chance to influence a child comes in the first ten years. After that, peer influence mounts and your influence wanes. Use the early years carefully, therefore, to instill strong positive values.

3) *Peer influence.* Know your youngster's friends — and their parents. Come down hard if Robin should drift into a

negative peer group. On the other hand, encourage friendships with the right kind of youngsters (ones who don't use drugs).

4) *Get informed.* I salute your active interest in getting informed about adolescence and teen drug abuse. This will help a lot. Read books, attend meetings, keep in touch with Robin's school, and let Robin herself educate you too. She'll be your best teacher of what it's like to be an adolescent today.

5) *Keep in touch.* You've heard it said many times, but it's still true — open communication is an absolute must.

6) *Get help if necessary.* Don't hesitate to consult with a professional if there's trouble and it doesn't respond to your initial intervention. Too many parents delude themselves by assuming, "It's just a stage, she'll get over it." Good luck. I like Robin's chances for a successful adolescence. Why? You and your husband are planning ahead.

Predicting Teen Drinkers

Q: My husband and I know that alcohol is the Number One drug problem for teenagers. We try to set a good example by not abusing booze, and we talk to the kids (ages 11 and 13) about it too. Is there any way to predict which youngsters are going to be most vulnerable to abuse?

Alcohol is still the No. 1 substance abuse problem. Many teenage alcoholics get started at 11 or 12. Talk to your pre-teen about it. Set a good example.

A: First of all, we know that alcoholism tends to run in families. Sons of alcoholic fathers are well-documented in the medical literature as being especially vulnerable; although, in my own experience, I have found daughters of alcoholic mothers and fathers are also prone.

A study conducted at the University of South Florida suggests some additional warning signs. Over 600 7th and 8th graders responded to a 90-item questionnaire. In a follow-up one year later, the researchers found that the children who initially believed that alcohol would help them have more friends and do better in school were at greatest risk for problem drinking.

The lesson is clear. Kids often harbor gross misunderstandings about booze. The good news is that savvy and concerned parents, like you and your husband, are in the best position to correct these faulty ideas. Keep up the good work.

Adult Child of Alcoholics

Q: I'm a 32-year-old mother of an 11-year-old boy, Brad. I'm an alcoholic with four years of sobriety. My father died of

Children of alcoholics learn three things: don't feel, don't talk, don't trust. Ala-Teen is a good place for them.

alcoholism. I'm worried about my son. What are his chances of becoming alcoholic? Should he attend Ala-Teen ?

A: Alcoholism is a family disease. In my own professional work I have found that over half of my adolescent alcoholic patients have an alcoholic parent. The reasons are complex and probably include both inherited causes and environmental factors. Brad is certainly at risk.

My suggestion however, is that you start with yourself. As an adult child of an alcoholic you probably still have wounds that have not healed as a result of your own relationship with your father.

While I hope you're attending AA meetings for your recovery, I recommend an additional self-help group for you: The National Association of Children of Alcoholics. For membership information, write to NACoA, Suite 201, 31706 Coast Highway, South Laguna, CA 92267.

Children of alcoholics tend to learn three things: don't feel, don't talk, don't trust. If you want to break the chain of pain that binds your family, you will have to unlearn these traits so that you don't pass them on to your son.

And for Brad? Yes, I do recommend Ala-Teen, the self-help group specifically for non-alcoholic youngsters who have an alcoholic family member. Like NACoA, Ala-Teen heals hurts, and it's good preventative medicine.

Drugs and Pro Athletes

Sports figures are no more immune to drugs and alcohol than anyone else, but they are powerful role models for pre-teens. Help your youngster put them in context. Talk about them.

Q: How should we handle all these stories of pro athletes getting busted for drugs? Our sons, ages 11 and 12, are both sports nuts. They read about all these things. At first I was afraid that they would be suckered by a glorification of drugs. Then I worried that they'd suffer by losing their heroes. But neither happened. Now I'm worried that they're not worried. They seem to take it all in stride. Are drugs in sports so commonplace now that little boys don't even react when they read about the latest superstar who's just signed himself into a Rehab?

A: Sports figures, of course, are no more immune to alcohol and drugs than any other group. We sometimes expect more from them, however, because they are so revered by children. I'm pleased that you are tracking this matter so closely. I suggest further discussion with your boys. Why the apparent blasé attitude toward drugs? Their indifference may be hiding some strong feelings.

Apart from the matter of the pro athletes, let's recognize that your boys, at 11 and 12, are standing on the threshold of adolescence. It's a good time to talk to them about drugs anyway.

Teen Smoking

Q: Our daughter Nancy is 12. My husband and I are both smokers. Neither of us wants Nancy to smoke — but what are the odds of her becoming a smoker if both of us continue?

A: If you both smoke, Nancy's chances will be about 21%. But if you both quit, the odds of her taking up the habit drop dramatically down to 8-10%, according to a Johns Hopkins study.

I like these odds for Nancy — and for you. Why not quit now?

Teen smoking is heavily influenced by parental smoking. The best thing you can do, if you don't want your youngster to smoke, is quit.

Gasoline Huffing and Glue Sniffing

Q: My ex-husband, who has custody of our 12-year-old daughter, Mallory, says that she was caught at school "huffing gasoline." What is that? Is it as dangerous as glue sniffing? Should she get some kind of treatment?

A: Gasoline, when inhaled, is a mood-altering substance. Absorbed into the lungs, it can create a dizzy drunken state that can last a few hours.

Huffing refers to the practice of soaking a rag with gasoline, then inhaling through the cloth, using the nose and mouth, This is usually done by pre-teens or early adolescents in groups. Those youngsters destined for continued substance abuse usually "graduate" pretty quickly to things like alcohol, marijuana, and other substances. The major physical dangers are neurologic: tremors, abnormal movements. It is dangerous, but not as dangerous as glue sniffing.

Treatment? For your peace of mind, Mallory could be checked out by her pediatrician for any physical problems. I'm concerned, however, about chemical dependency. Consult with a psychiatrist who specializes in addictions or with a certified drug counselor. Let's make sure that Mallory isn't developing a High Octane drug problem.

Gasoline and glue sniffing, as preferred methods of drug abuse, are almost limited to pre-teens and early adolescents. Both practices are quite dangerous medically and can serve as gateways to experimenting with marijuana, alcohol, and hard drugs.

Psychological Aspects of Some Common Medical Disorders

Skinny Son?

Just as pre-teen girls are sometimes preoccupied with being overweight, pre-teen boys may be bothered by the perception of being underweight. It's understandable. Soon, as early adolescents, their prowess and self-esteem will be expressed through their bodies.

Q: Jeremy is 11. His father and I think he's just fine, but his grandparents are always calling him "skinny" and it bothers him. Yes, he's thin, but not skinny. What should we do?

A: This problem has at least two parts. The first, the scientific part, can be easily settled. Just take Jeremy to his pediatrician and ask that he be checked on a "weight for height" chart. The doctor will be able to tell you precisely where Jeremy fits within the standardized norms.

The second part of the problem, the psychological, is probably going to be more difficult. Why the grandparents' preoccupation with Jeremy's weight or looks? Maybe they have a different notion of body weight and looks than you do (i.e., they may belong to the "fat and happy" school of thought). Maybe they are implying that you're not doing your job correctly as parents. After you get the information from the pediatrician, I suggest you address these issues.

In the meantime, be sure to let Jeremy know that he's just fine with you.

Undereaters

Undereating is not, of course, synonymous with anorexia (self starvation), but it could spell trouble for pre-teen girls. Proper nutrition, including normal body fat, is necessary for menstruation.

Q: Last week I took my 11-year-old daughter, Celeste, to the pediatrician. Celeste is a little on the thin side, but I was surprised to hear that she was actually underweight. The doctor said she's an undereater, that she could have physical trouble in adolescence. Is this the same as anorexia nervosa?

A: No. Anorexia nervosa is self-starvation. It includes weight loss of 25%, a pursuit of thinness, and a distorted body image. Your daughter's problem may be a slightly exaggerated form of dieting, an anxiety to be slim and trim. She probably skips some meals and avoids certain kinds of foods.

Yes, this could spell trouble in puberty. Most girls experience menarch (the onset of menstruation) and their growth spurt between the ages of 10 and 14. They need good nutrition and normal amounts of body fat to grow and develop.

TV and Sweets

Q: Toni, our 11-year-old, is a TV addict. She watches several hours a day. That's bad enough, and we're taking steps to limit her access to the television. The thing that worries us even more is that she stuffs herself with candy while she's watching her programs. Is it due to all the ads for junk food or what?

A: A nutritionist at Cornell University has concluded that the more TV a child watches, the more candy she eats. Researcher Christine Olson and her colleagues report that programming during so-called children's TV hours tends to be saturated with sweet commercials, and this obviously is an important factor.

But the researchers also identified a couple of other important influences: 1) Parental consumption. The more sweets a parent eats, the more a child eats. 2) Parental attitude. If parents, for example, use candy as a reward for good behavior, children eat three times as many sweets as children of parents who disapprove of sweet munchies.

So, for the answer to why Toni has developed a sweet tooth look not only to your TV — but also to yourself.

Television is a powerful influence (usually negative) on pre-teen diet habits, but parental behavior is too. Use it positively.

A Junk Food Queen

Q: Meghen, our 11-year-old, is a junk food freak. Even her teenage brother calls her "the queen of junk." If it was up to her, she'd feast on a steady diet of soda, pizza, candy, french fries, and cheeseburgers. No matter what we try, she manages to sneak her "snacks" into the house. Is it useless to nag? Is her health in danger?

A: While I share your concern about Meghen's nutrition, I find it intriguing that she persists in sneaking her goodies into the house. She might be making a little "game" out of this business. For example, she's certainly succeeded in getting her brother's goat!

I'd suggest a consultation with your pediatrician. Chances are he'll say that, although Meghen's eating habits are far from perfect, she's in good health. This is usually the case. I hope so.

If the report is positive, I would advise you to back off. Your attempts to break Meghen of her "addiction" to fast franchise food may be backfiring on you. Your punishment may be just

Some so-called junk foods may not be quite as bad as you think. Before you make a big issue out of it, check with the pediatrician.

so much icing on Meghen's devil's food cupcakes. Try ignoring her eating habits for a while. "Ignoring the Negative" is a good principle for managing misbehavior.

And, oh yes, be sure that your son is part of the plan too. Some of Meghen's "junk" may actually be for his benefit.

Fitness and Sports Medicine

A pre-teen's excessive preoccupation with fitness may signal psychological conflicts or sexual worries.

Q: Thomas, our 12-year-old, wants to go out for basketball next semester, but he's afraid he might not be physically fit. I don't understand it. He's in perfect shape. Yet, he insists that a check-up by his pediatrician will not be good enough. He wants to see a "sports medicine specialist" at the nearby University medical center. Comments?

A: My major concern for Thomas is psychological, not physical. Why the fear of fitness failure? Does he secretly fear injury? Is he worried about his body, and is this his way of getting it checked? Pre-adolescents often have exaggerated or fantasized notions about body function. Often, these notions are sexual in nature. If so, Thomas may be too embarrassed to ask his pediatrician about them — especially if the pediatrician is a female.

Sports medicine doctors, by the way, are capable of excellent fitness screening. They're trained to be very thorough. The customary "sports physical" in a doctor's office is a basic check of vital signs, heart, and hernia. Such an exam will identify only 15-20% of athletic risks. Maybe John has heard these things from his buddies. Maybe it's fashionable at his school to see a sports medicine specialist.

I suggest splitting the difference. Why not start with your trusted pediatrician? Alert him or her about John's concerns. Ask for special attention to psychological factors. Later, a more extended check by the specialist could round out the work-up.

Bedwetting Treatment

Not common among pre-teens, but when it exists, the result can be remorse and shame.

Q: We've tried everything: punishment, rewards, fluid restriction, even the buzzer alarm — but our Lewis, 11, still wets the bed. Any advice?

A: Here are some guidelines:

1) *Physical exam.* About 25% of cases are due to correctable medical abnormalities. Don't overlook something physical.

2) *No punishment.* Punishment, shaming, and ridicule only make things worse. The problem is out of Lewis' control. He can't help it.

3) *Buzzer alarm.* New-style fluid sensors are available. You may want to give it another try. The general success rate is about 50-75%.

4) *Delayed voiding.* Encourage Lewis to "hold it" as long as possible. In this way he learns control and his bladder is enlarged and strengthened.

5) *Medication.* The standby is imipramine which is successful in about 50% of cases within 1-2 weeks. Other treatments include desmopressin, amantadine, and oxybutynin. Consult with your pediatrician.

6) *Hypnosis.* Experienced hypnotherapists report good success in childhood enuresis.

7) *Time.* Time is on Lewis' side. His bladder will mature; 50% of enuretics become dry without treatment within 4 years of consulting for the problem.

8) *Relax.* It's frustrating, sure, but try to relax. Family stress and tension only compound the problem. If all else fails, the best you can do is to go with the flow, so to speak.

Girls and Bedwetting

Q: Our Wendy is 11. She still wets the bed almost every night. I thought this was mostly a problem of boys. Should we take her to a psychiatrist?

Bedwetting is not generally a psychiatric problem, but a psychiatrist can be very helpful if self-esteem has been eroded.

A: Bedwetting (enuresis) is not generally a psychiatric illness. It is usually due to an immaturity of the bladder and/or neurological system. Over 99% of children simply outgrow it by the time they reach adolescence.

Psychiatrists only become necessary when a child is so shamed or punished that he or she develops low self-esteem, depression, or other secondary emotional problems.

You're right about boys. The incidence of enuresis is about twice as common in boys up to 11. Then it's about the same.

Girls, by the way, more often have diurnal enuresis (night and day) and a greater likelihood of infection as the cause. So, be sure that Wendy is fully checked by your pediatrician.

Bedwetting Families

Q: My 11-year-old son, Arnie, is a bedwetter. My husband was a bedwetter when he was a boy. Does it really run in families?

Bedwetting, for unexplained reasons, does tend to run in families.

What are the odds of my 9-month-old daughter also turning out to be a bedwetter?

A: Yes, enuresis or bedwetting does tend to run in families, but we don't know exactly why. There may be an inherited trait that causes an immaturity of the bladder or the nervous system controlling urination.

Consider these facts:

1) In 70% of families with an enuretic child, the symptom appears in at least one other family member.

2) In 40% of cases at least one parent (like your husband) has a history of bedwetting.

The odds of your daughter also developing enuresis are about 25%. Be sure to consult with your pediatrician about treatment.

Won't Take Her Insulin

Pre-teens are famous for refusing to follow doctors' orders. Pill-taking is a constant reminder that they're different from their peers and that they are less than perfect. Non-compliance calls for gentle urging and greater sensitivity on the part of parents — and doctors.

Q: Our 12-year-old daughter, Lynda, is a juvenile diabetic. She's followed her diet and given herself insulin shots for the past three years. We've been very proud of her. Lately, though, she's let her diet slip and "forgets" to take her insulin on some days. As you can imagine, her sugar is out of control. Her doctor has tried to talk to her, but it doesn't seem to do any good. We're getting frantic. What can we do?

A: The number one cause of treatment failure among pre-teens and early adolescents, in my experience, is "non-compliance," or failure to follow doctor's orders. Why? The emotional, physical, and social pressures of adolescence. Lynda is entering a new phase of development, a phase where "to be different" is to feel worthless and alone. She may be sensitive to having diabetes because it sets her apart from other youngsters. She desperately wants to be just like everyone else.

Another factor is what we call "adolescent narcissism," the preoccupation with self-perfection. Actually it's a common teenage defense against the reality that they are far from perfect. Their bodies are changing, their feelings are changing, their world is changing. In a last-ditch effort to deny the obvious, some teenagers become self-centered and strive to be perfect — against the developmental tide. Youngsters with chronic illnesses, like Lynda, have a special problem in this arena because they have a daily reminder (an insulin syringe, for example) that they are far from perfect. Some kids, then, stop taking medication. Their unconscious reasoning: "If I don't take the medicine, I don't have the disease." It's a dangerous mind game to play.

On a more conscious level there is probably an element of good old teenage rebellion in Lynda's behavior.

I hope these observations help. Have another talk with Lynda yourself. Listen to her. If it doesn't work, I'd urge a consultation. Lynda's problem is not usual. A child psychiatrist should be able to help.

Hypochondriac?

Q: One physical complaint after another: headache, stomach ache, fear of skin cancer, you name it and our Mary Christine, 12, has had it. She's got the fattest chart at the doctor's office, but there's never anything wrong with her.

A: When most people say "it's all in your head," they imply that the complainer is: 1) just making it up, and 2) can, by change of attitude, make it go away just as easily. Neither is true.

Sounds like Mary Christine is well on the way to hypochondria. She is obsessed with her body and overreacts to real or imagined symptoms. This is body language at its worst. Your daughter's symptoms are most likely an expression of, or a defense against, some deeper psychological conflict. Many hypochondriacs, for example, are depressed and need treatment for that condition. Mary Christine's next step? A child psychiatrist, not because "it's all in her head," but because her root problems are psychological, not physical.

The youngster with multiple physical complaints for which there are no medical answers may be a hypochondriac — but her symptoms are real, she's not making them up. She needs a psychiatric evaluation.

Physical or Mental?

Q: My daughter, Marcie, is 12. For the past three months she's had nausea and vomiting almost every day. We've taken her to several doctors including two specialists at the University Hospital. They all say that they can't find anything physical. The child psychiatrist says, while his tests cannot confirm that her emotions are definitely causing the problem, she is "under stress and needs psychiatric treatment." I still say it's physical. What should we do?

A: This is tough for you and for Marcie too: I suggest a two-pronged approach. First, have Marcie begin her psychotherapy. Then ask her pediatrician for a referral to the leading expert in pediatric gastroenterology in your area. In this way,

Sometimes it's both. Don't delay recommended psychiatric treatment, though, while you are searching for a physical cause.

Marcie can begin treatment that may very well help her, and you will feel that no stone is being left unturned.

Secondary Gain

A principal of psychosomatic medicine: symptoms, like behavior, may have meaning. What is your pre-teen getting out of her symptom? That's her so-called secondary gain.

Q: Francine, 12, has been out of school for six weeks because of pains in her arms, legs, and back. All of her medical tests (including CAT scans) have been negative. The doctors all say that it's "psychological." The latest specialist says she's getting too much "secondary gain." What is it? What can we do?

A: Secondary gain is a basic concept in medicine. It refers to the indirect, psychological benefits that a "sick" person may unconsciously enjoy as a result of being "ill." When the secondary gain is powerful and is allowed to continue, it becomes a strong impediment to the patient's getting better.

For example, Francine's illness has kept her from school. Are there reasons for avoiding school? It has also caused her to receive a lot of attention from you. Why might she crave this kind of attention? Finally, are there specific activities that her symptoms cause her to avoid?

All behavior has a purpose. One way to consider Francine's illness is to ask: For what purpose is she having these symptoms now?

What to do? Don't blame Francine. This is an unconscious phenomenon. She's not "making it up." Instead, take her to a child psychiatrist. Treatment is usually straightforward and effective. Among other things, you'll learn how to help her cope and remove that secondary gain.

Psychological Growth and Development

Contrary to what you might have heard about the terrible teens, most youngsters manage to get through their adolescence free of serious turbulence. The best predictor of a healthy adolescence is the feeling of competence, being good at something.

Teen-To-Be at Risk

Q: Our son, Bruno, is 11. He's had his share of academic and behavioral problems and they seem to be under control now, but what about when he becomes a teenager? We're afraid he'll "erupt" again.

A: Most teenagers, contrary to popular belief, get through their adolescence relatively unscathed and go on to have happy and productive adult lives.

On the other hand, most research (such as the classic study of Daniel Offer and a newer study by psychologist Emory Werner) suggests that one out of three youngsters experiences a turbulent adolescence. In the Werner study, conducted in Hawaii, 15% of the teens had a record of serious or repeated delinquency, and 8% of the girls became pregnant. Boys tended to have more trouble in early adolescence (12-14), while girls tended to have more trouble in late adolescence (16-18).

Bruno's early problems may put him at some risk, as you fear, but let's not assume the worst. The most important predictor of a positive adolescence is whether or not a youngster feels "competent," i.e., does Bruno have faith in his own ability to solve problems? If so, great. If not, help him develop self-confidence. Give him success experiences. Encourage him.

If he starts to slip when the juices of puberty begin to flow, don't wait for him to hit bottom. Keep in touch with the school. Seek psychiatric consultation if it's recommended or if you feel it's indicated.

The Pre-Teen Conscience

Q: My 12-year-old son, Bruce, is fine when he's alone with me and my husband, but when we put him in charge of his two younger brothers, 6 and 8, he's impossible: rude, tough, and a real dictator. Why the difference?

A: First of all, Bruce, like so many oldest children, may relish the chance to be "parental" with his younger siblings. Of course, his idea of "parenting" is apt to be stern and unbending — given the rigid structure of his early adolescent conscience. He sees things in blacks and whites — not shades of gray. Hence, when the younger ones do something wrong, he will tend to overreact. This dynamic, by the way, explains why youngsters of Bruce's age can be so cruel to peers too; this is "Lord of the Flies" style morality. In time, Bruce will develop more tolerance and flexibility.

Bruce may also harbor some garden-variety grudges toward his brothers. Most oldest sons do not easily tolerate "competition from below." Be careful that he and the other boys do not believe that you are sanctioning his dictatorial ways. His excesses should not go unnoticed or unpunished — for the sake of the younger boys, and for his sake too.

Pre-teens tend to see things in black and white: either all good or all bad. Help them develop tolerance and an understanding for the shades of gray, that there's good and bad in everyone.

Problems of Teenagers

A preview of coming attractions. The major problems your child will face in adolescence are likely to be stress of parental divorce and re-marriage, peer pressure to use alcohol or drugs, and sexual experimentation.

Q: Our daughter, Delores, is 11. We're trying to plan ahead for her adolescence. Just what are the biggest problems she will face as a teenager?

A: Applause, applause! Parents who think ahead are informed parents. Informed parents tend to be involved parents. Involved parents can remain in charge, and that's one of the major needs of today's teens.

What are the biggest problems they face? Recently a group of over 300 mental health professionals was asked this very question. Here's how they ranked the problems and the percentage of experts who identified each problem:

1) Stress of parental divorce and remarriage, 72%
2) Peer pressure to drink, 68%
3) Sexual experimentation, 59%
4) Peer pressure to try drugs, 49%
5) Depression, 46%
6) Pressure to succeed academically, 30%
7) Attempts at suicide, 29%
8) Fears of nuclear war, 23%

What is a parent to do? Talk to your teens about these things. Ask about other worries they may have. Talk to the parents of your teen's friends. Read about the issues. Stay informed. Keep in touch. We may not like the world our adolescents are inheriting, but we had better understand it.

Her First Menstrual Period

Physical changes, such as menstrual periods, should be discussed frankly — and before they happen — so youngsters know what to expect.

Q: My daughter, Colleen, is 11½ years old. Several of her girlfriends have already had their first periods. I'd like to save my daughter the shame and embarrassment that I felt when the "blessed event" arrived for me. Do you have any ideas about how I can prepare her?

A: A girl's first menstrual period can be good news or bad news, depending on her preparation and readiness for the event. Girls who have a close relationship with their mothers have an advantage. Colleen, for example, may already have had some instruction in a hygiene course about the anatomy and physiology of menstruation, and she has, undoubtedly, talked with her girlfriends about it. But nothing quite takes the place of Mom when it comes to personal instruction, support, and most importantly, setting the correct emotional tone and atmosphere.

Rather than experiencing the shame and embarrassment that you felt, Colleen should be made to feel grown-up and proud. The first menstrual period should be anticipated naturally and positively. Colleen should not be made to feel dirty or that menstruation is going to limit her life dramatically. She should not be frightened that menstruation means that now she "can get pregnant." Use the opportunity to discuss the general topic of sex with Colleen — especially her attitude toward her own body and the family's basic sexual values.

I would also alert you that Colleen may feel "different" or "abnormal" because some of her girlfriends have had periods and she has not. Be sure to reassure her that the range of normality is wide. Some girls, of course, do not experience menstruation until the age of 14 or 15.

When will Colleen actually have her first period? It is difficult to say. Menstruation is certainly occurring earlier with each succeeding generation. This is due, largely, to superior nutritional and health factors in our society. So, by all means have a good talk now with Colleen, but be sure to keep the lines of communication open in the months and years ahead. Your continued availability, positive attitude, and personal example of femininity will be very important to your daughter as she launches into the exciting, but unfamiliar, waters of adolescence.

Training Bra?

Q: Are training bras necessary? My 12-year-old, Pam, is at that stage, but I haven't pushed it and she doesn't seem to be interested. My sister, though, doesn't think Pam should be braless, especially since she likes to wear tight-fitting jerseys. What do you think?

Not necessary from a physical standpoint, but sometimes of great psychological significance to some pre-teen girls. Talk it over.

A: Training bras are generally not necessary — at least from a physical standpoint. Early breast bud development does not place great strain on the ligaments of the breasts. There may, however, be some emotional strain. Some girls ask for training bras because of peer pressure, others because they're self-conscious.

My best advice is that you talk it over with Pam. In fact, it gives you a chance to keep open a dialogue with her about sexuality and her physical development. Whether she opts for the bra or not, you'll be providing the best training any parent can give — open communication.

Early-Maturing Girl

Early developing pre-teen girls are especially vulnerable. Don't let them grow up too soon.

Q: Our Carmen, 12½, is very physically mature for her age. She could pass for 16. The trouble is she's unhappy about it. Comments?

A: Early-developing girls often feel awkward. They're out of step, they feel their late-developing girlfriends don't understand them, and they're far too threatening for most boys their own age.

The worst thing a parent can do is to allow these girls to grow up too quickly. Resist the pressure, therefore, to allow Carmen to hang out with older teenagers, or to date older boys — at least for the next few years.

Help Carmen channel her interests into internal sources of self-esteem: school work, hobbies, etc. Encourage her to talk to you about her feelings.

Time is on Carmen's side. Her friends will catch up to her soon. Then she'll feel "normal" again.

My Daughter, the Tomboy

"Tomboy" is terminology that should be a relic of the past. Girls should not be discouraged from pursuing what traditionally have been considered "masculine" interests such as sports.

Q: My daughter, Maryellen, is 12 years old and she's a real tomboy. She refuses to wear dresses. Her passions are baseball and basketball, which she plays as well as most of the boys. She avoids girls her own age and thinks they are "silly" because they go to mixed parties. She refuses to discuss these matters, even with my husband, who has also been closer to her than I have been. Do you have any advice?

A: In today's world it should not be considered so "abnormal" for a girl to be interested in such traditionally "masculine" pursuits as baseball and basketball. In fact the very term "tomboy" is, I believe, a relic of the past. Your concern is that Maryellen seems to be denying the fact of her own femininity. Such conflicts of sexual role identity are not unusual for boys and girls at the onset of adolescence. They must, however, be handled with tact and sensitivity.

I would be interested to know if Maryellen has begun menstruation and to know something about her reaction to it. Girls with underlying problems of sexual identity often react with shame, disgust, and even denial, i.e., insistence that it is not happening.

Certainly Maryellen's abhorrence of dresses may signal an effort to suppress her femininity. How does she dress? Loose fitting, "masculine" garments that hide the developing body are the preference for many such conflicted girls.

You mention that your husband has been "closer" to Maryellen than yourself. Perhaps this is a clue. Some girls who over-identify with their fathers feel that Dad actually prefers them to be more like a boy, i.e., more like him. They fear losing Dad's love if they become a woman. This dynamic can be especially powerful if these girls are raised in an atmosphere where the father dominates the family; where to be a wife and a woman means taking a back seat. A girl like Maryellen, poised on the threshold of womanhood, might easily "decide" to deny her femininity in the face of such gloomy prospects.

While Maryellen will need your patient understanding, I would advise you to take the initiative — with your husband's participation. Help her to express her feelings. But do keep in mind that there are many innocent explanations for so-called tomboy behavior. Many girls go through such a phase in early adolescence as part of normal development. Do not assume that your daughter necessarily needs to be whisked off to a child psychiatrist. Talk to her about male and female roles. Talk to her about sex; maybe she is frightened about premature sexual involvement. And don't make the mistake of concentrating on superficial things like her love for sports. It's possible, in today's world, for a woman to compete aggressively in traditionally "masculine" pursuits, but to remain proudly a woman. At the young age of 12, Maryellen simply has no life experience to call upon for assistance through these complex matters. She'll need Mom and Dad to help her over the rough spots. Don't forget that many successful and thoroughly feminine women of your generation were considered "tomboys" at Maryellen's age. I hope the word can be deleted from the vocabulary of your daughter's generation.

Dan or Danny

Q: We've always called our 11-year-old son Danny. Now he insists on being called Dan. It's tough to break the habit, but my husband and I are trying because we understand that he wants to leave his childhood nickname behind him. My question is this: were we wrong to call him Danny? Should he have been Dan or Daniel right from the start?

Pre-teens tend to shed their childhood nicknames. Jimmy wants to be Jim or James, Lizzie wants to be Liz or Elizabeth. It's a rite of passage. They prefer new nicknames, especially ones bestowed by their peers.

A: Not necessarily, as long as you can now make the switch. In fact, if you can now call him Dan, you would be participating in something of a rite of passage for your son.

It's interesting, though, that the overwhelming majority of children who are called Danny, or Chuckie, or Barbie, or Lizzie react strongly against their nickname sometime between the ages of 10 and 14. They resent the infantalization that the "ie" or "y" name tag presses on them. Parents should consider these reactions before bestowing nicknames.

On the other hand, pre-teens like new nicknames, especially when bestowed by their peers. It's not only a signal of recognition and acceptance, but also a step toward establishing a new identity — the self of adolescence and beyond.

Rooting Against the Home Team

How to be yourself, but be the same — a tough developmental hurdle for pre-teens and teenagers: how to carve out your own identity while not standing out too much from the crowd.

Q: John, our 11-year-old, is a sports nut. No problem. But the thing that gets me is that he can always be counted on to root against the home team — no matter what the sport, no matter if the game is pro, college, or high school. He really gets a charge out of it. His buddies consider him something of a renegade and this is starting to concern me. Why does he have to be so different?

A: John, in casino parlance, is a wrong-way bettor. He always goes against the flow. Why? All kids like to be special. This may be John's way of standing out among his peers. It's something of a developmental task for pre-teens: how to be the same as your friends yet somehow uniquely yourself.

Should you be concerned? Only if John's behavior is predictably oppositional in other areas of his life as well. For example, does he habitually insist on doing things his way at home or at school? Is he able to collaborate with peers in other activities? Take a close look.

Dreams of Glory

Dreams are the royal road to the unconscious. They serve two basic purposes: to express an unconscious wish, or to work out some problem left over from daily life.

Q: My 11-year-old daughter, Hillary, is always telling me about her dreams. Even though the scenes shift and most of the characters change, the main theme is always the same: Hillary is a movie star or heroine who is adored by the masses. It all seems innocent enough, but does it "mean" anything psychologically?

A: Dreams serve two basic purposes: 1) to express an unconscious wish, or 2) to work out some problem that exists for the dreamer in the real world. There are pitfalls in attempting to interpret a child's dreams, since dreams are highly individualized. While certain symbols, for example, tend to be somewhat common, they are by no means universal. Even Freud cautioned that "sometimes a cigar is just a cigar."

My general comments about Hillary's recurrent dream themes are these: she obviously wishes to see herself as a star — the center of attention. As her mother you can answer whether this represents, say, the wish of a shy and unconfident girl, or whether it is an accurate picture of how Hillary really functions in the world — whether she is just trying to work out the fringe details, so to speak, in her movie contract.

The best interpreter of the dream is Hillary herself. If the opportunity presents itself, you might ask her for her own analysis. Most youngsters love to talk about their dreams, if left to their own initiation. They don't appreciate breakfast table chatter that begins: "Well, what did you dream last night?" Careful not to pry too much or to offer "clinical" interpretations of your own. The dreams of children, as of adults, are prized and private.

Bragging

Q: A lot has happened in our lives over the past 2 years. First, my mother passed away. Then my husband and I were divorced. The children have handled it well — except my daughter, Lee, 11. She's taken to bragging a lot. Things like "My house is bigger than yours," "I'm smarter than you," etc. Could this be related to all the recent loses in her life?

A: You bet. Her bragging may be a compensatory defense to bolster her self-esteem and reduce her fears of loss and abandonment. Such a defense is not unusual among pre-teens.

You can help by gently confronting her. Help her appraise herself realistically. Then, ask about her feelings. Talk about grandma's death and the divorce. Get it out in the open. If the bragging continues or if you notice other inappropriate behavior, I'd definitely suggest a consultation with a child psychiatrist. Lee is at risk. Watch the other children too. And, above all, take care of yourself.

Bragging is a common defense mechanism of pre-teens. Try to understand the hurt beneath the bravado.

More Bragging

Excessive bragging and self-promotion is usually a tip-off of a self-esteem problem. Kids must learn that they will make a lot more friends in life by listening than by talking.

Q: Hallie, our 12-year-old, needs to impress her peers. She thinks it's the way to make friends. She's always bragging and talking about herself. The problem, of course, is that she is very lonely. Her efforts backfire. The kids (except younger children who don't know better) are turned off by her. Any ideas?

A: Sounds like Hallie has a self-esteem problem. A youngster who works so hard to puff herself up must feel pretty badly about herself. When the other youngsters turn away from her, the pain intensifies.

If Hallie really wants to impress her would-be friends, she ought to impress them not with herself but with something that is guaranteed to get their attention — themselves. That's right. Hallie will have to develop a genuine interest in other people, and communicate that interest by listening to them talk about themselves. Hallie will make a lot more friends by listening than she will by talking.

Imitation

Pre-teens are great imitators of favorite adults. Imitation, along with its unconscious equivalent, identification, is a mechanism allowing a youngster to try on other identities, so to speak. Healthy if not carried to an extreme — and if not done in spite.

Q: Charles is 12. Last year his hero was a pro football player. This year it's his teacher, Mr. Johnson. Charles has even started imitating some of Mr. Johnson's mannerisms: his Southern drawl and habit of scratching behind his right ear. At first it was cute, but now we find it annoying. Should we tell Charles to cut it out?

A: No. Charles' behavior is natural and probably not under his conscious control anyway. Rather than consciously imitating Mr. Johnson, Charles is probably unconsciously identifying with him. Identification is a normal mechanism of personality development. In fact, we all indulge in periodic identifications throughout our lives. It's a way of "trying on" some characteristics of a desirable person in order to better ourselves or handle anxiety.

Charles will get over it. There will be other Mr. Johnsons along the path to his final personality formation. The best you can do is to make certain that Charles has positive identification models to associate with during his formative years. The most powerful models a child ever has, by the way, are his own parents.

Heroes, Heroines and Wall Posters

Q: You should see Anita's bedroom! Anita is our 12-year-old and she has plastered her bedroom walls with posters, posters, and more posters. Some are of rock stars, others of TV and movie stars. I can't keep track of them; they come and go so fast. Is this just a stage, or what?

A: Hero and heroine worship, of course, can be seen at all stages of life. But, yes, it is the special developmental hallmark of pre-teens like Anita.

Identification with glorified and idealized heroes can be a useful and temporary defense for such youngsters. Because they are so unsure of their own identifies, they will identify with the current superstars. These identifications, of course, are temporary. One poster comes down and another goes up as Anita and her peers continue their quest for their own true selves.

I do believe, however, that you should be aware of Anita's interests. Ask her about her posters in a casual, non-judgemental way. Tell her that you're interested. In this way you'll keep in touch with her and her evolving personality. If she gets stuck on a certain type of poster (such as drug-oriented material), you'll have to take a stand. Otherwise, patience is the name of the game.

Heroes and heroines of pre-teens tend today to be rock stars, movie and TV idols, and sports figures. These celebrities serve a useful function as temporary, non-familial models of identification. They represent a small step out into the wider, non-familial, world. Mostly harmless, but they may not represent your own values; that too is part of the process as youngsters search for their own identities.

Keep the Golden Necklace?

Q: Our Janice is 12. Last week her boyfriend bought her a gold necklace worth about $100. I don't approve. My husband says we "have no right to intervene in these young people's lives." What do you say?

A: As parents you have a strong obligation to be involved in Janice's life. Your husband's choice of words — "young people's" — makes it sound like he's talking about a 22-year-old rather than a 12-year-old. She wants to grow up fast. Dad should be slowing her down.

How you become involved is the crucial question. What do you not approve of? Is it the cost of the bracelet? Its significance? The relationship itself? Be sure to sort out your feelings, then have a meeting-of-the-minds with your husband. It is very important for both of you to agree now on things like dating, relationships, gifts, and, yes, even the sexual values you want to communicate to Janice.

Pre-teens, on the threshold of adolescence, may be inclined to give or receive elaborate gifts. Not a good idea. Don't let them grow up too fast.

After you've worked it out, both of you should have a talk with Janice about all these subjects. If you use this issue constructively, Janice's suitor and his golden necklace will have done all of you a big favor.

Who's Afraid of the Bomb?

Most youngsters, contrary to some reports, are not preoccupied with nuclear destruction.

Q: I keep hearing about children with nuclear fears, nuclear phobias, nuclear nightmares. Our newspaper even reported an "epidemic of nuclear neurosis among American children." I have three children, 11, 13, and 16, and they have lots of friends. I've never heard any of them mention one word about anything nuclear. Should I be pleased, or am I missing something?

A: While I believe we should have a healthy concern about the possibility of nuclear war, I also believe the so-called epidemic of childhood nuclear neurosis is far-fetched. Dr. Robert Coles, professor of Psychiatry at Harvard University, agrees. In his study of 108 children he has found relatively little nuclear preoccupation among children. In fact, such concern, when he encountered it, was mostly limited to children of upper middle class, liberal white parents. Coles found nuclear fear to be practically non-existent among white and black working-class children, Pueblo Indian, and Appalachian children.

The basic issue, Coles suggests, may be a class issue. Children, after all, tend to assume the worries and values of their parents. Poor families, Coles points out, also worry about extinction, but they have more immediate threats than The Bomb to worry about: threats like "hunger, joblessness, and the turmoil of ghetto life."

Should you be pleased or are you missing something? Probably a little of both. While you can be pleased that your children are not suffering from nuclear fear, they probably should have a higher level of awareness of an issue that ultimately looms over all of us.

School

Pay Her for A's and B's?

Social rewards (encouragement, more time with Mom and Dad, expressions of love) are more effective motivators than monetary or material rewards.

Q: Our daughter, Terry, is 11. She's never been very motivated in school. She just does enough to get by. My husband and I are worried. We want her to do her best. Last week Jack, my husband, offered to pay Terry $2 for every A on her report card, and $1 for every B. She seemed to like it, but I'm not so sure. What do you think?

A: It's been said that a child's "work" is her school work, and if you subscribe to that theory, I guess it's a short leap to some sort of financial contract for the effort, but I don't agree.

Why? Well, first of all, the real "work" of childhood is to learn to grow up to be a self-disciplined, solid citizen. The real reward for a job well done should be the appreciation that you get from Mom and Dad — which is ultimately translated into self-esteem. The child who is paid to perform is robbed of these crucial psychological accomplishments. She's being bought and bribed.

At worst, your husband's plan is a kind of pre-teen payola. It may work for the short term, but it's doomed to failure. Why? Terry will not develop a love of learning for learning's sake. Her attitude toward school (and things like chores too) may become: "How much you gonna pay me for it?" And what about when she's 15 or 16? Two dollars won't get her attention anymore. You'll have to inflate your sales commission, with no end in sight.

The solution? Start with a conference with Terry's teachers. What's the problem? Then, start with something simple. By that, I mean, encourage her in the subject she likes best. Then build from one success to the next. Her reward? Your encouragement, interest, attention, and love. These are "social rewards" — much more valuable to children than a dollar bill.

Report Card Reaction

Q: Joey, our 11-year-old, brought home three A's, one B, and one D on his last report card. I reacted immediately to the D. I really came down hard. My husband complimented Joey on the A's and then asked about the D. It was much more effective than my approach. Why?

Praise the good grades before you inquire about the D's and F's.

A: Dad has learned the secret of Accentuating the Positive. His approach is generally much more effective. Put yourself in Joey's shoes. How would you want a supervisor to react to your job performance if your results were as mixed as Joey's?

She Hates Her Teacher

Be a partner with your pre-teen's teacher. If a conflict between child and teacher develops, listen to your youngster and offer to help resolve it only if she can't settle it herself.

Q: Tanya, my 11-year-old, hates her teacher. Don't ask me why. I'm not sure. It's a little bit of everything. For weeks I've listened to her complaints and patiently encouraged her to talk things over with the teacher. "I can't, I can't. You don't understand!" is her reply. I'm about ready to go to school myself even though I know I shouldn't. What do you think?

A: My mind is open at this point, and yours should be too. Student-teacher mismatches and conflicts do occur, and although I applaud your philosophy of encouraging Tanya to work things out for herself, be careful that she doesn't misinterpret this reaction as meaning that you do not care or that you think her teacher is right. Tanya needs your interest and your support. It is possible to give both without picking sides.

In this case you may have to make a trip to see Tanya's teacher. Be candid and open. Do not force the teacher into a corner, but don't let her completely off the hook either. Get the facts. Then, you might serve both sides well by helping the two of them work things out.

If, by the way, you become convinced that Tanya really needs a change of teachers, press for it — but only as a last resort.

The Best and the Brightest

Childhood superstars (academic, athletic, artistic) tend to share one experience in common: parents who actively supported their special interests.

Q: Our daughter Patricia, 11, is a whiz at math. It just comes naturally for her. We've encouraged her, but now we have some tough choices. How hard should we push? Should we help her by taking her to Math Club Activities at the local high school (she's been invited to join). Should we encourage her interest in chess by taking her to tournaments? Or, do you think too much parental involvement will turn her off?

A: Get involved and stay involved. Do it for Patricia, not for yourselves. If she realizes that you truly have her best interests in mind, she'll appreciate your involvement.

Yes, by all means, take advantage of opportunities like the Math Club. But, no, don't push. And, finally, make sure that Patricia enjoys a well-rounded life: fun, friends, family, good emotional and physical health.

You may be interested in a book by Benjamin Bloom and a research team at the University of Chicago. It's titled *Developing Talent in Young People* and it traces the childhood experiences of 120 superstars — mathematicians, Olympic swimmers, tennis players, pianists, and others. The researchers found that while their talents differed widely, these people had remarkably similar childhoods. They were blessed with natural God-given talent, and with parents who cheered and urged their success. They all had to work hard to achieve "stardom." It didn't come overnight. This means that Mom and Dad were there to create opportunities, to cheer them up when they were discouraged, and to urge them to keep practicing.

There comes a time, of course, when such a youngster is "on her own." But getting her there requires supportive and sensitive parents.

The Genius as Nerd?

Q: Our son Hayden, 11, is a genius. We've been told his IQ is 150. We want him to use all of his academic potential, but we don't want him to be identified as a "nerd." Any suggestions?

A: First of all, let's do away with the stereotypes of the genius as nerd or eccentric. A recent review of the child development literature, for example, concludes that gifted youngsters excel in almost everything they try. For example, high IQ youngsters walk and talk earlier than other kids, reach puberty earlier, have better physical and mental health, do better in school, have more hobbies, prefer older friends, and are more popular.

There are, of course, exceptions. The key is to give Hayden every opportunity to be a normal, red-blooded American boy. You certainly want to provide him with academic opportunities that will allow him to utilize his full potential, but don't neglect opportunities for fun and friends.

Pre-adolescents are very peer-related. Make sure that Hayden's peers share some of his interests and talents. Scapegoating of gifted children usually results when they are thrust into situations where their skills are envied by less talented youngsters. One of the major benefits of Gifted and Talented programs in schools, beyond the academic stimulation they provide, is the positive peer relations for youngsters like Hayden. If possible, have Hayden placed in such a program.

Talented pre-teens should not be scapegoated by jealous peers. They need a positive peer culture, which may require special school placement and after-school activities with youngsters of similar interests.

Why Boys Score Higher

Q: Our daughter Pam, 11, is an excellent student. We want her to excel academically, but we're concerned when we hear that boys continue to out-perform girls in school. Is it true?

Boys tend to be praised for good performance, girls for good behavior. Careful. Each needs both.

A: If you accept the SAT (Scholastic Aptitude Test) as a measure, it is true that boys out-perform girls. Boys have generally scored about 50 points higher in math, and in the last ten years, they're ahead on the verbal test too, but there is evidence that girls are catching up.

There's a real paradox here. Consider this: when children enter school, girls are generally ahead of boys in the basics: reading, writing, and arithmetic. But by the time they graduate from high school, boys have taken a significant lead.

Why? Professors Myra and David Sodker of American University believe they have the answer: boys get more attention (positive and negative) from teachers than girls. Furthermore, when girls are praised it tends to be for good behavior, not for good performance. The Sodkers, by the way, are trying to do something about this inequity. They've launched a program called PEPA (Principal Effectiveness, Pupil Achievement) to sensitize educators to the problem.

You can start your own PEPA program at home. Be an effective parent by praising and encouraging Pam's academic skills. You might even take the matter up with Pam's principal. You could be doing her, and a lot of other girls, a big favor.

Calculators

Don't fight high tech. Most schools allow calculators, as long as youngsters can also do their sums the old-fashioned way.

Q: We have two or three calculators around the house and we're fighting a losing battle. We don't think that our children, 11, 9, and 8, should use them. We think it's better for their development to do math the old-fashioned way: in their heads or with a pencil and paper. What do you think?

A: I see no harm in the calculator as long as the youngsters are also learning well in the traditional ways.

In fact, the National Council of Teachers of Mathematics encourages the use of hand-held calculators. The Council points to an analysis of 79 studies which shows that "students who use calculators along with traditional instruction can improve their basic skills with paper and pencil."

You may want to write for a free pamphlet *How To Be the Plus in Your Child's Mathematics Education.* Send a SASE to the Council at 1906 Association Drive, Reston, VA 22091.

How Kids Learn

There are advantages to small group learning over 1:1 tutoring, but some youngsters require individualized attention.

Q: Our 11-year-old, Ricky, needs some remedial work in reading and math. The school offers an after-hours program in small groups of 6-8 students. As an alternative, we could hire a private tutor. What is best, small group learning or one-on-one instruction?

A: Without knowing more about Ricky's specific needs and how he learns best, I can only answer your question in the abstract.

In general, I like small group activity because it provides not only skill-building, but social interaction as well, a skill every bit as important as content learning.

On the other hand, all students need occasional one-on-one help from teachers and it should always be available.

Teachers themselves are split on which they think is most effective. In a recent national poll they ranked small groups and individual instruction as about even; way ahead, by the way, of classroom lectures.

Your best bet: ask Ricky's teachers what they think. If Ricky were their son, and they could afford private tutoring with the teacher you've selected, would they do it?

Is Valentine's Day a Popularity Contest?

Q: Daniella, our 11-year-old, says she won't go to school this year on Valentine's Day. Last year she was embarrassed because, while she gave cards to all 30 children in her class, she received only 10 in return. How can I help?

Youngsters should plan to give, hope to get.

A: What is the customary practice at Daniella's school? You might check with other mothers or with the teacher. If Valentine's Day has deteriorated into a popularity contest for children, you'll probably find a lot of support for making changes.

On the other hand, maybe the problem belongs to Daniella. Maybe she's put her self-esteem on the line. Help her save face. She should plan to give, and de-emphasize the getting. It's the quality of the exchange that counts, not the quantity. It might help her if she could plan an after-school party for a few of her favorite classroom friends.

Finally, be sure that Daniella is aware of her own internal sources of self-esteem: her positive attributes, her interests, her skills. Better to build her self-esteem on this firm foundation than to risk it on paper hearts and cupids.

Homework Hassles

It's possible to take the hassles out of homework. The keys: keep it positive, help your pre-teen get organized, be an available partner to your pre-teen and her teacher.

Q: Howard, our 12-year-old, has a problem. He won't do his homework. We've tried everything: threats, rewards, punishment, even bribes, but it's the same old story — hassles, hassles, hassles. Any ideas?

A: Try this 8-step formula:

1) *Parental example.* That's right. The best thing you can do is to set a good example. Do you read books? Do you value learning for the sake of learning? I hope so. Howard is watching.

2) *Do not make homework itself a punishment.* I know one father who used to punish his daughter by making her do math problems. She grew up to hate math, and she wasn't too hot in her other subjects either.

3) *Get organized.* Help Howard set up a special time and place for homework every day. Keep it sacred. No interruptions. In the beginning you might even help him make a list, before he starts, of just what he has to accomplish in the day's study time. By the way, on days when there's no assignment, Howard should use the time to read a good book.

4) *Be available.* Yes, be available to help, but don't do the work for him.

5) *Limit TV.* One hour a day is plenty for most kids. Some parents don't allow any TV until the homework is completed. Use your judgement.

6) *Check and praise.* I suggest that you routinely check Howard's work when he's finished. Offer suggestions and offer praise, too. Pride in scholarship is what it's all about.

7) *No bribes.* If you have to offer a youngster rewards for doing homework, you're in trouble. Homework is a basic responsibility; it's Howard's "job." The reward is a job well done. This is an important lesson in life. Don't rob Howard of it with bribes.

8) *Communicate with teachers.* By all means, keep in touch with Howard's teachers. Work closely with the school. After all, you're all on the same team.

Won't (or Can't) Do Homework

Some children need some help getting organized. If that doesn't work, seek professional help.

Q: Our Charles, 12, has an IQ of 130, but he's failing every one of his subjects. The reason? Homework. I've been patient and helpful. I make a list each night of the assignments he brings home and I check his work before he goes to bed. You'd think that would nail it. Surprise! I learned yesterday from his teacher that he's been "forgetting" to bring home all of his assignments. I'm frustrated. Punishment doesn't phase him. What next?

A: The basic question is whether Charles is being willfully disobedient, or if his problem is due to some emotional problem or learning disability.

My suggestions: 1) Have Charles go up to each teacher after class and check the assignment for the next day. He should write it down and have it initialed by the teacher before he brings it home to you. In this way you'll close the gap on possible "forgetfulness." 2) Keep it positive. Offer him a small reward (not money) for each day he completes all of his assignments. Give this plan one month. If it doesn't work, consult with a child psychiatrist.

Back to School

Q: Our 12-year-old, Melissa, had some problems with math in 5th grade last year. She really got discouraged. We got her some tutoring help over the summer and she should be in pretty good shape to start 6th grade. Do you have any further suggestions?

Bolster your child's academic strengths, then help her shore up her weaknesses. Nobody's perfect. Help her be good at something. Self-esteem is at stake.

A: First, let me congratulate you for getting Melissa some help. You recognized that there was more at stake than division and multiplication. Melissa's self-esteem was starting to slip.

I suggest that you do not overemphasize the math when Melissa returns to school. Play it calmly and matter-of-factly. Express equal interest in all of her subjects.

Another tip: bolster Melissa's strengths. While it's important to provide help in her weak area, math, be sure that she has every opportunity to pursue her strengths, including extra-curricular activities and hobbies. Every child should be "good" at something. This ability creates pride, a healthy reservoir of self-esteem, for those "down" times when things, like math, might be giving a child, like Melissa, the jitters.

Types of School Phobia

Q: Our youngest, Jose, 12, refuses to go to school. We can't figure it out. He never had problems before. What should we do?

Pre-teens refuse to go to school for several reasons. The first step is to understand the specific cause, then take appropriate action.

A: Two things. First, it's very important to make sure he gets to school every day. Be gentle but firm. (We call this technique "therapeutic coercion.") The longer he stays out, the more difficult it will be to get him there.

Second, it's also important to determine why he's suffering from what we commonly call school phobia. Child psychiatrist Charles Popper and others have identified several sub-types:

1) *Realistic danger.* Has Jose been threatened by other children? Might he have other realistic fears?

2) *Familial permission.* Have you, in any way, given him "permission" to stay home? This is the childhood equivalent of adult "mental health days."

3) *Truancy.* Garden variety "playing hooky," or serious, chronic truancy is more common with older teenagers than with pre-teens like Jose.

4) *Psychiatric illness.* A wide range of disorders, from psychosis to depression to anxiety, account for many cases of school refusal. One of the most common problems, classic "school phobia," is based not, as the name implies, on irrational fear, but on separation anxiety — fear of leaving parents behind at home.

A child psychiatrist will be able to make the diagnosis, and then to advise the proper remedy.

Medication for School Phobia

Medication is useful in the treatment of some types of school phobia.

Q: Headaches. Stomach aches. Sprained ankles. It's been one excuse after another from our Wendy, 12, for not going to school. Her pediatrician says there's no physical problem. Now a child psychiatrist wants to put her on drugs. Isn't this drastic?

A: Medication is not drastic at all if Wendy is suffering from a mood disorder (anxiety or depression) or a more serious illness such as psychosis (loss of reality). The use of anti-depressants in the treatment of school phobia associated with depression is a widespread and accepted practice in child psychiatry.

Talk to the psychiatrist. Ask about the diagnosis and the rationale for the recommended treatment.

The fact that you refer to "drugs" instead of "medication" leads me to suspect some prejudice or misunderstanding. If you're worried about the possibility of addiction (none) or side effects (always possible) ask about it.

Work it out. Then, get behind the treatment program.

Look It Up!

Q: He's just plain lazy, that's what he is. My 12-year-old, Charles, refuses to use the dictionary. He's always coming to me to ask what various words mean. I've tried giving him a new vocabulary list every week, but that didn't work either. Help!

A: There are several problems with dictionaries as far as kids area concerned:

1) *Interruption.* It is an annoying interruption to go to a dictionary when you're in the middle of reading something.

2) *Context.* Dictionaries can be difficult, especially since they may not relate the definition of the word to the specific context in which it's being used.

3) *Motivation.* Given these problems, a child really has to be motivated to use a dictionary.

What can you do? Try to be available to Charles for information, but have him keep a list of the words that stump him. Then, after he's finished reading, have him look the words up and jot down the meanings. Then, make this list his vocabulary list. In this way, the words on the list will have relevance and meaning. He'll be more motivated to assimilate them.

Many youngsters just hate to look it up in the dictionary. Some tips follow on getting them started, but don't do it for them.

Four Eyes and Smarts

Q: My 12-year-old, Betsy, wears glasses and she has a theory. She believes that kids who wear glasses are smarter than other kids. She wants to do a research project on it. Can you help?

A: Betsy's vision may be very sharp. Her observations are underscored by a study by Israeli researchers who found that 27% of boys with IQ's over 128 (superior intelligence) wore glasses. By contrast, of the boys with IQ's under 80 (markedly below average intelligence), only 8% wore glasses.

Why this finding? Here are some possibilities suggested by the scientists: 1) Smarter youngsters read more and this affects their vision. 2) Nearsighted children naturally prefer near tasks, including reading. 3) It's possible that intelligence and nearsightedness may be related genetically. 4) Perhaps the parents of low IQ children tend not to provide them with proper medical care, including eyeglasses.

I'd like to see a copy of Betsy's report when she finishes it.

Believe it or not, some research shows that youngsters who wear glasses have higher IQ's.

Underachiever

Don't wait for them to get motivated on their own. If it happens at all, it may be too late. Take action.

Q: Mickey, our 12-year-old, is an underachiever. The teachers say he has the potential, but he just won't try. My husband says he was like that too as a boy, but he "grew out of it" and now has a Master's degree. Should we wait to see what happens?

A: No. There's too much at stake — and no guarantee that Mickey will follow in Dad's footsteps.

First, you need a diagnosis. Why does your son refuse to try? Have a conference with his classroom teacher. Request educational and psychological testing, either through the school or privately. A good medical evaluation (including eyesight and hearing) would also help.

Then, design a plan of action. It might involve a change in your expectations and discipline practices, some behavior modification techniques for Mickey, a change of classroom (or school), counseling, medical intervention, or all of the above.

Yes, some kids grow out of it, but, in my clinical experience, the underachieving child too often grows into the underachieving adult.

Breakfast and Grades

Research proves what mothers have been preaching for years: youngsters who eat breakfast make better grades.

Q: I'm a stickler for breakfast. All of my children except Michael, 12, eat a hearty breakfast. Last semester his grades fell sharply. Could there be some connection?

A: There are, of course, many possible explanations for failing grades, and I encourage you to talk it over with Michael and his teachers in detail.

On the other hand, there is some evidence of a connection between grades and breakfast. In a study of several hundred grade-school youngsters in Lawrence, Massachusetts, it was found that the children who habitually ate breakfast outperformed the other students by a small, but statistically significant, degree.

Natural Talent vs Hard Work

Girls who make good grades are often thought of as hardworking, while their male counterparts are called talented. I don't like it and I bet you don't either.

Q: I've got a beef. Our 12-year-old, Sharlene, gets straight As in science and math. So does the son of a neighbor who's in her class. It's ridiculous. The teachers praise him as a "natural talent." Sharlene? They call her "hard working." Comments.

A: I've got a beef, too. Your daughter's teachers are doing Sharlene a disservice. Apparently they're not aware that girls and women have steadily closed the gap on their male counterparts in math and science.

Researchers at Berkeley and the University of Wisconsin have demonstrated that the mathematical ability of males and females is now just about equal. They feel that the difference is now so negligible that it should be de-emphasized.

Still, the myth persists and teachers, as well as parents, tend to encourage their sons to pursue science and math while girls are urged toward the liberal arts.

I hope you'll give Sharlene every opportunity to excel in her science and math interests. And please show a copy of this information to her teachers.

Excellence or Perfection

Q: We have three children, ages 12, 10½, and 2. My husband and I are both high achievers and we want our kids to be successful. My girlfriend complains that we're pushing the children to be perfect. We just want them to perform to the best of their potential. How can you gauge the difference?

All youngsters should be required to perform up to their potential. Perfection is unattainable, but excellence is not.

A: Children who are, unfortunately, saddled by their parents' ambitions to be "perfect" are always being drawn toward unattainable goals. Consequently, there's a high degree of stress and frustration. And even when they do succeed, they're not very happy; after all, it's a hollow victory, since soon they'll be launched on another quest.

Perfectionists are often sad or depressed. They feel valued only for what they do, not for who they are. Hence, their self-esteem rises and falls continuously. They are very vulnerable to criticism, distrustful of others, and tend to be loners.

Not very appetizing, is it? Like you, I'm a strong believer in excellence, but not in perfection.

Paddling in Schools

Q: We just moved with our children, 12, 9, and 7, from a state where paddling of children in school is outlawed, to a state that apparently still allows it. We were shocked. We thought paddling went out with the Dark Ages. What is your opinion?

Paddling and spanking have no place in the teaching of discipline to children — either at home or at school.

A: The Dark Ages? Look again. Currently, 41 states allow paddling and in some of them it is used quite liberally.

I'm against it. Why? 1) There are more effective techniques for discipline. 2) Some teachers or administrators may abuse it or use it as a "first result." 3) Respect of children means winning their cooperation in positive ways — ways that teachers should know better than anyone — ways that will encourage children to respect and learn in return.

On the other hand, parents should support teachers in their efforts to maintain appropriate classroom discipline. Schools need your participation. The teacher who feels that he (or she) needs at least the threat of paddling in order to preserve order probably feels unsupported.

Baseball or School?

Encourage your youngster to work (and play) as well as he can.

Q: It's that time of year again: Little League baseball season. Billie, our 12-year-old, is an All-Star catcher. We only wish that he was an All-Star in the classroom too. We warned him when school began last fall that he wouldn't be able to play ball this summer unless he brought his grades up. Well, you can guess what happened: his grades remained at the C level. My husband and I, however, are starting to have second thoughts. Do you think we should hang tough, or should we allow him to play ball this summer?

A: This is a tough call, like calling a runner out at the plate, but, in principle, I would say "Play Ball!" Why? In general, it is not a good idea to restrict a youngster from a wholesome activity that he enjoys and at which he excels. Billie, for example, is probably discouraged in the classroom, but he's a star on the baseball diamond. Baseball may well be the peg on which his self-esteem hangs at this time. Let's not rip it away from him.

On the other hand, I appreciate your dilemma. You want him to perform at his potential in the classroom too; his future rides on his academic abilities as well as his athletic prowess.

A good place to start, therefore, is with Billie's school. Just what is his potential? Should he be getting A's and B's? If so, what is the problem? Devise a plan with his active cooperation. But if Billie's C's are really the best he can manage, you may be doing more harm than good by pushing him beyond his capabilities.

Many high schools are now adopting "no pass — no play" rules for athletes. I think it's a good idea. A C-average will certainly be good enough for Billie to participate, but like you, I want him to be the best he can be — behind the plate, and behind the books.

Bookworm

Q: My husband and I are both avid readers, so we're basically happy about he fact that Allan, 12, is also a bookworm. What worries me is that he always seems to have his head in a book. He doesn't even hear me when I call him to dinner. Is he going too far?

The pre-teen bookworm may be avoiding the world of real-life peers — the best book on growing up I know of.

A: I'm also basically happy for Allan. Today's children tend to avoid books. They turn to more passive information-gathering, such as television. Communication of all kinds, however, is based ultimately on the written word. That's why strong communicators tend to be avid readers, like you and your husband. Good reading habits are also closely associated with good study habits, good school performance, and a good knowledge base.

But there's another side of the story. Reading can be a form of escapism. Is Allan hiding behind the covers of his books? Does he enjoy fictional characters more than real people? Does he avoid social contact? Does he have other healthy interests besides reading?

Excessive reading can be a problem, but one symptom does not a neurosis make. So, get a read on your son's overall behavior — and on yourselves too. If he identifies with what he perceives as your own excessive reading habits, you may be well-advised to alter your own behavior. Balance is the key. You can book on it.

Tell Him His IQ?

Q: We recently had our 12-year-old, Harvey, tested for intelligence. The psychologist says that Harvey's IQ is 144. Should we tell him?

Standard intelligence tests are a useful measure of a youngster's potential but hard work and motivation are also necessary ingredients for success.

A: In my own practice I'm very selective about revealing specific IQ numbers to children — and to parents.

Standard IQ tests ("normal" is 100) are only one measure of potential success in life. Hard work and determination, for example, can make up a lot of ground; similarly, lack of motivation can spell failure even if a youngster has a high IQ.

Why was Harvey tested? I'd advise you to consult with the psychologist about this question. Your decision about telling Harvey his score can then be based upon the reasons for the testing and your son's own ability to utilize the information positively.

Specific Learning Disability

Specific learning disabilities, sometimes called dyslexia, are not uncommon. It does not mean your youngster has sub-normal intelligence. Einstein and Edison were probably dyslexic.

Q: My grandson, 11½, has something called "specific learning disability." What is it? Does it mean that he's below average in intelligence?

A: Specific learning disabilities are weaknesses in particular areas of functioning such as reading, writing, visual memory, or memory for sound, and a number of other things.

For example, some children have a tough time learning to read or write because their brain confuses or reverses letters such as "b-d" or "p-q." A child might read "dog" for "bog." Children who have trouble processing sounds also have a tough time learning; imagine, for example, mistaking "bun" for "gun."

Sometimes the term dyslexia is used to describe this type of disability.

Special educational techniques are available to help youngsters with learning disabilities. I hope your grandson will have such an opportunity.

By the way, you might tell him that he's in some pretty good company: Albert Einstein didn't speak until he was six; Thomas Edison was a school failure; and Nelson Rockefeller overcame his lifelong reading problem by becoming a master at speaking off the cuff.

Cure for Dyslexia?

No, there is no cure, but there is plenty of special education help available. Make sure your youngster gets it.

Q: Our 11-year-old son, Michael, has been diagnosed as dyslexic. He has problems with reversing letters, spelling errors, and remembering things that he's read. The school has put him in a special resource classroom and it seems to be helping, but is there any cure? I've heard about medication, diets, even "patterning exercises." Does any of it work?

A: There is no cure for dyslexia, but there are a number of special educational techniques that can help youngsters such as Michael.

Researchers from Johns Hopkins University recently reported that more than half of dyslexics who graduate from special schools enjoy a high degree of success. At one high school, for example, 58% of the graduates went on to earn college degrees, and 10% went on to graduate degrees.

Pills and diets? No, there are no quick cures. Dyslexia, or specific learning disability (SLD), is complex and requires skill and patience on everybody's part.

For more information, I recommend a book by Sally Smith: *No Easy Answers: The Learning Disabled Child at Home and at School.*

Is Dyslexia Inherited?

Q: Bryan, our 11-year-old, is dyslexic. My husband also had a reading disability when he was young, but he overcame it. Is dyslexia inherited?

There is some research evidence that dyslexia is inherited, but the findings are preliminary.

A: We have surmised for some time that many cases of dyslexia may well be genetically transmitted. Recent findings at the University of Miami have taken the problem one step further. Researchers studied chromosomes from 16 families with histories of dyslexia and have concluded that one out of three inherited cases is linked to a specific defect of chromosome 15; one of the 23 pairs of chromosomes that carry human genes.

These findings, while preliminary, may ultimately allow us to predict, at birth, which children will have dyslexia. These youngsters could then receive specific training at a very early age to help them overcome their difficulty with letter reversals, word recognition, and the other factors that contribute to their reading problems.

Don't let Bryan become discouraged. Dyslexia is not a sign of low intelligence. In fact, Bryan's in good company: Leonardo DaVinci, Albert Einstein, and, of course, Dad. Make sure he benefits from special help at school.

Boys and Dyslexia

Q: Our 11-year-old son, William, is dyslexic. He understands everything just fine, but he has a heck of a time with reading. Our daughters don't have the problem. We've been told that boys with dyslexia outnumber girls by 10 to 1. Why?

Dyslexic boys outnumber dyslexic girls 10 to 1.

A: The answers aren't clear, but there is plenty of speculation and some serious research being conducted.

A Harvard research team suggests that unusually high levels of testosterone in the male fetus might delay the development of nerve cells in the left side of the brain, thus causing specific learning problems later in life.

The answer lies somewhere in the complicated circuitry of the brain. Autopsies on people with dyslexia, for example, reveal that the left hemisphere of the brain is smaller than normal.

What does all this mean for William? Cheer up. Most dyslexics have normal, or even above normal, intelligence. They're just stymied somewhat in some specific area of learning. With a good educational program, and lots of encouragement at home, he'll probably do just fine.

You can tell him that many famous men of history have been dyslexic. General George Patton was dyslexic. So was Woodrow Wilson, who had so much trouble with letter discrimination that he didn't learn the alphabet until he was 9 years old. I bet William is ahead of the former President's pace already.

Mainstreaming

Most youngsters with learning disabilities want to be "mainstreamed," i.e., to attend regular classrooms rather than special programs. As pre-teens they may exert tremendous pressure for mainstreaming because they don't want to be different. Careful. Make sure they get what they need. Their futures are at stake.

Q: Daniel, our 11-year-old, has been in a special classroom for the past year because of learning disabilities. We were against it but we went along. Now his friends are calling him "Retard." We want him "mainstreamed" back into his regular classroom. Right?

A: I'm not sure. Yes, I know it hurts Danny and you when he's called names. And I'm familiar with the argument that a child's self-esteem can be injured if he's placed outside the academic mainstream.

But, before you act, consider the big picture. Can Danny's academic needs be met in a regular classroom? If not, it's no place for him.

Danny's self-esteem is a precious commodity. Protect it. Help him deal with the name-callers. Make sure he develops skills he can be proud of. Nobody can ever take those things away.

And remind him that learning disability is not at all synonymous with "retarded," a subnormal intelligence.

Visual Perception Problem

One type of learning disability is limited to visual perception problems such as the reversal of letters.

Q: The school says that Hunter, our 12-year-old, has a visual perceptual disability. What is it? What can we do about it?

A: Visual perceptual disability is one of the specific learning disabilities (SLD). It has nothing to do with how well Hunter sees (visual acuity), but rather with his ability to process and understand the information. For example, he may reverse letters (d or b, etc.) or whole words (saw for was, etc.). This, then, may translate into a reading problem, dyslexia.

There are many possible causes (genetic, biochemical, maturational, and perhaps nutritional). Your pediatrician, perhaps aided by a psychologist and psychiatrist, may be able to pinpoint the cause, but usually can't make a specific causal diagnosis.

What to do? First of all, Hunter will need special educational help. Since his intelligence is probably normal or even above normal, he'll learn to overcome his problem.

Also, keep in mind that if Hunter is also hyperactive or distractible he may be helped by medication, and if he develops emotional problems, he could be helped by counseling.

Don't despair. Many youngsters with this problem go on to success and happiness.

Auditory Learner

Q: Our 12-year-old son, Jeff, has always had trouble in the classroom. Last year the school finally tested him. We were told that he is an "auditory learner" and that he will get some special teaching approaches. How can we help at home?

A: About 80% of children learn primarily by "seeing" things. They are visual learners. Most education, therefore, tends to be geared to reading assignments, visual demonstrations, writing assignments, etc. The other 20% of children, however, tend to learn more by "hearing" things. Like Jeff, they are auditory learners. Why the difference? The reasons are rooted in the mysteries of neuroanatomy, neurophysiology, and psychological development.

Yes, there are specific classroom techniques for aiding auditory learners. And you can help at home. Try these techniques: 1) Encourage Jeff to repeat things to himself after he has read them. 2) Allow him to tape-record TV news programs while, at the same time, taking written notes. Quiz him on what he heard — first from the tape, then from the notes. Later reverse the process (notes first, tape second), and after a few months try removing the tape entirely. In this way you'll build upon his auditory strengths while helping him to build his visual skills.

Youngsters with visual perception problems generally learn best through hearing (lectures, tapes, etc.) rather than reading. Some creative steps may help.

Vision Training

Q: Our 11-year-old Tommy is learning disabled. His main problems are reading (dyslexia) and poor muscle control due to problems with eye-hand coordination. The special tutoring he

Vision training is still controversial. There have been some notable successes, but as yet there is no hard scientific evidence that it really works.

gets at school helps, but we've recently heard rave reviews about something called "vision training." What is it? Does it work?

A: Vision training is basically a series of exercises, such as walking on a balance beam while reading, copying patterns on a computer screen, and so forth, that are designed to improve focusing, perception, and coordination. The therapy is being largely promoted by optometrists, non-MD eye doctors.

Success stories abound, but ophthalmologists (MD's) are skeptical.

They point out that the successes are random anecdotal reports, and that vision training has not met the rigors of hard scientific (double blind) research.

Is this just a case of professional jealousy and turf-guarding? We won't know until the research is available.

In the meantime, you might want to consider vision training. It probably will do no harm. The cost, however, may be a hurdle. Get a firm estimate before you leap.

Keep up the tutoring, though, and give Tommy lots of attention and encouragement. That's probably the best medicine of all.

Sexual Development

Unanswerable Sex Questions

Most pre-teens want to talk to their parents about sex. Although some schools offer excellent courses on the anatomy and physiology of sex, parents still have the vital responsibility to teach sexual values. Do it now — before puberty hits.

Q: I'm a single mother. I have a girl, 11, and a boy, 13. I take sex education seriously and I've always talked to the kids about it. Now that they're older, however, they're starting to ask me questions that I can't answer off the top of my head. I feel so stupid. Then, I get embarrassed. Any suggestions?

A: First let me salute you. I wish more parents took sex ed as seriously as you do. Children learn their basic attitudes and values from their parents. You are setting a good example. Keep it up. Stupid? Embarrassed? Forget it. You are not supposed to be an expert. Next time the youngsters ask a tough question, just admit that you are not sure of the answer and make a project out of it. Offer to look up the information or tell them where to find it, and then be sure to talk with them.

Mothers and Sex Education

Q: I'm a single parent. I have one son, Michael, who is 12. I've started to talk to him about sex. My girlfriends are surprised. They think I ought to "find a man" to talk to him about these things. Do you agree ?

A: No. Sex education is a parental responsibility. Most kids really prefer to discuss these matters with their parents.

Interestingly, mothers seem to do most of the sex education these days, even in two-parent families, and regardless of whether the child is a boy or a girl. So, you are doing what comes naturally.

Your girlfriends may be concerned that if your talks with Michael become too explicit or titillating, it could create some sexual tension between the two of you. This could happen. Your best bet is to use sound judgement about how you approach these matters. Don't go into explicit detail.

If, after some initial discussions, Michael has some unanswered questions that you really can't answer, and you choose to defer to a trusted male adult (uncle, grandfather, etc.), I see no problem with calling in some masculine help.

Pre-teens who have the benefit of sex ed (both at home and at school) tend to delay their first sexual experience, and suffer less teenage pregnancy and venereal disease.

Sex Ed for the Whole Family

Q: An organization in our city is sponsoring something called Parent-Child Sex Education. Their basic idea is to approach sex ed from a family perspective. We think it sounds like a good idea, but our 12-year-old son is dead set against it: "Too embarrassing." We have several questions: 1) What do you think of these programs? 2) Should we force Marty to attend? 3) Should we go without him?

A: Generally I'm in favor of these programs. Their primary value, I believe, is to get youngsters and parents talking about sex and sexual values. These courses, if properly taught, can combine the best of two worlds: expert instruction and parental involvement.

Over the past five years such courses as the one you describe have blossomed all over the country. It's a good sign. In one survey conducted in the Midwest in the late 70's, it was found that only 15% of parents had discussed sex with their children. This is a shame. It's a shame, particularly because when parents are involved in the sexual education of their children, we know that the youngsters tend to delay their first

Parent-child sex ed is a healthy trend. Sex education programs exist for both pre-teens and parents. It may not be for your family, but do talk to your youngsters about sex — especially sexual values. They'll need all the help they can get for their adolescent years ahead.

sexual experience, and when youngsters have the benefit of school-based sex ed programs the incidence of teen pregnancy and venereal disease is lower.

In a recent survey of parents it was found that 30% have an interest in attending sex ed programs with their sons and daughters. It is a positive trend.

I think we can all relate to Marty's embarrassment. Try to work it through with him. You might admit that it can be a little embarrassing to Mom and Dad too. But force him? I don't think so. How about a deal? If he'll attend the first session with you, he can make up his own mind about returning.

Go without Marty? Obviously it would be best if he attends with you, but let's face it, parents have their own need to keep informed. Don't let your son's reluctance stand in your way.

Girls, Sex, and Horses

It is largely a myth that a pre-teen's interest in horses represents sublimated sexual drives. Let's not get too analytical here.

Q: Laura, our 12-year-old, is crazy about horses. I've read that girls' passion for horses has something to do with abnormal sexual development. True?

A: False. Researchers who have studied the intense bond that some children make with horses have discovered a wide array of healthy explanations: some youngsters develop the capacity to nurture by taking care of a horse, others develop a sense of mastery and control, others relate to their horse more as a friend or confidant. The sexual theory, although probably accurate in some selected cases, has been oversold.

Homosexual Seduction

A one-time homosexual incident will certainly not make your son or daughter homosexual, but it can lead to anxiety and fears. Listen. Reassure. Talk about it openly.

Q: Our 12-year-old, Robert, was recently seduced into a sexual act by a workman in the neighborhood. Robert told us about it himself. He was scared. We have so many questions and worries that I hardly know where to start. Will this harm Robert? Will this make him a homosexual? Should we talk about it, or should we all try to forget about it?

A: I'm encouraged that Robert came forward to tell you about the incident. He trusts you and he is clearly troubled by the event. He has a need to share the burden of conflict and fear with you and your husband. He wants to talk about it.

A one-time seduction of this sort can obviously be troubling to a youngster, particularly at the age of 12 when Robert is probably just launching into puberty, but it will not "turn Robert into a homosexual."

Robert, however, may have some questions about his sexual identity. He may feel guilty as well as frightened. By all means encourage him to talk. Listen to him. Don't let his worries go underground.

Consultation is generally not required in such cases, but if Robert's worries (or yours) persist, a visit to a child psychiatrist might help.

Trust Thy Neighbor?

Q: I'm the divorced mother of two boys, 12 and 9½. They are becoming very attached to the man who lives in the next apartment. Bill (not his real name) is 24 and single. He buys the boys gifts, takes them to movies, and invites them over to his place constantly. At first I was pleased, but now I'm getting a little worried. Bill doesn't seem to have any other friends. Isn't it a little strange for him to build his world around two little boys? The boys deny that anything is wrong, but still I am worried. What should I do?

Pedophiles are very clever at gaining access to children. It probably won't be a stranger in a raincoat offering candy. Be alert closer to home. The best defence? A well-educated youngster and open communication.

A: It's a dilemma. You are probably worried that Bill is a pedophile (child sex abuser) and is gaining access to your sons under the guise of being a long-sought father-figure. On the other hand, you don't want to accuse him unjustly and you are finding it increasingly difficult to justify a break in the relationship with your sons because you don't want to hurt them either.

I'm glad you talked to your boys, but their answer, "nothing's wrong," is too vague. Ask specifically what they do at Bill's place. Ask if Bill has made them promise to keep any secrets. Seek, at the very least, to limit their contact if you have any suspicions. It could be a measure of safety (but no guarantee) if you insisted that trips and visits to the movies, etc. be with both boys together, never just one. Also, have a frank talk with your sons, but don't make them feel guilty. And for now, resist the tendency to blame anything on Bill (unless you have more evidence). Finally, keep your index of suspicion up.

Spin the Bottle

Q: My 12-year-old, Ginger, had a boy-girl party last night. She didn't want me to chaperone, but I did. Imagine my shock when I went down to the basement and discovered the kids playing Spin the Bottle. I was too stunned to do anything, and I didn't

Yes, kids still play this little game. Another harmless rite of passage for the most part.

105

want to embarrass Ginger in front of her friends, so I went back upstairs. But, believe me, Ginger got punished as soon as the last guest departed. My sister thinks that I should have sent everyone home immediately. What do you think?

A: Spin the Bottle is a rite of passage in our culture. Most kids survive it. It will be played somewhere, sometime by most kids, usually without parental approval or knowledge.

But, in this case, you did have knowledge and you are obviously opposed to the game. My concern, therefore, is that by going back upstairs you gave tacit approval to it — certainly in the eyes of Ginger's friends.

Your sister's suggestion, however, appears to be too heavy handed. If you had it to do all over again, I'd suggest stopping the game by saying, "I don't allow this in my house." Such a statement would bring as much relief as disappointment to the assembled teens. The party could then continue.

One more thing. Although you must punish Ginger if she knowingly broke an important rule, let's get the anger out of the way. Instead, use the incident to talk to her about boys, sexuality, and family values.

Mom's One-Night Stands

Single parents must be especially careful to keep their sex lives private. Remember, your pre-teen is getting ready, the juices will be flowing soon. She'll learn more from what you do, than from what you say.

Q: I hope you don't think that I'm too prudish, but I think my recently divorced sister is setting a horrible example. She's dating again with a vengeance — including some one-night stands — in her own home. What will the effect be on her son, 12, and daughter, 9?

A: Your sister may be a victim of crazy-time, or post-divorce delirium. She may, of course, be attempting to reassure herself that she's sexually desirable. She may even be working on a pay-back number on her former spouse. Such activity is fruitless, empty, and dangerous, especially in the AIDS era.

It's bad enough for your sister, but to subject her children to her troubles is inappropriate, insensitive, and yes, potentially harmful to them.

The children need stability and support from Mom these days -- not soap opera. Mom may well require some counseling.

Yes, single mothers have needs too — and there are lots of them: 7 million raising 13.2 million children under the age of 18. No, it's not always easy, but most of them are able to juggle the needs of their youngsters with their own personal needs.

Talk to your sister. Support her, but please advise her to, at least, shield the children from her "dating vengeance."

Scare Him Out of Masturbating?

Q: One month ago, my husband surprised our 12-year-old son, Ryan, in the bathroom. Ryan was masturbating. My husband was as flabbergasted as Ryan. The only thing he could think to say was "stop that or you'll go blind before you turn 21!" Two weeks ago Ryan developed a nervous tic: his right eye blinks continually. Could this symptom be related to the encounter with my husband?

Masturbation is a normal part of pre-adolescence. Don't try to scare your youngster out of it. Neither try to suppress it, nor encourage it. Be non-judgemental, but use it as an opportunity for a talk about sex and sexual values.

A: Yes, indeed. Ryan's tic may be a drastic example of body language. The opening of his eye probably represents the natural drive towards genital excitement. The closing represents the prohibition of his conscience against sexual arousal. In addition, he may now fear blindness and retribution, and, of course, he's saddled with the shame of Dad's "discovery."

But I'm not suggesting that your husband is the villain in the act. He didn't exactly cause Ryan's problem. The conflict over masturbation was certainly present before your husband made his ill-advised comment.

Let's focus on the solution. As a first step, your husband could be very helpful to Ryan. A frank father-to-son talk is in order. Your husband should give Ryan a chance to express his feelings and to ask questions about sex. It is crucial for your husband to adopt a kindly, non-judgemental, non-punitive posture. He should also put things right about blindness. What should he say about masturbation? It's natural, most teenage boys do it, some worry about it. Enough said. Dad should neither encourage it nor attempt to repress it. Let Ryan work it out for himself — like millions of kids do. Like his Dad probably did himself.

The tic? I wouldn't mention it at all. If, after some good talks, the symptom does not go away or it is replaced by another nervous symptom, brief therapy with a child psychiatrist should do the trick.

Do It in Private?

Q: I guess it was bound to happen. The other day I walked into our family room and discovered our 12-year-old son, Charles, masturbating. I was too embarrassed to say anything, but I told my husband about it. He later had a short talk with Charles

Telling them that it's OK and that they should do it in private misses the point. Pre-teens are

often conflicted about masturbation. They need conversation and understanding, not blanket permission.

and told him that "All boys do it. Don't worry about it, but do it in private." What do you think of this approach?

A: It doesn't go far enough. Most 12-year-olds, boys and girls, are conflicted about masturbation. They are tempted by sexual urges on the one hand, and prohibited by fears and matters of conscience on the other. In fact, this inner struggle is part and parcel of growing up. If you side with just one side of the conflict (the sexual urge in this case), you can miss an opportunity to educate your youngster about the developmental, physical, and moral issues at stake.

I suggest that you and your husband have a series of talks with Charles about sexuality in general. I'm not talking just about the anatomy and physiology, but about family values as well.

Boy Likes Pantyhose

An innocent behavior of childhood, cross-dressing by a pre-teen may signal problems with sexual identity. Better to seek consultation than "wait and see."

Q: My grandson, Jason, is attracted to pantyhose. For years his mother has thought it cute and has allowed him to wear hers. He's 12 now, and I'm concerned. Last weekend he stayed with me and disappeared into the bathroom for an hour. He explained he "had a stomachache." Later I found one of my panty-hose crumpled up behind the hamper. Why does he do this? What should we do?

A: I can only speculate, but it is entirely possible that Jason is turning an innocent preoccupation of childhood into a sexual fetish of adolescence. Obviously, he may have been engaged in masturbatory activity in the bathroom. While this type of activity is often transient, and part of the "normal" sexual explorations of pre-teen and teenage boys, it can become a fixed habit and interfere with appropriate sexual maturation. The problem is that sexual development is subtle and any abnormal development may not become apparent for a few years. Therefore, it may be a bit risky to adopt "a wait and see" attitude.

I suggest that Jason's parents confront him gently, but firmly, about the incident. They should use this as an opportunity to talk to him about sex in general. Then, without becoming Private Eyes, they should keep an eye on Jason's overall development and behavior. Consult with the pediatrician if necessary, or with a child psychiatrist, if there are additional worries about Jason's sexuality.

And, one thing more, no more encouragement of pantyhose or cross-dressing of any sort.

Incest Victims

Q: I have just learned that my 11-year-old niece has been the victim of incest with her older brother, 15. What should we do?

A: The way the family handles things now will be very important. Your niece will need understanding.

Be on the lookout for these danger signs: 1) isolation from peers, 2) depression, 3) guilt and shame, 4) distrust of males or authority figures, 5) fear of intimacy, 6) falling grades, 7) loss of interest in previously enjoyed activities, 8) physical symptoms.

It will be important for your niece to be able to talk with a trusted adult about her thoughts and feelings. I believe in preventative counseling, by the way, even if there are no signs of problems.

Finally, your niece must be protected from her brother, even if it means moving him out of the house until things can be sorted out.

Know the warning signs. Listen. Ask questions. Take action.

Pre-Teen Sex Abuser

Q: Last year our 12½-year-old son tried to have intercourse with the 4-year-old daughter of my girlfriend. Recently he tried to do it with his 6-year-old sister. We scolded him. We told him that it's illegal and immoral, but he just tunes us out. He's very independent and strong-willed. We can't trust him. He saw a psychologist, but it didn't help. What should we do?

A: This, obviously, is very serious business. Your son is out of control. In addition to scolding and moralizing, you have to take control. This will mean some form of restriction and punishment. You'll have to demonstrate that if he cannot control his impulses, you will have to take over temporarily.

Don't give up the psychological treatment. If you weren't satisfied with the first doctor, seek another consultation. I doubt there will be a quick fix. So, be prepared for several months of counseling sessions. Pre-teens who victimize young girls usually have serious underlying problems. Your son may be struggling against poor self-esteem as well as sexual and aggressive impulses.

While you're waiting for the treatment to show results, help him find constructive outlets for his tensions. Success in sports or hobbies can also bolster his feelings of self-worth. Keep him busy on the constructive and healthy side of life. And yes, talk

The pre-teen who sexually abuses younger children has serious problems. It's not a phase. He needs professional help.

to him about sex and help him put his feelings into words —
another healthy discharge for his impulses.

Siblings

Treat Them Equally?

Don't treat them equally, treat them fairly.

Q: We have three children, ages 11, 8, and 6. I try my best to treat them as individuals. For example, I set higher standards of behavior for our oldest; she also has more chores to do, but she has more privileges too. The problem I run into might be called the Equality Doctrine. The oldest wants the "easy life" (fewer chores) of the youngest. It never ends. I'm tempted to throw in the towel. Any advice?

A: Yes. Forget the Equality Doctrine. Cling to the Fairness Doctrine. Not only is it impossible to treat all children equally, it isn't even in their best interests to try. Each of your youngsters is at a completely different developmental stage. Each has his own specific strengths, weaknesses, and needs. The best you can do is attempt to treat them not equally, but fairly. Peg their responsibilities and privileges to their individual abilities. The kids, as you suggest, might fight the plan, but you are on solid ground. It's not easy, but I applaud your approach. Keep it up.

Angry with Brother

Anger, including anger at siblings, is neither good nor bad. It's a natural emotion. Accept your child's feelings, but do not allow abuse. Try to channel it positively by asking for solutions to problems.

Q: I don't know what to say. My oldest daughter Lisa, 11, is always shouting to me that she "hates" her brother Martin, 8. How should I respond to all this anger?

A: Try these steps: 1) Accept her feelings, but redefine her conclusions, i.e., "You get very angry about some of the things that Martin does." 2) Allow her to express her feelings and to give you examples of Martin's alleged misbehavior. 3) Ask her if she has any ideas how she can improve her relationship with her brother, but resist the urge to solve the problem for her.

Sibling Abuse

Serious abuse of a child by one of his brothers or sisters often signals family pathology. Therapy, including family sessions, is usually indicated.

Q: My sister has three boys, 11, 7, and 5. I always thought they were a happy all-American family. Last week, however, I learned that the oldest boy, Lewis, was taken to a psychiatrist because he's been abusing his youngest brother, Patrick. My sister was crying when she told me about it: beatings, water torture — he even locked Patrick in a closet when his parents went out to the movies. What causes a boy to be so vicious toward his own brother?

A: Sibling abuse is much more common than most people think. I'm not talking about everyday sibling rivalry but of true abuse: the kind that Lewis has apparently been inflicting on Patrick. Although I can't comment on the specifics of this case without a lot more information, I can outline for you the most common dynamics that child psychiatrists usually uncover in these cases:

1) *Perpetrator as victim.* Very often the youngster performing the abuse is himself abused by a parent. Other times he's been neglected. Sometimes he's been neither, but he perceives himself as abused or neglected. The effect is the same.

2) *Identification with aggressor.* The child-perpetrator often identifies with an aggressive parent. For example, if Dad abuses Mom, the child may identify with his father and search for a handy victim — a younger bother or sister.

3) *Favorite child as target.* The target of the perpetrator's abuse is usually the sibling he perceives as the favorite of his parents. This is often the youngest child in the family.

4) *Displacement.* The abuser is usually a youngster who has repressed his anger and rage at his parents. Fearing retaliation if he targets them, he displaces his aggression onto easier prey.

Children like Lewis who are perpetrators of sibling abuse frequently go on to abuse other children, and even to grow up into spouse abusers or abusers of their own children. But there's a positive element to the story. Lewis has been discovered. He's in treatment. There's hope.

The Black Sheep?

Q: I guess you could say that Peter, 11, is the black sheep of our family. He's so different from our other children. He's testy, doesn't like to spend time with the rest of us, likes loud music, and most of all, he just isn't interested in school. In contrast, his sister, 13, and brothers, 15 and 9, are all good students and very well behaved. What causes one child, like Peter, to be such a black sheep?

The black sheep of the family may simply be trying to be special in her own way — something that all pre-teens value. Help her be special — on the positive side of life.

A: First of all, it's important to realize that, in a sense, each child in the family has a different set of parents. Each child comes along a different point in the development of the marriage. Secondly, each child, in a similar sense, has a different family too. And, of course, sibling position is another powerful influence. Peter, for example, is a middle child; he may feel trapped between his high-achieving brothers and sisters.

There are genetic and physical factors, too. All children come into the world with specific biological endowments. This influences such things as temperament, health, behavior, and intelligence.

Finally, let's remember that each child wants to be special. Here's where psychological and learned factors come into play. Peter may just be doing what comes naturally. He wants to be unique — to be different in some significant way from his brothers and sisters. Unfortunately, he's apparently chosen to travel, shall we say, a negative path.

Maybe he's doing the best he can under the circumstances. Maybe he can't compete with the others academically. It's OK to be different (and even desirable in many ways) as long as you do it in a positive way.

My advice? Accept that Peter has to be different, but don't label him as a "black sheep." Help him find some positive ways to be unique and special.

Television

How To Set Limits on TV Watching

Most pre-teens watch too much TV. Parents should limit TV watching, but enlist the cooperation of the youngster in the process. A six-step formula follows.

Q: Last week my husband and I kept a log of our 12-year-old son's TV habits. We were shocked. Over a 7-day period Kevin watched a total of 32 hours of television. It's incredible. How can we limit the amount of TV that he watches?

A: It is incredible. American children watch an average of 25 hours of television each week. I agree with you that this is excessive. Even if there were 32 hours of worthwhile programming for Kevin each week (which there probably is not), he pays too great a price in passivity and social isolation if he spends so much time in front of the tube.

How to limit Kevin's video addiction? Try the following steps:

Step One: Study his viewing habits. Not only how much, but what programs does he watch? Document the baseline.

Step Two: Decide how much TV Kevin should be allowed. As a general rule I suggest one hour per day.

Step Three: Make a list, with Kevin's help, of his favorite shows. Ask Kevin to make a case for why he should watch any particular program. Is it educational? Does it entertain wholesomely?

Step Four: With the TV guide to help you, make a list, with Kevin's help, of the programs that are acceptable to you.

Step Five: Do not use TV as a reward. If Kevin deserves some recognition for an accomplishment, reward him with an activity that he can do with Mom and Dad.

Step Six: It is a good idea to select a few programs for family viewing. Lively family discussion about program content can have a strong positive influence on children. The key is to eliminate the negative impact of television, and then to use TV constructively in Kevin's social, psychological, and cognitive development.

TV-Free Home?

Q: I've just read in our local paper about a 12-year-old girl who won a $500 bet with her father because she did not watch TV for an entire year. Sounds like a great idea. Do you recommend it for our 11-year-old son?

A: Your first step would be to talk it over with your son. If you can stimulate his interest in the proposition, and get his cooperation, you're on your way.

Keep in mind, however, a couple of points: 1) Alternatives. The basic idea is to teach your youngster that there are worthwhile alternatives to an excessive diet of television. What will he do with his newly found "free" time? If necessary, help him come up with some ideas, but don't push too hard on your own suggestions or he'll smell a setup. 2) Plan for success. A one-year moratorium on TV is a mighty tall order for most kids. Why not suggest a one-month trial instead, with some type of interim reward. From a behavioral modification standpoint this plan is more apt to be successful.

The average child watches three or four hours of television every day. This is outrageous. While there are several TV programs of educational entertainment value to youngsters,

Television, viewed intelligently, is a positive force. If you opt for a TV-free home, be sure to offer alternatives.

even the most ardent TV booster would be hard pressed to agree that there are three or four hours of daily programming sufficiently important to snare kids away from other pursuits like reading, spending time with the family, or even the hated "H" word, homework.

Watch TV and Do Homework?

Homework is best done without distractions.

Q: My granddaughter, Betsy, 11, is allowed to sprawl in front of the TV while she does her homework. My daughter allows it because she claims "all the kids do it." Well, I didn't allow her to do it, and she grew up into an excellent student. Betsy is not doing so well in school. I'm not surprised. How can you possibly watch TV and do homework at the same time?

A: I'm with you, although I'm sure that many successful students study in front of the TV.

First of all, most children retain more information when it's not competing with radio, TV, or the VCR.

Secondly, if learning is given equal prominence with TV watching, it simply isn't being given the priority it should have in Betsy's life. Thirdly, I'm a bit concerned that your daughter is caving in a little too easily here. To excuse Betsy's poor study habits on the basis that "all the kids do it" is weak and shortsighted.

Betsy's academic problems, of course, may be due to many things. Her Mom should really consult with the classroom teacher to investigate the matter. In the meantime, I suggest a planned study time in a quiet place each evening — before any TV is viewed at all.

TV Violence and Children

TV violence does tend to affect youngsters. Some identify with it and become more aggressive. Others become desensitized to it. The parent who limits and controls the TV viewing of children is wise.

Q: Our kids, like most kids these days, are TV addicts. The main difference, I guess, is that we're trying to do something about it. We limit Jason, 11, to one hour per day and Tuesday, 9, to one half-hour per day. What's more, my husband and I go through the TV guide every week and select the shows they're allowed to watch. They complain (boy do they complain), but we're convinced we're doing the right thing. What do you say?

A: You'll get no complaints from me. Television is a force for great good in our lives if we use it wisely. The parent who limits and controls the viewing habits of children is a wise parent.

In case you'd like some backup, here's the essence of a review of research conducted over the past ten years by Murray, Zuckerman, and Zuckerman on the influence of TV violence on the behavior of children:

1) Children learn and remember aggressive behavior from what they see on TV.

2) Children who are exposed to repetitive violence on TV become desensitized to it. They then tend to become more accepting of aggressive behavior in real life.

On the other hand, it should be pointed out that some children learn to inhibit their own aggression as a result of TV violence, but only if they're made aware of the negative and painful consequences of this type of behavior.

The best tonic, therefore, is a concerned parent who is available to talk to kids about what they're experiencing on the tube — a parent who is ready to undo some of the damage done by excessive violence on TV. A parent, I'm sure, like you.

Quiz

Pre-adolescence. The quiet before the storm. How much do you know about this important, but poorly understood, stage of development? Try your hand at this quiz, taken directly from the previous chapter:

1. True or False? Girls today tend to have their first menstrual periods at an earlier age than their mothers did.

2. With "the negative" 12-year-old, it's best to:
    A. Punish her consistently for all negative behavior
    B. Ignore as much of it as you can
    C. Have her see a child psychiatrist

3. The youngster who is "jealous" of a brother who has a serious illness (select all that apply):
    A. May need more attention
    B. May actually feel guilty that he himself is well
    C. Is just expressing one form of sibling rivalry
    D. Should be made to apologize

4. True or False? Pre-adolescents tend to be more sensitive to criticism than younger children.

5. Joint custody (select all that apply):
    A. Is always the preferred arrangement
    B. Is doomed when ex-spouses continue to disagree strongly
    C. Depends mostly on the cooperation of the children
    D. May suffer if one spouse remarries

6. True or false? The youngster who habitually pulls her hair out may be suffering from depression.

7. Your 11-year-old brings home a report card with one A, three B's, and a D. You should:
    A. First compliment him on the A
    B. Ask him immediately about the D
    C. Wait for him to say something about it

8. True or False? A pre-adolescent's intense love of horses usually signifies underlying sexual conflict.

9. Regarding TV watching, most 12-year-olds:
    A. Are old enough to make their own choices
    B. Require limits on how much they watch and what programs they should watch
    C. Should be offered TV as a reward for good behavior

10. The parents whose 11-year-old son is seeing a child psychiatrist:
    A. Should be kept informed of the child's progress
    B. Must not speak to the doctor so that confidentiality is preserved
    C. Have to know everything that's being discussed in sessions

11. When asked to decide a "moral question," right vs wrong, most 12-year-olds:
    A. Will be quite lenient
    B. Will consider the nuances, the "shades of gray"
    C. Will view things in absolute "black and white" terms

12. Your 12-year-old stepdaughter is embroiled in a continual conflict with you. How should you respond?
    A. Don't back down. Be firm. Show her that you're in charge
    B. Give her some slack. It's a phase. She'll get over it
    C. Put your marriage first. Work together with your spouse

13. Incest between brother and sister (select all that apply):
    A. Always results in later sexual conflicts
    B. Tends to occur in disrupted, isolated families
    C. Results in less guilt for the victim if he or she was actively coerced into the act

14. True or False? Twelve-year-olds must learn to handle money. It's a good idea, therefore, to start paying them to do chores that they used to do without payment.

15. It is extremely important to (select one):
    A. Treat all of your children equally
    B. Give an older child more privileges
    C. Treat all of your children fairly

16. Among pre-adolescents who suffer medical illness, the number one cause of treatment failure is:
    A. Child's inability to understand his illness
    B. Child's failure to follow doctor's orders because of psychological factors
    C. Severity of the illness
    D. Inaccurate diagnosis and treatment

17. When divorce is imminent, children should (select all that apply):
    A. Be approached by both parents together
    B. Be told all of the facts; they'll find them out anyway
    C. Be allowed to ask questions

18. Up to age 12, the greatest influence in a child's life is:
    A. Parents
    B. Other children, including siblings
    C. Teachers
    D. Television

19. Sex education should begin:
    A. At age 10 or 11 (i.e., just before puberty)
    B. When a girl has her first menstrual period
    C. In early childhood

20. Which is more effective in teaching good discipline to children:
    A. Punishment for misbehavior
    B. Comparing them to siblings and peers
    C. Praise for good behavior

21. Children of parents who smoke:
    A. Tend not to smoke, i.e., they can see first hand the perils of cigarette smoking
    B. Smoke at about the same incidence as children whose parents do not smoke
    C. Smoke at twice the rate of children whose parents do not smoke

22. True or False? The 11- or 12-year-old with a serious history of accident proneness may actually be suicidal.

23. True or False? There is an epidemic of "nuclear fear" among today's children.

24. Your 12-year-old son is not doing well at school. You've tried "everything" to motivate him, but nothing works. Should you offer cash rewards for good grades?
    A. Yes
    B. No

25. Your 11-year-old son has been caught shoplifting. You should:
    A. Take matters into your own hands. Call the store owner and pay for the stolen merchandise, then punish your son
    B. Be firm but reasonable. Don't let him know how angry you are
    C. Take your son back to the store and insist that he work things out himself

Correct Answers

1) True; 2) B; 3) A, B; 4) True; 5) B, D; 6) True; 7) A; 8) False; 9) B; 10) A; 11) C; 12) C; 13) B, C; 14) False; 15) C; 16) B; 17) A, C; 18) A; 19) C; 20) C; 21) C; 22) True; 23) False; 24) B; 25) C

3

Early Adolescents (13–14)

While Shakespeare may have wished that there was "no age twixt twelve and twenty," you don't have any choice. Your youngster is an adolescent now and you'll have to cope with it.

But what is adolescence? There are many ways to define it: "a stage between childhood and adulthood" is one way. Many parents would probably prefer something like: "those impossible years." Some truth here, of course. Teachers don't like to teach in junior highs, parents know that 13 and 14 sometimes seems like a throwback to ages 2, 3, or 4, and even pediatricians and child psychiatrists will admit that the early adolescent is the most difficult of all.

Why? Remember those inherent drives (aggression and sex) that have been "latent" for the last several years? Well, they're not latent any more. With the onset of puberty, the juices are flowing and the unconscious drives push to reign supreme once more. The early adolescent's life, so well-ordered for the past several years, is thrown into chaos. He has new feelings. She has a new body. They're not children; and although they would sometimes secretly like to retreat to those simpler days, they're ashamed to admit it to you. They're not adults; although they clamor for the privileges of adulthood, they want no part of the responsibilities that go along with them.

The early adolescent.

All dressed up and no place to go. Too old for a baby-sitter, but too young to drive the car. No wonder this is a time of tumult and rebellion for so many kids.

One word of advice: don't take it personally, they're really rebelling against their own immaturity.

The early adolescent. Maybe the best thing that can be said about this stage is that it should only last for about two years.

But, hold it! There are some important advantages in this stage. Because of the dramatic swings taking place, adolescence provides an opportunity for positive change as well as rebellion and all the rest. Remember, the adolescent combines some of the best of both worlds: the plasticity of childhood and a growing adult-like ability to view himself critically and to work constructively for positive change. In fact, it's your child's last best chance to achieve fundamental personality change before he becomes an adult — and we all know how hard it is then.

So why not start by carefully reading this chapter? Be sure to take the quiz and to restudy any questions you miss. Other advice: read more books about teenagers, get to know the parents of your youngster's friends, and, above all, get to know your own child. He'll teach you more about these years than any of the rest. Relax. It could be lots of fun.

Discipline

Principles of Punishment

Punishment, although not as effective as other techniques in the teaching of discipline, is necessary in raising teenagers. Most parents, however, don't apply it effectively. While you can't always control your teenager's behavior, you can (and must) control your own. Apply the principles. Be consistent.

Q: Our Tammy, 14, and Tommy, 12, are good kids. We rarely have to punish them. When we do, we seem to go overboard, then we feel guilty about it. Any tips?

A: Punishment, although the least effective technique in teaching self-discipline to youngsters, is a necessary ingredient in the proper raising of children. Some tips:

1) *Last resort.* Use punishment only after techniques such as rewards, ignoring the behavior, logical consequences, etc. have failed.

2) *Punish the event, not the child.* Preserve self-esteem by being clear that although you are punishing a piece of misbehavior, you still love the child: "Tommy, you know that I love you, but I cannot tolerate (the specific misbehavior) and it must be punished."

3) *Timing.* Punishment should be as immediate as possible after the misbehavior.

4) *Don't waffle.* Do it. No hesitation.

5) *Anger.* Punishment is best done matter-of-factly, without malice. After all, it is basically a teaching exercise in self-discipline. But if you're obviously angry, admit that you're angry at the misbehavior.

6) *Fit the crime.* Punishment should fit the crime — not too harsh, not too light. This is why you should have a variety of responses at your disposal, ranging from timeouts to restriction of various privileges.

7) *Don't get physical.* Spanking or striking a teenager is, at best, ineffective, and at worst, abusive. Physical punishment has no place in the teaching of self-discipline.

8) *Consistency.* If a particular misbehavior is worthy of punishment once, it's worthy a hundred times. Consistency of parental response is all-important. Inconsistency breeds confusion and invites further testing of limits. You may not always be able to control your teenager, but you must control your own behavior. Be consistent.

9) *Good graces.* Punishment should wipe the slate clean. Once completed, immediately allow your youngster back into your good graces. He's learned his lesson (you hope); now it's time to get on with life as usual.

Curfew? Just Try To Stop Me!

Q: My 13-year-old daughter, Charlene, broke a rule (curfew) a few weeks ago and I grounded her. Last week she broke it again and I've told her she can't go out. Now she says: "Just try to stop me." Dr. Novello, I can't. She just does whatever she wants. I can't lock her up. What should I do?

A: You've got a serious problem on your hands: A defiant teenager who has slipped out of parental control. Why? That's the question. If Charlene has basically been a good, well-behaved girl up to this point, I'd suspect that she's reacting to the physical and psychological tumult of puberty and adolescence. Maybe she feels that you don't understand her, or that your punishment is too harsh and unrealistic. If so, she may have concluded that her only hope is to take matters into her own hands. If this is the case you may be able to turn things around with a calm responsible talk with your daughter. Listen to her. Talk to parents of Charlene's friends. Be willing to compromise on some of your rules if they're too strict. But don't compromise your principles or family values.

On the other hand, if Charlene's actions are part of a long-established behavior pattern, compromise and reasonableness will not work for long. Her inability to control her own impulses will cause her, inevitably, to test the limits of your control again and again. If so, professional help is the answer.

At any rate, you can't afford to settle for the status quo. Someone has to be in charge of the family. That someone should be you, not 13-year-old Charlene. Whatever you do, put yourself back in the driver's seat. And do it quickly.

Early adolescents deserve more freedom than pre-teens but they must respect reasonable curfews. Talk to the parents of your son's or daughter's friends. Listen to your teenagers too, then make your own rules. The principle is to allow your youngster to grow in privilege and responsibility.

Guilt Trip

Q: My husband has an awful habit of deliberately making our children, 14, 10, and 9, feel guilty. He reminds them how much they make him suffer when they break a rule or mess up in school. He insists that they say "I'm sorry" and ask "forgiveness" if they've offended him for some reason. I say "Enough already!" What do you say?

A: True guilt can only be felt when a youngster has developed a conscience. Guilt is the weapon of the conscience. Although your husband's misguided maneuvers may induce some semblance of guilt in the children, he is mainly inducing shame.

The deliberate planting of guilt or shame by a parent is, at best, counterproductive, and at worst, abusive.

123

Guilt, however, is not all bad. Children need to experience guilt as part of growing up. It's how they ultimately develop their own conscience: that inner voice of good and bad, right and wrong, do and don't.

I do believe that your husband is wrong in trying to personalize the youngsters' guilt. It's better to ask them how they feel about not behaving properly or not achieving up to their usual standards in school. This is a more effective way of helping to build their own super-egos or consciences. And it takes Dad out of the position of the moral heavyweight.

To Scold or Not to Scold?

Good, old-fashioned scolding does have a place, but it must be done appropriately. No name-calling. Scolding must teach, not humiliate.

Q: We have three children, ages 13, 10, and 7½. Any time we scold them it just goes in one ear and out the other. What can we do?

A: Scolding can and should be a fairly effective technique of punishment. Try these tips:

1) *No name-calling.* Beware the tendency to shoot from the lip. Name-calling creates ill will and angry children.

2) *Criticize the event.* No one's perfect, but assume that your children genuinely want to do things right. Say: "I'm disappointed in the way you handled that. You can do so much better." Focus on the event, don't launch a blanket condemnation of your child as a human being.

3) *Teach.* Effective scolding should point out alternative ways of handling the situation.

4) *No guilt trips.* Avoid such zingers as, "How could you do this to your Mother who works so hard for you?"

5) *Be ready for action.* Repeated misbehavior, unaffected by repeated scolding, may also mean that something more is required — punishment. Let your youngster know what the consequence will be next time it happens. Then, forget the scolding. Take action.

Juvenile Court

Teenagers who are entirely out of parental control can be helped by the juvenile justice system. Seek its help before it seizes your child.

Q: I've tried everything. I'm ready to throw in the towel. My 14-year-old, Becky, is simply out of control. She calls me four-letter words, wishes I were dead, does as she pleases, and refuses to go for help. One of my friends has suggested that I contact the local juvenile court and have her placed in solitary confinement at a detention center for a couple of days to show her I mean business. Would this be a good idea?

A: First of all, I doubt the juvenile authorities would do such a thing. Secondly, I don't like the idea.

Becky is obviously a very angry girl. Punishment simply for the sake of punishment is likely to backfire. She will feel even more justified in opposing everything you stand for.

Yes, you need to reestablish parental control, but this has to be done wisely. You might, for example, consult with the juvenile court and ask for their help. Perhaps the court can use its leverage to insist that Becky gets the therapy she so desperately needs.

In the meantime, take care of yourself. Start by seeing a child psychiatrist yourself to get some tips on how to defuse the situation before you run out of options.

Positive Labels

Q: My son-in-law has a label for all of his kids: Bryan, 13, is "Slowpoke," Becky, 11, is "Brainiac," and Paul, 10, is "Rambo." The children hate the labels because they're so negative. Won't they be injured by this practice?

Labels may work for frozen foods, but they're bad for kids — unless you use them positively.

A: Labels may be good for food packages, but they're usually bad for children. They unfairly distill to one word the many complex things that a child really is. And, these labels can become internalized. Some youngsters eventually believe them, and we witness a self-fulfilling prophecy as they act in such a way to make the label's prediction come true.

If you're going to label a child at all, make it a positive label. Maybe Bryan, for example, is cautious and deliberate. Becky may be the scholar in the family. And Paul? He may be the assertive one, the one with gusto.

Labels usually do more for the labeler than for the labelee. Why does your son-in-law engage in this negative practice? What does he get out of it? Some self-examination may help him change — or to at least fix some positive monikers on Bryan, Becky, and Paul.

Divorce

Divorce Therapy

Q: My husband and I separated two weeks ago after months of haggling about it. I'm sure we're headed for divorce. We have

Parental divorce, even under the best circumstances, is especially tough on early adolescents

who so often are struggling with normative conflicts with their parents. Counseling, even when problems are not apparent, is a good idea for almost all divorcing families.

three children, 13, 9, and 7, and I'm worried about them. I've been reading about the problems that kids have because of divorce. In fact, I've decided to take them to a counselor for some preventive sessions. My husband thinks it's a good idea, but he refuses to participate. He says it's for the children, not for him. My question is this: should we go without him?

A: Yes, by all means. Although your husband's participation would be better for everyone (including him), it's not fair to deny help to the children just because Dad won't cooperate. The sessions can really help. The goals might include:

1) *Information.* The children will need to know something about what's happening and why it's happening. This will have to be explained in a way that each of them can understand, based on their individual needs and abilities.

2) *Feelings.* The children must be given a chance to express their feelings.

3) *Reassurance.* They'll need some reassurance that Mom (and Dad) are not abandoning them, that they haven't caused the break-up, and that you'll try to normalize their lives as much as possible.

4) *Plan.* What's going to happen? Where will they live? Who will have custody? What will be the visitation arrangements?

You can see how helpful it would be if your husband was present for the sessions. His very presence would be a most powerful message: "Mom and I may be divorcing, but we are not divorcing you." He would also be able to answer questions that only he can answer.

But go right ahead. I congratulate you for taking this step. I wish more divorcing parents would consider preventive counseling for children. It works.

Reconciliation Fantasy

Although younger children almost invariably cling to the magical wish that Mom and Dad will get back together, early adolescents tend to have a more balanced view of things. Many see themselves as better off in divorce — but be careful: they're also famous for "What? Me, worry?" bravado.

Q: I knew it would be tough on the children, but I had to do it. Divorce was the only solution for me. Surprisingly, the kids, 13, 11, and 8, all seem to be taking it pretty well. I expected that they'd be filled with wishes for their Daddy and me to get back together again, but they're not. In fact, I think they're relieved. Could I be missing something?

A: Maybe — maybe not. There are several factors that determine how children react to divorce and whether they clutch the fantasy that somehow, someday Mommy and Daddy will be reunited and they'll all live happily ever after.

The most important variable is the ages of the children during the pre-divorce turmoil, the children's awareness of the difficulties, the effects of the bad marriage on them, their relationships with each of the parents, their confidence in the custodial parent, and the nature of their continuing relationship with the non-custodial parent.

Children who are old enough to see for themselves and make up their own minds often do feel relieved by the divorce. Of course, if the post-divorce relationship continues to be marred by conflict between their parents, it never really ends for them.

You're correct in assuming that, for the most part, children do indeed harbor the fantasy that Mom and Dad will get back together again. But a recent study suggests that we might have to look again. In a survey of 368 children of divorce, Glynnis Walker found that 76% said it was just as well that their parents weren't married anymore. Of course, short of interviewing these children, I can't tell you whether their reaction is as much a defensive bravado as it is a mature response based on their own special situations. My experience is that young children generally hope for parental reconciliation, but that teenagers (like your 13-year-old) have a more balanced view of things.

My advice: give the children plenty of opportunity to talk about it, but, at the same time, try to put the divorce behind you. Get on with life. It's the best medicine for you — and for your children.

The Other Woman

Q: My husband left me six months ago for another woman. I'm getting over my anger but my daughter Alexa, 14, isn't. She wants to pay a surprise visit on the woman to tell her off. Should I let her?

A: The fact that you ask this question at all makes me suspect that you're not getting over your anger at all — you may simply be expressing it through Alexa.

Should you let her? Of course not. It is not in her interest, nor yours.

Help Alexa to work out her own feelings. Don't saddle her with yours. If she has legitimate anger at Dad, however, she should be encouraged to express it to him — but not by springing a surprise on "the other woman."

It's a rule that all reasonable parents know, but many violate: do not involve your children when you are working out your conflicts with an ex-spouse.

Stability of Two-Parent Family

Yes, children generally fare much better in stable, healthy two-parent families, but "staying together for the sake of the children" is bad advice if your marriage is unstable, unhealthy, and cannot be fixed. A loving, reliable single parent beats a sick two-parent family any day.

Q: I'm a divorced single mother. My children are 14, 10, and 7½. My kids are my top priority and they're doing pretty well, but I keep hearing about the advantages of the two-parent family. Should I be doing something different?

A: Like what? Getting married? No, I don't recommend it just for the exercise of creating a two-parent situation.

On the other hand, some recent studies demonstrate that teenagers tend to have fewer problems if they grow up in two-parent families, and furthermore, that those that do have problems tend to straighten out as adults. The study, by Professor Emmy Weiner of the University of California at Davis, followed the lives of all 698 children who were born on the Hawaiian island of Kauai in 1955. Among the various problems resolved were larceny, battery and assault, drug abuse, and mental illness.

Just what is it about two-parent families? More time, more money, more support, more role-modeling are some of the answers. But studies like these sometimes stimulate more questions than they answer. Although a healthy two-parent family is superior to a healthy one-parent family, I believe a healthy one-parent family is usually superior to a sick two-parent family. The answer, therefore, comes down to the quality of parents, not their quantity.

Ping Pong Custody

Early adolescents are well-known for threatening to "go and live with Dad (or Mom)." Do not be intimidated.

Q: The trouble is Jennifer, 14. My husband and I were divorced two years ago. I was given custody. Jennifer was really rocked by the divorce, but she and I got along fine — for about six months. Then she became impossible. One day she packed her bag and went to live with her father on the other side of town. I told him to return her immediately, but he refused. I think he saw himself as a rescuer or something. Well, another six months have passed and guess what? Right. Jennifer is having problems with her father and is begging to come back. I want her, of course, but this bouncing back and forth bothers me. It's not the best way to grow up. What should I do?

A: The three of you are playing a game of "Ping Pong Custody" and, believe me, it's a dangerous pastime.

Jennifer's motivations may be several. On the one hand, she may be acting out her wish to retain both of her parents:

she may even secretly wish to bring the two of you back together again out of concern for her "problems." On the other hand, Jennifer may simply be looking for the easy way out: play one parent against the other for the best deal.

Yes, the "back and forth" should bother you. Children cannot be allowed to run from problems. Divorced parents, no matter what unfinished business may still lurk between them, must stand together against this kind of behavior.

How to do it? First, a private talk with your ex-husband. Decide where Jennifer will live and agree to support each other in the decision. Then, both of you should have a warm, open talk with Jennifer. It's been tough for her. Listen to her. You both love her. Tell her the plan. Ask for her cooperation. It's in her best interest. If problems persist, don't hesitate to consult a child psychiatrist or a trained counselor.

Live with Dad?

Q: I've been divorced for five years and have custody of my children, 7, 9½, and 13. Debbie, the 13-year-old, is the problem. She and I bicker constantly because she just won't live by my rules. Her solution is to take a "one-year timeout" by going to live with her father in another city. In principle I'm against it, but I've just about had it. Should I let her go?

A: In principle I'm against it too. Children of divorce too often hit upon this handy expedient. Sometimes they use the threat of going to live with their non-custodial parent as a way of intimidating and forcing hoped-for changes; sometimes they use it as a ready cop-out from facing and working through conflicts with the custodial parent; sometimes it's borne of the belief that life with Dad (in this case) will be ideal and part of their secret wish to reestablish the family unit.

Your first line of defense should be to work things out with Debbie. Get professional help if necessary. A "timeout" with Dad should be the last resort. Remember: that "timeout" could "stretch out" for many years. There's a lot at stake here.

Summer Visitation Problems

Q: Here we go again: Summer is here and it's time for my two daughters, 13 and 15, to spend a month with their father who lives in another state. Last year they didn't want to go, but I forced them. They were miserable. This year they say they won't go. I really hate to force them, especially since I'm not, shall we

A "timeout" with the non-custodial parent should be the last resort. Teenagers should not be allowed to run from problems.

Summer visits with Dad were happily anticipated events for several years, but now your daughter is an early adolescent and she wants to stay home to

be with her friends. What should you do? Nothing. Encourage her to work it out herself with her father.

say, "fond" of my former husband. But he is their father. And I'm sure he'll accuse me of putting them up to it if they don't visit him. What should I do?

A: Your problem, of course, is not unusual. Like most adolescents, your daughters are probably peer-oriented. They don't want to be away from their friends this summer. They view their visit to Dad not as a pleasure, but as a disruption. There may be other issues as well — issues that are more directly related to their relationship to Dad.

I suggest that you take yourself out of the middle of this drama. Why not start by calling your former husband and giving him the facts just as you've outlined them to me. Then tell the girls that this is something they'll have to work out with their father. Given such an opportunity, the three of them may be able to work out a compromise.

By the way, I like your attitude. Even though you are not "fond" of him, you realize that your ex is the father of your children and you're reluctant to be a party to damaging that relationship. That is the key: act in the best interests of your girls. In the long run they'll respect you for it.

Better Visitation

There are many justified reasons for seeking changes in your legal visitation rights. Better to try to work them out directly with the youngsters and your ex before getting the lawyers involved.

Q: It was a big mistake, but when I was going through my divorce three years ago I was a practicing alcoholic. I allowed my ex-husband, under our joint custody agreement, to have full physical custody of the children. I'm allowed to see the kids, 13, 11½, and 10, only once a week on Saturday afternoons — and only if another adult of my husband's choice is present. This is horrible. I've been sober for over a year. Should I see a lawyer about getting better visitation rights?

A: First of all, let me congratulate you on your sobriety. It has to be your top priority now and for the rest of your life.

I'm sure the court's custody and visitation judgment was based on a number of factors, some related to your alcoholism, some not.

Nevertheless, it seems a good idea to review the matter. The best and most direct avenue, of course, is to talk it over with your children and your ex-husband. Going first to your attorney seems to me to be an adversarial way of dealing with a problem that will work or not work based mostly on the amount of compromise, cooperation, and goodwill you can generate.

Stepparenting

Q: My children, ages 13 and 8, are about to become stepchildren. I have had sole custody of them since my divorce from their father five years ago. I will be remarried in a few months. What can I do now to make things go easier for our soon-to-be stepfamily of four?

A: First of all, I'd like to congratulate you on your sensitivity and your willingness to do some advance problem solving. Your situation is not uncommon. In fact, one out of five American adults is a stepparent or will become one during their lifetime. At the same time, one of seven children in the United States (almost 18 million) is a stepchild.

I would suggest a series of heart-to-heart talks for the four of you, since all of you will have to make accommodations to each other. Some of the most important issues to address will include:

1) How are the children to refer to their stepfather?

2) What will be your husband's role, especially in matters of family values and discipline?

3) Your teenager will, in all likelihood, have the most difficult adjustment. What are his or her special concerns?

4) Is your former spouse in the picture? How will he be affected? How will he react?

5) What about grandparents and stepgrandparents?

You, of course, are going to be the one in the middle. Yet this can be a very satisfying position as you bring together the people that you love and blend them into a family. Yes, there will be some rough spots, but if you can remain realistic, if you keep the channels of communication open among the four of you, and if you help your husband and the children to learn to love each other, you can all share in a priceless gift: the joy of family.

Stepfamilies are made, not born. You'll have to work at it. The best time to start is before you remarry. Involve the children in a wide-ranging discussion of the coming changes in their lives.

Sing at Mom's Wedding?

Q: I'm the divorced mother of three children, ages 9½, 11, and 14. The oldest, Cynthia, is a wonderful singer. Next month I plan to remarry. When I asked Cindy to sing at the wedding she was, shall we say, negative. I don't want to push the idea, but I did have my heart set on it. What do you suggest?

A: Beware. Cindy is sending a signal: she thinks your remarriage is nothing to sing about.

A parent's remarriage may be especially stressful for an early adolescent. Share the facts. Absorb the feelings. Learn. Grow together.

It used to be the custom for a couple to sneak away, get married, and return to hit the kids with the news. Such guerilla tactics obviously leave too many wounds for the youngsters.

On the other hand, more enlightened approaches, such as yours, can backfire too. While I admire your openness, it could be harmful to Cindy if she's led to believe she'll let you down if she doesn't sing for Mom and her stepfather-to-be.

Listen closely to your daughter. Absorb her feelings. The issue here is not so much the singing performance as what kind of drumbeat the new family will march to. Use this opportunity wisely. Let Cindy decide freely about the plans for the ceremony.

Dress Code

The Designer Jeans Syndrome

The sometimes frantic quest to be "with it" often leads early adolescents into being preoccupied with designer jeans, athletic shoes, and other paraphernalia.

Q: My 13-year-old daughter, Andrea, has a new craze: designer clothes, especially jeans. Like most families we have a budget for clothing. Andrea will break the bank if we allow this to continue. I try to talk sense to her: "You're just paying for a logo or a trademark." Andrea won't listen.

A: Andrea has fallen victim to what might be called "The Designer Jeans Syndrome," a major affliction of our time among adolescents — and some adults as well.

No 13-year-old wants to be different. If the other kids are wearing Calvin's or Vanderbilt's, then Andrea must slip into similar denim. Why? The early adolescent feels so different and vulnerable on the inside that she adopts an exterior veneer of sameness as a defense. A certain amount of this is normal. It goes with the teenage territory.

On the other hand, Andrea's insistence that she wear expensive clothing may be a signal that her basic self-esteem hinges on these external trappings, and that you do not love her unless you buy for her. She may equate your money with your love. Obviously this is a much more serious state of affairs.

There is no reason to allow a run on the family bank. Such indulgence is not in Andrea's best interests. Instead, have a good talk with her. Why the excessive preoccupation with status symbols?

Athletic Shoeitis

Q: Our 13-year-old son, Steven, has the athletic shoe mania. He own five pairs and wants more. He says he has to color coordinate with his outfit, and that all the other kids do it. I say enough is enough. Do you back me up?

Status symbols such as athletic shoes can be important, but don't allow them to break the family bank.

A: One hundred percent. The athletic shoe mania, or call it athletic shoeitis, started as an inner city phenomenon among older teens, but is now spreading to younger kids in the suburbs and smaller towns. Why? The mania is fueled by some of the slickest and most creative TV advertising seen in years.

Every generation of adolescents has its fads. Most teens secretly feel strange and out of step and will only feel comfortable if they can be the same as everyone else; therefore, fads such as athletic shoes catch on more quickly with this age group than with any other.

Steven, like many other youngsters, is going too far. These shoes (I don't have to tell you) aren't cheap. Besides, while I'm not against Steven being style conscious, I do believe he can turn this into an unwholesome preoccupation.

Yes, it's time to take the air out of his Jordan's.

Tight Jeans

Q: My husband gets furious with our 14-year-old daughter, Christine, because she wears tight jeans. He claims that the boys will think she's looking for sex and that she'll get a bad reputation. Christine says that her dress is actually more conservative than the other girls. Yet, the two of them fight about it constantly.

Relatively harmless. Another signal of budding sexuality. Give her some leeway, but require a dress code that is generally consistent with your family values.

A: A recent study by researchers at UCLA does confirm that teenage boys tend to read sexual come-ons from things like tight jeans, short shorts, low-cut tops, and braless blouses. But what else is new?

I suspect that your husband's preoccupation with Christine's sexuality, and Christine's own constant bickering with Dad, may really be a case of father-daughter misunderstanding of normal development. Their arguments keep the two of them stuck together psychologically when each should be willing to let go a bit. Step in there, Mom, and help them work it out. Allow Christine some slack, but require her to maintain a dress code that is generally consistent with your family values.

Son Wants Long Hair

A statement of independence and autonomy — especially if it outrages Mom and Dad. Go along with it if you can. If you can't, insist on a haircut, but allow some other means of expression.

Q: My son, the hippie. That's what we call our Thomas, 14. He insists on wearing his hair in a pony tail. I think it looks stupid, but I'm willing to go along with it. My husband refuses to be seen in public with Tom and threatens to sneak in some night while he's asleep and cut it off. Any advice?

A: A not uncommon situation. Thomas is choosing to make a statement about autonomy and independence via his hairstyle. He's also managing to distance himself from you in the process. In a sense that's what early adolescence is all about. If only they wouldn't be so outrageous in the process.

What to do? Generally I urge families to play along — to a point. That point is the limit of your own tolerance. Long hair and/or pony tails infuriate some parents, especially those who have an excessive need to control or who unconsciously regard their adolescents as narcissistic extensions of themselves. Can you compromise on the hairstyle? If not, can you give in to some other whim in exchange for a haircut?

Thomas is seeking some way to make a statement that he is moving toward independence from you. Among all the things he could be doing, a pony tail is pretty tame. But if you cannot. tolerate it, allow him some other avenue of expression.

Friends and Dating

How Teens Spend Time

Friends vs family: Early adolescence marks an important shift in how youngsters spend their time. From being family-centered, they become peer-oriented, and the gap widens with time. Parents should not hang on, but they should hang in there.

Q: Our Jackie has just turned 13 and we're ready for some changes. We understand, for example, when she insists on spending more time with friends, less time with us. But how much time should she spend with friends?

A: This is a tough question. Yes, Jackie's world will increasingly become a world of peers. This is a natural and necessary step toward adulthood. The movement from family to friends, however, should be gradual and gentle. Just as the early adolescent who clings to the family and fears friendship is in trouble, the teen who leaps toward unbridled freedom and slips from parental control is also at risk.

If you'd like some guidelines, here's the result of a poll, "Whom Adolescents Spend Their Time With," that was published in *Being Adolescent* by Csikszentmihalyi and Larson: Classmates (in school) 23%, friends 29%, alone 27%, and family 19%.

Generally speaking, an adolescent can be expected to spend progressively less time with family and somewhat more time with friends as she develops through early, middle, and late adolescence.

Remember though, that like all teenagers, Jackie has her own needs and will develop her own pace toward maturation and emancipation.

Just Talking

Q: Laurene, our 14-year-old, is very peer-conscious. We expected it, but we have a hard time accepting the fact that she doesn't "do" anything with her girlfriends. "We just talk," she says. Should we insist on more structure or goals?

A: Good luck. "Just talking" with friends is important to early adolescents, and you can bet that Laurene will do even more of it over the next few years. For example, Csikszentmihalyi and Larson (*Being Adolescent*, Basic Books, 1984) found that high school students talk with friends three times as often as with family members. In a more recent report, Raffaelli and Duckett (1989) report in the *Journal of Youth and Adolescence* that 9th grade girls, like Laurene, spend 9 hours a week just talking to friends, while boys spend almost 4 hours.

Youngsters learn and grow from this activity. While your interest in goals and structure is exemplary, and I encourage your efforts, you may be fighting a losing battle.

Make sure, however, you remain in Laurene's conversational loop. It is interesting to note that the 1989 report cited above revealed that the early adolescents in the study maintained their family communications; friends did not totally replace family.

Teenagers learn and grow from talking to their friends, but they should still be talking to their families too.

Teen Friendships

Q: We've been through it before. I'm talking about how teenagers prefer their friends to their families. When our oldest daughter went through this phase, we really didn't handle it very well. We were hurt and I think we overreacted. Now Debbie, our 13-year-old, is obsessed with making friends and is starting to ignore the family. Any advice?

What do teenagers seek in friends? According to a recent poll: reliability, honesty, sensitivity, sense of humor, mutual interests, and intelligence. Sounds promising. If only they would define these characteristics the way their parents do.

A: Yes. Don't let it become an either-or situation. Allow Debbie plenty of opportunity to make (and keep) friends, but insist that she stays friendly with her family too. After all, she needs both.

You might help her further by talking to her about the importance of friendships. What is a good friend? What qualities should she seek in friends?

A recent poll of adolescents addressed this question. Teenagers were asked to pick the most important ingredients to be found in a friend. Their responses: reliability 86%, honesty 83%, sensitivity 75%, sense of humor 75%, mutual interests 63%, and intelligence 52%.

One more word of advice. Resist the temptation to become a best friend to Debbie. Be friendly, yes, but remain a parent. The two roles, friend and parent, are not as compatible as you might think. Her ability to make extra-familial friends is a hallmark of her passage into the adult world.

Her First Mixed Party

Teen parties can get out of hand. Begin now by establishing the rules: parents as chaperones, no gate crashers, no alcohol or drugs, no unsupervised comings and goings by guests.

Q: Shelly, 13, is planning her very first mixed party. We're very proud of the way she's gone about it. She mailed her own invitations, consulted with us about the food, favors, music — everything. Well, almost everything. This morning she dropped a bomb. "And you guys can come back home after it's over," she announced. "What?" I asked. "Nobody's parents stay home for parties. That's baby," was her response. I didn't know what to say. Any advice?

A: Plenty. Stay home. Be unobtrusive but be in charge. Here are some tips:

1) *Official welcome.* Stand at the door with Shelly to greet all her guests and their parents if they'd like to drop by for a moment.

2) *Gate-crashers.* Watch out for them. They're notorious at teen parties. It will be much easier for you than for Shelly to turn them away.

3) *No alcohol or drugs.* Not now, not in later teen years either.

4) *Containment.* Limit the party to one or more rooms. Declare the rest of the house off-limits.

5) *Supervise.* Walk around but try to be inconspicuous. Know what's going on at all times.

6) *No early exits.* Some kids use bona fide party invitations as an excuse to slip out on their own, sometimes to use alcohol. No matter what the excuse, I recommend that you call the

youngster's parents for permission. After all, they have entrusted their child to your care.

In other words, do the reasonable things that you'd like done by other parents if Shelly was going to their home for a party. Then, enjoy.

Hobbies, Sports, and Other Interests

Video Games

Q: Allan, our 14-year-old son, is obsessed with video games. He spends all of his spare time (and a lot of his allowance) at a local video arcade. Are these video games bad for him? What about the kinds of teenagers who hang around such places?

A: While there are some who believe that video games are only a fad, I do not doubt that video games, and electronic games of all sorts, will continue to capture the rapt attention of youngsters (and many adults) for years to come. And why not? These games are fun. They are a challenge to the player's cunning and dexterity. They are also a kind of social organizer for some youngsters who build their network of friends around this common interest.

There is, however, a down-side risk for some kids. Video games can encourage passivity and isolation. You might not believe this if you dropped into a local Video Alley some day and watched the players jumping back and forth, feverishly manipulating the controls of a laser-spewing space ship. The players, and the onlookers too, appear to be almost totally engaged in the games. But these games are primarily "one-man-against-machine" affairs and do not encourage teamwork or even face-to-face competition. Passivity and isolation is not good medicine for teenagers if carried to excess.

Video games, furthermore, do very little to stimulate creativity on the part of the players. And, some of the game themes are violent and destructive. Again, these are negative features.

You are worried about what kind of youngsters Allan might be hanging out with at the video parlor. I'm afraid I can't help you very much with this question. Video games are popular with almost everyone these days who has a quarter in his pocket. Any place with a machine or two, even quaint Mom and Pop

The good news: video games can stimulate dexterity and a sense of mastery. The bad news: they can lead to social isolation if pursued in excess. Good or bad? Neither. Balance and moderation are the keys.

stores, can be christened as the local hangout. You should certainly ask Allan about the guys that frequent his favorite video haunt. You have every right to know about what he does with his time — and with his quarters too.

I'd suggest a go-easy, cautious approach. Keep your eyes on the "bottom line": Allan's behavior at home; his relationship to you, family, and friends; his performance at school; his health; how he feels about himself. Do not allow him to abandon other hobbies in favor of Nintendo. Insist that he retain balance in his life. If he can pull off this balancing act, and if you're satisfied that there are no other negative factors where Allan is personally concerned, I don't see any harm in some occasional video fun.

Teen Song Lyrics

It's designed to turn you off, but parents should know something about their teenagers' musical preferences. Know the groups and what they stand for, know the music, and above all, listen to the lyrics.

Q: I guess I shouldn't be shocked, but I am. I listened to the lyrics of a few songs that my daughter, 14, has been playing in her room lately. One song was about "getting a new drug." The other was about satanism and "the number of the beast."

When I asked Chrissy about it, she laughed. She said, "Nobody listens to the words, we just like the music, the beat." She also scolded me for invading her privacy. Am I out of line?

A: Not at all. Parents should be tuned into the music that their children favor. And don't fall for the "I-don't-listen-to-the-words" disclaimers either. As with any song, the words and the music do indeed go together.

I suggest, however, a less confrontational approach. Tell Chrissy that you're interested in what interests her. Sit down with her occasionally and listen to her music. If you don't understand the lyrics, ask questions in a spirit of non-judgmental openness. Open up some conversation.

By the way, if you're convinced that certain rock groups or specific songs violate your family values, don't hesitate to ban them from the house. I realize that teenagers will point out that there are any number of opportunities to hear the music elsewhere, but I believe it's important for mothers and fathers to remain informed, involved, and in charge.

Karate Killer?

Karate is still a favorite hobby of many early adolescent boys and some girls. Martial arts, which stress self-discipline, can be very helpful to teenagers' development.

Q: Our Danny, 13, enrolled in a karate school about two months ago. Because he's small for his age and lacks self-confidence, my husband thought it would be good for him. So did

I — until last night. It was the first time I had ever visited the place. I was surprised. The teacher kept yelling "kill, kill" as the boys practiced the kicks. I don't like it. What should we do?

A: The martial arts (karate, tae kwon do, kung fu, judo, etc.) can be very beneficial to young boys and girls — if properly taught.

Youngsters can gain in many ways. Physically they can develop better reflexes and posture. Emotionally they can learn respect for structure and rules. They can develop better concentration and self-discipline. All of these things can add up to the self-confidence that Danny apparently lacks.

Yet while lack of self-confidence might be bolstered by confidence-building activities, I would urge you to discover the real psychological roots of Danny's problems.

Finally, the martial arts lessons may help; but the karate school or teacher that stresses the aggressive use of force is not doing a youngster any favors. I suggest you look elsewhere.

Quitter

Q: We have given Richard, our 14-year-old son, all the advantages but I'm afraid he's a quitter. Piano at 8 — he quit. Private school at 10 — he quit. Tennis lessons at 12 — he quit. Karate last summer — yes, he quit that too. Now he wants us to buy an electric guitar so he can form his own rock band. It's silly, we tell him. First you have to study guitar, then you form a band. Since we know he'll quit, my husband and I refuse to buy the guitar. Still, Richard pleads for "one more chance." We'd like to give it to him, but we've told him many times that we're finished throwing money away on him. Any suggestions?

Because early adolescence is a stage of such profound change, youngsters will often start and drop hobbies with the same regularity that adults change their socks. Understand this phenomenon, but know where to draw the line.

A: Richard sounds like a dreamer, and why not? He's been allowed to take the easy way out time after time. He has not been given the opportunity to learn the joy of hard work and accomplishment. You and your husband obviously feel his failures more than he does. You should not pay the price for his lack of commitment, his poor tolerance of frustration, and his lack of self-discipline.

It's time to turn the tables. If Richard wants another chance, fine. There's no reason to be angry or punitive. You can help him find a way to earn money for guitar rental and lessons, or have him check at school to see if free lessons are available. Be helpful and supportive, but don't make it easy for him. Yes,

Richard needs success, but it's got to be his success. If he fails, it's got to be his failure.

Sports Drop-Out

Once the teen years hit, youngsters may prefer the mall to sports. Both informal and organized sports are among the healthiest activities for them.

Q: We always thought that our David, 13, would be the athlete in the family. Surprise. In this year alone he's quit both soccer and baseball. Now all he wants to do is hang out at the mall with his friends. Should we insist on sports?

A: Probably not, but you should get him out of the mall.

It's a fact that early adolescents tend to begin falling away from sports activity. Some experts say that before adolescence, youngsters do not pay much attention to skill and performance differences, but once they hit their teen years, they become painfully aware and begin to judge each other (and themselves) pretty harshly. The poor performers, in an effort to protect their fragile self-esteem, begin to drop out.

Another factor, of course, is negative peer pressure. I'll bet that David's mall buddies are not sports enthusiasts.

Sports, both informal and organized, are among the healthiest activities for teenagers. Apparently you know this fact. Talk it over with David. You probably cannot "insist" on sports participation, but you could sure "urge" it.

Pets

Pets are often a conflict-free refuge for early adolescents. Youngsters can sometimes learn more about nurturance and responsibility from dogs and cats than they might from people.

Q: We'd like to get a pet for our children, ages 14 and 12. What do you recommend, a cat or a dog?

A: The psychology of pet ownership has always interested me. I can learn a lot, for example, by watching a child interact with his or her pet. Generally, I'm in favor of pets for kids, especially if the youngsters are required to take care of the animal. Such children can learn something about nurturance, responsibility, and even self-confidence through the process.

Cat or dog? Most people prefer dogs, but cats require less care. How involved will the children be? Is this their idea or yours? Goldfish, of course, take even less trouble.

The key is to select a pet that will fit your family's lifestyle and that will match your youngsters' temperaments. A calm household could be disrupted tremendously by a hyped-up terrier, while very active children might get easily bored by a docile sheep dog.

So, take your time. The worst pet of all is one that is purchased on impulse.

Money and Allowance

How Much Allowance?

Q: It's a constant battle. Our 14-year-old, Donald, always wants a bigger allowance. How much do you advise?

A: 1) *Expense account.* Donald should be given enough money each week to cover his necessary expenses such as school bus fare, lunch money, and perhaps some discretionary or entertainment needs. The amount should be readjusted for the summer months. He gets this amount weekly — no strings attached.

1) *Incentive cash.* You might consider some extra allowance that you give Donald based on whether or not he performs certain jobs around the home beyond his basic chores (which he should be expected to do without payment). This is how Donald might earn extra money for special events.

2) *No advances.* Use the allowance to teach Donald something about money management: no deficit spending, no advances.

3) *Renegotiation.* Take the hassle out of it. Why not agree to renegotiate once a year — on Donald's birthday.

For your information, a 1987 Rand Poll reported that the average allowance for 13- to 15-year-old boys is $13.50 per week. Use this fact, but be careful. Allowances mean different things to different parents. My final point: don't be pressured into paying out more than you can afford.

Early adolescents should receive an allowance. The principles: 1) No strings attached to weekly money for legitimate needs, 2) Extra cash for selected special projects, 3) No advances, 4) Renegotiate every year.

Mothers and Fathers

Father-Son Rivalry

Q: Something's happening. My husband, Robert, used to have a very nice relationship with our son Greg. But ever since Greg became a teenager (he's now 13), Robert is always competing with him. They argue about everything and Robert has to have

Oedipus re-visited. Early adolescence can re-kindle competition between fathers and sons that may not have been experienced since the age of 3 or 4. A certain amount is developmentally natural, but it can get out of hand. Wise fathers beware.

the last word. When they play basketball in the driveway, Robert delights in beating Greg. What's happening?

A: First of all, with Greg's entry into adolescence, the nature of the father-son relationship is changing, and it can be awkward for both parties. If your husband is a competitive type, he will naturally try to erect a competitive relationship with his son. It's what he knows. It's comfortable for him. Some competition between father and son can be healthy, but not if Dad has to always be the winner.

Why does Dad have to win? Is he perhaps psychologically threatened by Greg? Why? Here's a common reason: Greg is coming into his own. Everything is possible for him. All the doors of life are open to him. On the other hand, if your husband's own life has not lived up to his expectations, he may be brought painfully face to face with that realization in the person of his own son. Therefore Dad denies his own fallibility by beating down the budding promise of his son. This, of course, is definitely not healthy.

What to do? As a loving third party in this unfolding drama, you are uniquely positioned to help your husband disengage from this unhealthy competition. Talk to Robert. Gently share your observations. Ask him if he's aware of the rivalry. If it's based on unconscious forces, your confronting the facts will bring it to Dad's conscious attention. Then, he'll be able to improve the situation.

If he can't and things continue to escalate, I suggest you ask your pediatrician to have a talk with Dad.

Dads and Daughters

Many fathers tend to withdraw from recently pubescent daughters whose budding sexuality can be cumbersome and awkward to both parties. Under-involvement sends the wrong message, but so does sudden over-involvement. Steer a comfortable middle course.

Q: My husband wasn't very involved with our daughter when she was younger. But now that Hillary is 14 he's spending more time with her. Won't this confuse her? Is he just trying to make up for lost time? What good is it now?

A: A recent study conducted by Emory University researchers concludes that teenage girls benefit greatly from involvement with their fathers. A 28-year study showed that high-achieving girls tended to have fathers who taught them to drive, who supported athletic interests, and who were emotionally available to them.

These fathers provided their daughters with a healthy role model for assertiveness and competition. I hope Hillary's dad will do the same.

If Hillary is confused, she ought to talk about it. If Dad is trying to make up for lost time, no harm in that as long as it's done with good judgement. What good is it now? It's good. Remember: many fathers tend to withdraw from recently pubescent daughters whose budding sexuality can be as cumbersome to Dads as it is to the girls.

Mothers and Sons

Q: Our son Jason, 13½, is an only child. We've always been close. Lately he's been pulling away from me, doesn't want to be hugged, or even seen with me in public. Is this just a phase? What should I do?

A: Two developmental issues are intersecting to give you some temporary problems. First of all, early adolescents commonly recoil from public appearances with Mom and Dad. Why? You are a reminder of Jason's childhood. He's still searching for a new relationship with you. Don't take it personally. Give him a little slack.

Secondly, Jason's reluctance to be hugged by Mom may be a signal of a different brand of discomfort. Touching you now takes on sexualized overtones. Again, give him some space, especially in public.

Yes, it's a phase. As early adolescents change, parents must change too.

Early adolescent sons tend to withdraw a bit from Mom. They seek independence and a comfort zone for newly-awakened sexual drives. Give them some slack — especially in public.

She Hates Me and Loves Her Father

Q: My 13-year-old daughter, Renee, is in bad shape. She cries in school. She's getting headaches every day. She fights constantly with me and blames absolutely all of her problems on me. By comparison, my husband can do no wrong in her eyes. I've had it. What can we do?

A: Renee may be caught up in a common early adolescent conflict: viewing you as a competitor for Dad. What to do? Be sure that both you and your husband remain united, understanding, and evenhanded. You cannot afford to be forced into the bad guy position: be sure that your husband, for example, shares in the discipline and supports you in the face of Renee's abuse.

Also, look beyond the obvious. Renee's preoccupation with scapegoating you for all of her problems may be a handy smoke

Early adolescent daughters, in a variant of that oedipal theme, may compete with Mom for Dad's attention. Go with the flow, but don't allow her to divide and conquer.

screen. She may be dealing with other conflicts and worries that have nothing at all to do with you.

If Renee's problems persist, seek consultation before all of you get locked into a rigid battle without end.

Too Traditional?

The so-called traditional family (working father, stay-at-home mother, and children) is approaching extinction.

Q: Our children, 14, 12, and 9, complain that our family is too traditional. Dad works at an office, I'm a housewife, no divorce, no stepchildren. Basically the kids are very happy about these things, but they complain that we don't really understand their friends whose parents are divorced or whose parents both work outside the home. I know the intact, nuclear family seems to be a minority, but we're not *that* unusual, are we?

A: Yes, you are. Consider these facts: 1) In 1955, almost 60% of families were so-called traditional families like your own. 2) In 1990, that number is down to 20%. What's happened in the last 31 years? Two things. First of all, the divorce rate has reached 50%. And secondly, more and more mothers have entered the work force; currently over 60% of mothers who have school-age children are employed outside the home.

If your children feel abnormal, they are — if you define normality by the numbers. For one thing, over 60% of today's children live with just one parent before they reach their eighteenth birthday.

But why do your youngsters complain? Teens and pre-teens are peer-related. There's tremendous pressure to fit in, to be like everyone else. It's interesting, in a way. Your children probably feel like children of divorce felt many years ago.

Hear them out, and stress the importance of the stability you have built into their lives. Try to understand their friends a little better too. Finally, be sure to take the position that no family is perfect. Your nuclear family may be different, but it's not necessarily better in all ways.

Values for Kids

Today's parents cherish pretty much the same values that parents wished for their children over 50 years ago: independence, tolerance, loyalty to church, and obedience.

Q: My husband and I have three children, 14, 10, and 8. We're pretty conventional and conservative. My girlfriends think I'm too traditional. Well, so be it. As I look around, I think today's parents want the same things for their kids that parents have always wanted. Comments?

144

A: You have a point. A recent survey by the Institute of Social Research at the University of Michigan seems to support your observation. The researchers, in 1988, repeated a survey that was originally done in 1924 that asked mothers what traits they believed were the most important to instill into their children.

Here are the results. In 1924: 1) independence, 2) tolerance, 3) loyalty to church, 4) strict obedience. The 1988 results? Exactly the same.

Or, as you yourself have probably said to your girlfriends: The more things change, the more they stay the same.

Mamma Mia's Day

Q: I'm Italian and I'm proud of it. I think I deserve a little more respect on Mother's Day. My daughter, 16, gives it to me, but my son, 13, thinks I go too far. He says I'm "too Italian" and that I think I'm still living in the old country. Is it too much to want to be honored on my Day?

Yes, every day should be Mother's Day, but the developmental drives of early adolescents may disappoint you on the second Sunday of May. Relax. It's just a phase.

A: Of course not. But, then, I don't know what you mean by "respect." Your son should respect you every day of the year. I get the impression that he may feel a little crowded by you. Unlike most girls, boys at this age have a need for some psychological distance from Mama. In our American society it is the norm for girls to retain a closeness to their mothers that most boys do not preserve in growing up into adulthood. This, of course, is a generalization; but perhaps it will help you to gain some perspective on the situation. The cultural norms for mother-son relationships do vary from nation to nation. It doesn't necessarily make Italian Style any worse (or any better) than American Style — just different.

Goodbye Dinner Hour

Q: The family dinner hour was always sacred when I was a child and I've tried to preserve the tradition, but it's a losing battle. My children, 14, 11, and 7, are home from school by 4:00 p.m. and they're starved. They want their dinner quickly so they can do their homework and be free when their favorite TV show comes on at 8 o'clock. My husband doesn't get home from work until 8 o'clock. Then, he wants dinner — and he expects the kids at the table too. What a hassle. What should I do?

Family dinner hour is a tradition worth preserving. It builds cohesion, communication, and camaraderie. And please turn off the TV while you're eating.

A: First, you've got to stop being a slave. When do *you* relax? You must spend the whole evening in the kitchen.

I'm a strong proponent of the family dinner hour. It builds cohesion, communication and camaraderie. How to do it? Why not give the youngsters a simple snack when they come home, to tide them over? They can work on their homework until Dad arrives. Then, it's family dinner time.

What about their TV shows, you ask? Two choices. If you can afford a VCR, why not tape for after-viewing? If not, I believe the family should take priority over television any day.

Adoption

The adopted early adolescent may take his drive for independence one step further than non-adopted youngsters. Even though adoptive parents know it's coming, it can hurt: "You're not my real parents." But he'll get over it and so will you.

Q: Our 13-year-old adopted son suddenly seems to despise us, while, at the same time, insisting that his "real" parents must be perfect. My husband and I have tried to always understand our boy's special needs, but it hurts — a lot.

A: My heart goes out to you and to your husband — and to adoptive parents everywhere because, as a group, you are among the real unsung heroes of this world. The love and devotion shown by couples who choose to adopt reflects the highest of human qualities. Therefore, it's even more painful to see you criticized unfairly by your son. But, I've seen many such situations. In fact, it goes with the territory.

Your son is going through a normal developmental crisis which is sometimes called the "family romance." As an early adolescent your son (and he is your son) is conflicted and frightened about many things. Many 13-year-olds don't appreciate their parents: your son, as he gives you up as the parents of his childhood and grows to relate to you as the parents of his adolescence, is momentarily clinging to a fantasized notion of his biological parents, i.e., if they are perfect, he is perfect. In other words, you son's conflict has less to do with you or his biological parents than with his own internal conflicts.

Try not to take it too personally. It is, indeed, a well-known phase of development that your son is facing. He needs your sensitivity, your understanding, your love. Encourage him to express himself. With your help, he'll get through it and all of you will be stronger because of it.

Aunt and Uncle Power

Loving non-parental adults (such as uncles and aunts) can exert a very powerful and positive influence on children. Such involvement and encouragement can even offset negative parental influence.

Q: My sister is a wacko. She's an alcoholic, she's paranoid (only eats packaged food so she won't "get poisoned"), and she humiliates her children, 13, 11, 7, 4, and 3. My husband and I try to spend a lot of time with the kids, but we're frustrated.

Can it possibly be enough to offset their mother's negative influence?

A: Yes, it can. Studies of children who survive and flourish in spite of childhood neglect, trauma, or other hardship suggest that the key is the availability of a reliable, consistent, encouraging, and loving adult. It can be a grandparent, a neighbor, or an uncle and aunt.

Keep up the good work. Let the kids know that they are OK, but that Mom has problems. Also, I encourage you to be aggressive in getting help for Mom. If her illness results in clear negligence or abuse, the children should be removed from the home.

Psychological Growth and Development

Adolescence: A Definition

Q: I am 13. I am writing an English paper on adolescence. What is your definition?

A: Adolescence is an age between. It is that exciting, and sometimes tumultuous, no-man's land between childhood and adulthood. It is impossible, however, to define adolescence chronologically, i.e., "the years 'twixt twelve and twenty." It must be approached developmentally, and that's why your question is not so easy to answer.

The definition I use is a practical, operational one: adolescence is the psychological reaction to puberty. Thus, I distinguish between adolescence as a psychosocial event, and puberty as a purely physical process. (Already I'm in trouble. There are exceptions: some early-developing youngsters, for example, are pubertal before adolescent; some late physical bloomers may actually be somewhat adolescent before they experience puberty. But aside from these exceptions, my definition works.)

But when does adolescence end? When I've asked this question of adult audiences over the years, I've gotten some interesting replies: "At twenty," "Never," "When he becomes a doctor or a lawyer."

Adolescence begins with the onset of puberty. It ends when the four tasks of adolescent development (independence, sexual maturation, conscience formation, identity) are completed.

I say that adolescence ends when the four tasks of adolescent development are completed. Individuals, of course, complete them at different rates. And yes, some never really complete them; they go through life, for better or worse, as adolescents in adult bodies.

The four tasks of adolescence:

1) *Independence and autonomy.* The battle cry of all 13-year-olds: "Leave me alone. I want to be free." It may look like they're rebelling against the world, but they're really rebelling against their own immaturity.

2) *Sexual maturity.* The essential task here is to blend two drives: The purely sexual drive with the drive toward intimacy and love. When the two drives become merged the person can be called sexually mature. When does it happen? Well, it begins in early adolescence, but the task is not completed for some years. And, for some individuals, it just never happens. They can have sex without love, or love without sex, but never do the twain meet.

3) *Conscience formation.* By mid-adolescence (15-16) many youngsters, using abstract thinking, are capable of discerning the subtle shades of gray as they contemplate moral and ethical issues. Early adolescents, by contrast, usually see only black or white; they are concrete (rather than abstract) thinkers.

4) *Identity formation.* The late adolescent (17 or 18 and beyond) begins to contemplate questions such as, "Who am I?" "Where am I going?" His quest for identity may end quickly or be spread over several years.

Finally, I'm reminded that Goethe once said that "continued life means expectation." To the extent that adolescence is a stage of life where expectations and possibilities are highest, I hope that all of us retain some of the spark of our own adolescence.

Independence: The First Task

Early adolescents must give up childhood (and the parents of their childhood) in order to fully enter the next stage of their life. It's a rocky road for some, but most youngsters under savvy parental guidance will make it just fine.

Q: We knew it would be tough, but nothing prepared us for this. Our problem is a 13-year-old named Roger. Talk about rebellion. His favorite words are "leave me alone," "get out of my life," and "I want to be free." That's when he's not shouting four-letter words at us. He used to be so sweet. On the plus side, though, we can say that his school work is still OK, and, after all his ranting and raving, he does follow our decisions.

Is Roger's rebellion normal? Should we be worried? How long will it last?

A: Roger is struggling with the first task of adolescent development: independence and autonomy. Like a lot of kids, he's overreacting a bit, but I like your observation about school and his acceptance of your disciplinary limits. This tells me that Roger's rebellion is still containable. He's not out of control.

What is this developmental task all about? Well, it's not about becoming "free" in the adult sense of the word. It isn't about the total freedom that Roger seems to crave. It's all about freeing yourself from childhood and entering adolescence: the way station between childhood and adulthood. It's also about freeing yourself from the parents of your childhood and finding a new set of parents, the parents of your adolescence.

Although you and your husband symbolize a lot of this struggle for Roger, he's not really rebelling against you at all. He's rebelling against his own immaturity. Roger is both attracted to the passive joys of his lost childhood and repelled by this attraction at the same time. So he takes it out on you. He externalizes what is basically an internal conflict.

Hang in there. Don't allow the four-letter words, but absorb as much of the rest as you can. He'll get over it. When? Hard to say, but most teenagers work through the basics of this first developmental task in 1 to 2 years. The fine-tuning, however, is an ongoing process that will require much more time.

Sexual Development:
The Second Task

Q: My daughter, Kelly, is 13. I've spoken to her a few times about sex and I'm pleased that she can come to me with questions. Here's one I couldn't answer: at what age is a teenager ready to have sex?

A: As a child psychiatrist, I'm going to approach your question from my area of expertise: child development. But I hasten to point out that other crucial factors must be considered: most importantly, your own religious beliefs and family values.

From a physiological standpoint, most teenagers are capable of performing sex by at least 12 or 13. But, in my opinion, they are not yet ready to "have sex" as fully mature sexual beings.

Why? The second basic task of adolescent development is sexual maturity. This task is not completed until the individual integrates the basic sex (erotic, genital) drive with the drive to intimacy (love, commitment). The first drive is experienced

The ultimate goal of full sexual development is to combine the sexual (or genital-erotic) drive with the capacity for love, intimacy, and commitment. No, it doesn't happen overnight, and some adults, unfortunately, never succeed at this task. Nevertheless, parents are the best guides for this important aspect of human growth.

much before the latter. When do the two drives merge? At 13? (I've never seen it.) At sixteen? (Very doubtful.) Let's face it: some people never complete this task. Even as adults they are doomed to a life of sex without commitment, or love without sex.

When will Kelly be ready? Talk it over with her. But remember, "being ready for sex" has many dimensions — the least important of which is anatomical.

Early-Developing Girl

Girls, of course, tend to develop physically and psychologically faster than boys. This can be both a blessing and a curse. It calls for wise parental handling.

Q: My daughter is 13, but thinks she should be treated like an adult. The latest crisis is that she insists that she plans to date an 18-year-old boy (young man?) whom she met at the beach last summer. She is physically mature for her age, but I'm just not sure about this dating business. What do you think?

A: On the one hand I can certainly sympathize with your daughter's predicament. Momentarily she has outgrown her natural peer group. Because she is an early-developing girl, she doesn't find 13-year-old boys very interesting, and vice versa. This plight is not uncommon for many adolescent girls today as they tend to enter puberty at a progressively earlier age. Adolescent psychiatrists refer to this phenomenon as the "secular trend." In 1800, the average age for the onset of menstruation was 17.5; today it is within the 12th year, with many girls having their first period at 10 or 11 years of age.

But what about psychological maturity? There's the rub. Girls such as your daughter may appear, on the surface, as though they are 13 going on 23, but deep down there beats the heart of a frightened child-woman.

It is a very rare event to find a 13-year-old girl who is ready to date an 18-year-old boy. Nothing in the experience of these girls can prepare them, psychologically, for the young adult dating game.

As a matter of fact, I have witnessed a number of psychiatric casualties among such young girls who have been allowed to propel themselves beyond their developmental capabilities: premature sexual experience resulting in confusion, guilt, or pregnancy; drug abuse because of peer pressure that they are not equipped to withstand; anger at their parents who have "enabled" them to lose control.

My last point may be your clue. Your daughter is raising this issue directly with you for a purpose. While appearing defiant and perhaps issuing an ultimatum about her "plans," she is inviting you to say "No!"

I would urge you to say "No." It's not that you do not trust her. It is not that you do not love her. The fact is that she is not emotionally ready for such dating.

Your daughter, of course, will probably not agree with you; she may argue with you and complain about you to her would-be boyfriend — but I would guess that somewhere, deep down in the heart of her childhood, she will be secretly thanking you for having the courage to protect her from her own immaturity.

Late-Developing Boy

Q: My 13-year-old son is the shortest boy in his class. Lately he's been pestering me to buy him elevator shoes. What would you say?

A: Late-developing boys can have it rough. Boys at this age are forever comparing themselves physically to other boys. They worry not only about such things as height, but about facial hair, deepness of the voice, pubic hair, and penis size.

The late-developing boy, like the early-developing girl, is temporarily without a peer group. He is vulnerable. Preserving self-esteem is the key.

Just telling your son that he's a late developer and that he'll do a lot of catching up over the next few years will not be enough. A "few years" seems like an eternity to such a 13-year-old. Yet it would be reassuring if you could point out that the average height for males in your family is satisfactory by his standards, or that his father might have also been a late developer, etc.

Your son obviously needs a "lift" right now. But he needs an emotional lift, not one made of shoe leather. It's his self-esteem that needs a lift, not his body stature. What are his particular assets and skills? What is he good at? Many small-statured boys learn to compensate by becoming "giants" in areas where brawn is not a factor: academics, music, hobbies. In fact, studies of high school reunions have shown that 15 or 20 years after graduation it is not usually the ex-football star or former cheerleader who is most successful in life: it is the youngster (like your son) who might have developed late physically, but who was able to compensate in some other area of life. Help your son to define his self-esteem in some other way than through his body. Such tactics will give a bigger boost to his ego than elevator shoes.

Teen Troubles

Although early adolescence has always been a difficult and awkward stage, and although the basic developmental tasks faced by contemporary teenagers are the same as we faced, today's teens do have it tougher, in many ways, than we did.

Q: Thank God our teenagers, 13 and 14, don't seem to have any major problems. But their friends! It makes me cry: drugs, depression, runaways, you name it. Do you think today's teenagers have more troubles than we did as kids, or is it just my imagination?

A: Your question is a tough one — from a statistical and scientific standpoint, adolescence has always been a time of turmoil.

My clinical intuition, however, is that you're right on the mark. Today's teens face deadlier problems, such as drug abuse. They also must cope with more family breakups and a higher divorce rate. Finally, the sexual "revolution" takes its toll too: venereal disease, teenage pregnancy, and the psychological fallout of premature sexual encounters.

You might be interested to know that other parents agree with you. A recent national poll found that 72% of the adults surveyed believed that today's teens face more problems than we did as kids.

Teenage Rebellion

Extreme teenage rebellion, contrary to some beliefs, is not the norm. A truly rebellious, out-of-control early adolescent probably needs professional help. Get it now. She may not outgrow it.

Q: My 14-year-old son is becoming impossible. He rebels at all of our rules and values. Is this normal or does he need help?

A: A certain amount of rebellion, I'm afraid, goes "with the territory" of adolescent development. These are, indeed, the years that try parents' souls.

About a third of all adolescents become so rebellious that limit-testing and conflict become the norm of their existence. They are apt to become involved in truancy, drug abuse, or other anti-social activity. Most of the 10-15% of American teenagers who see a psychiatrist come from this group. Most of these youngsters are not really "bad"; they need help to deal with the psychological conflicts of growing up.

Another third of U.S. teenagers are periodically rebellious, but are generally within parental control. They may warn you that they'll run away if you don't let them go to the rock concert, but when you really draw the line, they obey you. These youngsters basically feel pretty good about themselves, have friends, and are performing up to their potential in school most of the time.

Finally, there is another third of adolescents who show little or no overt rebellion. Although psychiatrists used to think that these youngsters were only repressing "normative" rebellion, and would grow up to become neurotic 25-year-olds, more recent research by Dr. Daniel Offer and his Chicago colleagues suggests that they tend, by and large, to grow up into happy adults.

Your son is apparently in either the first or the second group. Which is it? Is he totally out of control? If so, he needs the help of a child psychiatrist. Is he unhappy? Is he failing to achieve his best in school? Are there additional symptoms? I would suggest that you assess this brief psychological inventory, and that you also reflect on your son's earlier years. Youngsters who have had difficult behavioral problems in childhood are certainly more at risk during their adolescence. Yet, while even Shakespeare wished that there was no age "twixt twelve and twenty," the good news is that help is available for troubled adolescents while you're waiting for the grown-up to arrive.

Privacy

Q: She thinks she's Greta Garbo or something. I'm talking about Louisa, our 13-year-old. Her favorite words are: "I want to be alone." I understand her need for privacy, but how much is too much?

A: The need for privacy is probably greater in early adolescence than at any stage of development. Why? Privacy provides a retreat from the parents they still associate with their childhood — a reminder of their immaturity. Early adolescents, like Louisa, also tend to be very self-absorbed; hence, privacy comes naturally.

How much is too much? Tough to say. Insist on some level of family interaction every day, perhaps at meal time. Don't allow Louisa to set up a pleasure palace (TV, stereo, telephone, etc.) in her room, either; this just encourages more withdrawal.

Finally, keep an eye on the bottom line: her health, behavior, friends, school performance. If these factors are moving in the right direction most of the time, she'll probably survive her early teens — just as Mom did.

The need for privacy is probably greater in early adolescence than at any other time of life. Allow privacy — but not total withdrawal.

Privacy of Bedroom

An early adolescent's bedroom is often the symbol of his need for privacy. So, make it private, but not off-limits to Mom and Dad.

Q: I feel silly asking this question, but Josie, my 13-year-old, has me going around in circles. Do I or do I not have a right to go into her room? Josie says her room is her property. She demands absolute privacy. I understand her desire for privacy, of course, but I don't think her room should be off-limits to Mom. Should it?

A: No. But, first, let's look at this through the eyes of an early adolescent. Josie's whole life is changing. Nothing seems to belong to her any more. Her feelings, her body, her ideas are all foreign to the little girl who was your daughter just a short time ago. Josie, therefore, has to cling to something in her changing world — her room. It may be much more than her castle. It may represent her own identity.

Yes, Josie needs privacy. She's probably self-conscious about her pubescence too. But declaring her room off-limits? That's going a bit too far.

Teenage Vanity

Early adolescents, because their bodies change so rapidly, are spectators of their own creation. That's why they spend so much time in front of the mirror.

Q: Our 13-year-old son, Daniel, is forever admiring himself in the mirror. He turns to his side, checks his profiles, flexes his muscles. It's cute, but it's troubling too. He never used to be like this. When will he get over this fascination with himself?

A: Teenage vanity, sometimes called adolescent narcissism, is not unusual in early adolescents like Daniel. First of all, his body is changing rapidly. His furtive glances into the mirror may be to reassure himself of his evolving body image. Teenagers also have a natural fascination with their bodies, their feelings, and their thoughts. Adolescence is a new beginning; a rebirth, and they are spectators, in a way, of their own creation. A little vanity, therefore, is healthy. Too much, however, can lead to self-absorption, self-indulgence, and isolation. Keep your own reflection out of the mirror, but keep Daniel's narcissism under observation.

Early Teen Humor

If they didn't laugh, they might cry. Pre-teen humor (with its attendant giggling) is often a necessary defense against the pain of growing up.

Q: Giggle, giggle, giggle! You guessed it — I have a 13-year-old daughter. Why do they giggle so much?

A: Laughter and humor, as I'm sure you know, can be used as a defense against fears, uncertainties, and uncomfortable impulses. In psychiatry we sometimes call this reversal of affect, i.e., you tame your worries or fears by turning them into a joke.

Early adolescents, like your daughter, generally have a lot of fears and uncertainties on their minds. They stand uncomfortably poised between childhood and adulthood — caught between two worlds.

In one study of early adolescent humor, researchers interviewed girls, ages 12 to 14, from middle class backgrounds. The most common topics of their humor were: bodily changes of puberty, menstruation, boyfriends, curiosity about parental sex, masturbatory fantasies, and pregnancy fantasies. This is all pretty heavy stuff for a youngster who literally still has one foot in childhood. If they didn't laugh a little about it, they might be easily overwhelmed.

So, put up with those giggles. They may be helping your daughter to cope. But one more thing: keep in touch. Talk to her about the things she's worried about. It's no laughing matter.

Old Time Religion?

Q: My husband and I were both raised as churchgoers, but we've moved away from formal religion in our adult lives. We don't really have anything against it, but we prefer to translate those beliefs into our everyday lives rather than subscribe to any one religion. Imagine our surprise when Lance, our 13-year-old, announced that he plans to start attending services at a local fundamentalist church! We'll let him do it, of course, but we're curious. Is it just a stage?

A: Early adolescents, like Lance, sometimes turn to intense religious practices as a defense against emerging sexual and aggressive drives. They also seek direct answers to complex questions about "right and wrong," or "good and bad." Some teenagers, like adults, turn to formal religion for the feeling of community and universality that it provides. The church, for some, becomes a kind of extra-familial "family," a developmental transition out of their biological family and into the outside world.

On the other hand, Lance may be sending a message. He may well feel that something is missing from his life, that he's looking for answers to some ultimate questions of existence such as "Who am I?" and "Where am I going?"

In their quest for autonomy and independence, early adolescents often appear to rebel against long-held parental values and beliefs — including religious preference. While you should allow your beliefs to be questioned (you may even grow in the process), it is not necessary to sacrifice them.

Although you have chosen to allow Lance to experiment with another religion, many parents would not be so accommodating, and I don't believe it is necessary. You can allow an early adolescent to question your beliefs without sacrificing them. It's basically a matter of your family value system and where you choose to draw the line. It can, and must, be drawn somewhere, otherwise you are failing to provide any guidance at all. If you believe strongly in your religion, I'd suggest that you put the matter of Lance's change of preference off for a few years.

Insult Artist

Early adolescents can be real insult artists. It's a defense (called externalization) against their own deficiencies. They have to learn that nobody's perfect — a tough lesson to learn for some youngsters.

Q: Ray, our 13-year-old, has become a real insult artist. It started with calling his friends names: Wimpy, Sissy, Fatso, etc. Now he even mimics adults. It was cute at first but now it's getting out of hand. Why does he do this?

A: Ray is probably using a typical defense mechanism of early adolescence: externalization. He is unconsciously projecting his own deficiencies onto other people. When he criticizes others, he believes that he boosts his own ego. No, it's not cute. In its fullest form externalization is the stuff that blind prejudice is made of. You can help Ray by gently reminding him that he's not perfect. Nobody is. Help him admit some of his own flaws. If he can accept his own imperfections, he won't have a need to lay them on other people.

Changing Relationship to Parents

How to say goodbye to the parents of their childhood. It can be difficult for both early adolescents and their parents.

Q: My 14-year-old daughter, Adrian, seems to have an identity crisis — my identity. She doesn't know what to call me. Sometimes it's "Mom," sometimes it's "Moms," sometimes it's "Mother." To tell you the truth, I find it a bit irritating. Just what do most young girls call their mothers these days anyway?

A: You have, of course, always been Adrian's mother and you always will be, but the way in which your daughter has needed you has changed from one developmental stage to the next. It is not surprising, therefore, that she would search for some new way to address you from time to time.

The childish "Mama" or "Mommy" gives way to "Mom" or "Mother." The recent teenage fad of adding "s" to Mom or Dad is probably related to the preppie craze. While this particular way of addressing you will, therefore, probably not outlast the fad, it is most interesting. Adrian, like so many adolescents, wants to stay on familiar terms with you as long as she can be "cool" in the process.

In some ways this phenomenon encapsulates the adolescent dilemma: how to maintain parental ties while moving out into the larger world?

Psychiatric and Behavioral Problems

What Is a Psychotherapist?

Q: The school psychologist referred our 14-year-old daughter, Karen, to a woman who calls herself a psychotherapist. She seems very nice, but there are no diplomas on her wall and I'd like to know what a psychotherapist is, but I'm too embarrassed to ask. Can you help?

A: A psychotherapist is someone who uses any type of talking therapy to help people. The term is a very broad one. For example, a psychiatrist (MD) performs psychotherapy. So does a psychologist (PhD and MA), social worker (MSW), nurse (RN, MSN, etc.), pastoral counselor, and a list of other people. In fact, in many states you don't really need any special training or certification to call yourself a "psychotherapist." Your daughter's psychotherapist, therefore, could be any of these things.

Your best bet is to ask directly. You have every right to know something about her credentials, training, expertise, license, and certification.

In general, I prefer to see patients at least start out with a diagnostic evaluation conducted by a psychiatrist, the MD. Although he or she may later refer the patient for talking therapy to someone with another degree, you'll have some assurance that the whole process is under competent medical direction.

When Is Therapy Over?

Q: Terence, our 13-year-old, has been seeing a psychiatrist for the past two years because of behavior problems and poor school performance. He's been going once a week and we've been going about every two weeks for a parent conference. It has really helped. The problem is that whenever we ask the

All professions that use talking therapy are psychotherapists. The term applies to a psychiatrist (MD), psychologist (MA or PhD), social worker (MSW), nurse therapist (RN, MSN), pastoral counselor, and others. Psychiatrists (MD) are the only ones trained to fully diagnose mental illness and rule out (or rule in) the presence of physical illness. That's why a psychiatrist should usually be consulted first.

Parents, in most cases, should be involved in the treatment of their early adolescent. Confidentiality will prohibit you from knowing what is being said, but you have every right to know how things are going, and what you can do to help.

doctor when Terry can stop sessions, she either makes us feel guilty or puts us off with, "We'll see in a few months."

My question may seem stupid but here it is: How can you tell when therapy is over?

A: Not a stupid question at all. I've had it asked of me in my practice many times over the years.

The answer actually should be provided at the very beginning of the therapy, when the following questions should be answered: What's the problem? What will be done about it? What are the goals of treatment? Approximately how long will it take? How much will it cost?

The answers to these questions provide a road map. Without them the therapy is in danger of becoming an aimless journey rather than a medical procedure.

Your first step is to get answers to those questions from Terry's doctor. If she doesn't think he's ready to terminate, why not? Your next step, if you're not satisfied, would be to get a second opinion.

Abrupt terminations can be harmful. Talk it over with Terry. Ultimately you may decide to limit the therapy to a set number of future sessions with an agreement to return if things don't work out.

Counseling Can Hurt

Communication between the counselor and the parents helps avoid misunderstandings about the work of therapy.

Q: Penny, our 13-year-old, is seeing a counselor. She's had about six sessions. After her last appointment, she came out crying. She says she can't take it — that it hurts too much. We thought it was supposed to make her feel better. What's going on?

A: No pain, no gain. The work of therapy goes through many cycles, but you can be sure that if it is to succeed, Penny will have to get in touch with some feelings. Otherwise, it's just an empty intellectual exercise. So, yes, there will be some hurt. The skillful therapist, however, won't let it get out of control. Talk to the counselor. Ask how you can help.

Cartoon Therapy?

Sometimes a psychiatrist's techniques are described by the youngster in a way that puzzles parents. By all means ask the psychiatrist for more information about specific techniques.

Q: Our Harold, 14, started seeing a psychiatrist last week. He says the doctor just shows him cartoons to see if he'll laugh. What's going on? Are we wasting our money?

A: Harold's doctor may be just trying to break the ice; to loosen him up and make him feel comfortable. On the other hand, the psychiatrist is probably gauging Harold's response as part of the overall evaluation. We know, for example, that the more disturbed or conflicted a youngster is, the less he laughs.

One more thing: if Harold is not very motivated for therapy (and most 14-year-olds are not), he may be exaggerating the cartoons in an effort to devalue the treatment and to convince you to discontinue the sessions.

Finally, be sure to discuss this concern and any others directly with the psychiatrist. As Harold's parent, you have every right to know what techniques the doctor is using and his rationale for them.

Sounds like funny business, in a way, but the work of psychiatry is serious. It should also, of course, be cost effective. You and Harold have every right to expect your money's worth.

Residential Treatment Center

Q: Tina, our 14-year-old, has severe behavior problems: she lies, steals, skips school, and refuses to obey her father and me. Her psychiatrist says she should go to a residential treatment center. Is it like a hospital? How expensive is it?

A: A residential treatment center is something like a boarding school with therapy. Although programs vary in design and intensity, most offer a therapeutic milieu setting with some behavior modification, a structured schedule, group and individual therapy, and accredited schooling.

RTC's are not hospitals. They are not usually staffed by doctors and nurses. They tend to be long-term (1-2 years), where a hospital is more short-term (days to weeks). RTC's are for youngsters who require out-of-home therapeutic placement, but who do not require hospitalization. RTC's vary widely in costs. Some are covered by medical insurance.

Be sure to visit before you decide on a placement for Tina — and take her along too. Another tip: get names of families who have had youngsters in the programs; call them. Some RTC's are excellent. Others are seriously lacking. Shop carefully. Tina's future is at stake.

Anorexia Nervosa

Q: My 13-year-old daughter is on a diet craze. At first I saw no problem with it, but now it's out of control. She has gone from

Hospital treatment is for short-term (i.e., days) treatment of acute conditions such as suicide and other psychiatric illnesses. Residential treatment centers (RTC's) are like boarding schools with intensive therapy and offer longer term (i.e., 1 to 2 years) treatment for youngsters requiring it.

The cardinal signs of anorexia nervosa are: loss of at least 20% of body weight, food avoidance, obsessive pursuit of thinness, and distorted body image.

159

125 pounds to 100 pounds and still has an obsession with losing more weight! She looks in the mirror and says that she's fat. I hear her doing sit-ups in her room at three o'clock in the morning. She refuses to eat. I've heard of "anorexia nervosa" but never thought it could happen in my family. Should I keep trying to talk sense to her or is it time to seek help?

A: It is definitely time to go for help. Your daughter has lost 20% of her body weight, has an obsessive pursuit of thinness, food avoidance, and suffers from a distorted body image. These are all symptoms of anorexia nervosa — a serious disorder that primarily strikes young adolescent girls. Additional symptoms usually include increased energy output, hyperactivity, and cessation of menstrual periods. Some youngsters secretly curb their hunger by going on occasional eating binges and then forcing themselves to vomit (bulimia).

Anorexia nervosa can be tragic. While most cases can be treated successfully on an outpatient basis, some youngsters require several months of psychiatric hospitalization. Such interventions can be lifesaving, yet up to ten percent of these poor youngsters actually succeed in starving themselves to death.

I'm not trying to play "scare tactics" with these facts. I believe that parents should have accurate information about such serious conditions. Treatment is usually a team effort on the part of the pediatrician and a child or adolescent psychiatrist. Now is the time to call the team into action.

Young Anorexic

Anorexia is a serious illness primarily affecting adolescent girls as young as 13.

Q: My 13-year-old niece, J.C., has anorexia nervosa. She's so young. I thought this only happened to older kids. Does her young age mean that her treatment will be more difficult?

A: Probably not. As a rule of thumb, the younger the anorexic, the easier the treatment.

Early adolescent girls, like J.C., tend to develop anorexia (the compulsive pursuit of thinness) in response to the onset of puberty and the resultant sexual conflicts.

Each case, however, is distinct and J.C.'s prognosis will rest on several factors: her earlier psychological history, the severity of her underlying conflicts, the willingness of J.C. and her parents to participate in treatment, and the skill of her physician.

Bad or Depressed

Q: Our son, Mark, is 14. He's got a lot of problems: he won't follow rules, his grades are poor, he gets into fights, and he's angry all the time. Yesterday he got expelled from school because be broke a window. The principal calls him "bad," but the school psychologist says he's depressed. Who's right? What should we do?

Adolescent depression wears many masks. Since early adolescents typically put feelings into action, the depressed teen may actually appear angry or violent. Proper diagnosis is crucial.

A: Adolescent depression is not at all like typical adult depression. Depressed teenagers often exhibit the kind of behavior that Mark is demonstrating. Teens try to avoid feelings by putting them into action. Mark's aggression and anger, therefore, may only be cover-ups for the hurt that he is really feeling.

While Mark's behavior is certainly unacceptable ("bad" from the school's standpoint), it is not at all helpful to label him as a "bad boy" if, indeed, his underlying depression is at the root of his behavior.

What to do? Mark needs a comprehensive psychiatric evaluation by a psychiatrist who has knowledge about adolescent problems. This evaluation would include a thorough developmental history, direct discussions with Mark, family history, and psychological testing. If depression is present, it will be diagnosed. Then, proper treatment can be started.

Hysterical Paralysis

Q: Timmy, our 13-year-old, has never had any emotional problems. Last week he suddenly developed a paralysis of his right hand. He couldn't move it at all. We rushed him to the Emergency Room and the doctors examined him. We were petrified but we weren't prepared for their diagnosis. They said it was psychological and that we should take him to see a child psychiatrist. They called it "hysterical paralysis." Timmy isn't hysterical at all. In fact, he doesn't seem upset in the least. He's doing better than we are. What should we do?

Hysterical neurosis (or conversion disorder) is a relatively rare condition marked by a dramatic symptom (such as sudden paralysis or blindness) that, paradoxically, does not seem to concern the patient. Treatment is usually quite effective.

A: Hysterical neurosis or conversion disorder is relatively rare these days, but it can be treated successfully by a child psychiatrist.

Think of it as body language in the extreme. There is something that Timmy "can't handle." Psychologically, he probably has a drive to touch something and a stern prohibition (from his conscience) against touching. Instead of being overwhelmed by anxiety as might otherwise happen, his psyche "solves" the conflict by paralyzing his hand. Now he can't act.

You're probably wondering what it is that's causing all this trouble. I can only guess. There's a good chance, given his age, that he has a conflict about masturbation. But wait; keep this to yourself. There are other possibilities. Let the psychiatrist figure it out.

By the way, I'm not at all surprised that Timmy is not upset. If he were, I'd be more concerned that the E.R. doctors missed the diagnosis. One hallmark of psychological paralysis, you see, is what we call "la belle indifference" — apparent indifference to what should be a most disturbing symptom.

Don't worry. A good child psychiatrist will get Timmy through this crisis quickly.

Medication for School Phobia

Current treatment for school phobia often combines medication with talking therapy and behavior modification.

Q: Our daughter Rita, 14, has developed school phobia. She's deathly afraid that something horrible (she doesn't know what) will happen to her at school. She goes every day, but can hardly function. Talking therapy isn't helping much. Her social worker wants to refer her to a psychiatrist for medication but our pediatrician says it's too dangerous because of her heart problems. What can we do?

A: The most commonly used medications for school phobia are tricyclic antidepressants. As your pediatrician cautions, they can be dangerous in certain types of cardiac conditions.

Your first step would be to consult with a cardiologist. Depending on her diagnosis, she may be able to tolerate these medications, especially if she is closely monitored with periodic electrocardiograms.

Another option would be newer (non-tricyclic) antidepressants. A child psychiatrist could discuss them with you.

Accident Proneness

True accident proneness often has its roots in low self-esteem and a tendency to turn aggression inward. Treatment is necessary before it escalates into self-destruction.

Q: I'm beginning to think our 13-year-old son, Patrick, is accident prone. In the last 3 months he has on separate occasions: 1) broken his arm in a fall, 2) suffered a concussion in another fall, 3) accidentally cut himself (10 stitches) with a knife, and 4) dropped a hatchet on his foot which sliced off two of his toes. Is there such a thing as "accident proneness"? How do you prevent it? Hurry.

A: Yes, there is such a thing as accident proneness. Either Patrick has had a run of incredibly bad luck or he is a sure-fire accident-prone adolescent. I sense your alarm. You must worry that he is a time bomb waiting to explode. You must fear: "What's next?"

Let me help. First, the obvious question: Is there any recent stress in Patrick's life that might be causing him any psychological pain? Sometimes physical pain is unconsciously preferable to vague, but overwhelming, psychological pain such as anxiety or depression. Secondly, look back to Patrick's childhood. How did he customarily handle disappointment? Most accident-prone adults, as a matter of fact, tended to have many "accidents" even as children. Thirdly, how does Patrick handle anger? Can he express it directly or does he bottle it up inside of himself? Accident-prone teenagers customarily hold on to their anger, then turn it back against themselves in the form of an "accident." Lastly, what about Patrick's self-esteem? The truly accident-prone person doesn't feel very good about himself. His "accidents" are an unconscious weapon of self-punishment.

If Patrick fits this profile, I would definitely recommend a consultation with a child psychiatrist.

Master Manipulator

Q: I'm worried about my nephew, William. He's 14 and I don't trust him. He's becoming a master manipulator. He uses people for his own ends, usually to get things he wants. He pits people against each other and never gets "caught" doing anything wrong himself. He lies and cheats, but believe me, he's smooth as silk. He'll even apologize about some things if he thinks he can gain some advantage. The worst thing about all this is that his mother (my sister) is completely ignorant of Billy's deceit. In fact, in her eyes he can do no wrong at all. What do you suggest?

A: You can be sure that Billy did not become a master manipulator overnight. For the benefit of our readers whose children are younger than Billy, and for whom there is still time to avoid his fate, I'd like to point out that manipulators (or "users") generally start out as spoiled little darlings in the nursery, graduate to grade school tyrants, cheats, and liars, and then move up to pubescent con men and women. Parents should be alert to these traits.

Manipulators often have self-esteem problems. They use other people to bolster their fragile egos. Difficult enough to deal with in early childhood, they can get very nasty in adolescence.

163

Your sister, like many adults in the orbit of these charmers, may be smitten by Billy's polish. She may even be encouraging it — consciously or unconsciously.

I find it interesting that you do not give concrete examples of Billy's misbehavior. This may be symptomatic of the problem. It's very tough to pin things on these youngsters. They're smooth. They're slippery.

What to do? That's tough. I doubt that Billy feels he has a problem. His mother is oblivious to his deceit. If you don't feel right about talking to him privately about his behavior, at least don't let him manipulate you. If he does, call him on it. And, be sure to give Billy some success opportunities that do not require manipulation on his part. It will help him to learn that he can get what he wants through honesty and consideration of other people.

A Runaway Daughter

The peak incidence of runaway is at ages 13 to 14. It usually signals a desperate effort to fix an emotional or family problem. Psychiatric consultation is indicated. Better safe than sorry.

Q: My 13-year-old daughter, Elizabeth, has just returned from a two-day runaway. It was the first time that she's ever run away from home. You can imagine our anger and our relief when she returned. My question for you comes down to: What does all of this mean? Does Elizabeth need help?

A: Runaway teenagers are a national epidemic of sorts. About 10% of all boys and 9% of all girls run away at least once between the ages of 12 and 17. But there are runaways and there are runaways. Most need psychiatric treatment, but some do not.

Try some of these guidelines:

1) If Elizabeth's runaway was in the context of long-standing behavioral, academic, or personal problems, then you would be well advised to seek consultation.

2) If Elizabeth was on her own for 48 hours (e.g., rather than "hiding out" with friends) and traveled beyond your local area, then a consultation is in order.

3) If Elizabeth was reacting to family problems, better seek help.

4) If there are any other factors that sufficiently concern you, why not, at least, get a psychiatric opinion? Better to be safe than sorry.

For your information, about 3% of teenage girls run away more than once. Each time the runaway tends to be longer — and more dangerous. Repeated running away, in my clinical experience, is symptomatic of serious developmental and psychological disorder.

Is Runaway a Family Affair?

Q: Our 14-year-old son, Jerry, ran away for a couple of days, but returned home safely. Our pastor has suggested that we go to a psychiatrist for family counseling. We'll do anything to help, but why family counseling?

The treatment of choice for runaway is often family therapy, but it should be individualized for the adolescent. Be sure to ask for specifics.

A: The peak incidence of runaway is at age 13-14. At this stage of development, most youngsters are struggling with parental conflicts: how to gracefully separate from the parents of childhood and accommodate to the parents of adolescence; how to achieve some independence at the price of losing the passive joys of earlier years. There are also emergent sexual issues that can complicate the psychological puzzle.

Family therapy, as a first step in resolving some of these issues, is often the treatment of choice. But, bear in mind that the form of therapy must be individualized to Jerry. Ask your pastor why he feels so strongly about a family approach in your case. Then, be sure to ask the same question of the psychiatrist who evaluates Jerry.

Lonely Teen Girls

Q: She won't admit it, but I think my 14-year-old, Jenna, is lonely. Comments?

Researchers have concluded that teenage girls are among the loneliest creatures in our society.

A: Teen girls may well be the loneliest people on earth. That's the conclusion suggested by one researcher. John C. Woodward of the University of Nebraska has researched loneliness for 20 years and has studied almost 3,000 individuals. He has found that adolescent girls feel more lonely than all the other groups he has studied, including preschoolers, alcoholics, divorced people, and the elderly.

Early adolescents, like Jenna, are caught awkwardly between the two worlds of childhood and adulthood. Even their own would-be peers are unpredictable and uneven in their development. They're bombarded by new feelings, new worries, and by the uncertainty of new bodies too. In my own clinical practice I find that teen boys are also very lonely — they just don't admit it as readily as the girls.

By the way, the oft-prescribed solution, "keep them busy," only goes so far. Jenna, and other early teens, need a lot of encouragement and support from Moms and Dads. It requires sensitivity, patience, and time — all important qualities for parents of teens.

Strange Sleepwalker

When sleepwalking begins in early adolescence, there are often psychological reasons such as stress or inhibited aggression.

Q: Our Matthew, 13, has a strange and embarrassing problem. Last night he got up, walked in his sleep down to the kitchen, calmly urinated in the oven, then returned to his bed. We've all been under stress lately. What should we do?

A: Sleepwalking occurs because of a partial arousal from the deepest stage of sleep, Stage IV. It usually happens about three hours after sleep onset. In children up to age six, these events are usually just an exaggeration of the normal sleep-wake cycle; young children grow out of it.

When sleepwalking, however, has its onset in adolescence, there are often some psychological explanations. You mentioned stress. Matthew's sleepwalking may be a symptom of it.

Research into adolescent sleepwalking by Klockenberg at the Karolinska Hospital in Sweden may be helpful to you. The findings suggested that sleepwalking teenagers tend to inhibit aggression. They don't express feelings well. It is suggested, then, that the sleepwalking may be a mechanism of discharging (acting out) bad feelings.

What to do? The main danger is Matthew hurting himself if it happens again. Do what you can to safety-proof the environment. Medication can help in the short run. The long-term solution, however, is to resolve the family stress and to encourage Matthew to express his feelings in words.

Stuttering and Brain Chemistry

Stuttering is not usually a psychological disorder. New scientific evidence points to biochemical abnormalities as possible causes. Until medication is available, speech therapists are the professionals to see.

Q: Our son Hughie, 13, stutters. He's been seeing a psychoanalyst for three years. No luck. He still stutters. The analyst says that Hughie still "hasn't revealed his conflicted aggression toward his parents." We are getting impatient. Should we switch analysts?

A: Maybe you should switch from analysis. Hughie may be getting the wrong kind of treatment.

There is growing evidence that stuttering is not a purely psychological problem at all. It is much more likely to be a physical phenomenon.

University of Texas researchers, using sophisticated diagnostic techniques such as magnetic resonance imaging (MRI) and single photon emission computerized tomography (SPECT), have developed good evidence that stuttering may well be caused by biochemical abnormalities rather than emotional disturbances such as "conflicted aggression."

The MRI, for example, showed that 24% of subjects had abnormalities in brain structures, and the SPECT demonstrated 76% of patients had low metabolic activity in these same structures.

These discoveries are pointing toward new (as yet experimental) avenues of treatment, including the use of medication to dilate brain blood vessels, and medication that is commonly used to treat movement disorders. Until these novel approaches are proven to be reliable, I suggest that you consult with a speech therapist. While I'm reluctant to suggest that you terminate Hughie's analysis abruptly, such a consultation certainly will not hurt, and may well help him a great deal.

The Checker

Q: Our son, Mason, 14, is a checker. He checks everything two or three times: Did I lock the door? (Check). Did I tie my shoes? (Check). He's always been neat and careful, but this is excessive. Will he grow out of it? Does he need help?

A: Sounds like Mason, once a fastidious child, has developed a full-blown case of obsessive-compulsive disorder (OCD) in his adolescence. Obsessions are recurrent, unavoidable thoughts. Compulsions are recurrent, unavoidable actions. In mild form the symptoms may be irritating, but do not interfere with daily living. In severe form (such as washing one's hands 50 times a day or more), symptoms can be disabling. Psychiatrists who specialize in treating OCD often lump the symptoms into categories: neat freaks, washers, checkers, and hoarders.

OCD is much more common than most people think, because most sufferers, like Mason, function pretty well in other areas of their lives and tend to hide their symptoms. They only seek treatment if the illness becomes so severe that it significantly interrupts their lives.

No, Mason probably will not grow out of it. Up to one half of all adult cases of OCD have their onset before age 15.

Yes, he needs help. A psychiatrist can make the definitive diagnosis and then provide treatment, which may combine medication with behavior modification. Recent scientific studies

Compulsions are recurrent, unavoidable actions. Up to one-half of all adult cases have their onset before 15. Young patients become very anxious if their ritualistic behavior is interrupted. OCD may be caused by biochemical abnormalities. New treatment combines medications with behavioral therapy.

suggest a biochemical cause for OCD. A new medication, Clomipramine, offers promise.

Knuckle Cracking

Nervous habits, like knuckle cracking, can sometimes assume compulsive proportions. The key to change is the youngster himself.

Q: Our 13-year-old, Mark, is a compulsive knuckle cracker. He's been at it constantly for over two years. He can even crack the joints in his toes. The kids at school laugh at him. Our pediatrician examined him and said there's no physical damage — yet.

Is this just a habit, like thumbsucking, that will go away by itself? What should we do?

A: Thumbsucking, which usually begins in the first year of life, is primarily a self-soothing mechanism. Knuckle cracking, like Mark's, is more a nervous habit, sometimes of compulsive proportions.

What happens if Mark is interrupted from his cracking? Does he get anxious? If so, it's a clue that the habit is a compulsive ritual he's using to ward off anxiety, and may be a symptom of obsessive-compulsive disorder.

What to do? The key is Mark himself. If he sees it as a problem and wants to do something about it, it can be cured. Because the habit is so severe and chronic, I suggest getting some help. A consultation with a child psychiatrist who is skilled at behavior modification techniques would be a good place to start.

Superstitions vs Compulsions

Dealing with superstitions does not usually involve therapy. Environment plays an important role.

Q: My 13-year-old, Flora, has a lot of superstitions: black cats, crossing her fingers, ladders, lucky charms, wishing on stars. Is this the same as obsessive-compulsive disorder? Should we try to break her of the habit?

A: Superstitions are qualitatively different from the rituals of obsessive-compulsive disorder (OCD). Superstitions like those of Flora are based on a magical belief in something that either brings good luck or defends against misfortune. Rituals such as compulsive hand washing, checking, counting, or arranging things in certain habitual ways are a defense against the emergence of anxiety. Superstitions are usually playful; even children of 7 or 8 usually view them as magical and harmless. A child who engages in ritualistic behavior, however, is deadly serious about it. If interrupted, she becomes very anxious.

Little is written about childhood superstitions in the child psychiatry literature. Leonard et al., reporting in the *Journal of the Academy of Child and Adolescent Psychiatry*, January 1990, believe, as I do, that superstitions do not appear to lead to dysfunctional obsessive or compulsive behavior.

Break her of the habit? Educate her. Humor her. Set a non-superstitious example. Most children become less superstitious by 9 or 10 unless the superstitions are encouraged and supported by their environment.

Teen Suicide and TV News

Q: Last night on the TV news there was a story about a local teenager who killed herself by jumping in front of a train. My son Jason, 14, saw the report and was as turned off by it as I was. Why do they have to report these things? Doesn't it just add to the problem? Won't it give some kids the idea to kill themselves too?

A: It has been assumed for some time by psychiatrists that TV coverage leads to an increase in teen suicide due to a contagion or imitation phenomenon. A new study, however, from the Institute of Social Research at the University of Michigan challenges this assumption.

Kessler and his colleagues analyzed the relationship between network TV news stories about suicide and the actual number of teen suicides from 1973 through 1984. These investigators found no significant association between the newscasts and the suicides.

Nevertheless, teen suicide should be a concern to all adolescents and their parents. There were 22,184 suicide deaths by 10- to 19-year-olds in the years from 1973 to 1984. I'm pleased that Jason is "turned off" by the subject, but I hope that you and he can face it squarely and talk about it in a way that sheds light and understanding.

Although there have been conflicting reports, a comprehensive study has shown there to be no relationship between TV reporting of teen suicide and subsequent suicides. Don't be afraid to use such news stories to talk to your early adolescent about the issue. Another case where talking helps.

Teens and Hyperactivity

Q: Willard, our 13½-year-old, first started taking medication for hyperactivity when he was 9. At that time we were told he would "outgrow" his need for it when he reached adolescence. Well, he's a teenager now, but his doctor says he still needs the pills. Comments?

Early adolescents are famous for refusing medication, and many hyperactive 13- to 14-year-olds may have heard years ago that they would outgrow their need for medication at puberty. New evidence shows this is not always the case. Compliance with doctor's orders for these youngsters may, therefore, be difficult.

A: It used to be thought that hyperactive youngsters invariably "outgrew" their illness at puberty, but now we know that some hyperactive adolescents continue to benefit from medication. The benefits, however, are not generally as dramatic as for younger children. A recent report to the National Institute of Mental Health by Dr. Rafael Klorman confirms these conclusions.

Willard should, however, be carefully evaluated (perhaps by psychological testing and special rating scales) before a final decision is made. Also, best results are obtained when treatment also includes supportive talking therapy, behavior modification, parental counseling, and other helpful techniques.

Drugs, Alcohol, and Smoking

Teenage Smoking

You've-come-a-long-way-baby department. Teen girls are heavier smokers than teen boys.

Q: My husband and I, both former smokers, have just discovered that our 13-year-old daughter, Rebecca, is smoking a half-pack of cigarettes a day. We've preached until we're blue in the face about the health hazards, about our own fight against nicotine. Nothing seems to work. Any suggestions?

A: You might be interested to know that while the overall rate of cigarette smoking for teenage boys has declined steadily over the past several years, the rate for girls has increased. This situation has even gotten to the point where today more girls (12.7%) than boys (10.7%) regularly smoke cigarettes.

One of the influences on Rebecca, therefore, may be peer pressure. She may have selected female teen role models who are smokers — probably because they come closer to the overall image that she would like for herself. This is unfortunate. One of the keys is for you to help her carve out a more positive identity, more wholesome activities, more appropriate models of behavior.

How? Preaching and moralizing and scare tactics won't work. Rebecca has seen all the anti-smoking ads. References to your victory over "cancer sticks" may even backfire on you: if Rebecca's smoking is partly an anti-authority rebellion, you'd be playing into her hand.

Early adolescents, like Rebecca, generally respond to arguments that appeal to their budding sense of autonomy, e.g., by not smoking, Rebecca will show more self-control and independence than by smoking. Health warnings that target the immediate consequences of smoking, rather than the potential effects of 20 or 30 years of two packs per day, also work, e.g., yellow stains on teeth and fingers, bad breath, smelly clothes. These messages nicely appeal to the natural narcissism of most 13-year-olds.

One more tip: if you're really serious about not wanting Rebecca to smoke, do not allow her to smoke in the house or in your presence. To do otherwise would telegraph a mixed message. It would proclaim that Mom and Dad are not really serious, that you're just "blowing smoke," so to speak.

Teen Smoker

Q: I suspected it, but I finally caught her. My 14-year-old Cheryl smokes cigarettes. How can I get her to stop? Will it help if my husband and I quit too?

One of the greatest predictors of teen smoking is parental smoking.

A: Parental smoking is certainly a powerful influence. In families, for example, where both parents smoke, 15.1% of girls are smokers, compared to 6.5% if neither parent smokes.

There are, of course, other influences too: 1) peer pressure, 2) the adolescent attitude that since the major consequences of smoking are long-term, they can quit some time in the future and avoid any problems, 3) social, media, and advertising pressures, 4) smoking as a defiant and illegal practice, and finally, 5) the allure of nicotine itself, a powerfully addicting substance.

If Cheryl has been smoking a half-pack or more a day for over a few months, she may well be addicted in both a physical and psychological sense. Therefore, the intervention to help her quit will be very similar to the adult approach. It seems to me that Cheryl has perhaps inadvertently presented the entire family with a wonderful, life-saving opportunity. Why don't all three of you try a stop-smoking program together?

Stages of Drug Abuse

Q: My 13-year-old son, Jesse, confessed to us that he's tried pot — once. We were shocked, but we realize that most kids these days are going to try it. Should we be more alarmed? What are the chances he'll become hooked?

The four stages: 1) experimentation, 2) actively seeking a high from alcohol or drugs, 3) preoccupation with getting high, loss of other interests, new "friends," 4) addiction/ dependency.

A: Jesse wants you to know something. Be understanding, but be very clear that you're against drugs. And be watchful too. Teenage drug abusers go through four distinct stages:

1) *Experimentation.* Most kids do experiment with pot. It's so readily available. Thankfully, most kids try it once or twice and never do it again.

2) *Seeking a high.* Youngsters who liked the "high" may actively seek it. They go out looking for drugs, but may only use them periodically, the so-called weekend warriors.

3) *Preoccupation with high.* In this stage the teenager becomes preoccupied with getting high. He orients his life around drugs. His friends change. His attitude changes. He's in bad trouble.

4) *Chemical dependency.* In the last stage, the youngster is so accustomed to being under the influence of drugs that he needs them just to feel "normal." He's lost touch with his former straight life and everything it stood for.

I'm encouraged by Jesse's honesty. It's a good sign. Don't lose touch with him.

Parents Last to Know?

Yes, parents are usually the last to know. There's nothing to be gained by feeling guilty about it. Take action. Get help.

Q: My 14-year-old granddaughter, Celeste, was just taken to a hospital for treatment of drug addiction. I can't believe it. I'm flabbergasted that her parents didn't do something sooner. I hear that her problem started when she was 11 years old. How could they have missed it?

A: It's easy. Let me explain. As a child psychiatrist I've found that it's typical for parents to be the last to know. Why? There are several factors:

1) *Under-educated.* Too many parents are simply under-educated about the early warning signs of teen drug abuse.

2) *Denial.* Even when they first suspect a problem, many parents tend to deny it. "Not my child," is their response. Unconsciously they may have a need to avoid the stark truth.

3) *Con job.* As teenagers descend into the depths of the drug life they get very good at hiding it from Mom and Dad. This con job is actually part of the illness.

4) *Minimizing.* When parents finally confront a youngster with the facts they often get a response that minimizes the problem: "Okay, I do a little pot and beer. Don't worry. I can control it. Just leave me alone." Too many parents fall for this propaganda.

5) *Bargaining.* Confronted again, the teenager bargains: "Just don't send me to hospital. I'll quit. I promise."

6) *Guilt.* Some parents feel blame for their child's drug problem. This kind of self-imposed guilt trip only delays treatment.

7) *Intimidation.* When things continue out of control, parents usually confront their youngster again. By now the child is probably chemically dependent. The scene gets ugly: "If you make me go for treatment, I'll run away. You can't make me."

8) *Motivation.* It's sad but true that some parents still subscribe to the theory that "you can't make them get help if they don't want it." This laissez-faire attitude may work for adult alcoholics, but it's foolish where teenagers are concerned. Adolescence is a crucial developmental period. There is no time to waste.

Where do Celeste's parents fit in this scenario? Don't be too hard on them. The good news is that Celeste is finally in treatment. But from here on Mom and Dad must stand squarely for abstinence and sobriety. Their understanding will be important, but they'll have to be tough too.

Daughter of Alcoholic

Q: My husband is an alcoholic. I've tried for years to get him to go for treatment. No dice. Now I think it's starting to affect our 13-year-old daughter, Sheryl. She's always angry with her father, avoids him, won't bring kids home from school. She's also angry with me, I think — maybe because she feels I can do something about my husband's drinking. I can't. But what can I do for Sheryl?

A: First of all, I'm not ready to concede that you can't do anything about your husband's alcoholism. Yes, he's the one that will have to be motivated for treatment, but have you examined your own role in his drinking? Are you part of the solution? If not, you may be part of the problem. How? By simply "enabling" him to go on drinking. By not establishing consequences. By making excuses for him.

You may not be able to control your husband's behavior, but you can control your own. That's the sticking point — and that may be why Sheryl is angry with you. She probably isn't satisfied with your passive acceptance of Dad's disease.

Do yourself and Sheryl a favor. Go immediately to the phone book and call Al-Anon for help. There's another organization

Teen alcoholism and chemical dependency is, ultimately, a family illness. Everyone suffers. It's your choice: you're part of the problem if your behavior allows a family member to go on using, part of the solution if you insist on treatment.

called Ala-Teen for youngsters like Sheryl; adolescents who know what it's like to live in the shadows of alcoholism. Al-Anon and Ala-Teen can help make both of you part of the solution.

Daddy Smokes Pot

The active ingredient (THC) of marijuana can be stored in the body for several weeks. That's only one of the reasons it is so dangerous for adolescents.

Q: "If he can do it, why can't I?" That's the question my 13-year-old daughter is asking. And I don't know what to tell her. You see, it's true. My husband keeps a stash of marijuana in our bedroom and smokes it two or three times a week. I don't know how Jenny found out about it, but I guess she probably smelled it or something. Anyway, she admits openly that she's tried it too and that she plans to go right on smoking — because "Daddy does it." I'm afraid to bring this up with Jack. He'll overreact, that's for sure. What should I do?

A: He'll "overreact?" What do you mean? You can't afford not to bring this up with your husband. Your daughter's health and safety (and his too, by the way) is at stake.

Pot is poison. It's bad enough for adults, but for a developing teenage girl it's deadly. The active ingredient (THC) can be stored in the body for weeks. Therefore, a youngster's behavior can be influenced by marijuana long after the last glow of the joint. It's especially harmful to short-term memory, the type of retention that's needed to learn new things in school.

Marijuana and alcohol are usually the ticket of entry into the world of even more serious drug abuse, such as PCP and hallucinogens. Act now.

You're "afraid" to confront Jack? Maybe Jenny's experimentation is designed to get him to do what you're afraid to do — confront him.

Drug Abuse Treatment

There are many types of treatment options available, ranging from outpatient to intensive hospitalization. Consult an expert to determine your youngster's specific needs. Talk to parents of teenagers who have been in treatment; they are excellent resources.

Q: Our 14-year-old son, Michael, has a drug problem. It's taken us a year to face up to it, but now we know there's no denying it. What's more, we're determined to make sure he gets help. But where to turn, that's the question.

A: First, let me congratulate you for your determination. You know that Michael will fight against treatment. Denial, bargaining, minimizing — they're all part of the illness.

There are a number of programs around the country for teenage drug abusers. Some are excellent, some are not so hot. Here are the basic criteria to look for:

1) *Illness*. Chemical dependency should be viewed as an illness. Teenage drug users are not "bad" or morally deficient. They have an illness requiring treatment.

2) *Diagnosis*. Many programs are long on treatment, short on diagnosis. Not all drug abusers are alike. Medical and psychiatric diagnosis is an important first step.

3) *Residential*. The first phase of treatment (approximately 2 to 4 months) must usually begin in a hospital or residential facility where de-toxification can occur — and the youngster can be kept safe from "his chemical."

4) *Family*. Treatment must involve the family as partners.

5) *Abstinence*. The goal of treatment must be sobriety, complete abstinence.

6) *Psychiatric, medical*. The program must be able to treat concomitant psychiatric and medical illness.

7) *No cults*. Some programs resemble cults. Avoid them. You may be trading one problem for another one.

8) *Recovering staff*. In addition to physicians and nurses, good programs have some staff members who are recovering drug users. They lend credibility and role-modeling for youngsters and provide drug education.

9) *AA*. The philosophy of AA and its 12 steps should be at the core of the program.

10) *School*. The program should offer ongoing academic classes, preferably for credit, while the youngster is in treatment.

11) *Aftercare*. Successful programs offer a year or more of structured aftercare. This post-hospital or post-residential phase is the key.

12) *Lifestyle*. The program must promote a new lifestyle, free not only of drugs, but free of the "wrong friends." It must replace old values with a new, positive outlook on life.

Home Drug Tests

Q: We have two teenagers, 14 and 17. We're scared to death about drugs. What's your opinion of home drug testing kits?

A: In general, I'm not in favor of them for kids who do not have a previously established drug problem.

First of all, it introduces a strong element of suspicion into what should be a relationship built on honesty and trust.

Secondly, the tests themselves can be misleading. A negative test, for example, doesn't necessarily mean a youngster is clean. Every test has a minimum detection level. Small amounts

Drug testing is a very tricky business. Tests can be beaten by resourceful cheaters and all tests have limitations. Do not rely on them as sole-source indicators for your teenager's abstinence from substances of abuse.

go undetected. Then again, some substances, such as alcohol and cocaine, are essentially cleared from the body in about 36 to 48 hours. So timing is a factor.

There is also the possibility of interfering substances (such as prescribed medications) causing falsely positive results.

Finally, the test performed is only a screening test. Drug treatment programs, therefore, always require a second, more sophisticated assay as a confirmation test.

It gets complicated, doesn't it? That's why I believe the best defense against teen drug use is positive parental example, good communications, awareness, and trust. Keep your eyes and ears open, but don't launch into the testing business unless there's a clearly established problem and your teen is involved in some form of treatment. Then, the professionals can help you judge the results.

Drug Scares Don't Work

The best antidotes to teen drug abuse are firm family values, parents who are actively involved in their youngsters' lives, and the right kind of friends.

Q: We have two teenagers, Debbie, 13, and Mathew, 14. We don't want them to get into drugs. My husband tries to scare them with articles about the health and legal dangers of drugs, but I'm not so sure these tactics work. What do you think?

A: You're right. The overall experience with the scare tactic school of thought has not been encouraging. Why? Some kids just treat it as so much adult or parental overreaction. Others see peers or adults using drugs without any apparent ill health effects. Still others fall back on that powerful denial mechanism of adolescence: "Not me. I'm invincible. Drugs may harm someone else, but not me."

In my own experience, I find the most powerful anti-drug antidote to be firm family values. Teens who don't do drugs have made a conscious decision that they won't accept the values and lifestyles of the drug world.

So, help Debbie and Mathew develop a strong, positive self-image. They should each be good at something (school, hobbies, etc.) and their lives should be busy and full.

Just Say No?

Awareness of the teen drug problem is a good starting point, but remember that peers are the greatest single influence on teen drug use.

Q: We have two teenagers, 13 and 16. They recently participated in one of those "Just Say No" rallies at their school. Do you think that such programs are effective?

A: Former First Lady, Nancy Reagan, deserves tremendous credit for focusing the nation's attention on the teen drug problem. Her "Just Say No" campaign was a good beginning. But, in my opinion, it's up to parents, community leaders, and ultimately the teens themselves to solve the problem.

The greatest single influence on teens, for good or bad, is other teens. In a study of 350 Midwestern high school students, a Colorado State University psychologist found that peers had five times more impact on teen drug use than other factors. Their research concluded, therefore, that peer counseling in high schools is one of the most encouraging answers to the problem.

The cue for parents is clear: know your teen's friends, and exert all your influence to keep your son or daughter away from the losers and to stick with the winners.

One-Time Drunk?

Q: My 14-year-old niece was recently treated in an Emergency Room because she was drunk out of her mind. She swears she never did it before and will never do it again. Her parents don't seem to be worried about it. I am. Are you?

A: Yes. Parental unconcern can be dangerous. Acute drunkenness is very often a warning signal. We know, for example, that 20% of these youngsters will go on to full-blown alcoholism.

Teenagers at highest risk are kids who have had ongoing behavior problems at home or at school, or who suffer from shyness, or have difficulty making friends. These youngsters also tend to have a family history of alcoholism or mental illness and come from unstable home environments. (By the way, a very strong risk factor for boys is if Dad is an alcoholic.)

Interestingly, those teenagers who were just "experimenting," and are at much lower risk for alcoholism, not only tend to be healthier psychologically, but their parents typically are very anxious and concerned about the event.

Forget your niece's own protests for the moment. Does she fit the "at risk profile"? If so, talk to her parents. If not, relax — but keep an eye open.

Teen Drinking at School

Q: My daughters, 13 and 14½, say that a lot of kids at their school come to class drunk. Are these kids just showing off? What should my girls do about it?

Consider the at risk profile when a teenager is involved in a drinking incident. Low-risk teens tend to have parents who are very anxious and concerned about the incident.

Concerned classmates can work as a group to try to help problem drinkers. Peers are often aware of alcohol problems among their friends well before parents or teachers.

A: I'd be concerned even if it was "just showing off." Teenage problem drinkers are almost always known to their friends before parents or teachers ever suspect it.

In a September, 1989 survey by the national Parents' Resource Institute for Drug Education (PRIDE) it was found that 3.5% of the adolescents surveyed admitted to drinking before or during school. My hunch is that the vast majority of these youngsters have serious alcohol problems requiring treatment.

What to do? I suggest your daughters get their numbers up. I bet there are other concerned classmates too. After they've compared notes the youngsters should, as a group, approach each drinker. They should express their worry and offer to help. They ought to make it clear that if the drinkers will not or cannot stop, the next step will be to notify the school and their parents.

A tough assignment? You bet. Lives are at stake.

Why Kids Use Steroids

Steroids use among teens is not limited to athletes. Many adolescents use muscle-building steroids solely to pump themselves up — with chemistry. A dangerous practice.

Q: I thought only athletes use steroids. My son Tommy, 14, is not an athlete — far from it. But he says that kids like him are getting the drugs from "jocks" at school. Why? Do they get high?

A: Most people, like you, have been led to believe that the current dangerous practice of anabolic-androgenic steroids (AS) use is limited to athletes. Not so.

A recent national survey of male 12th graders reveals that 35% of the users were not athletes. Why do they do it? Most want to improve their appearance. They want to be bigger and stronger. Some say that peer pressure, "keeping up," is a factor.

Teenage boys have always placed a premium on stature and strength. It's a matter of self-esteem. Now, unfortunately, some of them believe they've found the "magic bullet." Well, call it black magic. Steroids are dangerous for the well-publicized professional and Olympic athletes who use them, but they're especially diabolical for adolescents because of the disruption of normal growth, secondary sexual characteristics, hormonal regulation, liver function, and psychological development.

AS are not mood-altering drugs, however. No highs, buzzes, or mellowing out. They are not addictive, but they are physically dangerous.

Better that Tommy finds a healthier source of self-esteem, such as academics and hobbies.

Psychological Aspects of Common Medical Problems

When to Switch from the Pediatrician

Q: Our 13-year-old daughter, Wendy, has been going to the same pediatrician since birth. She's always loved her doctor. But recently she's complained about all the "little kids" at his office and has asked to go to a family physician or an internist. What do you think?

A: Wendy's dilemma is real. It is symbolic of her underlying developmental struggle to leave her childhood behind and to move, as gracefully as possible, into the adult world.

I would suggest a private talk between Wendy and her pediatrician. After all, pediatricians are experts in these matters. They face this crisis with pubertal youngsters frequently.

By the way, the pediatrician's policy may determine the answer. Some pediatricians typically care for children only until puberty, others until high school graduation, still others remain available to their patients until young adult life.

Some pediatricians specialize in the relatively new field of adolescent medicine. They either restrict their practice exclusively to teenagers, or they set aside specific days solely for adolescent patients. In such an office, for example, Wendy would not have to sit in a waiting room filled with newborns and toddlers.

Before making a switch, encourage Wendy to discuss the pros and cons with both you and her pediatrician. Perhaps there are some hidden agenda items. For example, Wendy's pediatrician is a male. If Wendy has just become pubertal, the issue may be more complicated than meets the eye. Maybe she's just uncomfortable with a male doctor, but feels too embarrassed to talk about it. You, as a parent, and the pediatrician, as her physician, can be very supportive to her by helping her to express the full range of her thoughts and feelings.

She Won't Take Her Medicine

Q: Barbara, our 13-year-old, is a juvenile diabetic. She has been taking insulin for several years. In the past few weeks she

Early adolescence is the time when boys and girls may get squeamish about seeing a pediatrician. All those infants and toddlers in the waiting room are too close a reminder of the childhood they themselves are struggling to leave behind.

For early adolescents with chronic illnesses (diabetes, etc.) the mere act of taking medication every day is a message that they are not perfect creatures. Down deep they are keenly aware of this fact, but it is a difficult fact for early adolescents to face up to.

has been very negative about taking her medication. It's getting to be quite a battle. She needs her insulin. What can we do?

A: Early adolescents are notorious for refusing to take medicine or following doctors' orders. It is as though the medication is a constant reminder that they are somehow "damaged," less than perfect. The underlying illness represents a psychological insult to their budding "adolescent narcissism": their preoccupation with their changing bodies, feelings, and thoughts. Since so much is changing in their world, they strive mightily to control themselves. Sometimes this takes the form of rigid dieting — or refusing to take prescribed medication.

Barbara's diabetes, now that she is a teenager, is much more of a psychological liability for her; it marks her as being different from her friends. Being different, of course, is a curse for most 13-year-olds.

Barbara's battles with you, then, are less about insulin than they are about her own self-esteem. Rather than confronting her own feelings about being damaged or different (a painful confrontation) she is taking the fight to Mom.

I would suggest that you sidestep the battle. Put the focus on Barbara's feelings rather than on the insulin. How does she feel about being diabetic? What does it mean to her now that she is a teenager? What does it mean in terms of her peer relationships? And, most important, does she have any new fears about her illness?

Don't hesitate to get some support from Barbara's pediatrician. You might schedule a talking session just for Barbara and her doctor. Pediatricians are experienced in dealing with this common developmental phenomenon. They understand teenagers and are experts at getting them to take their medicine.

How Much Sleep?

Early adolescents are champion sack rats. Most require about 9 hours of sleep each night.

Q: Our son, Joe, is 13. He's become a regular sack rat. I mean he seems to sleep all the time. I can just barely get him up on school mornings, and on weekends — forget it — he'd sleep all day if he could. I realize that teenagers need a lot of sleep, but isn't this too much?

A: Sounds like it. Most research suggests that early adolescents, like Joe, need about 9 hours' sleep for optimal daytime functioning. Middle (13-16) and late (17+) adolescents need slightly less — about 8 hours.

But it's tough to say how much sleep any specific individual needs, since sleep requirement is based on specific physical and psychological factors.

Joe likes to sleep on both school days and weekends. If his snooze time was only a Monday through Friday affair, we'd probably conclude that he wasn't too enthused about getting up for school. But it leads me to wonder whether Joe is sounding a general retreat from the world. Sleep is often used as a psychological mechanism of social withdrawal by teenagers. Think about it.

Is It the Hormones?

Q: Our Danny is 13, and you know what that means — he's becoming Mr. Moodiness. I know it's just a stage, but what causes it? Hormones?

A: Yes, mood swings are not uncommon among early adolescents like Danny. The causes are most likely a combination of physical, emotional, and social factors.

Recently, however, researchers at the National Institute of Mental Health suggest specifically that hormones may well be linked to mood changes in teenagers. For example, in the NIMH study, boys with high levels of androgens, produced by the adrenal gland, were more likely to be rebellious. The researchers also found that early-developing boys were better adjusted — perhaps because they had lower levels of androgens and higher levels of the sex hormone, testosterone, at the onset of puberty.

Girls? Well, the findings were not as clear cut. The researchers speculate that the influence of hormones is more complicated in teenage girls.

Danny is going through a stage, but it would be wrong to chalk it all up to hormones or to events beyond his (and your) control. He needs some sense of mastery. Talk to him. Help him rise above the level of his hormones.

One Breast Larger

Q: My 13-year-old daughter, Marcie, is mortified. One of her breasts is larger than the other. I've tried to tell her not to worry, that things will even out. They will, won't they?

A: Yes, you can reassure Marcie that "things will even out." But this kind of reassurance to a 13-year-old sometimes doesn't

The daily ups and downs of early adolescents characterize this stage of development like almost no other phenomena. Hormonal changes are a major factor, but so too are the new psychological crises they face day in and day out.

Breast development (or lack of it) is, of course, a cause of considerable psychological trauma for many early adolescent girls.

go very far. "Next year," for example, seems like forever — Marcie has to face her friends today. Try, therefore, to let her know that you understand her feelings too.

As you probably know, female breast development is usually uneven. If Marcie is developing much earlier than her own peers, however, she may not be aware of this fact. It's always so painful to be out of step (too far behind or too far ahead) of your peer group in adolescence.

It is true, of course, that in some cases a woman's breasts may not "even out" enough to be cosmetically acceptable and that plastic surgery (reducing the larger breast, usually) may be considered. But don't rush into it — certainly not while your daughter's body is still developing.

Son Has Big Breasts

Gynecomastia (female-type breast enlargement) is not unusual among the boys. Medical consultation and parental understanding can win the day.

Q: Our Roger is humiliated. He's 13 and he's got the biggest breasts in his class. He refuses to undress for gym class and walks around slouched over all the time. The pediatrician says it's temporary, but Roger doesn't believe it. Help.

A: The pediatrician, of course, is correct. Breast enlargement, or gynecomastia, is fairly common in teenage boys. Why? As the male sex hormone, testosterone, gets turned on during puberty, some of it may be converted to the female hormone, estrogen, and stimulate breast development. In most cases, however, this is transitory and disappears in about six months.

These six months, however, can be an eternity in the life of a teenage boy.

My advice: let Roger get his feelings out before being too quick with the reassurances. Talk to his gym teacher. He's no doubt encountered this problem before and may have some ideas.

Pimple Face

Acne is only skin deep. Dermatologists have many new treatments available. But who will treat the emotional scars of a youngster hit by severe acne? Emphasize his personal assets.

Q: Our 14-year-old son, Victor, has a terrible case of acne. He's so ashamed. It's starting to cause him psychological problems. Just last night, for example, we learned that the kids at school call him "Pimple Face." How can we help him?

A: The logical first step is to take Victor to a dermatologist. There are some new developments in the treatment of acne that may really aid your son. For example, some dermatologists are using new skin medications in combination to treat severe cases of acne. Among them are benzoyl peroxide, retinoic acid cream (vitamin A acid), antibiotic ointments, and retinoic acid tablets. So you see, there's a lot new when it comes to this old plague known as acne.

It's important that you not allow Victor to seclude himself. Don't let him hide from those name-callers. Yes, it's very tough on him, but it's crucial that he preserve his self-esteem. Stress his strong points. Help him to put his best foot forward, even if his face isn't cooperating.

Braces, Ughhh!

Q: Well, we just came home from the orthodontist's office and the verdict is in: Ericka, our 13-year-old, needs braces. Her reaction: "Ughhh, creepy, forget it, no braces for me!"

I kind of expected this reaction, but the orthodontist says she really needs those things. How can I get her to accept them?

Another cosmetic reminder that all is not right. That's why it's especially tough to start orthodontic work on an early adolescent.

A: Ericka, as an early adolescent, is a creature of the moment. Therefore, telling her that while she may not be happy now with braces, she'll thank you in later years, probably won't work. Try it, of course, but don't count on it.

I wonder if any of Ericka's school friends have braces. If so, it might help to chat with them. They may be able to dispel some myths that may be floating in Ericka's mind.

Don't push. Tell her that you'll give her some time to think it over. You should also consider arranging a private talk between Ericka and the orthodontist; most of these specialists know something about child psychology. In the meantime, be patient. Don't force the issue until and unless you have to.

Son Wants Circumcision

Q: My son, 13, wants a circumcision. He says he wants to look like all the rest of the guys. Should I take this seriously?

A: Yes, to a point.

Listen to his concerns. Being like the rest of the guys is painfully important to an early adolescent. The penis can take on symbolic significance as well; boys sometimes compare their "manhood" in this way.

But manhood, as you know, is made of other stuff. Help your son realize it.

Most American boys tend to be circumcised, although there is little medical indication for it. The uncircumcised early adolescent boy who wants to be like his peers in every possible way may suddenly shun the locker room.

There are no cosmetic shortcuts to manhood. Not nose jobs, not weight lifting, not elevator shoes or designer clothes. Not even a circumcision will do it.

Therefore, I do not recommend a circumcision for your son unless there's a bona fide medical reason for it. Your pediatrician can help make the medical decision, but the psychological decision should already be clear.

Fat Cat

So-called baby fat does not magically disappear in later life. Fat teenagers tend to become fat adults. A reasonable, well-balanced diet and a healthy exercise program are the answers. But you can't force it on them. Make them part of a team effort.

Q: Our 13-year-old son, Gary, is a real fat cat. I mean he's about 40% over his ideal weight, according to our pediatrician. He's always been heavy as a child, and we've always chalked it up to "baby fat," but now I'm getting worried. Should we put him on a diet?

A: The myth continues to linger that "baby fat" somehow disappears in later life. The facts are that most obese children were obese infants, and 60 to 80% of obese teenagers grow up into obese adults. Merritt's studies have concluded that "it is unusual for an obese child who becomes an obese teenager ever to attain normal weight status."

Yes, it's time to become concerned. But be cautious. Efforts to put Gary on a diet may backfire. It sounds coercive. Instead, try to gain your son's active cooperation. Make it a team effort: Gary, his pediatrician, and you as parents.

School

Underachiever

The early adolescent who does not perform to his academic potential (as measured by standard tests) may have specific learning disabilities or psychological problems. Identify the problem, then plan the solution.

Q: Our 14-year-old son, Thomas, is a classic underachiever: above average intelligence, below average performance. His IQ is 118 but he makes C's and D's. Worse yet, he's very comfortable with these grades. He's a good boy, and we love him, but we're just sick about his attitude and school performance. What's the cause? What can we do?

A: Academic underachievement brings a lot of youngsters to my office. The cause is often psychological, after purely cognitive factors, such as specific learning disabilities, are ruled out.

Among the most common causes:

1) *Fear of failure.* A teen may suffer low self-esteem and lack of confidence. If he tries and fails (as he believes he will, no matter how much you reassure him about his 118 IQ), he will suffer even more pain. So he covers his inadequacy of self-confidence with a camouflage inadequacy — poor grades.

2) *Revenge.* Children of high-achieving parents may underachieve to retaliate against Mom and Dad.

3) *Fear of competition.* Some bright youngsters view the academic arena as competition. If they are passive or have problems with aggression, they may simply scale down their performance rather than compete.

4) *Being special.* All kids want to be special. If your family already has an academic super star, Thomas may choose to be "special" because of failure.

5) *Prolonged dependency.* The teen who secretly fears growing up may underachieve in order to prolong dependency on his parents.

6) *Peer acceptance.* If a teen craves peer acceptance from the "wrong friends" (often poor performers) he will, of course, adopt their values — a bad attitude toward school.

7) *Parental expectation.* Some parents push for happiness over grades. Although both are achievable, kids will generally take the easy path and opt for happiness over hard work.

8) *Boredom.* Occasionally the failure is the school's problem. The bright youngster who is not challenged and stimulated may simply stop trying.

What to do? Start with a school conference. Explore these possibilities and others. Work with the school. Map a plan of attack. Make Thomas, if possible, a part of the plan.

Since so many of the factors I've listed are psychological in nature, a consultation with a psychiatrist may also be in order.

But I'm Trying My Best!

Q: "But I'm trying my best!" How many times I've heard those words. But I've never understood my daughter's anguish until now.

Let me explain. Karen has never been a good student. My husband and I always assumed she just wasn't trying. In fact, even her teachers reported consistently that she "had the potential but wasn't using it." So we pushed her. We punished her. We pleaded with her. But nothing worked.

Karen is 13 now. Two months ago we took her to a psychiatrist because she was withdrawn and unhappy. She

Plan a special educational approach to deal with learning disabilities, as soon as you learn they exist. Your love and determination can help.

didn't have any friends. She said she felt like a failure. The doctor ordered some psychological testing and what do you suppose we found? Karen has learning disabilities! No matter how hard she tries, she just can't do the work. She was telling the truth all these years. We were only adding to her pain with all our punishment.

My husband and I are mortified. We feel guilty — and we're angry too with all those teachers over the years who failed to identify her problem.

How can we make it up to her? What should we do now?

A: I understand your feelings, but don't be too hard on yourselves. Karen's story is not a rarity. Let's not look back. After all, I can't say for sure that Karen's troubles could, or should, have been diagnosed at some particular point in the past.

Let's look ahead. Karen will require a special educational approach. Ask the psychiatrist and psychologist to consult with her school. If resources are not available through the school, you'll have to arrange for private tutoring by a teacher trained in learning disabilities.

Karen will probably need psychotherapy too. Her "failures" have damaged her self-esteem. She sounds depressed.

As for you and your husband, I'm sure you'll want to express your profound regrets to your daughter, but don't dwell on that theme. Instead, focus on your love for her — and your new-found determination to help Karen build a brighter future.

None of the Above

The methods of testing become more complicated in junior high. Specific skills on how to take tests must be developed.

Q: Christy, our 14-year-old, is bright. She excels at essay exams, but gets very frustrated and does poorly with multiple-choice tests. Any suggestions?

A: First of all, if Christy has to have a problem with one type of exam, I'd rather see her with the multiple-choice problem. Why? Essay exams are a truer test of her knowledge and ability to communicate it. Still, she'll have to master the "forced choice" type of test, especially if she's planning on a college career.

Here are some tips:

1) *Read carefully.* Is the question calling for the single correct answer or the "most correct" response? The frustrated, anxious student often jumps to the first "correct" response she sees, but it may not be the answer being sought.

2) *Answer first.* Before looking at the choices, try to come up with the best answer in your head.

3) *Select the response.* Now choose the most correct answer from the choices given.

4) *If you're not sure.* Go through each of the choices and eliminate the options that just can't be correct. This is a process of elimination.

5) *Best guess.* After eliminating what you can, make your best, educated guess. Don't leave the question blank. In most tests, unanswered questions are counted as incorrect responses.

Four Stages of Learning

Q: Our son James, 13, is a very good student and I guess I shouldn't complain, but I just don't like the way he goes about it. He doesn't think. He just memorizes. Consequently, he often fails to apply the new ideas that he learns. Comments?

There's more to learning than simple memorization of facts. Help your youngster apply what he learns. That's the best way to make it stick.

A: Bravo. Too many students (and some teachers unfortunately) equate memorizing with learning, cramming with concept formation. James may well pass tests with flying colors, but he probably forgets the material as soon as the exam is completed. A good test-taker maybe, but not a student or scholar. The real aim of education is not to see how many facts a child can amass, but to develop the capacity to think and reason.

Real learning usually occurs in four stages:

1) *Introduction.* When a teacher first explains fractions, for example, the student is being introduced to a new concept.

2) *Internalization.* Next, the student works problems. He practices so that the concepts are etched in his mind. Memorization of basic principles is part of this process, but lasting internalization also requires comprehensive understanding.

3) *Application.* Facts and concepts are useless unless they have relevance and applicability. When the student measures ½ cup of sugar for a cake or 3 centimeters for a model airplane, he's applying his knowledge.

4) *Teaching others.* It's not often appreciated, but children also learn by teaching. In this act they utilize the three previous steps in a new way and gain even further understanding and mastery.

Don't let James stay stuck at stage two.

How Much Homework?

A recent study reveals the average early adolescent spends 6 hours per week doing homework. But your teenager may need much more. It's true: kids who do the most homework get the best grades. Get involved — but don't do it for them.

Q: My Leslie is 13. She never seems to have any homework. She says she does it all at school. I'd like to get her in the habit of independent study. Should I insist that she spend time reading every day at home whether or not she has any assigned homework?

A: Frankly I like the idea, but be careful. If your plan is perceived by Leslie as coercive or punitive, it is likely to fail. And, before instituting your "learning-for-the-sake-of-learning" program, I urge you to talk to Leslie's academic counselor. Why doesn't she have assignments that will require homework? She should, in my opinion.

According to a report by Leone and Richards in the December 1989 issue of the *Journal of Youth and Adolescence,* the average early adolescent spends six hours a week doing homework. Interestingly, the researchers found that students doing the most homework tended to get the best grades, and that some element of parental help with homework was also associated with better academic performance.

If Leslie's school will not assign her homework and if her grades are up to her potential, you might suggest an evening course somewhere, an enriching hobby, or a homegrown book-of-the-week club where the two of you read and discuss the same literary works.

Report Card Feedback

The way you react (or don't react) to your youngster's report card is very important; it sets the tone, establishes a family value. Use report cards to encourage good work and to plan ahead for more of the same.

Q: I dread it. Report cards are coming. My husband and I always end up in some kind of tussle with the children, ages 14, 10½, and 8. Any suggestions?

A: Try these guidelines for giving realistic and effective report card feedback:

1) *Know child's potential.* The most important question to be answered by any report card is simply: "Is my child performing to his or her full potential?" But, the only way to know is to be aware of what that potential is. Do your homework. Talk to teachers long before the report card comes. And, by all means, let your youngster know what you expect ahead of time.

2) *Listen.* Let your children do the talking. Ask them to explain their grades and evaluations.

3) *Accentuate the positive.* Start by praising the highest grades. Establish a good-feeling tone.

4) *Examine the bad news.* "You slipped in math." "This C- is not like you, what happened?" Don't fly off the handle. Be frank but reasonable about poor grades.

5) *Action plan.* Help your child devise a plan, in writing, for improving some aspect of his performance or behavior for the next grading period.

6) *No cash rewards.* Many parents do it, but I don't encourage it. Pride in a job well done and praise from parents should be reward enough. No cash.

Should Parents Be Teachers?

Q: Our Donald, 14, is lazy. He just won't study. My husband has set up a "study hall" every night between seven and nine o'clock where he tutors Donnie in all his subjects. And the screaming — I can hear the screaming all the way upstairs. Comments?

Short of tutoring him yourself or doing the work for him, there are several things you can, and should, do to encourage good academic performance. Get involved.

A: Parents should be parents, not teachers. The best you can do for Donald's education is to:

1) Value learning yourself and be a good role model.

2) Provide him with the best school and educational opportunities possible.

3) Provide a quiet place for study.

4) Help him get his work organized, if necessary.

5) Keep in touch with Donald's teachers.

6) Expect your son to perform up to his full potential.

7) Give Donald the friendly encouragement he needs.

But become a tutor? I'm generally against it. First of all, it can cause conflict, since Dad as tutor is not neutral; he brings a lot of psychological baggage into that "study hall." Secondly, why not get an expert? If Donald really needs a tutor, why not hire one?

Parental Roles at School

Q: We have two daughters, Melissa, 13, and Melanie, 11. Their school likes parents to be involved. My husband and I like the idea, but our girls don't. What should we do?

There's definitely a place for parents in middle school, from chaperoning field trips to advising on projects.

A: I also like parental involvement at school. Your daughters, of course, are at an age where they're trying to break away from the intensive parental influence of childhood. Don't take it personally, but don't back down entirely either.

What to do? Talk to other parents. What are they doing? Then, do your part. Explain to the girls that you're not trying to check up on them, but that you have an obligation to the school and to them.

For your interest, here are the most common roles for parents in middle schools, according to a recent national survey: 1) field trip chaperon, 2) classroom chaperon, 3) visiting speaker, 4) clerical aide, 5) tutor, 6) instructional aide, 7) project advisor.

Too Much Control at School

The ideal school for most early adolescents combines firm structure with a warm, supportive environment.

Q: Our 13-year-old, Mary, has just entered a new middle school and we're concerned. The school is so rigid. The teachers emphasize rules, policing, control. Mary's former school was warm, personal, relaxed. Comments?

A: In my experience, middle schools (or junior highs) tend to be more controlled than either elementary schools or high schools. There are, however, some good reasons for this: Early teens generally experience a lot of emotional turmoil because of the onset of puberty, the hoped-for promise of more freedom as adolescents, and other factors.

On the other hand, this is the very stage of development that such youngsters require gentle understanding, a sympathetic ear, a helping hand, a warm heart.

The ideal school, therefore, would combine firm structure with emotional support. Mary, for example, may not need the structure, but I'm sure many of her classmates do.

The answer? Start by talking to teachers, administrators, and other parents. Learn as you go. I hope you can get Mary what she needs.

Cooperative Learning

A relatively new concept being promoted for middle schools, it emphasizes group skills over individual achievement. I have my doubts about it.

Q: Our Tommy, 13, is in the eighth grade. We agree that middle schools are a mess. But a lot of the parents in our Parents Council are up in arms about the new report that recommends something called "cooperative learning." What is it? What do you think?

A: The recent report of the Carnegie Foundation recommends sweeping changes in the way that middle school (grades 6 through 9) education is provided.

The report includes a number of excellent ideas such as smaller schools or "schools within schools," and an emphasis on critical thinking rather than the rote memorization of facts. But the concept of "cooperative learning" has me concerned too.

Basically, the cooperative approach emphasizes group skills and team learning. Students of varying abilities join together under the supervision of teachers who stimulate problem-solving skills. Students are not tracked according to their individual achievement levels. While this may be beneficial for the slower learners, the more gifted students may be short-changed.

Changes are needed in our middle schools but, like your Parents Council, I have concerns about the "cooperative learning" concept.

No Pass — No Play

Q: Our son Andrew, 14½, is an excellent athlete (football, basketball, baseball) but only a so-so student. Our school board is now considering a "no pass — no play" rule for athletes. Next year, if the rule is passed, all athletes will have to maintain a C average to participate in sports. Andrew doesn't like it. Do you?

A: Yes. We exploit gifted athletes by giving them a free academic ride. What happens when Andrew's sports days are over? He'll need more than locker room nostalgia to prepare him for a career and other responsibilities.

Your school system may be going with a trend. Several states, including California and Texas, have brought to a halt the special treatment of high school athletes.

Several states now require student athletes to maintain a C average to be eligible for sports participation. Hooray.

All-Boys School?

Q: Our 13-year-old, Randy, will enter high school next year. My husband wants to send him to an all-boys school. I think he'll be better adjusted if he goes to a co-ed school. What do you think?

A: There is no evidence that I know of to suggest that boys who attend all-boys high schools (or girls who attend all-girls high schools) turn out any better or worse adjusted than youngsters who attend co-ed schools.

The adjustment I'm referring to, of course, relates not only to the need for healthy friendships, but also to the entire

An all-boys school for your son? An all-girls school for your daughter? There are pros and cons. The best test is your youngster's own preference and his or her own comprehensive needs.

spectrum of development: intellectual, emotional, spiritual, and behavioral.

Don't focus too narrowly on the single question of hetero-sexual relationships: Would girls be distracting for Randy in the classroom or would they promote better understanding? Either, of course, could result. Don't forget, though, that Randy would have many influences outside of the school setting (including yourself, and sisters if he has them). Finally, most same-sex schools promote activities with a "sister or brother school" to encourage mixed experiences.

My suggestion: take Randy's own wishes into account. Then find the school that will best meet his comprehensive needs. If it's an all-boys school, fine. If it's co-ed, that's fine too.

Three Schools in One Year

Before you change your early adolescent's school because of academic or behavioral problems, look again. The problem may be the adolescent's, not the school's. If so, there is no geographic cure.

Q: Our daughter, Paula, is 14. In the last two semesters she's been in two different schools. First she begged us to remove her from public school because she didn't like the teachers. We obliged. She entered a parochial school. Now she refuses to go to class; she says all the girls at the school are on drugs. She wants to attend another school. By the way, her grades have fallen over the past two years from A-B to C-D. She's irritable and hangs out with undesirable kids. What should we do?

A: Paula's school problem is a symptom, not a cause of her troubles. Changing schools again will not solve the problem.

What's the problem? I don't know. The way to find out is to seek a diagnostic evaluation with a psychiatrist or psychologist who specializes in adolescent work.

If Paula balks at the idea, tell her that you can't decide the school issue without the consultation, i.e., that she can present her case for changing schools to the consultant. Then, let the expert handle it from that point.

Sexual Development

My Daughter Won't Talk About Sex

Q: I've raised five girls. My youngest is 14. Just like her older sisters, she refuses to discuss sex at all. What am I doing wrong?

A: Try on some of these common mistakes for size:

1) *Waiting until it's too late.* Sex education begins in early childhood with a youngster's first innocent questions about where babies come from. Sex education is also "taught" through a parent's attitude about the body, touching, intimacy, and the opposite sex. If you wait for puberty, it's usually too late.

2) *The cram course.* Don't overwhelm youngsters with the answers to questions that they're not asking yet. Take it a step at a time.

3) *Two ships passing in the night.* Some parents make the mistake of talking down to youngsters. For example, using a birds and bees metaphor to today's pre-teen is off-base. Other parents, sometimes because of their own discomforts, hide behind technical, sterile language that sails right over the heads of most youngsters. Such miscommunication results in two ships passing in the night.

4) *The unspoken signal.* Some parents talk about sex out of a sense of obligation, but they're clearly uncomfortable with it. Teenagers are quick to pick up these signals. Unconsciously, they'll try to take Mom or Dad off the hook by refusing to talk, and thus taking the "blame" for the noncommunication.

Many children, of course, are embarrassed about talking to parents about sex. Early adolescents, such as your daughter, often have a need to de-sexualize their parents. They can imagine anyone in the world talking about sex, except their own mother or father. They usually get over it in a year or two. I admire your sense of parental responsibility. Keep trying.

Parents must take the initiative in sexual education especially where sexual values are concerned.

Sex Ed

Q: Our 13-year-old daughter is eligible for an optional sex education course next semester. On the one hand we think it would be good for her to learn the "facts," but we're concerned that she will be encouraged to actually try the real thing. What do you advise?

Sex ed may not lead to less sexual activity on the part of teens, but it tends to lower the rate for pregnancy, venereal disease, and AIDS.

193

A: I appreciate your concern and your dilemma. You are not alone. Thousands of other American mothers and fathers must face this very question.

Before answering directly, let me make a few basic points that I believe represent the common wisdom among child psychiatrists:

1) Sexual education of children is a lifelong process. It begins with the first innocent question of the 3-year-old: "Where did I come from?" Parents should actually anticipate such questions, but answer them only with enough information to satisfy the child's curiosity. Do not overwhelm them with details that they cannot understand. Allow them to grow slowly into their knowledge about sex.

2) In my opinion it should be parents, not schools, who should provide sex education to their children. But it is a sad fact of life that very few parents talk to kids about sex today. A study in Cleveland, for example, showed that barely 10% of the surveyed parents had ever talked to their children about sex.

3) Yet, if parents prefer to turn over the responsibility of teaching the "facts" to the schools, it should remain the parents' obligation and responsibility to teach the moral values regarding sex. Schools, in fact, are generally better equipped to teach the biology and anatomy of sex; teachers can use movies, illustrations, etc. Mothers and fathers, however, should communicate the family values about sexuality.

4) One word of caution: while there are some very fine sex ed courses available, there are also some disastrous programs conducted by untrained persons. I would urge you to examine the curriculum and even meet the teacher before making a decision.

In answer to your basic question, there is no strong evidence that teenagers who have had sex education courses are any more or any less sexually active than other teenagers. In one follow-up study at George Mason High School in Fairfax County, Virginia, it was shown that sex ed courses did not result in an increase in sexual activity: 44% of the students who had completed the course reported that they were "sexually active" — this is about the national average for all U.S. teenagers today. The study did, however, reveal startling differences in two areas: contraception and pregnancy. Only 4.4% of the girls at George Mason had become pregnant (admittedly still a high figure compared to when we were teenagers) versus a very alarming 11.6% of all teenage girls in the United States.

I hope this information helps you to make the decision that you feel is right for your daughter. It's not easy to be the parent of a teenager today!

No or Not Now?

Q: My daughter, Stephanie, is 14. I have always preached that she should simply say "No" to sex until she's married. My sister claims that my ideas are old-fashioned. She says that Steph ought to say "Not now" and to wait until she's at least a senior. What do you say?

Family values, and the youngster's feelings, need to be openly communicated — especially when sex is the subject.

A: It's a different sexual world out there for today's teen from the one we knew. The Alan Guttmacher Institute, for example, reports that 70% of unmarried females have had sexual intercourse by the age of twenty.

Your sister may feel that she's being more realistic than you are — given today's realities. On the other hand, sexual intercourse is a profound human experience. While teenagers are certainly ready for it in a physical sense, they lack the psychological maturity that brings intimacy and commitment.

It's important that you communicate your values to Stephanie and that she is comfortable talking to you about her feelings.

Your sister's "Not now" approach has some advantages, but I don't like the artificial target of Stephanie's senior year. It implies tacit approval to something that you, her mother, are against.

This is a problem for all parents of teenage girls — and boys too.

Excessive Interest in Daughter's Sex Life

Q: My sister is a divorced mother with a 14-year-old daughter, Karen. Lately my sister has been complaining bitterly about Karen's "promiscuity." She can even detail nights when boys stay overnight in Karen's room. I'm not a psychiatrist, but when my sister tells me these things with a smile on her face, I've got to believe that Karen is doing exactly what her mother wants her to do.

It is important to draw a fine line between being totally disinterested in your early adolescent's sex life, and being overly interested. Both extremes can signal conflicts being experienced by Mom or Dad.

A: Sounds like Mom is sending mixed messages to Karen about sex. You're also suggesting that Mom is perhaps vicariously sharing in her young daughter's sexual exploits. Both of these phenomena, sadly, are not uncommon.

Why? There are many reasons. A parent whose own sexual life, for example, is unfulfilled, may unconsciously encourage sexual activity in their teenager. They then identify with their son or daughter and share in the excitement, while alternately being repulsed by it. Another dynamic is the parent who over-values sexual attractiveness as a trait in a son or daughter; hence, the teenager's sex appeal becomes "proof" of their value as a person.

By the way, I wonder how Karen feels about all of this? As a good aunt, a trusted third party, you could be crucial to her. Why not have a quiet, non-judgmental talk with her? She may need your help.

Teen Sex and Single Mothers

Teen daughters of single mothers are three times more likely to experience sexual intercourse.

Q: I'm a single mother. I date, but I'm careful to keep my social life separate from my two daughters, 13 and 15, and our home life. Recently I learned that both of my girls are sexually active. My girlfriend says that daughters raised without fathers tend to get involved more in sex no matter what you do. Can you explain?

A: From a strictly statistical standpoint your friend is correct — to a point.

Research conducted by Planned Parenthood and the Carolina Population Center confirms that adolescent girls living in stable single-mother households are three times more likely to experience intercourse than girls living continuously with their natural mothers and fathers. The researchers, Susan Newcomer and J. Richard Udry, concluded that the presence of a girl's natural father has in inhibitory effect where adolescent coitus is concerned.

Statistical studies, however, can only go so far. Your friend says "no matter what you do." I'm not so pessimistic. Such teen sex activity is a product of many things: search for male acceptance, acting out aggression toward the mother, peer pressure, too much unsupervised time, drug or alcohol use, vicarious identification with a sexually active single mother, and other factors.

The solution? First, talk to your girls about sex. Transmit your values to them. Search for the real meaning of their sexual activity. In this way, they'll be more than mere statistics.

Padded Bra

Q: Sherrie, our 13-year-old, is a slow developer. Most of her girlfriends have breasts and are wearing bras. Sherrie, of course, feels left out. She wants to wear a padded bra. If I give in, won't I be giving her the wrong signal about her body and her sexuality?

A: A perceptive question with no easy answer.

Breast development is the most visible sign of puberty and physical maturation. Our society is also quite breast-fixated. These two issues can combine with a late-developing girl's own self-consciousness to create some real problems for youngsters like Sherrie.

First I would recommend that you utilize Sherrie's request as an opportunity to talk to her about the body and sexual values. You obviously don't want her to become preoccupied with only the external, physical aspects of her sexuality.

On the other hand, I see no real harm in a padded bra. Chances are that Sherrie won't be needing it very long anyway.

Before buying your early adolescent daughter a padded bra, talk to her about sexuality. Don't let her become preoccupied with the physical aspects of sexuality and to equate physical attractiveness or bra size with self-esteem or sexuality.

Tell Son about Menstruation?

Q: Our son, Jerome, is 13. Six months ago my husband had a talk with him about sex. Now he wants to know about menstrual periods. My husband says he doesn't know much about it, and that I should do the explaining. What do you think?

A: In principle, I believe that sex education is a job for both mothers and fathers. In fact, I like to see parents doing it together — as a team. In this way you can communicate an important value: that sex is natural and part of a loving marital relationship.

So, by all means, talk to Jerome about menstruation. It's something he should know about. But ask your husband to be present for the talk too.

One more thing — sex education is an on-going process. It can't be packaged into neat little talks. Give Jerome the basics and encourage him to come back for more information as questions arise — as arise they surely will.

Boys, as well as girls, should be educated about menstruation. As with all sex ed, it's best if Mom and Dad do it together as a team.

Wet Dreams

Wet dreams are normal physiological events of early adolescence. Talk about them, of course, but usually there is no need to make a big deal about it.

Q: I'm a single mother. I think my son, 13, is having wet dreams. What exactly are they? What should I do?

A: A wet dream is a nocturnal emission of sperm from the testes and of fluid from the prostate gland — the normal male ejaculate. These ejaculations usually occur with sexually oriented dreams and are experienced as an orgasm. Usually the dreamer is awakened, but not always.

Boys sometimes feel ashamed of these episodes and rarely talk about them to parents.

My advice: no need to confront the issue directly. On the other hand, I do hope you're involved in your son's sex education. If so, you might raise the general subject at some opportune time. If your son picks up on it, you could discuss it.

The tell-tale emissions could, of course, be the result of masturbation. If so, my advice is the same.

Punish Victim of Incest?

Teenage victims of incest must first be protected from the offending adult. The second step is counseling. Youngsters must usually work through a complex of hurt, shame, and guilt.

Q: My girlfriend's daughter Francie, 13, is an incest victim. I just got the news yesterday. I was stunned, but not as stunned as when I heard the next bit of news: Francie has been "removed to a shelter home for her own protection." Meanwhile, her father, who has been ordered to get therapy, stays in the home. What is this? He should get out, not her! Why should she be punished further?

A: Immediate protection of the victim is the first order of business in these cases. But protection, as in this case, can take some mighty strange twists. Yes, Francie may well feel that she's now a double victim.

In similar situations I've found such youngsters embittered and distrustful of the would-be helpers in their lives.

Whenever possible the child victims of incest or abuse should remain in the home with the safe, nurturing, protective parent. The offending parent should be barred from visits except in the presence of therapists or court-appointed officials. This arrangement should continue until or unless rehabilitation of the entire family can be confirmed.

There may be some extenuating circumstances in Francie's case, but like you, I'd sure like to know what they are.

Father-Daughter Incest

Q: I have a terrible problem. Please help. I have just learned that my husband has been having sex with my 14-year-old daughter, Becky, for the past 3 years. I'm horrified. Apparently Becky had kept the secret until last week when she confided in a girlfriend who took the story to a school counselor. Becky was then interviewed by someone from Juvenile Court. I was called yesterday by a social worker from the court. I don't know where to turn. Is my daughter ruined? Will my husband, who is a good man, be arrested? What should I do?

Experts are available to help all of the family members involved in incest. Look past the first reactions of rage and fear and examine the situation.

A: The first reactions in a situation like this are usually panic and rage and fear. Let's settle down and examine the picture.

There are two basic types of incest:

1) *Assault.* The victim of incestuous assault is like a rape victim. She requires immediate intervention and protection. As defenseless victims, these girls generally do not suffer from the same level of shame or guilt that may strike girls in the second category. The father who rapes a daughter may be suffering acute psychiatric illness or alcoholism. He needs help too.

2) *Misguided love.* This type of incest may start with innocent hugging between a lonely or sexually conflicted father and an attention-starved daughter. As the relationship proceeds to sexual intercourse, the girl does not, at first, think anything wrong of it. As she grows older she becomes aware of the taboo, but feels compelled to guard the secret — for many reasons.

Becky reached out to a friend. Why now? I'm also concerned that Becky did not confide in you. I'm sure you're concerned too. Does Becky feel you would not do anything? Why? As a child she may assume that you have known about the problem and have allowed it to continue. Listen to her. Help her.

I hope that the Juvenile Services people will be sensitive to all three of you. Incest requires immediate separation of Dad from Becky. Your husband, of course, will have to deal with the law, but I hope he also gets the help he obviously needs. Becky very clearly is asking for help. She needs it. There are experts available who can help all of you.

1-900-PORNO

Q: I couldn't believe it. My phone bill last month was $525.00. When I looked closer I noticed that the calls had gone to (900) numbers. Curious, I called. Smut. Heavy breathing. Sex talk.

Adolescents' use of 1-900-PORNO telephone lines is leading to changes in local legislation affecting telephone services. Technology often lags behind teenagers.

And who placed these calls? My 13-year-old son, Kenneth, and his buddies. What should I do?

A: These (900) numbers are gaining in popularity. There are a number of legitimate uses: sports news, stock market reports, even messages from Santa Claus.

Unfortunately, the porno peddlers have also gotten into the act, and according to the Federal Trade Commission, there are no special rules governing child access. Although federal law does ban the sale of pornographic material to minors, the telephone titillaters get around this by simply sticking a message at the beginning of the tape that says something like: "If you are under 18, hang up now." What an invitation to a curious teenager!

What can you do? I'm told that some vendors will refund fees on disputed calls. You sure ought to try. In some parts of the country your phone service may be able to block your telephone from placing (900) calls — at your option.

Kenny? You could use this as an opportunity to talk to him about sex, of course — and to provide him with a chance to pay you back. That ought to precipitate some heavy breathing.

Scarfing

It's a form of autoerotic asphyxiation and it can be deadly.

Q: Last week a 14-year-old boy in our neighborhood died as a result of something the kids call "scarfing." His parents found him hanging by a belt around his neck. What is this all about?

A: Scarfing is a form of autoerotic asphyxiation. It's been known for centuries. It's a practice that combines masturbation with cutting off blood supply to the brain, using a scarf or belt wrapped around the neck. Some porno magazines have extolled its virtues because the asphyxiation causes a "rush" that enhances the orgasm.

Scarfing is a grisly affair. It's estimated that 500-1,000 individuals (mostly teenagers) die each year from the practice — but the numbers are undoubtedly higher since many of these deaths are chalked up to suicide.

Dietz and Hazelwood, co-authors of *Autoerotic* Fatalities, say that possible warning signs are neck abrasions, and a youngster's tendency to emerge from the seclusion of his room with a flushed face and bloodshot eyes.

My Son, the Sissy?

Q: My husband thinks that our son Adam, age 13, is effeminate because he likes to sew and to paint, and wants to take ballet lessons. My husband and Adam battle constantly. Larry, my husband, thinks that Adam should be interested in "masculine" things like baseball and cars. Larry shouts. Adam cries. Now I'm starting to battle with my husband too, especially when he calls Adam a sissy. Help.

Boys who have interests in things considered traditionally feminine may be neither effeminate nor sissy.

A: Adam seems to be interested in things that have traditionally been thought of as feminine. Such a label is, indeed, unfortunate, since men and women share such interests. After all, a great many masculine men have been world-famous tailors, clothes designers, painters, and dancers.

Your husband seems to be confusing effeminate behavior with these tradition-bound feminine areas of interest. Effeminate behavior describes a boy who exhibits exaggerated female mannerisms: a swishing gait, smacking lips, a dramatic toss of the head, a drop of the wrist. These mannerisms generally result from over-identification with a powerful mother or from growing up without sufficient models for male behavior; they sometimes result as a reaction to a harsh, unaccepting father. Mannerisms, however, and interests are two entirely different items.

Down deep, of course, your husband fears that Adam might be headed for homosexuality. Why not face the fear? Talk it over with your husband. Tell him that so-called feminine interests are not necessarily indicators of homosexuality at all. In fact, effeminate behavior is not even a positive indicator of male homosexuality.

Finally, it seems to me that there is a good deal of father-son conflict in this picture. This is not an unusual phenomenon with 13-year-old boys and their Dads. In fact, maybe Adam has learned to pull Dad's chain. Maybe Adam's feminine interests are, at least in part, a way of getting back at Dad. Without getting caught in the middle, you might try to interpret Adam to his father. Help your husband to understand Adam and to increase his tolerance. Once the conflict is de-escalated to manageable levels the two of them will be able to really start relating — man to man.

Siblings

Sibling Rivalry Never Dies

Sibling rivalry can last well into adult life. It is interesting to note, however, that sisters (rather than brothers or brother-sister combinations) tend to work things out best over time.

Q: Our daughters, 14 and 16, fight like cats and dogs. I've heard that sibling rivalry mellows with age. True?

A: Sibling rivalry can be a lifelong battle, but yes, it does tend to mellow. Your girls are very close in age and, from a developmental standpoint, need many of the same things from you and your husband. They are, therefore, natural competitors. As they grow older this clash of needs should largely disappear — unless they continue to search for things they didn't get in childhood. You might be interested to know, by the way, that sisters tend to become friendlier over the years than do brothers or brother-sister combinations.

Yes, your girls may well work it out.

Teen Mutilates Sister's Hair

Rivalry is normal, revenge is not. Parents should generally allow siblings to work out their rivalries among themselves, but should not leave hostile, destructive acts unpunished.

Q: Debbie, my 14-year-old, is jealous of her younger sister, Mandy, 8. This time she went too far. My husband and I have always made a fuss over Mandy's beautiful, long, blond hair. Last night Debbie sneaked into her room while she was asleep and chopped off Mandy's hair with a pair of scissors. Mandy, of course, is horrified. She thinks we ought to let her return the favor. Advice please.

A: Debbie is obviously suffering from a serious case of sibling rivalry and I'm very concerned about it. First of all, I have to ask why she is so threatened by an 8-year-old. Is Debbie really struggling with low self-esteem? Are there other problems in her life: behavior, feelings, school performance, friends, health? If so, Mandy may be a handy target for the anger Debbie really feels toward herself or others.

I also have to ask whether you may tend to favor Mandy over Debbie. It's impossible (and not necessary) to treat the two of them equally — just fairly — according to their needs. Are Debbie's needs being met?

Punishment? You bet. Debbie must be punished for this incident. Restriction and loss of a favored privilege for about two weeks is the best approach. As for Mandy's "returning the favor," I don't like it. Punishment is for Mom and Dad to handle

— thoughtfully and sensitively. It should teach, but not smack of revenge.

Television and Music

Teens and TV Ads

Q: Our son Jay, 13, is a walking encyclopedia of TV commercials. He can recite the jingles of dozens of ads. The thing that bothers me about it, apart from the materialism, is that most of the advertisements are for junk foods and beer. What can I do to combat this bad influence?

A: Teaching a youngster to be an intelligent viewer of television and a thoughtful consumer is an important lesson. You can start by limiting the amount of time Jay spends watching TV and by exercising some control over his choice of programs.

Commercials, of course, are more difficult to restrict, so I suggest a modified approach. Why not try to capitalize on Jay's interest by making it a learning experience? Ask him to select his favorite jingles and to explain to you why he thinks they're effective. Try to make him aware of the message, the intended audience, and the tone adopted by the writers. An effective ad must be credible, original, relevant, and strike a responsive emotional cord in the viewer. Do Jay's favorites meet these tests? How would he improve them?

If you can engage Jay's curiosity, you might be able to shift him from a rote memorizer of commercials to an astute student of the art and science of advertising.

Yes, even TV commercials can be made into a learning experience for your adolescent. In fact, they can be especially instructive in our consumer-oriented society.

TV vs Music

Q: Our oldest, Colleen, is 14. There's good news and bad news. The good news, less TV. The bad news, more stereo music. Comments.

A: According to a recent study, Colleen may be doing just what comes naturally. Larson, Kubey, and Colletti report in the *Journal of Youth and Adolescence* (1989) that adolescents watch less TV than pre-adolescents. The researchers conclude that this is attributable to a decrease in TV-watching done with the family, especially on weekend mornings and evenings.

Early adolescents tend to watch less TV than pre-adolescents. Many of them turn instead to popular music. The question, "Who's your favorite group?" replaces "Did you watch Cosby last night?" Make it a point to learn something about your teenager's musical preferences. You'll learn a lot about her or him in the process.

My own experience is that music becomes a powerful organizer of peer relationships among early adolescents. The question, "Who's your favorite group?" when asked by and of a teenager, is rich in context and meaning. It serves as a resumé of sorts: "Who are you? Can we be friends?"

Interestingly, the study also concluded that adolescents who frequently listen to music are those who spend more time with friends. Colleen's shift in media interest, therefore, may signal her shift from the world of family to the world of peers.

One additional tip: just as you should know your youngster's TV-viewing habits, make it a rule to learn something about her musical tastes — a valuable lesson in understanding her newly unfolding values and personality.

Quiz

Early adolescence. The time that tries parents' souls — and the time that tests everything you've ever learned about raising children. So why not try this test? A score of 80% or more won't, of course, guarantee a trouble-free time for you and your teenager, but it will mean that you're well-informed. And that's a giant step in the right direction.

1. Which one of the following is a symptom of anorexia nervosa?
    A. The 13-year-old who is always dieting
    B. Loss of 10% of body weight
    C. Disturbed body image, i.e., everyone says she's very thin, but she thinks she's "fat"

2. Anorexia nervosa (select all that apply):
    A. May require hospitalization
    B. Ten percent death rate
    C. Affects boys and girls equally

3. Your 13-year-old daughter is physically mature for her age. She wants to date a 17-year-old boy. You should:
    A. Allow it. She'll only see him secretly anyway
    B. Sympathize with her, but say "no"
    C. Invite the boy over to "check him out," then decide

4. The rebellious adolescent who is consistently out of control won't accept punishment, breaks rules at school, displays anti-social behavior, etc.:
    A. Is just going through a phase. He'll get over it
    B. Probably needs professional help

5. True or False? The 14-year-old who shows little or no rebellion at all is just repressing her normal drives. She may need help so she won't grow up to be an adult "neurotic."

6. It's very important to talk to early adolescents about sex, especially sexual values, but do most parents do it?
    A. Yes
    B. No

7. True or False? Teenagers who have had sex ed courses in high school report a higher incidence of sexual activity.

8. An adopted 13-year-old boy begins to fantasize that his "real" parents are nobility or movie stars. This means:
    A. He has an underlying anger at his adoptive parents
    B. He is compensating for his own imperfections
    C. He'll want to search for his biological parents soon

9. Your 13-year-old daughter has had the same pediatrician since birth. Now she wants to switch to another doctor. This could be due to (select all that apply):
    A. Too many young infants and children in the waiting room
    B. Her natural rebellion. Most kids switch at thirteen for this reason
    C. If her current doctor is male, she may want a female, but isn't communicating it to you

10. True or False? Effeminate behavior in a 13-year-old boy is a strong indicator of homosexuality.

11. Your 13-year-old daughter has just returned after running away from home. Which of the following factors would indicate the need for psychiatric consultation? (Select all that apply):
    A. It was her first runaway. She stayed overnight at a girlfriend's home
    B. She was gone for three days. She won't say where
    C. This is her second runaway
    D. Her grades have been slipping lately. She seems angry and upset

12. The father who continuously criticizes his daughter for wearing clothing that is "too tight" may:
    A. Be having a tough time coping with her emerging sexuality
    B. Be wrong. Teenage girls express their personalities in their clothing. He should let it go

13. True or False? Teenage girls tend to be heavier smokers than boys.

14. True or False? By age 14 most youngsters have a pretty well-defined sense of morals and should be able to stand up against peer pressure.

15. True or False? In early adolescence it is not uncommon for a girl to prefer her father over her mother, and for a boy to side with his mother against Dad. This is a temporary repetition of the "oedipal triangle" usually seen at age 3 to 5.

16. A 13-year-old girl reports to you (a family friend) that her father has been forcing her to have sex with him for the past three years. What should you do?
    A. Tell her that you'll help her. Have her stay with you. Then call Juvenile Services for advice
    B. Insist that she tell her mother about it
    C. Advise her to warn her father she'll report him to the police if it continues

17. Teenage drug abuse. Parents (select all that apply):
    A. Are often the last to know
    B. Should insist on going for help even if the youngster threatens to run away
    C. Regularly search kids' rooms to look for drugs
    D. Should not blame themselves

18. Treatment for teenage drug abuse:
    A. Is usually successful on an outpatient basis
    B. Usually requires hospital or residential treatment

19. True or False? If your 14-year-old admits to "experimenting" with alcohol or marijuana, you should seek professional consultation since there is a high likelihood of her developing a more serious problem.

20. Your 13-year-old son stayed out past his curfew. The next day you learn that he also lied to you about what he was doing. You should:
    A. Punish the curfew breaking, but not the lying
    B. Punish the lying. It's more important than the curfew
    C. Punish him for both offences
    D. Help him express his feelings

21. A classmate of your 14-year-old daughter has committed suicide. You should:
    A. Not talk about it since it might be contagious
    B. Not mention it unless your daughter brings up the subject
    C. Mention it and give your daughter a chance to talk about it

22. Sibling rivalry is normal and never really dies, but which combination of siblings tends to evolve into the friendliest relationship in later adult years?
    A. Two sisters
    B. Two brothers
    C. Brother and sister

23. The first developmental task of early adolescence, which may take the form of some apparent rebellion, is:
    A. Identity formation
    B. Conscience formation
    C. Trust
    D. Independence and autonomy

24. True or False? Thirteen and 14-year-olds generally require more sleep than 17-year-olds.

25. Teen (rock) song lyrics:
    A. Don't worry about them. Kids just listen to the music
    B. Can be a powerful influence on youngsters. Parents, therefore, should pay attention to the words as well as the music
    C. Just reflect what's going on in society. There's not much you can do about it

Correct Answers

1) C; 2) A, B; 3) B; 4) B; 5) False; 6) B; 7) False; 8) B; 9) A, C; 10) False; 11) B, C, D; 12) A; 13) True; 14) False; 15) True; 16) A; 17) A, B, D; 18) B; 19) False; 20) C; 21) C; 22) A; 23) D; 24) True; 25) B

4

Middle Adolescents (15–16)

The middle adolescent stage generally spans the years from 15 to 16, but may also include some 14-year-olds and some 17-year-olds. These are, basically, the high school years. This stage, in some ways, is analogous to the latency years, 5 to 10, that follow the tumult of the early childhood years.

The middle adolescent stage, therefore, is a time of settling down, settling in. Less conflict now. Less rebellion. More fun. The youngster has weathered the onset of puberty and has more energy to plow into things like school work. She's less self-absorbed and genuinely more interested in her family and the world around her. Her friendships, too, are more stable, and she's beginning to develop an adult-style conscience — the capacity to "stand alone," if necessary, against her peers if she disapproves of their ideas.

The middle adolescent is easier to live with — the consolation prize for Mom and Dad. But the grand prize is on the horizon; just one more important stage to go. Believe me, there is an adult-to-be lurking in there somewhere.

Discipline

Motives for Misbehavior

*There are many
explanations for why
teens misbehave.
Here are four basics:
1) attention-getting,
2) desire for power,
3) revenge, and
4) avoidance of failure.*

Q: I've read a lot of books about raising children. I guess I'm doing all right since my children (16 and 12) are doing well. My question is a little academic: What really causes children to misbehave?

A: It's an academic question, but it has a lot of practical implications. If you know why a child misbehaves, you should know how to handle it.

There are many psychological theories. Some are more relevant than others, but no theory is all-complete. Freud, for example, stressed the unconscious and the influence of child-hood experiences on adult personality. Freudian psychoanalysis remains a strong influence in American psychiatry.

Alfred Adler, on the other hand, believed that all behavior has a purpose. Adlerians believe that kids misbehave by choice rather than because of unconscious forces. Adler's disciple, Rudolf Dreikurs, identified four basic motives for misbehavior:

1) attention-getting,
2) desire for power,
3) revenge,
4) avoidance of failure.

Next time one of the kids misbehaves, stop and ask yourself: What is the hidden goal of this behavior? Then, alter your response so your child does not get what he's after. Once he learns that his old behavior no longer works, he will be forced to try something new. You hope, of course, that the "something new" is behavior on the positive side of life.

Taking Control of Misbehavior

*A pattern of serious
misbehavior calls for action.
Take control. Yes, your
teenager may fight it, but
later she'll thank you for it.*

Q: I'm a single father. I have custody of my oldest son, Ricardo, 15. Yesterday I returned home at noon to pick up a report I had forgotten. The first thing I noticed was that the car was gone. I stayed home all day, fuming. Finally Ricardo returned at 6 o'clock, parked the car, and walked right by me like I didn't exist. Frankly, I'm scared. The last time I punished him he ran away for two days. And he's always threatening to go and live with his mother, who's an alcoholic and drug addict. I feel trapped. What should I do?

A: You've got to take control — and quickly. You simply cannot allow yourself to be blackmailed and intimidated by Ricardo's threats and behavior. It will only lead to more misbehavior.

This is serious. Ricardo not only broke the law by taking the car, but he also made you vulnerable for his actions too. Such behavior is often symptomatic of hostility toward a parent.

When I observe this kind of scenario — out-of-control teen and frightened parent — I know it's time to call for help. An immediate consultation with a psychiatrist is a good place to start.

Finally, a word to other parents: Don't let this happen to you. Teens, like Ricardo, don't suddenly slip from parental control. The early warning signs are usually pretty clear. The time to get assistance is early — not late. Ricardo and his father can still be helped, but it would have been much easier a year or two ago.

Should Stepfather Discipline?

Q: We need help. I have three children, 15, 13, and 10½, from a previous marriage. After being single for seven years, I recently remarried. The problem is: Who should discipline the children? Frank, my husband, says it should be him. The kids, however, resent him and won't obey him. This upsets him so much that he doubles the punishment. Don't you think the problem can be solved if we both do the disciplining?

Stepparent as disciplinarian: Not usually a good idea, especially with teenagers. Stepparents should get respect, but they're better off leaving the discipline to the biological parent.

A: No. I believe you should be the disciplinarian. Why? Your youngsters are two teens and a pre-teen; they're at ages where discipline is tough and resentment of stepparents runs high. They are also accustomed to you (seven years, remember?)

It's a set-up for failure if Frank positions himself as the tough, take-charge disciplinarian. You should certainly consult with him on rules, punishment, etc., but you should be the one to act.

Frank's role might be that of a "good uncle" who is given due respect and courtesy, and who will be able, with time, I hope, to earn the love of his stepchildren.

The Teenage Ultimatum

The teenage ultimatum, "If you make me___, I'll___!" is a well-known phenomenon. Don't take it too seriously, and don't call their bluff. The ultimatum is really a question: "How far will you go to help me control my impulses?" Help. Take charge.

Q: My 15-year-old son always threatens me that he'll quit school or that he'll run away from home if I force him to do something that he doesn't like. I can't live with these threats. What can I do?

A: Such adolescent ultimatums are not generally threats at all. Your son is actually implying an important question when he appears to threaten you. His question goes like this: "To what extent are you prepared to go in order to set limits upon my behavior?"

Giving in to his threats only invites more limit-testing. Be gentle, be understanding, but be firm — especially where important family values are at stake.

Ultimatums: Calling Their Bluff

A potential runaway may become a "throwaway" if you call her bluff. Act immediately to locate a missing child.

Q: Our 15-year-old daughter, Laura, has not gotten along with her father for 3 or 4 years. She's threatened to run away on several occasions. One week ago my husband called her bluff. He told her to "Go ahead. Things will be a lot happier around here without you anyway." That night, while we were asleep, she left. We haven't heard from her since. My husband says not to worry; she'll be back when she runs out of money. I'm scared to death. What can I do?

A: Laura took your husband at his word. On some level she probably does feel at fault for the feud with your husband. When he called her bluff, he just rubbed her nose in her own guilt — and convinced her that he does not love her. Such are the dynamics, not of runaways, but of "throwaways."

Don't sit around waiting for Laura to return. Your husband's cavalier attitude may well mask his own guilt over what has happened. He may be too proud, or too angry, to admit that he was wrong. I would start by calling Laura's friends and notifying the local police. Additional help may be sought from the National Runaway Switchboard, 2210 N Halstead Street, Chicago, Illinois 60614.

Logical Consequences

Q: My husband insisted that our 16-year-old son quit his part-time job after he overslept on what would have been his second Saturday at work. Christopher, my husband, says that Doug has to learn "responsibility." I agree, but it seems to me that his punishment was too harsh in this case. What do you think?

A: I am definitely in favor of things like hard work, part-time jobs for teenagers, and responsibility. But I agree that your husband seems to have overreacted in this case.

First of all, why should Dad choose to tackle this problem at all? There are so many times when he will have to set limits, establish values, say "no." Why here? It seems to me that your husband may have gone out of his way to make trouble for the family and to poison the atmosphere between Doug and himself. What's more, Dad is depriving Doug of a valuable lesson in life: when you oversleep, you have to answer to your employer.

That's right. It would have been better for Dad to express his displeasure, but allow the punishment to come in the form of Doug having to go in late to work and face his boss. He might have received a reprimand or a loss of pay. He might have even lost his job. That is life teaching about life, a very powerful teacher of responsibility. More powerful even than Dad's response, and certainly without the cost of father-son conflict.

By the way, this technique is called Logical Consequences. Use it. Allow your children, whenever possible, to learn from the direct consequences of their own behavior. There does not have to be a parental solution to every problem that comes up in a youngster's life. In fact, mothers and fathers should stay out of these things as much as possible. Avoid hassles whenever you can. Keep your powder dry for the hassles that are really important and that only you as a parent should confront; when a youngster's health or safety is involved or when a core family value is at stake.

There does not have to be a parental solution (punishment) to every misbehavior. Use logical consequences, allow your teen to learn directly from the consequences of his mistakes. Let life teach about life.

Is This Logical?

Q: I like the technique of logical consequences, i.e., whenever possible, parents should let children learn directly from the consequences of their behavior. But I'm puzzled. I think my daughter is trying to use the technique against me.

Let me explain: When Kerri, 15, came to me for an advance on her allowance to attend a concert, I said, "Sorry, the logical

When using the technique of logical consequences, consider the factors of defiance, pattern, and family values. But remember to rely on your own parental understanding, self-confidence, and common sense.

consequence of spending your money so quickly is that you may not be able to buy something later in the week." I thought that was it. But Kerri's answer stumped me: "Well, OK, I'll borrow the money from my friend Jennifer. The logical consequence is that now I'll owe her money instead of you!"

I let Kerri borrow the money from Jennifer. Is it right or wrong?

A: Right or wrong? Tough to call. The answer depends on several factors:

Defiance. If you felt Kerri was acting in defiance and testing to see who's really in control, you should have forbidden her to borrow from Jennifer.

Pattern. If Kerri has established a pattern of trying to outmaneuver your disciplinary efforts, you have a problem on your hands.

Family values. If you have established a firm family value against borrowing and deficit spending, then you would have been on solid ground in saying "No."

On the other hand, children deserve consistency from parents. If you're going to change the rules, you ought to give a brief, factual explanation. In the final analysis, logical consequence is a good technique. It works. But like any technique, it's just something you use until the parent arrives. No technique will ever replace parental understanding, self-confidence, and common sense.

Toughlove

Toughlove is a shape-up-or-ship-out parenting philosophy that can work wonders with some out-of-control teens, but it is easily misused. Caution is advised.

Q: What is Toughlove and what is your opinion of it?

A: Toughlove is a philosophy designed for parents who have out-of-control teenagers. It is based on a get-tough credo that urges parents to seek support from each other, to confront teenagers, to stop being enablers of teens' misbehavior, to insist that they face the consequences of their actions, and to ultimately give them an alternative: shape up or ship out.

The fact that Toughlove groups have sprung up all around the country is proof that a great many parents want to stand up against teenage misbehavior: drug abuse, runaway, truancy, sexual promiscuity, and parent abuse too. This is a good thing. In my opinion we've paid a great price for decades of permissiveness in child raising — the if-it-feels-good-do-it mentality. It's time to save these children from their headlong dash to self-destruction.

Toughlove, however, is a mixed blessing. While its popularity is certainly calling dramatic attention to the plight of troubled teenagers, and its emphasis on parent self-help groups is laudatory, I have some problems with the approach.

First of all, Toughlove can be easily misunderstood and misapplied; some parents respond to the "tough" but not the "love." In the hands of some zealots it could become an excuse for abuse.

Secondly, it is important to realize that Toughlove should not be used as a general parenting philosophy; it is specifically useful for some families who have tried everything else with an adolescent (understanding communication, parental discipline, psychiatric consultation), but to no avail. Toughlove is the end of the line.

I also regret that the Toughlove doctrine defines a successful outcome as one in which the "family has found new ways to adapt," or in which the parents are pleased — even if the teenager has been sent packing. Unfortunately, the adolescent's adaptation is not a part of the equation.

Finally, the Toughlove formula does not take individual differences and developmental factors into consideration. Some teenagers, for example, are so negative or oppositional that they have no alternative but to "ship out" if confronted face to face by a roomful of adults — as sometimes is prescribed. Teenage bravado compels others to "save face" by continued defiance when their fragile defenses are so bluntly battered.

Toughlove is an extreme solution — that can be useful for some extreme problems. I would urge parents, however, to emphasize consistency and firm, but loving, disciplinary techniques in the early years of childhood so that drastic solutions, like Toughlove, will not be necessary in the teenage years. Remember that most out-of-control teenagers were once out-of-control children.

Divorce

Divorce: Anniversary Reaction

Q: I always get depressed on New Year's Eve. It reminds me of the good times that used to be — before my divorce eight years ago. I can't even stand to let my two teenage daughters, 16 and 19, go out to a party because I don't want to be left alone. They resent it. I can't help it.

The anniversary of a traumatic event (divorce, death of a spouse, etc.) can be very difficult. It is permissible to express your feelings to your teenagers directly, but do not overwhelm them with your problems.

A: You are suffering a form of "anniversary reaction." New Year's Eve is a sad reminder of things past. Many people suffer such reactions at this time of year.

The fact that party-goers seem to have so much fun is another reason that you probably prefer to stay home on this would-be special night. Their gaiety is a stark contrast and painful reminder of your own loneliness.

I appreciate your dilemma. It was easier to keep the girls at home in years past, but now, as teenagers, they naturally want to join their friends. The fact that you are concerned enough to write to me tells me that you do not feel good about burdening them with your private grief. Part of you, at least, realizes that you may be doing them some harm.

But I'm also concerned about you — just as I'm sure that your daughters are concerned about you too, and would probably feel guilty about leaving you at home alone if they thought they were abandoning you to your misery. It would certainly put a damper on their celebration.

Why not try to break out of the New Year's Eve blues this year? Why not go out with some friends while the girls attend their party? Or, treat the girls to an early restaurant dinner, and then allow them to join their own friends?

In other words, take care of them on this special night, but also take care of yourself.

Dress Code

Teen Dress Code

Teens dress to be like other teens — and to be different from their parents. It is symbolic of their quest for autonomy and identity. So, remember your own adolescence and give some slack — but you have a right not to let it get too outrageous.

Q: Our friends say that we shouldn't let it bother us — but it does. Our 15-year-old, Clarence, goes around looking like a slob all the time: T-shirt, torn jeans, tennis shoes (untied!). We've given up trying to influence the way he dresses when he goes out with his friends (they're sloppy too), but don't we have a right to demand appropriate attire when he's out in public with us?

A: Think back to your own adolescence. Did you dress for your parents or for your peers? If you were like most of us, you dressed according to the prevailing teenage standards of the times; you dressed for your peers.

Why? In spite of all their rhetoric to the contrary, adolescents are among the great conformists in this world. They want desperately to be just like their friends. Hence, they have their own elaborate dress code, language, music, and value system. At 15, Clarence's world has flip-flopped. Everything is changing. His insistence on dressing and acting just like his peers is actually a defense mechanism: "If I'm like everyone else, I must be OK." It's a variant of the well-known "safety in numbers" coping mechanism.

The torn jeans and untied shoelaces probably bother you most of all because you fear that they are a poor reflection on you as a parent. Relax a bit. You're in good company. Most parents go through this stage with adolescents.

But, yes, it's reasonable to set some standards and limits on Clarence's clothing. I suggest that you sit down with him and make a list of acceptable and unacceptable apparel in specific situations: church, family events, school, etc. There should also be some consequences if Clarence does not cooperate. One mother I know simply threw away her daughter's tattered jeans after she wore them to a family dinner party. Her daughter was angry, but she got the message.

So, the formula is this: be understanding, give a little slack, be reasonable, but remain in charge.

Mothers and Fathers

Formula for a Winning Family

Q: We have four children, 16, 14, 12, and 9½. We're proud of our family. We think it's a winner. How can we keep it up?

A: Winning families have a lot in common. Here are six basic features of happy, successful families based on the research of Lewis and others:

1) *Values.* Successful families know what they believe in.

2) *Power.* Parents are in control, but they are benign leaders.

3) *Closely knit.* Winning families are close, but each member is encouraged to be an individual.

4) *Problem solving.* Winning families are able to spot problems ahead of time and solve them. They are also able to seek outside help when necessary.

5) *Communication.* These families clearly share ideas and feelings. They listen to each other.

Want to make your family a winner? Follow these six steps: 1) firm values, 2) parents in control, 3) encourage individual interests, 4) solve problems, 5) communicate facts and feelings, listen well, 6) laugh together.

6) *Feeling tone.* The atmosphere is usually warm and optimistic. Winning families also share a good sense of humor; they laugh together.

Still think your family is a winner? I hope so.

Use Empathy

In my opinion, empathy is the single best quality for a mother or father to possess: to hear with a youngster's ears, to see with her eyes, to feel with her heart. If you've got it, you don't need much else to be a successful parent.

Q: I've had it. Marti, our 16-year-old, is impossible. She'll come into the house all upset and when I ask, "What's wrong?" she snaps, "Nothing," and runs up to her room, shouting at me all the way. Any suggestions?

A: Use empathy. Forget the facts, go for the feelings. Instead of asking, "What's wrong?" you might simply say, "It must be pretty tough," or say nothing at all, just reach out and give Marti a hug.

Empathy is the ability to feel with another person. Empathy is the ability to hear with another person's ears, to see with another's eyes, to feel with another's heart. When it happens, it's one of the most powerful communications two people can ever experience.

So next time, try to put yourself in Marti's shoes. Dare to feel what she feels. Communicate it to her. She'll feel understood, supported, relieved. Sooner or later, the facts will come out too.

Parent Abuse

Physical abuse of teenagers against parents is not a rare event. Sniff it out immediately. Do not let it escalate. Seek help if necessary.

Q: Please help. My 15-year-old son, Richard, has been beating me up for the past 3 years. It started with insults, slapping, and spitting in my face. Last week he kicked me in the stomach. Yesterday he showed me a knife, and swore that he'll cut on me if I "hassle" him. I'm afraid to tell his father about any of this because my husband is always looking for excuses to beat up on Richard. Next time, I'm afraid they'll kill each other. What should I do?

A: You need help and you need it fast. Richard's violence is escalating. He's warning you that he's out of control. Everyone in the house is in danger.

You, for example, have let yourself become a willing victim. Your explanation is that you've done it to protect Richard and his father from each other! A perilous bargain.

The root cause of the trouble may be your husband's own violence toward Richard. And I wonder, by the way, if your husband has been violent toward you? Children who engage in violence toward a parent usually pick on mothers rather than fathers. There are many reasons for this, but one fairly consistent fact is that they pick up the cues from what they see happening between Mom and Dad.

Parent abuse is not uncommon. A recent study revealed that 9% of youngsters are guilty of at least one aggressive act against a parent each year. Once unleashed, these attacks tend to grow more ugly and more serious.

Believe me, you may be sitting on a time bomb. Don't wait for disaster to strike. Get help. A local psychiatrist, a mental health clinic, or an agency such as Family Protective Service should be able to help. Be prepared for a recommendation that Richard and/or his father may have to move out of the house temporarily, as a safety measure, until the conflict can be resolved. Don't delay.

Teenage Bedroom Is Pleasure Palace

Q: I blame my husband. My husband blames my daughter. And my daughter blames everybody.

Here's my problem: Kandy, 15, won't come out of her room. She's up there every spare minute she's got. I blame my husband because he's bought her a stereo, a TV, and a telephone — all of which, of course, are in her room. I don't think it's healthy. I think she ought to spend time with the rest of the family, right?

Yes, teenagers need privacy, but if their bedrooms are outfitted as pleasure palaces (TV, stereo, phones, etc.) you may see them only for meals.

A: I can see it now. Kandy ensconced in her Pleasure Palace: stereo, TV, telephone. What 15-year-old could ask for more?

I'm not generally in favor of stereo, TV, or telephone in a teen's bedroom. Just as you're learning, it can lead to seclusion and avoidance.

My advice: move the high-tech to another room, unless you can work out a deal with Kandy that she must be out of her room at certain designated times.

Privacy: Read Her Diary?

Q: Last night while our daughter Sherrie, 16, was at choir practice, I caught my husband in her room reading her diary. He was embarrassed, but said that he had a right to do it since he had to know what she's up to. I think it's wrong. What do you think?

Do not violate your teenager's privacy without cause. The trust you will lose isn't worth it.

A: I agree with you. First of all, privacy is a very important commodity to teenagers. They need it for many reasons, including its value as a method of establishing personal identity.

Secondly, the parent who violates a teenager's sense of privacy, without cause, risks damaging the critical sense of trust that you must maintain with your children.

I do not subscribe, however, to the notion of privacy at all costs. For example, a teen who violates family values (drugs, sex, etc.) has probably jeopardized his right to privacy, at least to some degree, until he can reestablish his parents' trust in him.

But Sherrie? Seems to me that Dad is the guilty party.

Why not pursue a middle course? If there's something Dad wants to know, why not sit down with Sherrie and ask her face to face?

Stay-At-Home Mothers: A Defense

No need to be defensive about being a stay-at-home mother even in these days of women in the corporate boardroom. Parenting is still the most important job a woman (or man) ever had.

Q: I'm a housewife and I've always been proud of it. I never felt I had to "find myself" in the career world and, fortunately, I have not been forced to go to work out of financial necessity. I've enjoyed the full-time job of being a wife and mother because I've felt the job satisfaction was high. Imagine my shock when my 15-year-old daughter turned from a TV program on "Women of Achievement" and asked me matter-of-factly: "Mommy, why did you grow up to be nothing?"

A: The most important job anyone ever has in this world is the job of being a parent. While women should certainly be free to pursue success in the world that has long been the exclusive preserve of men, those, like yourself, who choose to be full-time mothers should not be made to feel they're somehow wasting their lives away on diapers, dishpans, and den-mothering.

Yet you are too often the unintended victim of these "Successful Women" programs. If success spells business or career and the kids see Mom not in a gray flannel suit, but in an apron; not wielding an attaché case, but lugging the wash up from the basement; they may, in their naiveté, ask some penetrating questions.

While your daughter's question obviously threw you for a loop, I hope you were not intimidated and that you did not become defensive. In fact, you can use her question as the springboard for a good talk with her. She is, on another level, asking a question about herself: "What will I grow up to be? What are my possibilities? What does Mom want for me?" She is growing up into a world of expanded opportunity and increased complexity for women. It is a mixed blessing. Whichever way you cut it, the career woman, the full-time stay-at-home mother, and the working mother all face unique demands and conflicts. Your daughter will need your help in sorting it all out.

Deborah Fallows of Washington attempted to sort it out in an article entitled: "The Myth of the 'Successful Woman' — and the Costs It Neglects." Herself a successful careerist who decided to devote full-time to raising her two children, she complains that "there is a narrow-mindedness, ignorance, condescension, and indifference about motherhood." She ends her thought-provoking article by concluding that "if the success of women is to be judged in terms of performance at work alone, then the contest we're all in becomes as trivial and silly as a beauty pageant — and the rewards as meaningless, elusive, and above all, temporary."

Money and Allowance

It's My Money!

Q: Our 16-year-old, Lara, has been on a fashion jag — and it's breaking the family bank. Her latest extravagance was a $100 pair of boots that she charged to my account. I got so furious that I told her she had to get a job; she'd have to pay out of her own pocket if she insisted on throwing money away. I thought my troubles were over, but they were only beginning. You see, Lara got a job. She earns $90 a week, and she insists that it's her money, to do with as she pleases. I feel trapped. I did tell her to get a job, but somehow I feel that $90 a week is too much money for a 16-year-old to throw around. Do you agree?

A: Yes. Don't let yourself be trapped. Go with your best judgement. There is a great deal at stake here. You have an obligation to teach Lara proper money management. It's an important lesson in growing up.

I'd suggest that Lara turn her checks over to you as a custodian. You could then reimburse her an adequate weekly allowance to cover her reasonable expenses. Let her participate in pegging the amount. The remainder of Lara's earnings could go into a savings account for college or when she turns 18.

Middle adolescents should be pretty reliable at handling money, but it's a mistake to give them too much of a good thing. Even money they earn at a part-time job should be at least partially controlled by parents.

Friends and Dating

Boyfriend in Bedroom?

There are limits to privacy. Enforce them. Entertaining the opposite sex in the bedroom should not be a prerogative of middle adolescence.

Q: My 15-year-old daughter insists that she has a right to invite her boyfriend up to her room and to close the door. She says it's her right to privacy. My husband and I have let it go on two occasions, but we're unsettled about it.

A: The Bill of Rights of most teenagers would probably begin: "Leave me alone." But don't take it too seriously. Your daughter may be testing you. She knows that any "rights" she may have flow directly from your own responsibility as a parent.

Follow your instincts. They're right on target in this matter. Two teenagers in a bedroom behind closed doors — with the tacit approval of parents — is not a good combination.

Does Mom's Divorce Cause Daughter's Boy Problems?

Parental divorce can have a powerful effect on how a teenager relates to the opposite sex. Watch the early dating years carefully. Talk about problems.

Q: I'm the twice-divorced mother of a daughter, age 15. Tammy's father left me when she was a baby, and I've never mentioned him to her. My second husband and I were married for six years, but we split last fall. Tammy loves him, but he doesn't even return her phone calls. In the past she's taken out her anger on me, but now there's a new twist: she takes it out on her boyfriends. She's very pretty and the boys flock to her, but she ends up trashing them. I'm worried. What should I do?

A: Tammy probably feels abandoned and "trashed" by her father and stepfather. Down deep, she may well feel there's something unlovable about her, and now she's in a position to turn the tables: she will be the one to do the trashing. Consciously or unconsciously, her game is now Revenge.

Tammy needs therapy, not to help her get along better with boys, but to help her feel better about herself. The "family secret" about her father will also have to be unearthed as she gets in touch with a host of feelings about her past, her present, and her future.

Mom's Chasing Daughter's Boyfriend

Q: My 16-year-old niece, Leslie, broke up with her boyfriend, Jack, 17, three months ago. No problem — except, ever since then, her mother has been inviting Jack to the house. She says she likes Jack, they're friends, and she's ashamed of how Leslie treated him. Recently she bought Jack a computer, and now says that she's going to help him buy a car. What's going on? Seems to me that Mom is chasing Jack. It gives me shivers.

Mothers (and fathers) must preserve the generational boundary with their teen's boyfriends (or girlfriends). Competition for the friend's attention signals serious problems.

A: Mom's behavior is certainly inappropriate and unacceptable. No matter how she may rationalize it, she has, at the very least, gone beyond the boundaries of good parental judgement.

If she was disappointed in Leslie's treatment of Jack, a good mother-daughter talk would have been sufficient. Now Mom has blurred the generational boundaries by calling Jack her "friend," and perhaps even treating him better than she does her own daughter.

Why is this happening? Hard to say. There are many possibilities. Among them: Mom's own immaturity, naiveté, or lack of judgement; competition with Leslie; acting out of anger against Leslie; acting out of her own impulses or fantasies.

Whatever the reasons, Mom's behavior must stop. It's bad for Leslie, for Jack, and for Leslie's mother too.

Extravagant Gifts

Q: Our 13-year-old son, Andrew, wants to buy his girlfriend a diamond ring for Valentine's Day. My husband and I think he's going overboard. We've tried to talk him out of it, but he's insistent. He says it's his money, which it is, and that we're just trying to break up his relationship with Tammy. What should we do?

Mid-adolescents want to be adults. Buying a friend extravagant gifts may become their ticket of admission to adulthood. It can also cover up low self-esteem.

A: Yes, it sounds like Cupid's arrow has zapped Andrew good. He'll need your gentle, but firm, understanding to cure him of this case of adolescent romanticism.

Do not let Andrew paint you into a corner. It sounds to me like you're objecting only to the lavishness of the gift, not to Andrew's choice of Tammy. As far as the cost of the diamond is concerned, have you had a policy about Andrew's access to his savings? Frankly, it is not a good idea to lead youngsters to believe that money deposited from birthdays, part-time jobs, etc., is entirely at their discretion; it can lead to problems for 15-year-olds on Valentine's Day.

Andrew wants to be taken seriously. Try to understand his predicament. Why the grand gesture? Is he unsure of himself with Tammy? If so, it is better for him to learn, at 15, that diamonds will not solve the problem. Help him to examine his motives and to settle on a personalized gift that will be really "special" for his girlfriend. You'll be better off setting a dollar limit on how much he can spend for Tammy's gift than on dictating what he should buy her instead of the diamond. Basically, Andrew just wants Tammy to be his Valentine.

Preppie, Jock, or Freak

Teenagers want to belong. Cliques offer a handy, though temporary, solution to the problem. Clique membership is like trying on a suit of psychological armor.

Q: Our 15-year-old daughter, Kelly, doesn't seem to fit in with any of the cliques at her school. She complains that she's not a "preppie," not a "jock," and not a "freak." The interesting thing is that Kelly is comfortable with all of these groups. The kids accept her, but she just can't exclusively identify with any single one of them. It bothers her.

A: Every American high school has its well-defined cliques. This phenomenon of group identity goes with the territory of middle adolescence. The major attraction is that it allows youngsters who feel unsure of their emerging values and personalities to latch onto an instant identification. It takes some of the anxiety out of their uncertainty. It removes some pain. It serves as a defense — but only temporarily. As youngsters continue to develop, they tend to discard one clique or label for another, like trying on a new suit of psychological armor. This process continues until a young person is able to stand apart from peer groups and say, "This is who I am" — until he can define himself as an individual, not as part of Group X, Y, or Z.

Kelly's identity at this time might be that of a teenager who doesn't really need a group. It seems that she would be welcomed if she chose. I'm encouraged by her ability to transcend the sometimes impenetrable boundaries of these adolescent enclaves. Kelly's only real problem may well be that she's a little further along in her psychological development than most of her friends — always a mixed blessing if you're a teenager.

New Wave Teenagers

Theater of the absurd, teenage style, designed to turn you off and tune you out.

Q: My sister and brother-in-law came to visit last weekend. They warned us in advance that my niece, Suzanne, 16, was "different." They didn't warn me enough. Pink hair with blue spikes, four earrings in each ear, leather. It would have been bad enough if it was Halloween. She says she's New Wave. What is it? She wouldn't tell us. I guess she thought we were really out of it. Actually, her parents don't know much about it. And they're not in favor of it either. They say it's like a modern Beatnik. Does it mean she does drugs? What is it?

A: Labels are notoriously uncertain where teenage fads are concerned. By the time the adult world understands them, the kids have dropped them and moved on to something else. Suzanne's coiffure and dress sound Punk: the badge of identity that distinguishes her musical tastes. New Wave is a term that identifies young people who rebel against the system. Their beliefs are sometimes vague and contradictory — part of the paradox of the movement's appeal. Many New Wave youngsters, for example, are fans of hi-tech. They shun health food for junk food and artificial foods. They identify with rock music videos. For some it's a theater of the absurd. They hold a mirror to society (or to their vision of society) and reflect it back to the world in all its garish and grotesque excesses.

Drugs? Don't jump to conclusions. Many of these youngsters do not use drugs.

What should Suzanne's parents do? I'm struck that, while they're not in favor of her new look, and they're uncertain about its philosophical meaning, they obviously allow her to dress like a Punker. I believe they should be more consistent. If they do indeed feel strongly about this issue, they should enforce some kind of reasonable dress code on Suzanne. It's a matter of family values, good discipline, and parental control.

Should other parents allow their teenagers to dress like Suzanne? I don't think so. Youth does have a certain duty to rebel, but not to deface themselves in the process. A thoughtful challenge of adult values can be growth inducing. But pink hair with blue spikes won't get you taken very seriously.

Druggie Friends

Q: Jesse, our son, is 15. Oh, he's had his ups and downs, but basically he's a good kid. The thing that troubles me is not Jesse, it's his friends.

They look like dope fiends. He admits to me that they use marijuana, but he insists that he has never tried it. "Get away from them," I tell him. But he won't listen. What do you think? Won't these guys lead him astray?

"OK, so my friends use marijuana, but I don't." Don't believe it.

A: Teen drug users tend to hang together. It's unusual for a dedicated non-user (as Jesse claims to be) to truly be part of a druggie inner circle. It's possible, of course, that Jesse is telling you the truth, but I'd advise you to keep your eyes wide open. Will Jesse's "friends" lead him astray? Hard to say. But I doubt they'll do him much good.

Apparently you agree. You've told Jesse to stay away from these youngsters, but I take it that your warnings have gone unheeded. Why? Were you serious? Did you tell Jesse what would happen if he continues to associate with these marijuana users?

My advice: have a very serious talk with your son. Tell him that you trust him, but that you just don't trust his friends. Be straight with him. Tell him that, as his parent, you simply cannot allow him to jeopardize his health and safety by associating with "friends" who do drugs. Tell him that you realize that you can't follow him around twenty-four hours a day policing his friendships, so you'll rely on him to follow your rules. If he doesn't, there will be some consequences, such as loss of privileges.

At this point, of course, you're probably saying, "Sure, doctor, but what if he continues to hang out with those guys and simply hides it from me?" He may. But at least you're giving him clear guidance and something to think about. The rest is up to him.

But don't let down your guard. Observe Jesse's behavior, attitude, grades, and other indicators. Don't be a private eye about it — but don't avert your eyes either. There's too much at stake.

Confidants of Teens

A middle adolescent's closest confidant is usually a friend of the same sex. Don't fret about being displaced as your youngster's best friend. Your proper role is to be a parent — first, last, and always.

Q: I guess I knew it was coming, but it still bothers me. I've always been a best friend to my daughter, Wendy, 15. We seem to be growing apart, and I asked her about it last week. After some prodding, she finally admitted that her friend Missy is now her closest confidant — that she tells Missy things that she can't tell me. Have I done something wrong?

A: Probably not. As you mention, you knew it was coming. Most teenagers gradually come under the influence of peers. It's a natural part of growing up.

A recent survey of 1,370 adolescent girls, conducted by Who's Who Among American High School Students, confirms the fact. Respondents were asked to identify their chief confidants. The results:

Female friends
38%

Mother
27%

Boyfriend
13%

Other
6%

Sister
8%

Nobody
3%

Brother
5%

What can you do? Be a mother, first, last, and always. Be open, receptive, and as non-judgmental as possible. Be friendly. But don't expect to be Wendy's best friend.

Teenage Telephonitis

Q: My husband and I probably have more battles with Katie, our 15-year-old, over her extensive use of the telephone than over chores, curfew, homework, and everything else combined. Why are teenagers such phone junkies?

A: The telephone is important in a youngster's psychological development. To young children, for example, it is a symbol of the adult world. Learning how to dial on your own is a big deal, and something of a minor rite of passage.

To teenagers, however, the telephone takes on much richer meaning. It is a very real link to the world of peers; a ready reminder that friends are just seven digits away. In this sense, the telephone is an important psychological device. This explains why teenagers usually react so fiercely to punishment that restricts them from the telephone; their open line to the adolescent world of peers is severed and they are yanked, momentarily, back into the childhood world of family.

The telephone also allows for instantaneous, impulsive communication, the perfect device for impulsive adolescents. I bet Katie sometimes calls friends just minutes after she has left them on the school bus.

The telephone, curiously, is an intimate means of communication since it puts the parties, literally, ear-to-ear and mouth-to-mouth, but it also allows for psychological distancing. Many teenagers, like adults, are more comfortable on the telephone than in face-to-face conversation. Adolescents,

The telephone is more than just a means of communication to teenagers. It has rich, complex meaning in the making and sustaining of friendships.

227

especially, find that personal subjects are better handled by phone. How many times I've overheard teenagers say, "Let's not get into it now. I'll talk to you about it tonight on the phone."

Finally, the telephone is single-channel, e.g., it is limited to the spoken voice: auditory communication. Since adolescents, like Katie, are developing their ability to express themselves verbally, the telephone is a kind of communications laboratory.

I hope Katie's telephonitis is under control. I also hope that you now have a greater understanding of what "I'll call you!" means to a teenager.

Ski Weekend

Coed weekend outings are a sign of the times. A good experience for mid-teens — with chaperones and proper rules.

Q: "But everyone's going." Those are the words of Bette, our 15-year-old. She wants to go with her friends on an unchaperoned ski weekend. We're against it. What do you think?

A: It was unheard of when we were kids, but today's teens are more accustomed to such activities. Still, I'm not in favor of it without qualifications.

Here are my guidelines:

1) *Chaperones.* At least two adult chaperones for every six teenagers.

2) *Planning meeting.* All the youngsters and their parents should have a meeting before the event to get to know each other.

3) *The rules.* Expectations about behavior, curfew, drinking, etc., should be clear. Consequences for infractions should also be clear.

4) *Keep in touch.* Each teenager should call home at least once during the weekend at a prearranged time.

5) *Have fun.*

Teen Trashing

Teen parties can easily get out of hand. They can, and must, be properly supervised by adults.

Q: Last week while my neighbors were away, their 16-year-old son had a party. I couldn't believe it. There must have been 200 kids there. We finally called the police, but it was too late. Those teenagers did about $10,000 damage to the house. My own daughter, 15, says this has happened before. What goes on? A new fad?

A: Teen parties, in many communities, are getting out of hand. What usually happens is that the host (or hostess) volunteers his (or her) home while Mom and Dad are away. Although he may only invite a few friends, the word quickly gets around and the party is crashed, with or without the host's implied permission. When you mix in alcohol or drugs, the result can be what's being called trashing.

The solution: better informed parents, better supervised teenagers, and yes, alert neighbors.

Hobbies, Sports, and Other Interests

Teens and Jobs

Q: "I want a job!" It's become a battle cry for our 16-year-old son Ricky. We're not dead set against it, but we are afraid that if Ricky does take on a part-time job, his school work will suffer. He, of course, promises that his grades will actually improve if he gets a job since he'd be "more motivated." What do you think? Should we let him take a job contingent on his grades?

A: "Get a job." Remember that old rock 'n roll number from our adolescent days? It was a big hit. And why not? Jobs and teenagers have gone together for years. Getting a job is a rite of passage for many adolescents, a passport into the adult world.

There are other reasons why jobs are so important to teenagers. Some kids, especially if they're not academically or athletically gifted, define themselves through their jobs. Their work proclaims who they are to their peers. It's a matter of identity. Other youngsters only feel good about themselves if they have a lot of money to throw around. Their equation is: job = money = self-esteem. This is dangerous, of course.

And, finally, there's the matter of financial necessity. Some boys and girls have to work to help support the family or to save for college. They're among the real unsung heroes and heroines in my book.

So, which category is it for Ricky? Understanding his motivation should help you decide. But don't fall for his promise of motivation if you let him get a job. School performance should not be contingent on anything. Sounds like he's holding it up for ransom.

Getting a job is another rite of passage for many middle adolescents. Should you allow it? Watch the bottom line: school performance, health, wholesome peer and family activities. If your son or daughter can fit a job into that mix, I see no problem. But what's the real motivation for a job?

Fast-Food Job?

Part-time teen jobs can teach responsibility and self-reliance. The best ones expose adolescents to new interests and healthy adult role models, and build genuine new skills. Take a close look at any potential job for your teen, and discuss it with her.

Q: Gerri, our 16-year-old, is badgering us about getting an after-school job at a local fast-food restaurant. We're not in favor of it. We want her to concentrate on school, and she doesn't need the money. Her answer is that a job would be educational for her and teach her more responsibility. She thinks she's got us there. What do you think?

A: Careful. Most teen jobs in fast-food factories do not impart many lasting skills that can be directly translated into educational gains. How long does it take to learn to operate a cash register or a milk shake machine? And, once you've learned the new "skill," what then? What new career path has suddenly opened to you?

No, I don't think Gerri's argument cuts much mustard, or french fries either, for that matter.

But, on the other hand, I am in favor of part-time jobs for teens as long as the work does not interfere with school and other important aspects of their lives such as friends and family.

The best jobs, by the way, are those that expose adolescents to new interests, healthy adult role models, and that build genuine new skills that can be further developed later in life.

Gerri is right about one thing. Teen jobs can teach responsibility and self-reliance. For many adolescents, a part-time job is a rite of passage into the adult world. If all her friends are working, Gerri may feel left out. Why not talk it over with her?

Nursing Home Volunteer

Volunteerism, a healthy alternative to a paying job, is an important value in our society. Middle adolescence is a good time to experience it.

Q: My daughter's school is starting a volunteer program at a local nursing home. The kids will spend time talking to the residents so they won't be so lonely. Bree, 15, wants to do it, but I'm afraid it will be too depressing. What do you think?

A: There are several such programs around the country. The word I get is that they're generally quite successful. Both the residents and the teenagers report that they get something out of them.

From a developmental standpoint, I believe that adolescents fifteen and older do best, since they are less self-absorbed than early teens and are beginning to deal with broader issues, such as growing up and growing old.

Maybe you're trying to shield Bree too much. Let her try it for a fixed number of visits. If she doesn't like it, she should be able to quit.

Is Winning Everything?

Q: Our son is 15. His baseball coach stresses the win-at-all-costs mentality. It really has David and his teammates stressed out. What is your opinion?

A: It's better to win than to lose, but winning isn't everything. A better philosophy for baseball (and for life) is to practice hard, play to your top potential, plan to win within the rules, and let the chips fall where they will. If you win, be gracious in victory. If you lose, be gracious in defeat, knowing that you can hold your head high because you gave it your best shot.

I think you and the other parents should have a talk with the coach. Not only is he stressing his players, but he's failing in his role as a teacher of baseball — and of life.

If you keep score, it's better to win than to lose. But learning how to play to your potential and to be a gracious loser is important too.

High School Football

Q: Kyle, our 15-year-old, is determined to go out for football next year. My husband and I are both against the idea. It's just too dangerous. We tell him this, but, of course, he doesn't listen. Can you give us any facts to build our case?

A: I'm not interested in teaming up against Kyle. There may be some very good reasons for his wanting to be part of the squad: camaraderie, competition, physical fitness, the team experience, peer pressure, self-esteem — to name a few.

Yet, what you say has more than just a grain of truth to it. Football can be dangerous.

Researchers at Penn State University recently concluded a 12-year study of 2,730 players. These players sustained 2,186 injuries and were out of action for 11,730 days. Knee injuries were the most common. Ankle injuries were next.

One alarming finding was that the injury rate appears to be on the upswing. Between the first half of the study and the final six years, the injury rate increased 27%. Why? Players are getting bigger and stronger and, say some, the sport itself is getting more violent.

In fact, the team physician who conducted the study has suggested that schools should stamp a Surgeon General's

High school football injuries are apparently on the upswing, but most teen boys still find the advantages outweigh the disadvantages.

warning on footballs: "This game may be hazardous to your health."

You requested some facts and I've tried to provide them. But I'm a football fan, and I'd like to add that most experts believe that injuries can be reduced by better conditioning, coaching, officiating, and equipment.

Car Crazy

The automobile, like no other symbol, represents adult-like freedom to mid-teens. A gentle reminder is in order; with privileges come responsibilities.

Q: Our 15-year-old son, Donald, is obsessed with getting his driver's license next year and with saving enough money to buy his own car. It's all he talks about. Why is he so car crazy?

A: The driver's license and the car have replaced things like fertility ceremonies, Bar Mitzvahs, and Confirmation as the real rites of passage for today's teenagers. The automobile represents, for most US adolescents, the symbol of entry into the adult world.

No wonder Donald is so anxious to get behind the wheel. The state grants a large measure of responsibility and privilege to him when he is handed that little piece of paper that entitles him to take a powerful machine out on the highway. Donald's ability to drive a car will demonstrate to him and to his world that he is achieving mastery and competence — two vital ingredients in the growing-up process. Donald's intensity about having his own car may indicate his need for the car to be a symbolic projection of himself, maybe with its own special body work and other frills, that will shout for all to hear: "Look. This is me. I'm one of a kind. I'm grown up. I'm free."

Donald and many other boys and girls do learn a lot about growing up from automobiles. The lesson, however, isn't one of carburetors and chrome — it is a lesson that with adulthood freedoms go adulthood responsibilities. Be sure that this gets built into the equation and Don should have miles and miles of happy highways.

A New Car

When driving a car is a privilege that can be earned, your teen has the opportunity to learn and grow. Try working out a specific plan for use of that prized automobile.

Q: We have a daughter, Marcy. Her grandfather had promised her he would buy her a car when she turned 16. Well, she's 16 now, and Grandpa made good on his word. The car is parked in our driveway. But my husband and I don't think Marcy is ready to have her own car. She's just not responsible. Her grades are poor. She won't study. And she doesn't listen to us. We've got a problem. Marcy and her grandfather insist they had a deal, and that we shouldn't intervene. What do you say?

A: Intervene. Grandpa's good intentions will only compound your problems. It's important for you, as Marcy's parents, to be in charge.

Why not use the car as a behavioral lever? Sit down and work out a plan with Marcy. She can have the car in two or three months if her grades and behavior improve. Be specific. And be clear that Marcy must continue to demonstrate responsibility after she's earned the privilege of the car, or you'll have to take her wheels away from her. In other words, it's up to her. Give her a chance to intervene on her own behalf.

Hard Rock

Q: Our 16-year-old daughter, Rachel, is into hard rock. My husband and I object to it because of its emphasis on drugs and sex. But the more we object, the more Rachel persists. Are we off base? What should we do?

I know it may be tough, but do listen to the music. Study the lyrics. Your youngster's choice of music will teach you a lot about her.

A: The adolescent's world, in some respects, is supposed to be foreign terrain to mothers and fathers. Music and lyrics that sound like so much cacophony to adult ears are all the more appealing to teenagers because they have succeeded in offending adults — thus keeping them out of a corner of the teen domain.

Rachel may be attempting to define herself in opposition to your own tastes. This is not so bad. Many teenagers go through such a phase. Your concern, however, goes beyond mere taste to substantive matters, like values and behavior.

What is the real signal of Rachel's infatuation with rock? This question calls for a reasoned discussion between her and you. Forget the music for a moment. How is Rachel doing in her life? Is she happy? Is she reasonably obedient? Is she doing her best in school? Does she have interests beyond rock music? Does she have good friends? After answering these questions, look to the broader horizon of her values. Don't talk around your real worries. Get them out of the closet. It's not the music you object to, it's sex and drugs, and the wrong friends. Be honest. Give Rachel a chance to express herself without condemning her.

In other words, lend your ears to Rachel. If she's in trouble, it's probably not caused by the rock 'n roll beat at all, but because she's dancing to the beat of her very own drummer.

Hard Rock and Teen Suicide

Talking to a teen about his choice of music will help you understand his feelings. Music is one of many influences, though. Be sure to also keep an eye on things like his behavior, choice of friends, interests, grades, and physical health.

Q: Our 16-year-old, Nino, is a very moody boy. He spends a lot of time alone in his room listening to rock music. A neighbor told me yesterday that the parents of a teenager in California are suing a rock group because their son took his own life after listening to their song about suicide. What should I do? Is this music so powerful?

A: It's powerful, but not that powerful. There are many factors that contribute to teen suicides: family history of suicide, drugs and alcohol, depression, and isolation, to name a few of the more lethal predictors. Rock music that glorifies or encourages a suicidal solution, however, can create a deadly environment in which a teen may be more likely to act upon his own dark impulses.

Recent research by psychiatrist Donald Tashijian and music therapist John Sappington suggests that a teen's choice of a specific sub-type of rock 'n roll may predict his or her problems:

Acid rock: Anger and deep-seated conflict.

Heavy metal: Isolation.

Folk rock: Poor self-image, poor communication with parents.

Nino's moodiness and isolation may, of course, be within the limits of normal behavior. It's hard to say for sure. So, begin by asking him about his feelings. Throw him a communication lifeline. Then, keep an eye on things like his behavior, choice of friends, interests, attitude, grades, and his physical health too. Changes for the worse in two or more of these factors should alert you to seek a consultation.

One more thing: talk to Nino about his choice of music. It may sound like so much noise to your ears, but remember, it may well reflect what's going on in your son's head.

Psychiatric and Behavioral Problems

Don't Wait for Motivation

Most teenagers can easily think of two dozen things they would rather do than see a psychiatrist.

Q: Our 15-year-old son, Steven, is really in trouble. He's skipping school regularly, he gets high two or three times a week, he stays out all night whenever he pleases. The worst thing is his open defiance of my husband and me. We have totally lost control. We took him to a therapist last month, but Steven just sat there and wouldn't say a word. The therapist sympathized with us, but said that there's nothing he can do until Steven gets "motivated for treatment." In the meantime our son is ruining his life and ours. How do we get him motivated?

Therefore, waiting for a troubled teen to get motivated for therapy on his own does not usually work. Don't wait for him to hit bottom, take the bottom to him. Make sure he gets the help he needs.

A: You may wait a long, long time before Steven is able to admit that he needs help. Don't count on him to suddenly admit that he has a problem. The very nature of his psychological problem is probably working against it.

The therapist obviously subscribes to a philosophy that works with many adults and those few adolescents who are sufficiently self-observant that they can admit their own flaws.

Steven needs more active interaction at this time. Look for a psychiatrist who specializes in treating adolescents, and who takes a harder line. Such a therapist will be able to advise you on how to make sure Steven gets the kind of help he obviously needs.

Let's not wait for Steven to get motivated. Look on his problem like a ride on an elevator. He doesn't have to hit bottom. He can get out on any floor he (with your help) chooses. In essence, I advise you to take the bottom to him. Make sure he gets help.

Family Therapy

Q: I'm not a psychiatrist or anything, but I think I've figured out my nephew's problem. It's his parents. Danny is 15 and he's been in trouble for years: poor grades, trouble with the law, you name it. His parents have a terrible marriage. They can't agree on anything, except Danny. In fact, the only time they really ever spend time together is with principals, psychiatrists, or probation officers — all for Danny's benefit, of course. Danny is deathly afraid that his parents will get divorced and that, I think, is the clue. Is it possible that he stays in trouble just so his parents will stay together?

Parental involvement of some kind is always crucial to psychotherapy with adolescents. At times, the family itself becomes the focus of treatment. It is especially useful in establishing new patterns of healthy interaction.

A: You may have something here. It is not unusual for children to be the glue that binds a tenuous marriage. Sometimes this can take the form of misbehavior that is unconsciously designed to pull Mom and Dad closer together. It is, of course, a poor solution to the problem but, perhaps, the only one available to a desperate youngster. Sometimes one or both parents participate in this charade; they unconsciously perpetuate the child's behavior problems because they realize it's all they've got. They'd rather have a youngster with problems than a broken marriage. Not a good deal for anyone. The solution: family therapy.

Group Therapy

Adolescents grow in groups. Therefore, group therapy is a natural for them, despite the misgivings that some parents have about it.

Q: A psychiatrist has recently recommended group therapy for our 15-year-old daughter. We do not object to therapy. She needs it. But we've got some worries about the group. How can other kids with problems help our daughter? Won't she catch some of the problems of the other boys and girls? Will they talk about her to the other kids at school?

A: Your questions are entirely legitimate. First, let me say that the choice of treatment (individual, family, group) is a crucial clinical decision. You can assume that the doctor considered the advantages and disadvantages of each approach before recommending the group. Yet, you have every right to ask why he specifically believes that group therapy is the most appropriate treatment plan for your daughter.

The other youngsters in the group are probably struggling with a wide variety of problems. Some of them may have strengths in areas where your daughter is weak. They can help her. At the same time, your daughter will have the opportunity to reach out and help other youngsters in the group. Adolescents grow in groups because they are so peer-related. A well-functioning adolescent group is a powerful therapeutic tool.

While your daughter may temporarily pick up some bad habits, she will not develop the illnesses of the other group members. And remember, she is also susceptible to catching some good habits too!

Confidentiality is a must for all therapy groups. The psychiatrist will insist upon it. The most powerful motivator, for the other youngsters not to spread stories about your daughter is that they know she could easily retaliate. Call it a kind of therapeutic détente.

Psychiatric Hospitalization

The course of last resort, hospitalization is the most intense and powerful treatment in adolescent

Q: We have just learned that Jessica, our 15-year-old niece, has been in a private psychiatric hospital for the past five months. We knew she was having problems (running away, drug abuse, etc.), but we didn't realize it was so serious. Isn't five months a very long time to be in a hospital?

A: It must seem a long time to anyone unfamiliar with psychiatric hospital treatment. And it may even feel like forever to a 15-year-old, but a hospitalization of five months is actually not considered very long for those youngsters who require this type of intensive treatment. Adolescents generally require much longer hospital stays than adults because of several factors:

    1) unlike adults, they may not have a memory of what it's like to be well,

    2) they lack the life experience and personality strengths to solve problems quickly,

    3) they're less likely to admit to having problems,

    4) they generally go through a lengthy resistance phase before accepting therapy,

    5) the treatment is much more complex, involving the family, school, and a number of specialists in adolescent psychiatry.

    While I'm pleased to learn that your niece is receiving treatment, and I hope it's going well, I'm concerned that you just recently learned of her hospitalization. Why were you left in the dark? I hope Jessica's parents were not ashamed to tell you earlier. Such secrets and silence only add to the stigma of psychiatric illness. Jessica needs everyone's love and support.

psychiatry. But be forewarned: teenagers usually require longer hospital stays than adults.

Ink Blots

Q: What can you learn from ink blots? That's what I want to know. Our 15-year-old daughter just had psychological testing and she says she had to look at those ink blots. I thought it was just for serious cases. My daughter is normal.

A: The Rorschach Test (ink blots) has been around for many years and is usually part of any psychologist's battery of tests.

    A skilled psychologist can learn a great deal from what the subject says about the various cards. This test is called a projective test because it allows the subject to project ideas and feelings freely — without the usual cues that we depend on to help us understand things.

    Yes, the interpretation is somewhat subjective, but the experienced psychologist will analyze each response based on standards that have been developed over a long period of time.

The Rorschach Test (ink blots) is mysterious to most people, but in the hands of an experienced psychologist, it can reveal a great deal of information.

No, the responses to any single ink blot may not tell too much, and even the entire Rorschach Test itself must be analyzed within the context of the complete battery of tests, but, taken together, the overall composite of results can be very helpful.

Finally, nobody's perfect. Your daughter may or may not have some problems. You sound a little defensive. Don't let it get in the way of her getting help if she needs it.

Medication for Schizophrenia

Finding the correct medication in the optimum dose (not too much, not too little) for schizophrenia calls for expert consultation. Because the field is so complex, some psychiatrists specialize in psychopharmacology.

Q: Debbie, our 16-year-old, has been hospitalized twice for schizophrenia. She's taking Thorazine, 200 mg/day. Her treating psychiatrist says she needs more medication. A consultant we brought in says she needs less. How do we know who's right? Are there other medications that can be used?

A: First of all, there is tremendous individual variation of response to antipsychotic medications like Thorazine. Debbie, therefore, may need more, but she may do better on less.

Also, there is a myth that "if a little is good, more must be better." Researchers in Sweden have demonstrated through the use of sophisticated PET scanning that 90% of the nerve-end receptors requiring blockade are effectively blocked by Thorazine in the dose range of 200-400 mg/day in most cases.

Over the past several years, psychiatrists have been using lower doses of these medications, and getting good results.

My inclination, therefore, would be to go with the consultant's recommendation, but to have Debbie monitored very closely so the dosage can be increased quickly, if necessary.

Yes, there are several other medications used to treat schizophrenia. They are all referred to as major tranquilizers.

Street Drugs vs Medication

Psychoactive medications are almost never a preferred substance of abuse for teenagers. Yet, it never ceases to surprise me that some teenagers who would willfully accept pills and other substances from a street dealer balk at taking legal medication prescribed by a psychiatrist.

Q: Our 15-year-old daughter, Tamara, was recently admitted to a psychiatric hospital for treatment of drug addiction. We've learned that she's been doing drugs for the past two years: marijuana, PCP, LSD, cocaine — everything. She's starting to make some progress now, and says she wants to lead a drug-free life. We were stunned last week, however, when her psychiatrist told us that Tammy is depressed and that he plans to treat her with drugs! We don't understand. And we've refused to allow the drug treatment. What do you think?

A: First of all, it's very important to make a distinction between street drugs, like marijuana, and medication, such as antidepressants. The former are substances of abuse, the latter are therapeutic agents which, if used appropriately, can be of enormous benefit.

Depression comes in many forms, not all of which respond to medication. For example, drug abusers often become depressed as a result of the mood-altering substances they carelessly stuff into their bodies. This form of depression generally clears as they become sober. Another form of depression, sometimes called "reactive depression," results from the shame, guilt, or remorse of having failed many people, including oneself. This type of depression does not respond to medication. But a third type of depression does. This depression is rooted in biological and biochemical causes; it's often hereditary.

My suggestion: Have another talk with the psychiatrist. Ask him to define Tammy's depression. Why does he believe it will respond to medication? If he makes a good case, allow a trial. After all, he may have uncovered an important clinical finding. If Tammy had diabetes, you wouldn't object to insulin. If she has a medically treatable form of depression, you'll want her to receive all the help she can possibly get.

Medication for Depression

Q: Roberta, our 15-year-old, has been seeing a psychiatrist because of depression. Last week he said he wants to put her on drugs. My husband and I are worried. We didn't think she was so sick. Is there any chance of addiction? What about side effects?

A: Depression in adolescents basically comes in two forms. First, there's the situational depression that anyone can experience when things seem to be going against him/her. This depression is usually caused by a loss, either real or perceived. The treatment, when needed at all, is usually talking therapy.

The second type of depression is caused by chemical and neurological factors. It often runs in families. This is the type of depression that usually responds best to medication.

And let's make a distinction between drugs, as in street drugs, and medication, as in pharmaceuticals prescribed by doctors.

No, these medications are not addicting. They do not give a high. They are not substances of abuse.

Some types of adolescent depression are effectively treated with antidepressant medication. Side effects sometimes get in the way and adolescents are less tolerant than adult patients. Two new antidepressants, however, are relatively free of side effects.

All medications have side effects. Roberta's doctor should carefully list them for you. He'll also do periodic blood tests to rule out hidden problems.

Don't be alarmed. If Roberta's depression responds to medication, she'll be very fortunate. You and she will be relieved to know that while she does have an illness — it is treatable.

Two basic types of antidepressants have been mainstays for years: tricyclics and monoamine oxidase inhibitors (MAOIs). Because MAOIs require dietary restrictions, I rarely use them with teenagers. Two new antidepressants (Prozac, Wellbutrin) are quite effective and relatively free of side effects.

Tranquilizers for Teens?

Anti-anxiety medications (minor tranquilizers, such as Valium and Xanax) are rarely indicated for adolescents.

Q: Last week we took Sherry, 16, to our family doctor because she's nervous all the time. He prescribed a mild tranquilizer, Xanax, and told her only to use it when she "really needs it." So far, she's been careful; she's only taken three tablets. She says they help. My husband and I don't like pills. What do you think?

A: I think Sherry should see a psychiatrist. She needs a careful diagnostic work-up first. Then, the proper treatment plan can be designed.

Minor tranquilizers are rarely indicated for adolescents. They treat the symptom (anxiety), but not the cause, and they can be habit-forming.

Your doctor, no doubt, is trying to be helpful. If Sherry had a heart problem, he'd refer her to a cardiologist. For her emotional problem, he should refer her to a psychiatrist.

Refuses "Mom's Drug"

If a substitute medication is available, start with that. A part of psychiatric treatment might be to explore the reasons why a teen refuses the medication her mother takes: perhaps misinformation, fantasy, or unconscious psychological conflict.

Q: For the past two years I have been taking an antidepressant called imipramine. It's really made a difference. I feel 100% better. Recently, a psychiatrist diagnosed my 15-year-old daughter, Melanie, as depressed. He recommended medication, and when he heard my imipramine story, suggested it for Melanie too. The only problem is that Mel refuses. She'll think about medication, but will not take my drug. Should we try to talk to her? Is it worth the fuss? What are the options?

A: The purely psychological aspects of prescribing are every bit as important as the pharmacological reasons. Every physician knows this and now you know it too.

240

Melanie's reluctance to take your medication may be rooted in misinformation (does it mean she'll have the same side effects or suffer exactly the same symptoms as you?), fantasy (one teen patient of mine fantasized that she would actually become her father if she was treated with his medication), or unconscious psychological conflict (at 15, Melanie is struggling to be independent from you, perhaps the medicine symbolizes a lingering link of dependency).

You and Mel's psychiatrist could explore these issues. I, however, would probably opt for a reasonable option (desipramine or nortriptyline) to get the treatment going, and later explore these issues in Melanie's psychotherapy.

Poor Mental Health Insurance

Q: Maryann, our 15-year-old, is very depressed. When her psychiatrist recommended hospitalization, we all agreed immediately. Then reality set in. We learned that our insurance will only pay 20% of the bill. We're desperate. She needs the hospital, but we can't afford it. What can we do?

A: Your plight, unfortunately, is not unusual. Insurance carriers have been cutting back on mental health benefits for the past several years.

Your short-term options, I'm afraid, are limited. You might see if the hospital will reduce its charges and/or offer you a generous payment plan. Another alternative would be to explore public sector (state hospital) alternatives.

I also urge you to contact your employer's insurance office and register your dismay. If more people request adequate mental health coverage, employers and insurance carriers may respond.

Interestingly, the National Association of Private Psychiatric Hospitals recently surveyed over 1,000 adults about psychiatric insurance coverage. An overwhelming 79% said they'd be willing to pay the $5 more per month in premiums that it would take to provide better coverage.

Is My Insurance Carrier Crazy?

Q: Our son, 15, has a serious drug problem. After researching available programs, we put him in a residential center that charges $10,000 for the year of treatment it's estimated he needs. That's the good news. The bad news is that our insurance company refused to pay. But, bless their hearts, they did offer

Unfortunately, psychiatric illness is often discriminated against by many health insurance plans. Mental illness should be covered on a parity with medical and surgical illness. The time to speak up is now — before you need it.

If you think there are good reasons for a specific residential treatment program (RTC) to be covered by insurance, arrange a meeting. Important factors are the quality of treatment, the qualifications of the RTC, and the quantity of savings.

241

an alternative. They said they'd pay the full tab at a local hospital-based 28-day program. Total cost: $20,000.

Who's crazy, me or them?

A: I'm afraid you and your son are caught in a crazy-quilt bureaucratic morass.

Insurance carriers tend to pay for hospital-based programs that are accredited by the Joint Commission on Accreditation of Health Care Organizations (JCAHCO). Although some residential treatment programs (RTCs) are certified, many are not. Insurance carriers, however, fear they will open Pandora's Box if they pay for the ever-growing number of non-hospital programs, even though many of these programs offer excellent treatment at costs far below expensive hospitals, and even though some of them are indeed certified by JCAHCO.

I suggest that you arrange a meeting for yourself, your employer's insurance director, and a representative of your carrier. Stress the quality of treatment, the qualifications of the RTC — and the quantity of savings. It seems to me you may have a powerful argument.

Mental Illness Awareness Week

Mental illness does not have a poster child. Few celebrities lend their name to depression or anxiety. Efforts to destigmatize mental illness are very important. It must start at the grass roots.

Q: My niece Peggy, 15, goes to a high school in Texas that sponsored a Mental Illness Awareness Week. She's always been worried about the depression that runs in our family. The doctor who lectured to the students was able to answer her questions. In fact, Peggy wrote to me about new medicines that are now available. I'm very impressed.

A: So am I — by the program and by your caring niece.

The American Psychiatric Association has sponsored an annual Mental Illness Awareness Week since 1983. For the most part, the program has been conducted through the media. Peggy's school is in the vanguard, as I know of very few school-based programs. An excellent idea.

Such a program could teach youngsters not only about things like depression, suicide prevention, and drug abuse, but encourage them to seek help for themselves or loved ones. It could also serve to increase tolerance and understanding for people in psychiatric treatment — all of which could serve to help demystify and destigmatize psychiatric illness.

If any readers are interested in developing such a program, write to: Public Affairs, American Psychiatric Association, 1400 K St. NW, Washington, DC 20005.

Mood Swings

Q: Cheryl, our 15-year-old, is like an elevator: up and down. I'm talking about her moods. One minute she's elated, on top of the world. The next minute, she's crying, at the bottom of a dark pit. Is this normal?

Mood swings are the order of the day in adolescence, but if excessive, may signal a serious psychiatric disturbance.

A: Adolescence is the best of times and the worst of times. Nothing matters as much as it matters in adolescence. Hence it's normal for teenagers to experience sudden highs and lows. Moodiness or mood swings are the order of the day. Normal? Yes.

On the other hand, it is not normal if these mood swings are excessive in degree or frequency. How high does Cheryl fly? How low does she fall? Are these episodes precipitated by real events or do they occur spontaneously? How long do they last? What helps? These are all important questions.

There's another very important question too. Do you have a family history of mood disorder? I'm talking about severe depression that's required psychiatric treatment, or manic-depressive illness where depression alternates with giddy, unreal highs.

The second possibility, you see, may be that Cheryl is suffering from a psychiatric illness. If so, this form of illness is very treatable with medication and talking therapy.

My advice: talk it over first with your family doctor. If a psychiatric consultation is indicated, then she will be able to steer you in the right direction.

Teen Depression

Q: We just came back from the psychiatrist's office. He says our 16-year-old, Christina, is depressed. I believe it. I knew something was wrong. But how could I have missed it?

Depression in adolescence is The Great Pretender. It is often masked by behavioral problems and, therefore, often overlooked by parents and even misdiagnosed by physicians.

A: Teen depression is a great masquerader. It wears many masks. Sometimes depressed teens turn their sadness into aggressive behavior. Some run away. Others turn to alcohol or drugs. And even when they're aware of bad feelings, most kids tend to keep feelings to themselves.

According to a study of 150 depressed teenagers conducted at the University of Missouri-Columbia School of Medicine, two-thirds of the parents of these youngsters were completely in the dark. Obviously, you've got lots of company.

The chief investigator in the research, Dr. Javad Kashami, suggests that depression may be present if an adolescent has at least three of the following symptoms for two weeks or more: changes in sleeping or eating habits, restlessness or lethargy, loss of interest in favorite activities, extreme guilt for no reason, difficulty concentrating, or suicidal thoughts.

The good news is that Christina is in treatment now.

Agitation, Anger, or Depression?

Treatment is available for depression: talking, mostly. Antidepressant medication can also be useful.

Q: Our daughter Shari, 16, was hospitalized last year for depression and she's been seeing a doctor once a week ever since. She's doing well and we're so relieved. At first we were shocked to hear that she suffered from depression, but we've talked to a lot of other parents of depressed teenagers. It's not uncommon, is it?

A: No, but accurate statistics are tough to come by. One of the reasons is that adolescent depression is often missed entirely or misdiagnosed. Why? Adolescents typically do not suffer the familiar adult symptoms of depression: sadness, hopelessness, decreased appetite, sleep disturbance, and so forth. Often they appear agitated and anxious, and they convert those feelings into behavioral symptoms such as school refusal, misbehavior, or running away.

The President's Commission on Mental Health (1978) estimated that 20% of all people treated for depression are under the age of 18. And treatment, as you know, is available. What kind of treatment? Talking mostly. But antidepressant medication is useful for some youngsters who suffer from a biochemical form of depression.

Thoughts of Death

Suicide is very difficult to predict, but among the best predictors are previous attempts, depression, substance abuse, and a family history of suicide or suicide attempts.

Q: What should I do? Nathan, our 16-year-old, told me last night that he's been wondering about what it would be like to die. He even admitted that "once in a while" he's thought of jumping out of his bedroom window. Doctor, our son is a well-adjusted boy: honor roll, friends, the works. He's happy most of the time, and has never been depressed as far as I know. Is this normal behavior, or does he need a psychiatrist? I'm scared, but I don't want to overreact. Please help.

A: The mere fact that Nathan has confided in you is a good sign: he wants to talk about his feelings. He may want you to simply reassure him that almost everyone has such thoughts "once in a while." But is he preoccupied with taking his life? Is there more to his story? You'll only know if you ask him to tell you more.

Based on a report by Levy and Keykin in the *Journal of the American Psychiatric Association*, November, 1989, among the major predictors of teen suicide are previous attempt, depression, and substance abuse. In my own experience, I've found that a family history of suicide or suicide attempt is another predictive factor.

But be careful. Many adolescents who "succeed" at suicide do not fit this narrow clinical profile.

Talk it over with Nathan. Tell him that you're worried. A one-time consultation with an expert may well allow both of you to rest easier.

Cry for Help

Q: Our neighbor's 15-year-old daughter tried to kill herself last week by cutting her wrist. My son, 16, scoffs. He says she was just trying to get attention. I'm shocked. I think she's crying for help. Who's right?

Seemingly superficial suicide gestures must be taken seriously. The cry for help must not go unheeded.

A: You are. Self-destructive behavior in adolescence, even if it's patently manipulative, is symptomatic of trouble. Remember, only one in 200-400 adolescent suicide attempts actually results in death. The others are either failed suicide attempts (the true intention was actually death), or superficial suicidal "gestures" that are designed to get attention, to manipulate someone, or to get help.

I can't be sure about your young neighbor based on the information in your question. Did she really wish to die? Was it macabre theater? Whatever the answer, she needs help.

Teenage Suicide

Q: We are shocked and frightened. Our 15-year-old son has just been admitted to a psychiatric hospital because of a suicide attempt. He took an overdose of aspirin. If my husband had not come home earlier than planned last Saturday night, Jamie would have died. We're all very lucky, but we keep asking ourselves why, and we wonder if we missed something? Should we have known how badly he must have been feeling? What can we do to help?

Sobering statistic: The suicide rate for adolescents has more than doubled in the last 40 years.

A: My heart goes out to Jamie and to your family. Yes, Jamie is a very fortunate boy. He's getting treatment now, and he has an excellent chance for a happy and healthy adulthood.

But what about all the "Jamies" around the country who have not been as fortunate as your son? We're faced with an epidemic of teenage suicide today. In fact, suicide now ranks as the second leading cause of death among adolescents — second only to auto accidents which, of course, include a number if disguised suicides. The suicide rate for early adolescents (12-14) has increased 32% since 1968, and the rate for all adolescents has more than doubled since 1951. It's reported that 12% of all suicide attempts in the U.S. today are by teenagers.

I'm not reporting these statistics to alarm our readers, but I do feel that we must all be knowledgeable and sensitive to this phenomenon.

For example, you ask if you might have been able to pick up some signals or some early warning signs that Jamie was contemplating hurting himself. Without a detailed history I cannot know for certain, but it seems to me that a heightened awareness that these things can and do happen with alarming frequency is a first step.

Here are some other guidelines you might consider:

1) These teenagers usually have a long history of behavior problems dating back to childhood — preventative treatment in the early years is the key for them.

2) 20% of all adolescents who attempt suicide have a parent who has attempted suicide.

3) Most teenagers show a marked increase in behavioral problems (truancy, testing limits, uncontrolled rage, social isolation, etc.) just before the attempt.

4) Most youngsters do give some kind of "message," since most of them do not really want to kill themselves — they just want people to know how much they hurt inside, or they want to change something in their life. One girl started giving away her prized record collection. Another youngster told his buddies cryptically that he "wouldn't be around any more." A number of kids "signal" through their bodies; they develop psychosomatic symptoms such as headaches, blurring of vision, and stomach problems.

5) The final precipitant is usually some form of loss, real or imagined, such as the loss of a girlfriend, or the loss of self-esteem, which results in depression.

What can you do to help? A great deal. Jamie, more than ever, needs you in his corner. You probably feel a lot of other things in addition to shock: guilt and resentment, for example.

It's natural to feel these things. Work them out in family therapy as you assist your son in rebuilding his world.

Yes, Jamie was lucky. You've described a serious attempt, not a manipulative gesture. Your husband got to him just in time. Jamie has been handed a gift of life.

Talk About Suicide

Q: We are parents of three adolescents, 15, 16 and 18, so you can understand our interest in teenage suicide. It's been in the news a lot lately. Most expert advice seems to focus on the need to talk to worried kids about their feelings — including whether or not they might be feeling suicidal.

I must say this scares me. I mean, wouldn't you maybe give the idea of suicide to a teenager who wasn't otherwise even thinking about it?

A: I can easily understand a parent's reluctance to probe for suicidal feelings with a troubled teen. In fact, most people, other than mental health professionals, probably should have a healthy respect for getting in too deep. But don't hesitate to go at least halfway.

By this I mean it is important to communicate on a feeling level with teenagers. If your adolescent has been withdrawn and depressed, or if you suspect that he or she may be self-destructive, by all means ask about it. Talking about it will not cause a youngster to commit suicide. In fact, it probably will help. At this point, however, I urge you to call for reinforcements. A teenager who admits even to fleeting thoughts of suicide is beyond home remedy. He or she needs skillful professional help.

Parents should not be afraid to talk to their teenagers about suicide. It won't plant an idea in their heads that's not already there. Talking helps. If your youngster admits suicidal thoughts, seek help.

Teen Suicide Prevention

Q: Our son Paul, 16, has attended a suicide prevention program at his school. Do these programs work?

A: If you talk to students and school officials you hear that the programs work in several ways, depending on the purpose and design:

1) They increase awareness of teen suicide.

2) They educate students about general mental health services.

3) They tend to destigmatize depression and other mental illnesses.

School-based suicide prevention programs are a good idea, but there are not enough of them.

4) They help school officials identify specific youngsters at risk.

5) They create a positive peer culture.

6) They may assist students in developing problem-solving and coping skills.

But do they really work? Do they actually prevent suicides? I know they do. I've had suicidal teenagers referred to me from such programs. They're alive now thanks mostly to timely intervention by friends and teachers.

The irony is that, from a public health perspective, these programs reach only a very few teenagers. Columbia University researchers point out, for example, that in 1986 there were only 100 school-based programs in the U.S., reaching only 180,000 adolescents.

Teen Homicide

The recent spate of teens shooting teens (usually drug-related) is chilling. Adolescents may laugh it off, but it's only a defense: whistling in the dark. Encourage them to reveal their real feelings to you.

Q: We live in a large city where there have been a number of teen shootings and killings. Our son, 15, jokes about it. Is this just his way of coping, or do most kids think it's a big joke?

A: In my role as a medical reporter for a Washington, DC television station, I recently covered a shooting incident at a local high school. The youngsters I interviewed tended to fall into three basic categories:

1) Most of the kids were stunned and shocked. They poured out their grief — a healthy reaction to a vicious tragedy.

2) A few youngsters, mostly boys, were making jokes. One said, "This is cool, you know, like Miami Vice." Like your own son, they were using a psychological defense, called reversal of affect. It's kind of like the three-year-old who whistles in the dark to overcome his fears. It's not as healthy as getting your true feelings out.

3) The last group of students (about 10%), however, worried me the most. These kids did not seem to be phased at all. They seemed to accept the disaster as business as usual. They seemed to accept violence as an everyday item in their lives: no empathy for the victims, no rage at the perpetrators, no concern for their own safety.

In the case of your own son, don't accept his jocularity at face value. Give him some time. Then, gently inquire about his real feelings.

Teens on Teen Suicide

Q: My son, 16, has just completed a Suicide Awareness program at his high school. He said he learned a lot, but he won't go into details. What are kids saying about the subject?

A: A recent survey sponsored by Who's Who Among American High School Students provides some answers. Almost 2,000 youngsters were asked what factors they think contribute to adolescent suicides. Their ranked responses and the percentage identifying each factor:

In a survey asking teens what factors they think contribute to adolescent suicides, feelings of worthlessness had the largest percentage of responses.

FACTOR	PERCENTAGE
1. feelings of worthlessness	86
2. isolation and loneliness	81
3. pressure to achieve	72
4. fear of failure	61
5. drug and alcohol use	58
6. poor communication with parents	58
7. actual school failure	56
8. lack of parental attention	56
9. lack of family stability	49
10. fear of future	41
11. unwanted pregnancy	32
12. parental divorce	24
13. sexual problems	23
14. financial worries	14

Why Teens Run Away

Q: Our neighbor's 15-year-old son, Todd, just ran away from home. We're stunned. He seems like such a normal kid. Why do teenagers run away?

A: There are many reasons. Each runaway has to be analyzed individually because the answers may be complex.

Nevertheless, one study (conducted by psychologist Jack Rothman and educator Thomas David at UCLA) sheds some light on the problem. The research team surveyed a group of professionals and runaways themselves in two facilities. Here's what they found: 26% mentioned sexual abuse; 39% cited physical abuse as the reason for leaving home; and 46% of the respondents felt that parents actually pushed them out of the house.

In my own experience, however, I find that the stated reasons are often just a smoke screen to obscure deeper

Runaway is often a symptom of family dysfunction. The runaway teen needs help, and so may his entire family.

reasons. The only way to get at the root causes is a thorough, professional evaluation.

Runaway is a serious symptom of family dysfunction. When Todd returns, as most runaways do, you can help by encouraging his parents to get him and themselves to a psychiatrist or psychologist who specializes in helping teenagers.

Finding Runaways

You can take specific steps to find runaways. You'll feel better if you do such things as calling friends, calling hotlines, keeping in touch with police, hiring a private detective, and getting publicity.

Q: Please help. Our 15-year-old son, Danny, ran away for six days. He's never done anything like this before. We're frantic. We've reported it to the police, of course, but we haven't heard a word yet. What else can we do?

A: I know your anguish. It's important to do something. I can't guarantee that any of these things will work, but you'll feel a lot better if you take a more active role. Try this seven-step formula:

1) *Call friends.* Call Danny's friends and their parents. Ask for leads. Chances are that Danny, as a first-time runaway, is still in the area, and that at least one of his friends knows where he is. You might even offer a reward.

2) *Call hotlines.* Here's a list of some national hotlines. Call them: Child Find (800-431-5005), National Center for Missing and Exploited Children (800-843-5678), Runaway Hotline (800-231-6946).

3) *Police.* You've made a report. Good. Now keep in touch. Be persistent. Ask for reports to be forwarded to other police jurisdictions in your area.

4) *Private detective.* Some families who could afford it have told me that a competent private detective, with experience in tracking teen runaways, was the thing that brought their child home.

5) *Publicity.* It doesn't take a lot of money to get publicity. Put together an inexpensive poster with a recent picture of Danny. Display it everywhere you can. Send it to the local TV stations and then follow up with a call to the assignment editor. A long shot, but you might get some valuable air time on the news.

6) *Keep cool.* Information may come when you least expect it. Get it straight. Ask the right questions.

7) *No strings attached.* When Danny is found, or when he shows up on his own (as he probably will, based on statistical probability), accept him with no strings attached. After he's

safely back in the fold you can ask questions and try to put your lives back in order — perhaps with the aid of a family therapist.

Conduct Disorders

Q: The psychiatrist says our 16-year-old, Winston, has a conduct disorder. Winston is always getting into trouble: at home, in the neighborhood, at school. His behavior is atrocious much of the time. Punishment doesn't seem to work. And Winston doesn't accept responsibility for his actions; he's always blaming someone else for his troubles. The doctor has recommended group therapy. Can you tell us more about conduct disorder and how group therapy might help?

A: You've done a good job of describing conduct disorder. Unlike some youngsters who take too much responsibility for their problems, children who wear their problems on the inside, Winston wears his problems on the outside. He refuses to accept responsibility or to even feel the inner pain of his conflicts. Instead, Winston makes everyone else suffer — he blames and externalizes in the process of acting out his inner turmoil.

Punishment, as you say, doesn't usually work in these cases. Why? Since Winston doesn't feel he's to blame in the first place, he'll simply react to discipline with more righteous indignation, more self-justification that everyone is, indeed, out to get him. Individual therapy for youngsters like Winston is obviously very difficult. The psychiatrist, first of all, will only have Winston's version of events — and you can bet that will be self-serving. Then, if the doctor confronts him or tries to offer other interpretations, Winston will predictably react with anger. He will view the therapist as just another adult who simply doesn't understand him.

On the other hand, youngsters in a group will be more representative of the real world. Winston will act out his typical behavior problems in the group and there will be a better opportunity of demonstrating his difficulties in the here and now, rather than working only with Winston's self-reports as in individual therapy.

Group therapy, of course, is no guarantee of success, but it is a good treatment plan for conduct disorders in adolescents. One word of caution: be prepared for Winston to blame his next misbehavior on something he learned in the group. It would be a natural play for him to convince you that group therapy is a waste of his time. Insist that your son gives therapy a chance.

The adolescent with a conduct disorder is difficult to treat because it is his basic personality structure that is the problem, and he does not experience his difficulties as painful or dysfunctional. He often blames someone else. Group therapy can be an effective treatment.

Cruelty to Pets

Cruelty to stray animals is a warning flag. Cruelty to one's own pets is a fire-alarm alert. Get help.

Q: I came across an article about cruelty to pets. It said that this behavior in children often predicts later violence toward people. I'm worried. Our son, 15, has been vicious toward animals for years. He also has learning disabilities and is aggressive with his sisters. We've had him diagnosed by psychiatrists and neurologists, but he refuses treatment and my husband won't spend any more money on him. Last week he strangled his pet gerbil in his bare hands. Afterward, he cried. What can I do?

A: Your son is in urgent need of psychiatric treatment. Most teenagers can think of a dozen things they'd rather do with their time, but for your boy, there is no option. Rather than reacting to the violence, I suggest you respond to his tears. How does he feel after a violent episode? Does it scare him? Help is available.

You'll also have to get your husband to support the therapy, financially and emotionally.

Don't delay. Your son may well be a tragedy just waiting to explode.

Shoplifting

Shoplifting should not be taken lightly. It must be taken seriously. Punishment or some sort of logical consequence is indicated. So too is psychiatric consultation.

Q: Our Tony is 15. Last week he was picked up at a local department store for shoplifting. Yesterday the store manager and the juvenile court officer decided to drop all charges because he apologized and, on his own, wrote a beautiful essay about the evils of stealing. On the one hand, I'm proud and pleased, but on the other hand, I'm scared. Tony is a charmer. He's very slick at talking himself out of trouble. I was secretly hoping that they'd throw a scare into him. Now what?

A: The ball is in your court — where it belongs. Tony may have sweet-talked the officials, but what about Mom and Dad? If shoplifting is against your family values, there should be some form of consequence. A restriction or loss of privileges is in order. Or, you might insist on some type of community service such as volunteer work at a shelter or nursing home.

One more thing. Your question suggests that Tony's antisocial behavior is part of an established pattern. I don't like the sound of it. A consultation with a psychiatrist who specializes in helping adolescents is probably a good idea.

Fear of Flying

Q: My stepdaughter, Pam, 16, has a fear of flying. I mean she starts getting sick and anxious for a week before we take a trip. In all other respects, she's a normal adolescent. Will she grow out of it? Do teenagers respond to the same kind of treatment given to adults?

A: Fear of flying, to the degree that Pam is suffering, certainly qualifies as a phobia, i.e., an irrational fear. It's irrational because the act of boarding a flight is not an inherently dangerous procedure. Every year, for example, there are 500 times as many fatal highway accidents as there are accidents on scheduled airliners. And I bet Pam is not afraid to drive or ride in a car.

But so much for appeals to statistics and reason. These won't help Pam because her fear of flying is based on irrational, highly emotional mechanisms.

No, I'm afraid it's not likely that she'll grow out of it. But the good news is that treatment works. Techniques such as systematic desensitization, hypnosis, and other forms of behavior modification can help teenagers, just as they help so many adults. Bon voyage, Pam.

Teenagers respond to some types of treatment for phobias (irrational fears) that adults do.

Obsessive — Or Worse?

Q: I read an article about Obsessive-Compulsive Disorder (OCD). My sister, 15, may have it. Last year she began washing her hands 50-100 times a day. Then she refused to bathe. Finally, she said she was "dead" because she had no blood in her body. She was hospitalized for two weeks and it helped, but now she's home and getting worse. She won't sit on chairs where the dog has been, and is washing her hands again. Is this OCD? What can we do?

A: Your sister's rituals are certainly suggestive of OCD, but I'm concerned about her believing she was "dead." That symptom sounds more delusional and may represent a psychotic illness. Obsessive-compulsives are in touch with reality, even though their behavior may seem bizarre. Psychotic thinking is not in touch with reality, and indicates a more serious psychiatric illness.

My suggestion: get more information. Talk to your sister's doctor. What is her diagnosis? If she is suffering from a psychotic disorder, she should be on major tranquilizers. If she is

Repetitive, unavoidable thoughts (obsessions) or actions (compulsions) are the hallmark of obsessive-compulsive disorder (OCD), which is now treated successfully with medication and behavior modification. The symptoms, if extremely bizarre, may signal a more serious underlying disease.

suffering a severe case of OCD, she needs intensive behavior modification therapy and medication too.

Schizophrenia

Schizophrenia often has its onset in adolescence. It is a thought disorder, i.e., hallucinations, delusions, confused thinking. Schizophrenia is treatable.

Q: Our 16-year-old son has just been diagnosed as having schizophrenia. We took him to the hospital two weeks ago when he began hearing voices and describing plots that everyone was out to get him. We were frightened and shocked. Terry has always seemed so normal. Will he recover? How should we react when he gets home?

A: Schizophrenia is a serious psychiatric illness that usually includes symptoms of distorted thinking such as confusion, hallucinations, delusions, and irrational suspicions. Its onset is often in adolescence or young adulthood.

The acute onset of Terry's illness, and the fact that he apparently hasn't suffered any prior emotional problems, would place him in a category with the best chance of full recovery.

Unfortunately, the word schizophrenia has become one of those buzzwords, like cancer, that are misunderstood. Schizophrenia is a treatable disease. The treatment includes medication, talking therapy, and family support.

How should you react? A couple of family sessions with Terry's psychiatrist might help you to work through your own feelings, and then to plan for Terry's homecoming. Generally, the family can help by:

1) minimizing family conflict,

2) providing clear daily structure,

3) avoiding the twin dangers of excessive protectiveness or unrealistically high expectations.

Finally, beware the labeling of your son as "a schizophrenic." He has schizophrenia, a psychiatric illness. Terry should not be considered "a schizophrenic" any more than a person suffering from a peptic ulcer should be called a peptic.

Drugs and Alcohol

Teen Drug Scene

Good news: Overall teen substance abuse is down. Bad news: the decline in alcohol consumption is minimal, cigarette smoking has not changed, and PCP use is up.

Q: We have two teenagers, 15 and 17, and so we're concerned about drugs and alcohol. We've heard that teen drug use is declining. That's good, but why?

A: First of all, statistics, as you well know, do not tell the whole story. According to the 15th annual survey conducted by the National Institute on Drug Abuse, current use of illicit drugs by high school seniors dropped from 21.3% in 1988 to 19.7% in 1989. That's the good news, but let's look a little closer.

PCP use has actually increased (from 0.3% to 1.4%), and there has been no change in cigarette smoking. And as far as the Number One problem, alcohol, is concerned, there has been only a very small decline in daily use; in fact, 60% of the teens surveyed had used alcohol in the past 30 days.

So, while the overall numbers for all illicit drug use are encouraging, the results are mixed.

Why the (partial) success? I believe there are many reasons: involvement by concerned parents such as yourself; school, community, and government sponsored prevention programs; and media efforts, to name a few. The single most powerful influence (for good or bad), however, remains peer pressure. More teens are turning off to drugs, and turning off their friends to drug use too. That's the best news of all.

Why Kids Deal Drugs

Q: My 15-year-old nephew was picked up at school for dealing pot. He told his mother he needed the money. That just can't be true. Why do kids do this anyway?

Kids deal drugs for many reasons, but mostly to be popular.

A: The most common reason, believe it or not, is to be popular. Most juvenile pushers are lonely kids who crave the company of "friends." Parents should be alert to drug dealing if:

1) their sons or daughters suddenly acquire a host of new pals who call or come to the house at all hours,

2) they are flush with cash, or

3) they themselves begin to show signs of drug abuse, such as sudden mood swings, isolation, falling grades, and behavior problems.

The best antidotes? Strong family values, good discipline, parental supervision, and the encouragement to be good at something. The teenager with pride in himself will always have himself as his own best friend. That's the best deal he'll ever make.

Pediatricians and Drug Testing

Q: My husband and I think (but we're not sure) that our 15-year-old daughter, Colleen is using drugs. I called our

Drug tests can be beaten. The best "test" is your teenager's honesty.

pediatrician and asked him to do a drug test next week under the guise that I was bringing Colleen in for a routine physical. He refused. He said he would only do the test if I told Colleen the truth about why I was taking her to the doctor. I am very disappointed in this pediatrician. As a parent, I need help, and he's refusing to give it. Should I find another doctor?

A: No, as long as you and Colleen are otherwise satisfied with his services.

His position, in my opinion, is basically correct. He should not jeopardize his relationship with his young patient by playing detective for you. If you suspect drug use, the first line of defense is an honest confrontation between you and your daughter; then, if indicated, bring the doctor into the play, with your daughter's knowledge.

On the other hand, I do believe that pediatricians and adolescent medicine specialists should include drug screening as a regular part of all genuine routine exams of teenagers, but that they should certainly notify the youngster about what they are doing.

Drug testing, by the way, is not infallible — another reason why good, honest communication between parent and teen is still the best way to protect against substance abuse.

Drugs and Family Influence

45-60% of substance-abusing teens have a positive family history for alcoholism or drug abuse.

Q: I'm a high school teacher. Over the past few years I've witnessed more than my share of 16-year-olds who develop drug problems. My observation is that many of these youngsters come from families where parents or siblings are using drugs. What do you think?

A: In my own practice I've found that 45% of teen alcoholics or drug addicts have a positive family history.

A recent study conducted in St. Paul, Minnesota goes a bit further. This study surveyed 1,824 middle-class teenagers in 13 treatment centers located in five states. The results? Sixty percent of these adolescents reported that at least one other family member living at home abused alcohol or drugs.

This is why prevention must begin in the family and why treatment, to be effective, must involve the entire family.

Shyness and Substance Abuse

Q: Our Edward, 16, almost died last week after drinking an entire fifth of vodka. He was admitted unconscious to the hospital and spent two days in ICU. His buddies were scared to death. One of them told me that Eddie drinks because "it's the only way he has to relax." We are shocked. We didn't know he had a problem, he's such a quiet, well-behaved boy. The psychiatrist who saw him says that Eddie's shyness makes him vulnerable to alcohol and drugs. Is this what his friends were trying to explain?

A: I think so. Peers, not parents, after all, are usually the first to know about an alcohol or drug problem.

We tend to think of teen drinkers as wild troublemakers, but in my own experience, I've found that the quiet ones like Eddie, who wear their problems on the inside, may drink or drug in an effort to self-medicate. They find temporary solace from shyness, anxiety, or depression in a bottle, a pill, or a joint. This practice, however, can easily lead to chronic abuse.

Researcher Randy Page of the University of Idaho has reported in *The Journal of School Health*, January 1990, that shy boys use cocaine six times as often as non-shy boys, and hallucinogens seven times as often.

The answer? Eddie needs psychotherapy that will include relaxation techniques so he can overcome his shyness and learn healthy ways of dealing with the stress of everyday life. He may also benefit from Alcoholics Anonymous, especially a group specifically designed for young people.

Shy teenagers may be especially vulnerable to substance abuse. They use drugs, essentially, to self-medicate.

Locked Up, Covered Up, or Sobered Up

Q: Our 16-year-old son, Billy, has a drug problem. Everybody knows it but him. He refuses to get help. Should we force him?

A: Yes. Do whatever you have to do to get him help. Don't wait for him to admit he has a problem. It may be too late.

Chemical dependency is a very serious illness. In the words of one of my patients, a recovering 15-year-old drug addict: "You've got three choices. You can either be locked up (jail or institution), covered up (dead), or sobered up."

Billy is too sick now to make the right choice. You'll have to make it for him.

Now.

Druggies have three choices: getting locked up (jail, institution), covered up (dead), or sobered up. You may have to make the choice for them.

If You Use, You Lose

Don't bet on the illness of chemical dependency going away with time. Parents can help by attending Al Anon.

Q: My nephew, Randall, is 16. He's got a drug problem. He's been in two different programs, but left before finishing treatment each time. His parents are worried, of course, but they've developed a kind of fatalistic attitude. They are pinning their hopes on the future. They believe Randall will "settle down" when he gets older. Comments?

A: The future, for Randall, is now. Hoping that his illness, chemical dependency, will go away with time is like waiting for a miracle cancer cure. You can't bet on it.

Why did Randall leave treatment? What kind of treatment was it? Sounds like he needs a locked hospital program.

Mom and Dad should attend Al Anon. It will help, but betting on the future won't. Teen alcoholics and drug users grow up to be adult alcoholics and drug users. In other words, if you use, you lose.

Treat Drug Abuse First

Treating a substance abusing teen for something other than his drug problem is like pouring water into a pitcher with a hole in the bottom. It just won't work.

Q: Please help. Ryan, our 16-year-old, has just been kicked out of school because he refuses to attend. He admits, finally, that he's been using a lot of marijuana. The psychiatrist says that he's depressed and needs psychotherapy. My girlfriend, a recovering alcoholic, says that he needs treatment for his drug problem. Who's right?

A: They're both probably right, but for starters, I would go along with your girlfriend. Why? Until Ryan is clean and sober, talking therapy won't do him much good. It would be like pouring water into a pitcher with a hole in the bottom.

The best treatment for drug and alcohol problems is a well-structured program (maybe starting on a residential basis, depending on the severity of Ryan's illness) that would also include regular attendance at AA or NA meetings.

Once Ryan has established a good recovery, he could be reevaluated by the psychiatrist. If he still needs traditional talking therapy, he could get it then — after the hole at the bottom of the pitcher is repaired.

You might also inquire if there are any Dual Diagnosis programs in your community. Some psychiatric hospitals, recognizing that adolescents often present with both emotional problems and substance abuse, have established specialized units that treat the problems simultaneously.

Ex-Drug Users as Counselors

Q: My nephew, 16, just checked into a rehab for drug abuse. When we went to see him we were shocked. Most of the so-called counselors are ex-druggies — and they look it too. Comments?

Ex-drug abusers with a strong personal program of sobriety make very good drug counselors.

A: Sobriety wears many faces. Don't be put off (or fooled) by appearances. What matters most is the quality of a person's drug-free life and his skills as a counselor.

I believe that teen drug treatment programs should be staffed by a mix of former drug users (with at least one year of sobriety and a strong ongoing recovery program of their own) and non-users. The treatment team should combine skills derived from AA, NA, and other self-help groups as well as traditional medical, psychiatric, social work, and nursing backgrounds.

If you have questions about the quality of your nephew's treatment, ask for the names of families who have preceded him. Talk to them — and be sure to ask the tough questions.

Teenage Alcoholic?

Q: My former husband was an alcoholic. Now I'm scared to death that it is happening to my 16-year-old son Donny. I've confronted him, but he denies it. A friend of mine says that Donny will have to decide for himself that he needs help. What should I do?

Denial is part of the illness. Don't fall for your youngster's denial; don't be blinded by your own.

A: If you are convinced that Donny has a genuine problem with alcohol do not wait for him to ask for help. Denial is part of his illness. Take the bull by the horns. Insist that he gets help. AA is doing a very good job with adolescents now that it is recognized that alcohol is, by far, the most serious drug abuse problem for U.S. teenagers. A recent study, for example, revealed that 41% of high school students state that, on at least one occasion during the past two weeks, they have had five or more drinks in a row — and that 7% of them use alcohol on a daily basis.

Your friend is relying on an old adage that applies to some adult alcoholics, i.e., only when they truly hit bottom will they come to their senses and admit that they have a problem. We cannot sentence adolescents to years of misery waiting for them to get motivated. Donny may need a nudge or two from Mom.

259

He Only Drinks Beer

Alcohol is alcohol. Beer, wine, booze — it's all ethyl alchohol.

Q: We've finally got the goods on Justin, our 16-year-old. He admits he drinks three or four times a week, but insists it's not a problem because he only drinks beer, not hard liquor. Is beer less harmful than vodka, gin, or whiskey?

A: Don't let Justin jive you. Alcohol is alcohol, any way you pour it. For example, there is as much alcohol in one can of beer as there is in a glass of wine or a shot of booze.

Sounds like Justin has a problem and like most youngsters at the stage of discovery, he's denying it. Don't be an Enabler; don't enable him to continue down the path of alcoholism by allowing yourself to be convinced by his shrill protests. Get help. Try your local Alcoholic Anonymous. There are many AA groups designed especially for teenagers.

Wine Cooler and Teens

Talk with your teen about the reality that wine coolers have the same active ingredient as vodka. Remember to reaffirm your position on alcohol and drugs, and be observant.

Q: Last night my husband and I found some wine cooler bottles hidden in our son's room. Kevin, 16, says not to worry, they're "like cola" and not to be confused with "hard liquor."

Besides, he says he's only "holding them for someone else." What do you think?

A: First of all, I'm sure you realize that wine coolers (basically a combination of fruit juice and wine) are not "like cola." On the average they contain about 6% alcohol by volume, similar to beer.

Secondly, alcohol is alcohol. Whether it comes in coolers, beer, wine, vodka, or gin, the active ingredient, ethyl alcohol, produces the very same effects.

Yes, some teenagers are turning on to these new, sweet drinks. But don't be fooled.

And don't be fooled by Kevin's "holding" story. It may be true, of course, but I suggest a serious chat with your son. Don't overreact, but use this opportunity to reaffirm your position on alcohol and drugs. Then resist the temptation to be a private eye, but don't avert your eyes either.

A Girl on the Rocks

You are an Enabler if, by your action or lack of it, you allow your son or daughter to go on using alcohol or drugs. AA and Al Anon are everywhere, and still a good place to start.

Q: My 16-year-old niece, Angela, has always confided in me. Imagine my shock when she told me she's worried that she may be an alcoholic. She drinks alone and is "under the influence" two or three times a week. She's afraid to tell her mother. What should I do?

A: This much is certain: Angela wants help and she has picked you as her lifeline.

I'm impressed that Angela has surmounted the usual defensiveness and denial that is so characteristic of people with drinking problems. Either she's unusually self-observant, she's very scared, or she's in much worse shape that even she's letting on to you. In any event she needs help — now.

Alcohol is, by far, the Number One drug abuse problem for today's American teenagers. About 7% of adolescents are hard-core alcoholics; another 30-50% are confirmed moderate drinkers by the time they reach adulthood. Obviously there are a lot of kids on the rocks and I'm afraid that Angela may be one of them.

The bright spot is that help is available. I would suggest that, as a starter, you call your local Alcoholics Anonymous chapter and then arrange to attend a meeting with your niece. The AA people will be very helpful and will probably even have good ideas about how to assist Angela in bringing her mother into the picture, perhaps by attending Al Anon, the self-help group for friends and relatives of alcoholics. Some teenagers can be helped adequately on an outpatient basis, while others must initially receive therapy in a hospital or an alcoholic treatment center. Be sure that Angela is directed to a program that specializes in working with adolescents, since their psychological and developmental needs require unique attention.

Drink at Home?

Q: My husband allows our 15-year-old daughter, Vicki, to drink wine and beer at home. He says she should learn to "hold her liquor," and that if she's allowed to drink at home, she'll be less likely to drink or use drugs outside the home. I don't like it. What do you say?

Allow your youngster to drink at home? Better think twice about it.

A: I'm not in favor of the practice. First of all, let's be clear that alcohol is a drug and that it's still the Number One substance abuse problem among American teenagers.

Secondly, a recent study contradicts your husband's belief that at-home drinking diminishes outside drug use. Researchers at Seattle's Center for Social Welfare Research surveyed 480 9th-graders and their parents. Of those youngsters whose parents did not allow at-home drinking, 46% had tried marijuana. Of those teens whose parents did allow alcohol consumption at home, 56% said they had tried marijuana.

Alcohol is often the gateway to other drug use. I'm sure your husband believes he's helping Vicki, but in my opinion, he could be creating a problem.

Dangling Sobriety

Teenagers will be teenagers. Some recovering abusers will use the excuse of a meeting to get out of the house. Don't let them dangle their sobriety like a threat. Confront it.

Q: Brooke, our 16-year-old, is a recovering alcoholic. She graduated from a hospital treatment program six months ago and has been sober ever since. We're very proud of her, but we have a problem. We know that she has to attend frequent AA meetings and we support her in this. But she seems to be using these meetings as an excuse to get out of the house and to avoid her other responsibilities, such as homework. She really has us over a barrel. We're afraid to say, "No, you've got to stay home tonight," for fear that she'll start drinking again, and blame it all on us. Do you have some advice?

A: Brooke's behavior is sometimes called "dangling sobriety." She's dangling her sobriety in front of you to get her own way. Yet, as you suggest, it's a tough shot to call, and Brooke knows she has you caught in a dilemma.

The problem here is that while Brooke is a recovering alcoholic who's apparently committed to her sobriety, she's also a teenager. And, as an adolescent, she'll do all the things that kids normally do, such as avoiding chores and homework.

Here's my suggestion. Set up a meeting with Brooke, yourselves, and Brooke's AA sponsor, or her former counselor at the hospital. Talk things over. Express your dilemma clearly. While Brooke's sobriety must, indeed, be her top priority, she does have other responsibilities to meet. Her sponsor or counselor will understand. He or she should be able to help.

Marijuana

Pot is dangerous. It can be stored in the body for weeks, and it is often the gateway to other drug abuse.

Q: We recently confronted our 15-year-old son after we found some drug paraphernalia in his room. After some heated denials he finally acknowledged that he's been getting high about once a week. We suspect more. For example, his grades have deteriorated this semester, and he spends a lot of time in his room — alone. We're scared. What advice would you offer?

A: Too many parents might have been inclined to accept their son's denials at face value — not because they do not fear marijuana, but because they do not wish to believe that their own son could be a victim of it. I do not criticize those mothers and fathers. They love their children as much as you. Yet, there is a powerful denial mechanism that clicks into place when we are faced with problems in our own sons and daughters. It's kind of like whistling in the dark — deny the fear and hope that it magically goes away.

I am also pleased that you have not fallen victim to all of the pro-pot hoopla that so many so-called experts have touted for years. Believe me, marijuana is not harmless. I see far too many burn-outs, drop-outs, and wasted teenagers. And, don't forget that marijuana is often a gateway to other, even more serious, forms of substance abuse.

Another latent danger is that heavy users become so oblivious ("mellowed out") that they are completely unaware of how pot is ruining their lives. The active ingredient, THC, can be stored in the body for weeks, wreaking havoc on concentration and memory.

I cannot know for sure, of course, the extent of your son's marijuana abuse, but I definitely agree with your suspicion that he is low-balling his own estimate. As a rule of thumb, kids exaggerate their habit to their peers, and minimize it to their parents — when they tell parents about it at all.

And, there's the key. The fact that your son first left paraphernalia in a place where it could be found, and then "confessed" to you, can be taken as a sign that he wants help.

But don't expect him to ask you to take him to see a psychiatrist. Most teenagers are just far too defensive for that kind of motivation. Try, instead, to keep your channels of communication open to him. Be non-punitive and open, while, at the same time, making it very clear that you will not allow him to ruin his life by smoking pot.

What if he does it behind your back? Well, he might. But, as a first step, it is very important for him to know where you stand. Give him some guidelines and values to come up against. Give him structure and security. He needs it. If he admits that he cannot (or will not) stop using marijuana, I would suggest that you definitely insist on a consultation with a psychiatrist who specializes in treating adolescents.

Even though a majority of all high school students in most parts of the country have tried marijuana at least once, regular use of pot is not only harmful, but it is symptomatic of a teenager who is running away from the sometimes painful, but always necessary, tasks of adolescent development: separation from parents, autonomy, sexual development, conscience formation, and identity formation.

Marijuana vs Tobacco

Don't let the issue of tobacco obscure the reasons to stop using marijuana: it is illegal, alters perception and mood, interferes with learning, and is often the gateway to other forms of substance abuse.

Q: My husband and I are both longtime cigarette smokers. Our 16-year-old Patsy admits that she smokes marijuana. She justifies it on the basis that, "Well, pot isn't as bad on my lungs as tobacco is on yours." Is she correct?

A: No, she's not correct, and I don't like the sound of this argument at all.

First the pulmonary facts. Independent research at both the University of Arizona and UCLA has shown that marijuana puts more harmful material into the lungs than cigarettes. For example, about five times the amount of carbon monoxide is inhaled from a joint of pot as from a filter-tipped cigarette, and three times the amount of tar is trapped in the lungs.

Marijuana, besides being illegal, has other dangers, of course. It alters perception and mood, it interferes with learning, and it is often the gateway to other forms of substance abuse.

Your first job is to stop arguing the issue of which substance is most harmful. Your daughter's pot smoking has to stop.

Finally, it may well be that Patsy is trying, in her own imperfect way, to send you a message: don't smoke.

Pot and Soccer

Don't let side issues obscure the fact that your child has used drugs. Take action to help prevent future use.

Q: Kenny, our 15-year-old, was just kicked off the school soccer team for smoking pot after practice. We're against drugs, but we think the coach is being unfair. What about the other boys? Kenny says they do it too. We plan to appeal to the school board. Do you agree?

A: Not unless Kenny is innocent or the school's standard policy on such matters is not being followed properly in his case. In fact, you may be doing Kenny a disservice by focusing your anger on the coach instead of your son. Sounds like Kenny admits to using pot. This fact, therefore, should be your primary focus.

Talk to Kenny. What is the extent of his marijuana use? If he's gone beyond occasional experimentation, he may well have a drug problem. Be aware that he's likely to minimize his drug use to you. That's why a consultation with a drug counselor would be a good idea.

Don't be an Enabler. Anything you do to shield Kenny from the consequences of his drug use may only serve to enable him to go on using them. Use this event wisely and constructively.

The Path to Cocaine

Q: Our niece, 15, has just been admitted to a drug rehab program because of addiction to crack cocaine. We're sad, and although it's not a time to point blame, we're angry that her parents didn't do something earlier. When she started smoking, they shrugged it off. Later her beer drinking was viewed as "something all kids do." The same goes for marijuana. Couldn't they have predicted this would happen?

Teen cocaine users usually start with cigarettes, alcohol, and marijuana.

A: Things are always so much more clear in hindsight. No, I don't think they could have predicted addiction to cocaine, but they should (based on your information) have taken strong steps when they learned of her drinking and marijuana use (also the cigarettes, in my opinion).

For your interest, here's a profile of high school seniors who have used cocaine, as developed by PRIDE (National Parents' Institute for Drug Education): 43% first smoked marijuana at 11 or under; 58% smoked cigarettes before or at the age of 13; 60% drank beer before or at the age of 13.

So you see, teenagers don't suddenly find themselves on the cocaine highway; the path begins early and slowly. I agree with you: prevention and early intervention are the keys.

Cocaine Concern?

Q: You'd think that the cocaine-related deaths of celebrities and sports stars would scare kids away from the stuff, but I doubt it. My teenagers, 15 and 17, don't use drugs, but they maintain that cocaine is safe. Comments?

Coke kills, but many teens underestimate its dangers.

A: Your teens are, unfortunately, in the majority. In a recent survey conducted in Southern California, only 12% of adolescents admitted to being scared of cocaine. In fact, 3.6% said it helps them get better grades, 18%, better athletic performance, and 22% improved creativity. These attitudes are dangerous, as dangerous as cocaine itself.

Your youngsters need some cold cocaine facts. Tell them that coke is just slightly less addicting then heroin. Therefore, kids who believe it can enhance academic, athletic, or creative performance are not only fooling themselves, but they are endangering their lives. Coke is not chic. Coke kills.

First Crack, Now Ice

Ice has a lower price tag than cocaine, one of its major appeals to young people. It produces essentially the same effects as cocaine.

Q: My son, Mike, 17, knows an older guy they call "The Ice Man." Apparently he uses a drug called "ice." Is it just another form of cocaine, like crack?

A: No. Ice is a smokable, crystalline (ice-like) form of methamphetamine (speed). It can be easily manufactured synthetically.

Because ice, like cocaine or crack, is a central nervous system stimulant, it produces essentially the same effects: exhilaration, euphoria, alertness, increased heart rate and blood pressure. Like cocaine, it can also produce paranoia.

Both ice and cocaine are powerful psychologically addictive substances. One of the major allures of ice, especially to young people, may be its lower price tag.

I hope Mike cools out on "The Ice Man" real fast. Tell him to stick with the winners.

Psychological Aspects of Common Medical Problems

Food Fad Fever

Fad diets do not work if the goal is permanent weight control, and they may be dangerous for the growing adolescent body.

Q: Our Leslie is 16. It's been one food fad after another: vegetarian, megavitamins, liquids only, and even diet pills. I'm concerned about her physical health, of course, but I'm also concerned about why teenagers are so diet crazy today. Any ideas?

A: Food fad fever is raging hot among today's teens, especially girls. Part of the reason, of course, is that our society places a great premium on being slender. Another reason is that the sponsors of these diets are very persuasive and actively market young women and adolescent girls in print, on the radio, and on TV. Adolescent developmental issues are also at work: teens want to be independent, to control their bodies and their destinies. What easier way to control than through the food you put into your mouth?

The adolescent has a growing body. It demands a healthy, well-balanced diet. When teens such as Leslie fall victim to food fads, they run the risk of growth retardation, loss of muscle tissue, abnormal endocrine and menstrual functioning, and loss of important fat stores. Physical stamina is compromised and even intellectual sharpness can be dulled.

Leslie, therefore, could be jeopardizing not only her physical health, but her intellectual and emotional well-being too. Why not consult with your doctor? I hope Leslie can be given the dietary control she apparently needs, but on the healthy side of life. And don't forget the crucial second part of the solution: a good exercise program.

Can I Help My Daughter Lose Weight?

Q: My 16-year-old daughter, Sarah, has just signed up at a weight reduction clinic. Along with the diet and exercise program, they offer group counseling. Mothers are invited to participate. I'd like to help, but I don't want to turn her off. What do you think?

Effective weight loss for your teen means shedding pounds for herself, but it might help to have Mom in the picture.

A: Recent studies at the University of Pennsylvania suggest that teenage girls fare better at weight reduction if their mothers participate in program meetings, but not in the same groups as their daughters. Keep this fact in mind, but be sure to check it out with your daughter. Ultimately, she'll have to feel that she's shedding pounds for Sarah, not for Mom.

Diet Pills?

Q: Beth, our 16-year-old, is overweight. She's constantly on one of these newfangled diets, but they never work. Now she's insisting on diet pills. What do you think?

Diet pills? No way.

A: I say a loud "no" to the diet pills. First of all, there is no evidence that either prescription or over-the-counter diet pills work over a long term. Secondly, many of them have significant side effects, such as high blood pressure. Finally, many diet pills, as stimulants, can be mood-altering and, therefore, addicting.

I'm surprised the fad diets haven't worked for Beth. Most of them do — for a little while. That's why I don't recommend fad diets either. They're so special that no one can stay on them forever.

That's why the key to Beth's success rests on several basic things:

1) medical checkup,

2) motivation (I suggest she consult with a psychologist or psychiatrist who is trained in behavior modification),

3) a lifetime plan of eating what she likes, but eating much less of it,

4) an exercise program.

Secret Dieting

The now-thin adolescent girl, who still thinks she's fat and continues to diet, may be on her way to full-blown anorexia. Beware.

Q: My 15-year-old, Lynette, is dieting and I don't like it. She doesn't need it. I only found out about it by accident, and she keeps angrily setting lower goals as soon as she's lost a few pounds. What do you think?

A: I share your concern. Only overweight people should diet to lose weight. They should do it under supervision. They shouldn't need to hide it. They should be pleased with success and have no need to continually push their goals lower.

You are describing some possible early signs of anorexia nervosa. Another sign: the cessation of menstrual periods.

Don't be alarmed. Talk to Lynette. Watch closely. Talk to your pediatrician soon if concerns continue.

Anorexia and Femininity

The cause of anorexia is not known. Beware of simplistic notions such as "rejection of femininity."

Q: Our daughter Nora, 16, is anorexic. She has starved herself to the point that she looks like a concentration camp survivor. Still, she says she's fat. Her psychiatrist told us that the problem is Nora's "rejection of her femininity," i.e., she's making herself unattractive. Okay, she's skinny, but she seems perfectly feminine to me. Comments?

A: We don't know the specific cause of anorexia nervosa, the self-starvation syndrome. Therefore, many theories abound. What is at the core of Nora's illness? I don't know, but if you (and Nora) have more questions, please take them to her psychiatrist. Be sure that he has data that supports his conclusion, and that he's not simply fitting Nora into a preconceived framework.

I can tell you from my own work, for example, that not all anorexic patients have sexual conflicts.

Bulimia and Boys

Q: I thought only girls did it. But last week I heard that my 15-year-old nephew, Arnie, has been stuffing himself with junk food and then forcing himself to throw up. Any comments?

A: Bulimia is usually associated with teenage girls and young women, but it is not unheard-of in adolescent boys. In fact, one recent survey conducted by a health services corporation reported that teenage boys may be frequent victims of the disorder.

Bulimia is marked by binge eating (huge amounts of mostly junk food) followed by purging (self-induced vomiting or laxative use). Most of these youngsters complain about how fat they are, but unlike victims of anorexia nervosa, they don't lose much weight as a result of their symptom. This is why bulimia so often goes unrecognized.

Arnie needs a thorough evaluation by his pediatrician or family doctor, and a psychiatric evaluation too. If his bingeing and purging is serious, if it fits the criteria for true bulimia, he'll need psychological treatment. And let's not underestimate the physical dangers of bulimia. Repeated self-induced vomiting, for example, can cause large losses of gastric juice, which is rich in potassium, an element required for the heart to beat properly.

Although eating disorders are usually associated with adolescent girls, boys may be more frequent victims (especially of bulimia) than previously recognized.

Medication for Bulimia

Q: Trudy, our 16-year-old, has bulimia. She stuffs herself with food, then forces vomiting. Because she never really lost any weight, we didn't know about it until we caught her buying laxatives. Now she talks to a social worker twice a week and it seems to be helping. Is there some medication she could take?

A: There are several medications that are used successfully in the treatment of bulimia nervosa.

I recommend an initial trial with Fluoxetine, a new medication. It is relatively free of side effects. A good alternative, however, is Trazodone, up to a dosage of 400 mg. Patients who respond only partially to either of these two drugs often benefit when lithium is added.

If neither Fluoxetine or Trazodone work, a tricyclic antidepressant (such as Imipramine, Desipramine or Nortriptyline) may do the job.

Bulimia, an eating disorder characterized by binge eating followed by purging (self-induced vomiting, laxatives, enemas) is a potentially serious medical/psychiatric condition. Bulimia, because of the absence of obvious weight change, can easily go unrecognized.

269

Medication for bulimia? You bet. But don't neglect the talking therapy. The best treatment, in most cases, is a combination of the two.

Binge Eating and Depression

Depression often accompanies bulimia. This is one of the reasons that current treatment often includes antidepressant medication.

Q: Rebecca, our 15-year-old, is suffering from bulimia, or binge eating. For several months she's been secretly gorging herself on junk food, and then forcing herself to vomit. We've taken her to a couple of talking therapists without result. Last week she saw a psychiatrist who wants to treat her with antidepressant medication. Is this something new?

A: Yes. Rebecca's doctor is right up to date. Recent studies show that many bulimic patients suffer from depression, and that a significant number of them respond to antidepressant medication. In one study, for example, 70% of a drug-treated group showed decreased bingeing within six weeks, while none of the patients who received talking therapy had yet responded. In addition, 50% in the "drug group" showed reduced depression, while only 1% in the "non-drug group" felt less depressed.

One word of caution: medication may help, but it won't work magic by itself. Rebecca will also need patient and skillful talking therapy if she's going to make it all the way back.

AIDS and Adolescents

AIDS is a threat to adolescents. Do not be fooled by the relatively low number of currently identified cases among teenagers. Many young adults with AIDS no doubt became infected during their adolescence.

Q: Realistically, now, isn't the AIDS scare being exaggerated where teenagers are concerned? The number of confirmed AIDS cases among adolescents is very small compared to adults.

A: No, I don't think it's being exaggerated. Many young adults who are diagnosed with AIDS no doubt became infected during their adolescence. Remember: the incubation period for AIDS (the interval between infection and the appearance of symptoms) can take years.

Another important point is that many teenagers tend to be sexually active with multiple partners, and teenagers do not tend to use condoms; thus, the potential for spreading infection to others, before one knows of his own infection, is great.

Talk about AIDS?

Q: My husband and I, like most people, are concerned about AIDS. We have three children: Jonathan, 15; Tammy, 10; and Monica, 7. Should we talk to them about AIDS?

A: Some AIDS experts urge that children be taught about AIDS before they reach adolescence—even as early as third or fourth grade. This recommendation has caused some controversy.

I believe parents should talk to their children about sex. Such at-home sex education begins with a child's earliest and most innocent questions about where babies come from, and progresses to frank, explicit talks about sex and sexual values with teenagers.

It's important, however, not to force information on children that:

1) they're not asking for,
2) they don't need, or
3) they can't understand.

Jonathan, 15, could certainly use the AIDS information now. He's reading about it anyway. Talk to him.

Tammy, 10, is on the verge of adolescence. Use your judgement. No need, though, to get too graphic.

Monica, 7, is in my opinion too young to require the information. If she asks questions, answer in a general manner only: "It's a disease that's killing people, but you're safe."

The AIDS story is shifting weekly as new information becomes available. Keep informed. Use common sense and your own family values to guide you.

Middle adolescents require frank discussion about AIDS with Mom and Dad. Be guided by the facts, common sense, and your own family values.

He Won't Follow Doctor's Advice

Q: Our Sean, 15, hurt his knee three months ago playing football and had arthroscopic surgery. His doctor told him not to play any competitive sports for at least nine months. Yesterday he re-injured the knee in a pick-up basketball game. And I knew it was going to happen. He's been ignoring his doctor's advice for weeks. How can we get him to listen?

A: Adolescents are famous for ignoring medical advice. Why? There are several reasons.

First of all, teenagers are action oriented; they don't like limits placed on their newly found freedoms. Teenagers are also creatures of the moment. They want what they want when they want it. If Sean feels like basketball now, he's likely to do it. The

Teenagers are famous for not following doctors' orders. There are several reasons for this phenomenon: ego and denial are primary.

warning of future disability if he re-injures his knee just doesn't make much of an impact.

Teenagers also suffer occasionally from what we call adolescent narcissism. They defend against the reality of their flaws and imperfections by thinking and behaving as if they are perfect. Therefore, for Sean to resist the pick-up game might have been to acknowledge his wounds, his vulnerability. His joining the game, therefore, can be seen as a form of denial, a well-known psychological defense.

Finally, there may be an element of ego here too. If Sean's self-esteem is tied almost exclusively to his identity as a football player, he could be suffering quite a blow to his pride and self-identity at this time. Hence, his difficulty in accepting the surgeon's advice.

My advice? A good talk with Sean. Explore these possibilities and others. Help him accept his limitations and find new sources of self-esteem.

Teen Sports and Steroids

A short-term solution with long-term psychological problems, steroid use is to be condemned.

Q: Our son, Peter, is 16. He's a good football player, but he got pushed around this year by heavier boys. Next year, he says he's going to use steroids to build himself up. We think they're dangerous. What do you think?

A: You're right, but sometimes it's tough to convince a teenager about long-range problems when he can see a short-term gain.

These steroids do build muscle mass, but they can also cause shrunken testicles, stunted growth, high blood pressure, and liver damage.

There is some evidence that professional athletes are turning away from these so-called power pills. The National Football League, for example, tests for steroids now, and places penalties on their use, but the word hasn't yet filtered down to teenagers like Peter.

What to do? You might talk to the coach. If he would take a stand against steroids for the whole team (and perhaps do periodic testing) he could take the pressure off all his players.

In the meantime, make sure that Peter feels "big" in other ways. If he puts all his self-esteem eggs in the athletic basket, he's risking a blow to his ego. It's important for teens to have more than one source of identity, esteem, and pride.

Acne and Chocolate

Q: Gail, our 15-year-old, is a chocoholic. I guess that's not so bad, except that it gives her acne. She hates the acne, but she loves the chocolate more. Is there anything we can do?

A: Yes, relax. There is no objective evidence that chocolate, or any other food, plays any part in the formation of facial acne. Several controlled studies, in fact, have refuted the value of dietary restriction for acne.

I should add, however, that some youngsters and their parents insist that there's a direct link between facial flare-ups and certain items in their diet. For some such youngsters, there may be no convincing them of the scientific data I've just described. For them I wouldn't take a hard-line position. If they firmly believe that something they eat brings on their acne, they should drop it from their diet.

So, talk it over with Gail. Make her part of the plan. Will it be more chocolate — or a switch to raspberry ripple?

Myths persist, so I repeat: there is no hard, scientific evidence that acne is caused by chocolate or any other food. Chocoholics of the world, relax — unless, of course, you've got a weight problem.

Psychological Growth and Development

Conscience and Moral Development: The Third Task

Q: Our son, Christopher, is 15. He used to have a fine sense of morals. He knew right from wrong. He knew his own mind. Now he just goes along with anything that his "friends" tell him to believe. Is this just a phase? Will he regain his old conscience?

A: Yes, this is just a phase. No, I hope that Christopher does not regain his old conscience. He should be able to do better. Let me explain. The development of an adult-like conscience is the third task of adolescent development. Children go through three distinct phases of moral development.

The first phase, pre-conventional morality, is based largely on the fear of punishment and desire for reward. Events are viewed in primitive terms: black or white, good or bad, right or wrong. If you're good, you're rewarded. If you're bad, you're punished. Simple.

The development of an adult-like conscience is the third developmental task of adolescence. From a rigid sense of right vs wrong (black vs white) and a reliance on the peer group's sense of morality, your teenager should be able to start appreciating the complexities of life (shades of gray) and, on occasion at least, to stand up to his peers for his own personal beliefs.

This early phase of conscience formation is usually replaced in early adolescence by a second phase, conventional morality. In this phase, the peer group becomes the standard of morality. Teenagers are greatly influenced by peers. There is tremendous pressure to "go along with the crowd." Christopher, as a 15-year-old, seems to have adopted the position: "my peer group, right or wrong." His world is changing rapidly. He probably doesn't know what to believe. He clings to his crowd for support and direction.

Most youngsters, however, move on to a third phase of conscience development in their middle teens (15-16). This phase, post-conventional morality, is based upon rational, individual decision-making. Using abstract thought, a young person is able to consider not only the black and white of an issue, but also the many shades of gray.

When Christopher reaches this phase, he will be able to stand up against his peers, to look them in the eye and say: "I do not agree with you. No matter what you believe, this is where I, Christopher, stand."

The "Normal" Adolescent

No, adolescence is not an illness. There are many so-called normal teenagers and there are several ways to define normality.

Q: Our daughter, Darlene, is 15. My wife, who reads a lot of psychology books, is always making claims that Darlene is "normal." She seems fine to me, but then, I don't read all those books. So here's my question: What is "normality" anyway?

A: Zap. You obviously don't have to read books to have a lot of psychological savvy. And you have it. Your question is a very tough one.

Two of my colleagues, Drs. Offer and Sabshin, have addressed the subject of normality in adolescence. They point out that there are three basic ways to define normality:

1) *Average behavior.* This is "normality by the numbers," a statistician's view of normality. If a majority of kids do something, it becomes the norm. This approach has obvious flaws. It wouldn't allow Darlene, for example, much latitude to be an individual.

2) *Non-disturbed behavior.* This is the medical model way of looking at things. If you're ill or disturbed, you're not normal. Everyone else is "normal." But where do you draw the line? That's the problem.

3) *Happiness behavior.* This is the philosopher's perspective on the question. If Darlene is "happy," she's "normal." But what is happiness? Philosophers would say that ultimate hap-

piness is when you have everything you want, and nothing that you don't want. But when have you ever met such a "happy" person?

I said this is a tough question, and it is. I think the best you can do is to consider the sum of several bottom lines. Where does Darlene rate on things like:

4) physical health,
5) mental health,
6) attitude,
7) school performance,
8) family relationships,
9) friends,
10) dating and sex, and
11) values?

Now that it's clear I can't answer your question easily, I know you may not be able to resist tossing it at your wife. I'd be curious to know how she responds.

What Teenagers Want

Q: We have two teenagers: a son, 15, and a daughter, 16. It's tough being parents of teenagers today, but I think we're doing a pretty fair job. We try to understand what the kids are going through, but we also try to keep our eyes on the future — on the skills they'll need when they're adults. We've heard that today's teenagers, even though they may not admit it to their parents, want basically the same things we want as adults. True?

A: Yes, if you interpret a new national survey of teenage attitudes the way most observers are reading the data.

The National Association of Secondary Principals recently published a study in which they asked over 900 youngsters, ages 12 to 18, what they wanted most out of life.

The answers, in order, were:
1) career success,
2) happiness,
3) marriage/family,
4) general success,
5) financial success,
6) long/enjoyable life,
7) education,
8) religious satisfaction,
9) friends, and
10) personal success.

Believe it or not, today's teens want pretty much the same things out of life that we wanted.

Sound familiar? If so, you and your youngsters may be travelling down the same path. But why not take your own family poll? I suggest that all four of you make a list of the things you want most from life. Do it independently, then share your lists with each other. It should make for some very interesting conversation at the dinner table.

Type A Adolescents

It's true. Firstborns tend to be more success-oriented and goal-driven. But are they happy?

Q: Charlotte, 15, is our oldest. She's a real dynamo — much more competitive and aggressive than her younger brothers and sisters. I've heard a lot about firstborns being more success-oriented. Any comments?

A: Charlotte, like many oldest children, is on the fast track. She sounds like a classic Type A personality: self-directed, goal-oriented, driven to succeed.

Researchers at UCLA have concluded what many parents have suspected: firstborn teenagers do indeed tend to be so-called Type A personalities. Among a group of 184 teenagers studied, 66% of the firstborn (compared to 45% of middle and youngest children), were found to be like Charlotte — Type A.

The reason? Parents often project their own hopes and aspirations onto their firstborns. These youngsters then identify with their parents' lofty goals. This phenomenon, of course, can be good news and bad news. Firstborns who are endowed with the intelligence and stamina that it takes to be a high achiever can benefit from high expectations. Others, who may lack the necessary qualities, are driven beyond their capabilities and succeed only in becoming frustrated and discouraged.

The key is to measure Charlotte's happiness. Does she thrive on her success? Or is each success an empty accomplishment, only to be replaced by yet another victory?

Happiness

It's been said that you can't seek happiness. It sneaks quietly into your life while you're busy doing good things for other people — a good lesson for ourselves as well as our teenagers.

Q: We have three children, 15, 12, and 9½. All we really want is for them to be happy in life. How can we help?

A: Entire books have been written about this subject, but I'll try to answer your question briefly.

Happiness cannot be found by pursuing it. True happiness is when you have everything that you want, and nothing that you don't want. True happiness, therefore, is impossible — at least in a philosophical sense.

Happiness, says Kushner, sneaks into your life while you are busy leading a meaningful life yourself. Therefore, teach your children to love and to give back to other people without the thought of reward. The best way to teach them this value is by setting a good example.

It's Not Cool To Be Cool

Q: Our 15-year-old son, Daniel, belongs to the cool school. He never shows any feeling about anything. He says he's cool — that he doesn't have feelings. Is this a new craze or what?

A: Daniel, of course, has feelings. In fact, as a teenager, he is probably a cauldron of feelings. His cool facade may well be an attempt to repress them because he fears them or because he might be embarrassed by them.

Yes, some teenagers adopt this defense temporarily and he might be influenced by friends to some extent.

Your best approach is for you and your husband to set a good example by expressing your own feelings openly at home. Invite Daniel to not only share facts with you, but to express feelings as well. Don't clobber him though. Give him some slack. While it's definitely not cool to be cool, he may need a little time to sort out the feeling side of life.

Mid-teens are often better at expressing facts than feelings. The wise parent will help them do both.

A Teenage Macho

Q: Daniel, our 15-year old son, is a late bloomer. He's much smaller than the boys and girls in his class, still speaks in a high-pitched childish voice, and has not developed other signs of puberty. Lately he's adopted a kind of tough guy, or "macho," style of behavior. He bosses and pushes everyone around, and even got expelled from school for cussing at a teacher. Any advice?

A: Boys who are late in launching into puberty can have it tough. They are momentarily robbed of the single most-prized asset of all teenagers: a peer group. Efforts to compensate for this loss, and for their loss of self-esteem, sometimes lead them to misbehavior.

Beneath his macho exterior, Daniel probably doesn't feel very good about himself. He's embarrassed by his short stature and by the fact that, symbolically, he doesn't measure up to the other kids. Imagine his inability to compete athletically and his awkward social position. He may well be extremely guarded

The late-developing boy at 15 or 16 may slip into a macho identity to bolster his sagging self-esteem. Such bravado can be a burden for you — and for him — but there are better ways to handle his developmental struggle.

277

about exposing his body. I bet he avoids things like gym class and beach parties. It can be a miserable existence.

Late-developing boys generally follow one of several paths, depending on their psychological make-up and other factors:

1) *The path of least resistance.* These boys give up the battle of trying to make it in the adolescent world. They hang out with younger children.

2) *Lonely isolation.* Some boys choose to become teenage hermits. They watch a lot of TV — alone. They listen to music — alone. They go to the video arcade — alone.

3) *The banty rooster syndrome.* These boys are like Daniel. They defend against their hidden insecurities by putting on a show. They work hard at becoming the cock-of-the-walk. Such bravado often leads them into trouble.

4) *The driven achievers.* Some boys, especially those blessed with a high degree of intelligence, or some kind of special skill such as musical ability, actually benefit from their delayed puberty. They are driven to channel their energies into things like academic pursuits. This becomes the turf upon which they compete and try to make their mark in the teenage world. Often overlooked by their adolescent contemporaries, these are the guys who sometimes turn out to be the heroes of the 20th high school reunion parties: the artists, professionals, and business tycoons.

5) *What? Me, worry?* Believe it or not, some boys take the whole business matter-of-factly. They basically feel "OK" about themselves. They feel big enough inside to make up for being small on the outside.

Daniel needs your sensitivity. He needs attention — on the positive side of life. He needs to feel that he is good at something. Look for ways to reward his good behavior and try to avoid getting into power struggles with him. Instead, do your best to hook up with his hidden feelings of insecurity. Let him know that you understand. Reassure him that he'll catch up soon enough and that he doesn't have to prove his masculinity by being macho.

School

Will New Car Bring Better Grades?

Motivation for better grades: Although I'm generally opposed to the use of money and gifts as incentives for academic

Q: Paul, 16, has come up with a new twist. He promises to make better grades in school if we'll buy him a car. His father and I don't like the idea, but nothing else we've tried has worked. Should we give it a shot?

A: No. I'd like to shoot down the idea.

Paul's new twist amounts to extortion. Call it four-wheel blackmail if you like. You want results now — not a promise of future delivery.

Why can't Paul do better in school? That's the question. Consult with his teachers. Have him tested for ability, interests, and aptitude if necessary.

School performance, ideally, should come with no strings attached. Love of learning should be its own reward. Also, at 16, Paul should be able to understand that his future is at stake. But preaching this to him probably won't work either.

If he needs some behavioral modification to help get him motivated, you might tie his grades to a series of immediate rewards such as curfew or other privileges. A car? He'll have to demonstrate that he's responsible first; that he's capable of being in the driver's seat of his own life before he gets behind the wheel of his own car.

performance, many parents use the technique with some success. If you do, be sure to reward results — not future promises.

Mixed Math Results

Q: I can't figure it out. Lawrence, our 15-year-old, hated algebra and barely passed. But this year he's taking geometry and he loves it and his grades are excellent. He says the difference is the teachers. Could there be something else to explain the turnaround?

A: It might be explained by Lawrence's learning style. Algebra is very abstract, but geometry is more spatial. If Lawrence does better with shapes and designs than he does with numbers or abstract concepts, geometry may be a more natural, hence easier, subject for him.

Ask Lawrence's teachers about it. If I'm correct, you may be on to something very important to your son.

Geometry is easier for students with strong spatial skills. Algebra, trigonometry, and calculus appeal to those with highly developed abstract thinking ability.

School Suspension Doesn't Work

Q: Paul, our 15-year-old, has been suspended from school three times this year. It's supposed to help him shape up his behavior, but it's a laugh. Paul loves it. Since my husband and I both work, suspension is just a vacation for him. Comments?

Suspending students from school is usually an exercise in frustration. It doesn't work. Urge your youngster's school to come up with more creative solutions, such as in-school suspension — even if you have to be there too. It works and will save you time and grief in the long run.

A: School suspension doesn't work. From a behavioral standpoint, a negative consequence such as a suspension should:

1) be sufficiently punitive so that a youngster will want to avoid it in the future, and

2) teach something about appropriate behavior.

Suspensions for youngsters like Paul do neither. They succeed only in getting him out of the school's hair for a couple of days. This is a short-sighted and self-defeating non-solution.

I think an important missing ingredient is parental involvement. In the old days it wasn't the suspension itself that hurt, it was what Mom and Dad were going to do to you when you got home that made you shiver. These days with so many two-earner families, Mom and Dad are simply not available to hold up their end of the bargain.

The answer? In-school "suspension" with time spent performing meaningful, but onerous, tasks is one idea. Another idea I like is having parents spend a suspension day at the school with their youngster. Yes, I know, this plan may seem to punish parents, and it might, for the short term. But I like it because it works with a lot of kids. "Do anything," they say, "but don't have my parents come to school."

Son Leads Student Strike

Student strikes, even in support of worthy causes, usually are not taken seriously unless they are positive and constructive.

Q: Our Randy, 15, supports the local teachers in their drive for more pay. He's trying to organize the other students into boycotting classes to demonstrate what he calls their "solidarity." What do you think of the idea?

A: Not much. Even assuming that Randy's intentions are honorable, he and his followers may still be perceived as rebellious teenagers in search of a lark — and an excuse to get out of school. Better to put a positive spin on his support of the teachers: a petition and a meeting with the school board and/or a media interview. Such efforts, I believe, are much more constructive.

Women's College?

Women's college? There are advantages and disadvantages. If your daughter is interested, visit the campus, but don't rule out coed schools too early in the selection process.

Q: My Donna, 16, is a high school junior. She's one of the top students in her class. Her advisor, a woman, is pushing women's colleges — I'm not so sure. What are the pros and cons?

A: Your first step, of course, is to talk it over with Donna. What are her preferences? Then, I'd certainly want you to meet with the advisor. Why is she specifically suggesting this route for Donna? There may be some compelling reasons. It's a shame that so many brilliant girls lower their academic goals once they graduate from high school. And that's one of the arguments for women's colleges. It's been found, for example, that, compared to female graduates of coed colleges, alumnae of women's schools:

1) are twice as likely to pursue doctoral degrees, and

2) seven times more likely to be named as *Good House-keeping*'s top women graduates.

But there's a flip side to the argument. Many girls find that coed schools not only help develop social skills better, but that direct competition and collaboration with male students is good preparation for the real world.

No easy answers here, but Donna should get all the information available and visit colleges of various types before she makes this all-important decision.

Sexual Development

Teen Sex

Q: My daughter, 16½, claims that all her girlfriends have had sex. I don't believe it, but I do know that today's teenagers are a lot more sexually active than we used to be. Do you have any figures?

A: Yes. According to recent figures from the National Research Council, by the age of 15, 17% of boys and 6% of girls have engaged in sexual intercourse. By the age of 18, the figures are 67% for boys and 44% for girls. Keep in mind, however, that:

1) These figures could be lower or higher in various communities, and

2) We do know there is a national trend for teens to be experimenting sexually at ever-younger ages.

Your daughter seems to be giving you an invitation to talk to her about sex. I hope you accept it. As I often stress, parents are the best sex educators of all, especially when it comes to teaching values.

It's a different sexual world out there today. We may not like it, but it's important to understand it. Teens are having sex earlier and more often than when we were adolescents.

When Is a Teenager Ready for Sex?

When is a person ready for sex? When he or she is capable of merging two instinctual drives: the purely physical (genital) drive for sex, and the drive toward intimacy and commitment. Most teens can have sex, but they're not capable of making love.

Q: Wendy is 16 and I have a dilemma. I don't believe she should be having sex. She's too young. I worry about pregnancy and venereal disease. It's against everything I've tried to teach her about religion and morality. On the other hand, I realize most of the kids are doing it these days. When I ask her about it she kind of shrugs, "Well, I haven't done it yet, if that's what you want to know." In other words, she's telling me it could happen any day now — that's my dilemma. If I suggest birth control, I'm really giving her a double message: Don't do it, but if you do, be sure to protect yourself. I feel trapped. Any helpful hints?

A: You've captured the essence of the problem facing so many parents, and so many teenagers.

First some facts. There is no doubt that teenage sexual activity is on the upswing. It's a different sexual world out there today. In one study conducted by the Alan Guttmacher Institute, it was reported that 45% of 16-year-old boys and 32% of 16-year-old girls are sexually active. These figures, of course, are higher in some communities, lower in others.

But when is a person ready for sex, that's the question. The achievement of complete sexual development requires the merging of two distinct drives. The first is the anatomical and physiological readiness to perform the sex act. Since puberty occurs earlier today than it did several generations ago, we have the phenomenon of 12- and 13-year-olds with adult bodies and adult-like urges. But are they ready? No. The second drive, the capability to express intimacy and to sustain a loving relationship, with all the responsibility that goes along with it, is far beyond any 12- or 13-year-old I've ever met. It's also beyond 16-year-olds. Teens have sex. They don't make love.

You're frightened and concerned; Wendy, in spite of her evasiveness, may be, too. My advice: don't compromise your own values. Let Wendy know exactly where you stand. Then listen. Help. Ultimately, the dilemma has to be Wendy's, not yours. Help her own it. Talk with her, not at her.

Teen Too "Chicken" for Sex

Middle adolescents are often coerced by peer pressure into "trying sex" before they're ready for it. Understand. Listen. Advise — wisely.

Q: My 15-year-old son, Brian, tells me everything. He's worried because he's too "chicken" to have sex with his girlfriends. I told him that everyone is "chicken" at first; he shouldn't worry about it. But I'm afraid he might have a real problem here. Should I take him to see a counselor?

A: Hold it! You seem to be telling Brian to go ahead and have sex. I don't think that's what he's looking for.

Brian, like most boys and girls his age, is caught between two competing psychological forces: strong sexual drives and a moral prohibition against those drives. He may also be worried about his masculinity; his ability to perform the sexual act. Therefore, Brian needs your own understanding of these issues and your help in coming to grips with his emerging sexual self. If you're too quick to side with one of the forces, such as the sexual drives, you won't help. In fact, you may only add to his confusion, guilt, and shame.

Sexual inhibition ("chickening out") can be a problem in later years. But premature sexual activity by teenagers also causes problems. Don't be too quick with reassurances and advice.

A counselor? Not now. Instead, go back to Brian and offer to listen. Share his struggle. Listen to him.

Why Teens Say "No"

Q: Our Meredith is 15. My husband and I are against teen sex for many reasons, but mostly because of our religious beliefs. Merrie just tunes us out when we "get religious" with her. What are some other arguments we can use?

A: First of all, I doubt you'll argue many adolescents out of having sex. The best plan is to listen non-judgmentally to your daughter. She may have some pretty good reasons of her own. Help her grapple with her feelings and with things like peer pressure and her own values. Your values? By all means state them clearly. Give Meredith some guidelines so she can cope with this important developmental issue.

A recent poll by Planned Parenthood may give you some additional ideas about how to approach this problem. One thousand teenagers were asked: What would make you delay having sex? Here are their responses (they could choose more than one category):

Why do teens delay sex? Because of four basic fears: 1) sexually transmitted diseases, 2) pregnancy, 3) parents finding out, 4) ruined reputation.

CONCERN	PERCENTAGE
sexually transmitted diseases	65
pregnancy	62
parental reaction	50
reputation	29

Talk to Merrie. That's the key. And listen, listen, listen.

283

Should I Put My Daughter on the Pill?

Telling a daughter not to have sex, but putting her on the pill "just in case," is a classic mixed message. What are your values? Clarify them. Communicate them. Be clear.

Q: I've got a real problem. My daughter, Barbara, is 15 and is going steady. She's dropping hints that she and her boyfriend are about ready to start having sex. Now, I am absolutely opposed to it. Premarital sex goes against everything that I've ever taught my children. In addition, I see all this teenage pregnancy and the sorrow that it causes. I don't want it to happen to Barbara. What should I do? Is it better to stand by my morals and take the chance that she'll get pregnant, or should I take her to our doctor and have her put on the Pill?

A: You are describing an all-too-commonplace dilemma for today's parents — and for today's teenagers. But let's approach this problem one step at a time.

You say that Barbara is "dropping hints." It may be that she is confused and ambivalent about having sex. She needs less moralizing and more understanding. Listen to her. Hold your judgement in reserve. Help her to work out her conflicts.

Many teenage boys and girls get propelled into premature sexual experience because of peer pressure. Deep down they may feel that they are not yet ready for it. When a parent shoots from the hip with advice, they may react badly.

Please don't infer that I'm advising you to change your own values. To the contrary, stick to your morals. Let Barbara know where you stand, but do it gently, with understanding.

Remember, it's a different sexual world out there for today's adolescents: they're having sex earlier and more often than when we were teenagers. We may not like it, but it's a fact.

The Pill? Forbidding Barbara to have sex in one breath, and suggesting a trip to the gynecologist in the next, is a mixed message if ever there was one. You seem aware of the dilemma. Explain it to her — it's her dilemma too. Face it together.

Teen Contraception Clinics

Teen contraception clinics are a growing phenomenon, but do they work? Yes, if the goal is to lower teen pregnancy. What do I think? I prefer to see parents involved in these decisions.

Q: My daughter Wendy, 15, goes to a high school that plans to open a health clinic that will prescribe contraceptive devices. Won't the clinic just encourage more kids to have sex?

A: Currently there are many such clinics in this country. Half of them, with parental consent, will prescribe contraceptives. The experience in Baltimore is enlightening. In two high schools with clinics, the pregnancy rate dropped by 30%; in schools without the clinics, the pregnancy rate increased by 58%, and the youngsters in those schools tended to experiment with sex at an earlier age.

On the other hand, some school clinics have not been very successful in curbing teen pregnancy.

I believe, first of all, that parents should become much more involved in the sex education of their children — especially in the teaching of sexual values.

The clinics are somewhat controversial. They might be right for some school districts and unacceptable to others. Whatever the case, I personally favor parental involvement in the contraception decision.

VD

Q: Our 16-year-old daughter, Chris, has just been treated for gonorrhea. Imagine my surprise when she told me that she has had gonorrhea before and thought she was "immune." Is that possible? How can I help her?

A: No, it's not possible. There is no natural immunity to gonorrhea or the other venereal diseases. Teenagers like Chris, no matter how worldly wise they may appear to be on the surface, often have some strange and fanciful misconceptions when it comes to VD and sex.

Often, according to a Planned Parenthood survey, beliefs include:

1) VD is not really dangerous since it can be treated,

2) You don't need any treatment if symptoms disappear on their own,

3) You won't get pregnant if you jump up and down after intercourse — or if you stand while having sex.

How can you help? By doing what so few parents are doing today: talk to your daughter about sex. Not only about anatomy and physiology, but about venereal disease, AIDS, pregnancy, and most of all, family values.

Teenagers harbor a lot of misconceptions about venereal disease. Some of them are so fanciful as to be almost humorous to us. But VD is no laughing matter. The best medicine? Talk about it. Be a good sex educator to your adolescent.

Son Shuns Gay Father

Q: My former husband and I have been divorced for eight years. I've suspected for a long time that he's homosexual and I've lived with it in silence. Last week, however, he told our 15-year-old son, Raymond, that he's gay. Raymond is destroyed. He won't talk to his father. He won't even go near him. I'm frantic. What should I do?

Learning that a parent is homosexual can be devastating to a teenager. Will I become gay? What will my friends think? There is a loss of respect and trust, but most adolescents can grow to understand it if you give them time and honest information.

A: First, it's crucial for you to get your own emotions sorted out. Your reactions will heavily influence Raymond. There's no doubt that your husband should have discussed this with you before laying such a heavy trip on your son. The two of you, whatever your differences, might have been able to cooperate on a plan in the best interests of Raymond.

Keep in mind, though, that Raymond may well have also had "suspicions" about his father, and that he may be both relieved and destroyed.

Don't push Raymond toward his father precipitously. He may need a cooling-off period to collect his own thoughts. He'll also need your support and sensitivity. Raymond may feel cheated and abandoned by his father, and may even resent you for keeping the secret from him. He may worry about what his friends will think, and that he himself may become gay.

Listen to your son. Most youngsters can grow to accept. Whatever your reactions to these revelations, and whatever Raymond's immediate response, your former husband will always be Raymond's father.

Lesbian Mother

Intense emotions are involved, but it's really more of a psychological matter than a legal one. Keep the best interests of the children in mind.

Q: I've just learned that my ex-wife is a practicing lesbian. We were divorced last year and she has custody of our two girls, Patti, 15, and Joyce, 13. I'm stunned. I'm hurt. And I'm frightened for my daughters. I've already talked to my lawyer about going back for custody of the girls. What should I do?

A: First, talk to your ex-wife. Do it in the best interests of Patti and Joyce. Second, be aware that, even if Mom hasn't confided in them, they probably know. The worst thing, then, is to deny them the chance to air their questions and feelings.

This is really more of a psychological matter than a legal one — especially given the girls' ages. Try your best to work out your own reactions privately. As shocked as you are, try to be as helpful as you can be. A custody fight is not the answer.

Gay Support Group for Teens

I'm wary about gay support groups for teens. Yet, sexually conflicted adolescents must be able to share their worries with knowledgeable, non-judgmental, sensitive adults.

Q: I'm the concerned mother of two teenagers, 15 and 17. Our newspaper has been running a series on Gay Teens. Now there's some talk about the local high school forming a support group for them. This is dreadful. Won't it cause some confused kids to be pulled into the net? Besides, I've heard that you can't really be truly homosexual until age 20. Please comment.

A: Yes, the adolescent years are a time of turmoil and confusion, and it's not at all unusual for heterosexual youngsters to feel, or fear, momentarily, that they may be gay. It's so common that it's virtually a normative experience of growing up. On the other hand, in my clinical experience I can say that some teenagers can and do become homosexually oriented, i.e., the 20-year-old standard is mostly myth.

What happens is that homosexual teens repress their behavior, hide behind their shame and confusion, and suffer in silence. Some become depressed. Others may turn to drugs or alcohol. Some, in fact, attempt suicide. It is for these kids that support groups would be most valuable.

On the other hand, since it is common for adolescents to feel alienated, it is possible that vulnerable, but basically heterosexual, youngsters could be drawn inappropriately to such a group. This fact, and community opposition, has steered most schools away from such services.

My own opinion? These groups are still fairly new. Frankly, I don't know enough about their track record. Until I do, I am not in a position to give them a favorable recommendation. In the meantime, we can only hope that traditional therapists will sensitize themselves to the special needs of these youngsters, and that the teens themselves will feel less stigmatized in using existing services.

Television and Music

TV vs Newspapers

Q: We try to teach our children, 16, 14, and 11, to be careful and thoughtful about current events. For example, we'd like them to seek more than just one source of information before they make up their own minds about an issue. We're constantly disappointed, therefore, when they simply take what they get on TV news as gospel. Are we fighting a losing battle?

A: I salute your efforts. Don't give up. But you should be aware that your youngsters are typical of a generation raised on television. Not only are the fast-paced newscasts with their dramatic visual reinforcement so compelling, it's simply less work to get all your news from the tube.

Like adults, most adolescents get their news rather passively from television. You can help by questioning them about it. Seek the stories behind the stories. Discuss meaning and values. Make it an active learning experience.

Know your youngster's heroes and you know a lot about him. Yes, television often merely celebrates celebrity. An antidote? Talk up real, live heroes and heroines right in your own community.

In a recent national poll of over 100,000 children it was reported that 57% said they believe what they see on TV news, 47% believed newspapers, and 37% believed books.

TV Heroes vs Small Town Heroes

Q: We have three children, 11, 15, and 17½. I'm disturbed by their choices of heroes and heroines they see on TV: mostly rock stars and TV celebrities. They fail to see the genuine heroism of men and women right here in our little town — average people who work hard to make a difference for others. Any comments?

A: I find it hard to improve on your own comments.

From a developmental perspective, children are first attracted to superhuman heroes (Superman is still tops for most) who represent fantasied wishes, i.e., being able to fly, etc. Later, as adolescents, they adopt real-life heroes with real attributes, such as good looks, that they want for themselves.

You imply, and I agree, that many youngsters are attracted to superficial and illusory qualities such as money, fame, sexual prowess, or even celebrity for celebrity's sake.

It all comes back to family values, and I salute your appreciation of the many "local heroes" in all of our communities. They can teach our children a great deal about what is possible in life if you care enough to make it so. They may not make Good Morning America or the network news, but they make our lives better, day in and day out.

Quiz

The middle adolescent, 15 to 16, isn't quite as complicated as the early adolescent, but he does require special understanding. Can you answer at least 80% of the following questions correctly? If so, you're using this book wisely — or you already know a lot about teenagers. Whichever the case, keep it up. Your adolescent needs an informed parent.

1. Your 16-year-old son overslept on Saturday and was late for work. You decide to use logical consequences. Therefore, you should:
    A. Call his boss and make an excuse
    B. Punish him by making him quit the job
    C. Punish him by taking away the car for one week
    D. Let him explain it to his boss

2. When confronted by parents about alcohol or drug use, most teenagers will:
    A. Minimize it, if they admit it at all
    B. Tell the truth

3. Marijuana:
    A. Is harmless
    B. Can cause psychological damage
    C. Can cause both psychological and physical damage

4. If your 15-year-old has a drug problem, but refuses to go for help:
    A. There's nothing you can do about it. After all, she can't be helped unless she's really motivated for it
    B. It's up to you to do whatever is necessary to get her into treatment

5. Your 15-year-old son threatens to run away if you insist on a particular punishment for his misbehavior. What should you do?
    A. Be careful. Such an adolescent ultimatum should always be taken seriously and at face value
    B. Be understanding, but be firm. Proceed with the punishment
    C. He's asking for double trouble. Give him an extra punishment for talking back to you

6. The teenager who attempts suicide (select all that apply):
    A. Usually drops some hints before the attempt
    B. Often has a family history of suicide
    C. Usually has a history of behavior problems
    D. Often is reacting to a loss, either real or imagined

7. True or False? Late-developing boys (puberty delayed to middle adolescence) are more vulnerable to psychological problems than early-developing boys.

8. True or False? Most teenagers whose behavior is out of parental control were also out of control as younger children.

9. Group therapy for a 15-year-old:
    A. Is often the best form of treatment
    B. Should be avoided since adolescents are so susceptible to the negative influence of their peers
    C. Is dangerous because there's no confidentiality

10. A 15-year-old slaps his mother in the face (select all that apply):
    A. Forgive him if he apologizes
    B. Get help. There is a strong chance of abuse continuing and getting worse
    C. He must be punished

11. True or False? The best response, if your 15-year-old threatens to run away, is to call her bluff: find her a suitcase. This will communicate to her that you cannot be intimidated.

12. Most teenage sex:
    A. Takes place in parked cars
    B. Occurs during parties
    C. Takes place in the youngsters' homes

13. Your 15-year-old son has just landed a part-time job. He insists that the money is his and that he should be allowed to spend it as he wishes:
    A. Okay. It's up to him
    B. No. Allow him to keep some of it as spending money, but insist that the rest goes into a savings account

14. Bulimia (select all that apply):
    A.   Is characterized by binge eating
    B.   Is often associated with depression
    C.   Is treated by psychotherapy but not medication

15. According to a recent national survey, what do today's teenagers want most? (select one):
    A. More friends
    B. Marriage and family
    C. Career success
    D. More freedom

16. Today's teenagers and political beliefs:
    A.   Most share their parents' beliefs
    B.   Most disapprove of their parents' beliefs

17. True or False? Chocolate is a major cause of teenage acne.

18. True or False? It is not until 15 or 16 that the average youngster is capable of abstract thinking (to think about thought, to consider the "shades of gray" of various moral issues, etc.).

19. True or False? Due to better equipment and coaching, high school football is less dangerous today than it used to be.

20. True or False? Although the goal of sexual development is to ultimately combine the genital drive with love and intimacy, it is rare for a 15- or 16-year-old to have accomplished this task.

Correct Answers

1) D; 2) A; 3) C; 4) B; 5) B; 6) A, B, C, D; 7) True; 8) True; 9) A; 10) B, C; 11) False; 12) C; 13) B; 14) A, B; 15) C; 16) A; 17) False; 18) True; 19) False; 20) True

5

Late Adolescents (17+)

For the late adolescent, (usually high school seniors or beyond), it's time to get down to serious business. This is a time of making choices: Who am I? Where am I going?

This is the time that all of the crossroads of one's developmental road map begin to converge. All of the influences of the past, from whether or not she successfully bonded with mother and achieved basic trust in the first few months of her life, to things that happened just last week, play a part in her "getting herself together" ... a teen phrase, to be sure, but a phrase that captures the essence of the psychological work to be done: identity formation.

But when is this work really completed? If the onset of adolescence can be defined as the psychological reaction to puberty, it has a rather obvious beginning — puberty. But when does it end? At high school graduation? At 18? At marriage? No, no, no. It ends when the four basic tasks of adolescence are completed: 1) independence and autonomy from the parents

of your childhood, 2) sexual development, including the capacity for intimacy and love, 3) adult conscience formation, and 4) identity formation — who am I?

Some youngsters complete all these tasks by their late teens. Others resolve them during their young adulthood. And some people, of course, never do fully complete these tasks — they remain "adolescent," searching for themselves for much of their adult life.

Your job as a parent, however, is essentially completed when your youngster graduates from high school and moves out into the world. You've worked yourself out of a job.

Or have you?

No, a parent's job is never really done. Your child will always need you, but he should need you in different ways as he matures. Soon he'll need you as a friend and confidant and later you may even need him in ways that you've never imagined: for help, advice, and support. Yes, it goes full circle. That's the beauty of it.

Discipline

Go to Juvenile Court for Help?

No parent likes the prospect of turning teenagers over to juvenile court, but it can, and has, saved kids and families. Prior legal consultation is advised.

Q: Please help. My brother is 17. He used to be real nice — a Boy Scout and everything. Now he skips school and won't listen to anyone. He comes and goes as he pleases. My parents are at their wit's end. They're afraid to turn Scott over to the Juvenile Court, but that's about all we can do. What do you advise?

A: A teenager out of control is a grisly picture. There are many possible explanations, including drugs, anger, fear, depression, anxiety, and a host of other psychological conflicts.

Your parents have to get tough. Someone has to be in charge. It should be them, not your brother. The time to act is now. As a first step, your parents must do whatever is necessary to have your brother evaluated by a psychiatrist. He should not be given an option. If he refuses, your parents should certainly consider the Juvenile Court.

Why are they afraid of the court system? Most Juvenile Courts provide parents the opportunity to petition for their child to be declared in need of court supervision. Laws vary, of course, from state to state, so I certainly suggest that your folks consult a private attorney before approaching the court. Once the court takes supervision it can mandate treatment or other options, such as juvenile detention, based on a teen's record and needs and the court's facilities.

Strong medicine? Yes, but Scott is hurting and time is rapidly running out. Once he turns eighteen, your family's leverage will be almost zero: shape up or ship out.

Messy Room

Well, the logical consequence to a messy room is to close the door and let them live in the mess. But if you must intervene, be specific.

Q: We made a deal with our son David, 17. He could paint and decorate his room — if he kept it clean. Well the room is a god-awful black and silver, and resplendent with rock posters and a parachute draped from the ceiling. He loves it. We hate it. And the room is as messy as ever: dirty socks, empty soda cans — you name it. What do we do now?

A: Probably nothing — except keep the door closed. The logical consequence is that David has to live in that mess. Changing the rules now will probably be futile, and a battle that you can win only at the considerable expense of frustration and turmoil.

If, however, you can't resist the urge, talk it over with David. Rather then requiring that he "keep his room clean," be specific. Write down your standards. Conduct a once-a-week inspection and tie one or more of his privileges (curfew, car, etc.) to his passing muster.

Divorce

Ex-Husband Takes Young Wife

Q: It's disgusting. My ex-husband, 40, has just married a girl, 18, who's a year younger than our daughter, Roberta. I'm flabbergasted, but Roberta is completely destroyed. What can I do to help?

A: The best approach is to listen non-judgmentally to Roberta's concern. She may feel that she's been replaced as a daughter by Dad's new wife. She may feel competitive. She may feel awkward or embarrassed about what her friends may say. There are deeper explanations too: Roberta may unconsciously identify with her new stepmother, and hence, come face to face with the taboo of incest. You can help by listening, accepting, then listening some more.

Your ex-husband, by the way, is following a well-known pattern. In first marriages, only 2% of men marry a woman who's 10 or more years younger (May-December marriages), but in second marriages, men choose a May bride 50% of the time.

In second marriage, men choose a woman who is 10 or more years younger than themselves 50% of the time. This can obviously cause serious tensions with adolescent children who may view Wife No. 2 as a rival sibling.

Son Ignores Non-Custodial Parent

Q: My 17-year-old son, Mark, lives in another state with my ex-husband, whom I divorced three years ago. Mark visited me last month. After two days he refused to speak to me and wouldn't say why. Now, when I try to call him, my ex-husband just says, "He doesn't want to talk to you," and hangs up the phone. I'm desperate. What can I do?

A: I don't like the sound of this. Did something happen between the two of you? Could Mark have found something in your home, witnessed something, overheard something? I'm sure you've asked yourself these questions, but ask again. Another possibility is that Mark still holds you responsible for the divorce and is acting out his anger by refusing to talk.

Non-custodial parents often face unusual obstacles to maintaining communication with their children. It can get harder or easier as they reach late adolescence. Listen. Try relating more on an adult basis.

Mark's father, on the other hand, is acting poorly. Whatever his own feelings toward you, he is not acting in the best interests of his son by cutting off communication with you.

If you can't get through to Mark, pursue your former husband for some information. He owes it to you. Keep after it. Pull a surprise visit if necessary. Work through a trusted intermediary, if possible. Don't let the link be broken.

When you do get a chance to talk to Mark, hold onto your own anger. Listen. Do some bridge building. Don't demolish the fragile foundation of the relationship. Build a new one. Mark is now on the threshold of adult life. Treat him as such, even though he may not be acting in a very adult manner just now.

Friends and Dating

Dating Game Plan

Conflicts with your late adolescent about his or her dating practices? You might have avoided it with a well-conceived game plan a few years back.

Q: Older but wiser. That's what we'd like to be. Our Carrie, 19, is a college sophomore. Her teenage years just crept up on us and we winged it, so to speak. As a result, she dated a few boys we disapproved of, but we didn't know how to stop it. We had no rules. Now her younger sister, 14, and brother, 13, want to start dating. We need a plan. Can you help?

A: As with so many other responsibilities (chores, homework, curfew, money management, etc.) it is important to have a basic game plan that allows a teenager to grow in experience, privilege, and responsibility, according to his or her ability to handle the situation.

How you structure your own plan will depend upon your family values, your teenager's chronological age and developmental maturity, and local customs.

So consider the following outline, then adjust for your own circumstances:

11 and 12: chaperoned mixed parties only

13 and 14: chaperoned group dates, then unchaperoned double dates

15 and 16: unchaperoned one-on-one dates with advance parental approval (i.e., screening) of the prospective date, and perhaps a talk with the date's parents

17 and over: unchaperoned one-on-one dates without advance approval, but require that you meet the dates before the youngsters go out for the evening, and retain veto power over a second date with the same person.

Should Parents Screen Prospective Dates?

Q: Our Cheryl, 17, is a high school senior. She started dating at 15, and we had a firm rule: we insisted on meeting any of her prospective dates before she could go out with them. Now she says "seniors shouldn't be required to have their dates screened by Mom and Dad." Should we turn her loose now?

It's reasonable for parents of older teens to meet their child's new dates, and get better acquainted with their steady dates.

A: Turn her loose? You seem to be going from one extreme to another. How about a transitional step. If you are reasonably pleased with her judgement, why not allow her to accept her own dates, but insist that you meet the boys for a brief, get-acquainted chat when they pick Cheryl up at the house?

I also think it's a good idea to include steady dates in family activities. It's a good way to get to know them.

Dating Double Standard?

Q: Jack, our 17-year-old, has been dating for two years. We've never met any of his girlfriends. His sister Allie, 15, has just started dating and my husband insists that we meet her dates in advance. She's angry because her brother never had to go through this process. She thinks it's a double standard and that we don't trust her. What can we tell her?

It's not too late to exert influence in both teens' dating preferences. In the future, give privileges based on age.

A: That you blew it. You are employing a double standard. The implication is that you do not trust her.

What to do? I believe that parents of teenagers should exert influence in their son's and daughter's dating preferences. Therefore, I do not recommend that you change your plans for Allie. And, of course, it's a little late for you to now insist that Jack have prior consent from you before he asks a particular girl on a date. But you can make some changes that will be in the best interests of both your youngsters. Ask Jack to bring his dates to the house to meet you before they go out. Require Allie's prospective suitors to meet you before giving your approval for a one-on-one date, but when she's 17, give her the privileges that Jack enjoys.

True Love?

Time will tell — time with other teenagers, some limits on the amount of time spent alone together. Listening will help too.

Q: My 17-year-old son, Brent, is head over heels in love with a 16-year-old girl, Marcie. They're together all the time. They're both loners. They have no other friends. Brent has been withdrawn since his father and I were divorced three years ago. Now he wants to quit school and marry Marcie. He says it's true love. Comments?

A: These things always have to be examined from a developmental perspective. It may well be that Brent and Marcie are using each other as a defense against a world that they view as lonely and uncaring.

I sense your dilemma. You may be afraid to take a strong stand against the relationship for fear that you'll only push them closer together.

A kindly, reasonable approach is in order. Listen to Brent. Listen to Marcie. Talk to Marcie's parents too. Encourage them to slow down. They should spend time with other teenagers. Place some limits on the amount of time they can spend alone together, but don't attempt to sever their relationship. Then, time will tell. And time, in this case, is on your side.

Make Him Jealous?

Making dates jealous sounds adolescent and it is. Many kids test their dates (and their own self-esteem) by making them jealous in some way. Should you intervene? Some gentle advice is in order, but they'll have to learn themselves — just as we did.

Q: Mary, our lovely 18-year-old daughter, has it made. She's bright, attractive, and has a super boyfriend. But that's the problem — the way she treats poor Brad. She's always putting him to some kind of test. She admits, for example, that she likes to make him jealous — just to see if he really loves her. I warn her that one of these days Brad will have had enough, but she keeps right on with her little games. What can I do?

A: I'm not sure that you should do anything. Sounds like you're more concerned about Brad than Mary is. She may have to learn the hard way. You might be interested to know, by the way, that Mary's behavior is not unusual. In a study of 90 college students, researchers found that most of these young people actually used tests (especially jealousy) to see if they were loved. Only 21% of the students did the obvious thing: ask directly.

There are many possible psychological explanations for Mary's behavior: poor self-esteem, the constant need for reassurance, ambivalence toward males — to name just a few.

Our course, there's another side to this equation: Brad. I wonder why he puts up with it? He may have some growing up to do of his own.

File this information away, but I suggest that you do not try to be an armchair counselor to Mary and Brad. Sure, give some gentle advice, but let them work it out. Let the chips fall. Let them work it out themselves. They will both learn something about life as a result.

Beach Week

Q: Our 17-year-old daughter, Valerie, recently graduated from high school. She has notified us that she plans to spend a week in August at the beach with her former classmates. She says it's a tradition and that everyone goes. My husband and I don't know what to do. We're worried about Val spending a week in mixed company without supervision. But we also know that we have to "let go" sometime, especially since she'll be going away to college in the fall. Any suggestions?

Graduating seniors in most parts of the country have some sort of tradition like Beach Week: unchaperoned fun in the sun — and under the moon. If it's his or her first such jaunt you may be reluctant to give permission. But if not now, when?

A: I appreciate your dilemma. It is one that is faced in some form or other by all parents of recent high school graduates: how to let them grow up gracefully while still offering parental protection and maintaining family values.

Some parents skirt the basic underlying issues, and decide that a young person cannot take a trip because of financial reasons, or because the family vacation suddenly conflicts with the youngster's plans. I would urge you to be straight with Valerie. Just what is it that concerns you most? Valerie can probably read your mind on this matter anyway. Confront the issue directly. If your concern is the boys or the living arrangements, say so. But try to do this in an understanding manner. After all, Valerie herself may also have some concerns. An open discussion can be very useful at this time in Val's life.

It is also a good idea to maintain some contact with the parents of a teenager's peer group. Such a group is your own peer network: a useful source of information about things like beach week. Just what is the tradition? Does everyone really go? What are the pros and cons? Ask questions, listen, then make up your own mind based on your family value system and your understanding of Valerie's own readiness for such an adventure.

Suppose you say "No" and Valerie responds, "You don't trust me." What next? Be honest with your daughter. It's possible to trust her, but not to trust the situation. As long as she lives under your roof you have an obligation to protect her and to be consistent in applying your values. In the final analysis, young people respect this kind of consistency.

And if you really don't trust your daughter herself, I'd still recommend honesty on your part. If you don't trust Val, we really do have a problem on our hands. What is the problem? Whose it it? Face it and try to work it out. Otherwise, Valerie's college days may be marred with parent-daughter conflict and be painful for all of you.

You are correct when you imply that Valerie will be on her own anyway in the fall. It is a fact that we raise our children to eventually leave us. I hope you have had a game plan over the years for preparing Valerie for her new independence, responsibilities, and opportunities. If you have, you should feel reasonably confident about her ability to take care of herself — to do the right thing. In this case you can take a deep breath, cross your fingers, and help her pack the beach bags.

Fraternity Hell Night

We called it hazing and it can be dangerous. Kids will endure almost anything to belong, but let's hope they know enough to say "stop" if things go too far.

Q: Our 17-year-old son, Ted, recently pledged a high school fraternity. It means a lot to him and we're in favor of it, but we're concerned about what they call Hell Night. It's the night they initiate the new members — and it does sound like hell. They pour paint and feathers on the boys and make them eat hotdogs stuffed with Vaseline and other horrible things. Ted says everyone survives but we're worried. Comments?

A: These grisly induction ceremonies are usually called hazing. The initiates prove their loyalty to the organization by submitting to the rite of passage. The practice has been around for over 100 years.

There are no good statistics about the number of young men and women who are injured by the practice, mostly because few of them report their suffering to authorities. After all, they are willing participants in a secret ritual. In fact, the *American Journal of* Forensic Medicine and Pathology estimates that only 45% of injured inductees seek medical attention.

The problems are twofold: physical injury and psychological abuse. Civil laws and school codes prohibit hazing in some parts of the country. I suggest you check the laws in your area.

The most important step, however, is a good talk with Ted. Being accepted is important, but not as important as maintaining his dignity, his mental health, and his physical well-being.

He must show enough courage to say "no" to any prank that goes too far.

Hobbies, Sports, and Other Interests

Cults

Q: Our 18-year-old daughter is a college freshman at a Midwestern university. She recently wrote to say that she won't be coming home for her next vacation because she plans to go to the West Coast with some new "friends" (not fellow college students) who are doing "community work." We've always trusted her judgement, but this time we're scared. We're afraid that these friends may be members of some kind of cult. What should we do?

A: I appreciate your concern. It does sound a bit suspicious. Although cults are not currently making headlines, they have in no way disappeared from the American scene. Their recruiters are still very active on the street corners of large cities and on the fringes of college campuses. In fact, a prime target is the college freshman: away from the familiar value base of home for the first time, perhaps a bit lonely, and puzzling over the typical late adolescent identity crisis: Who am I? Where am I going?

Cultists sweep in with friendly reassurances to these sometimes lonely young people. A ready-made family atmosphere is offered as a replacement for the family back home. Quick and easy answers are glibly provided to complex questions. The young person's naive sense of trust is manipulated. In essence, the cult hucksters take advantage of young peoples' natural developmental vulnerabilities — sometimes with disastrous results.

What is a concerned parent to do? First of all, you have every right, and every obligation to your daughter, to find out more about these "friends." Just who are they? Just where do they say they're taking your daughter? If you do not like the sound of it, I would encourage you to gently, but firmly, refuse her permission to travel with them.

Late adolescents are prime recruitment targets for cults because these youngsters are often so unsettled in their own beliefs and self-identities. Cultists cleverly offer simple answers to the complex questions that the kids are asking: Who am I? Where am I going? What should I believe?

Of course, you're probably asking: "How can I refuse her permission? She's 18 years old. She's away from home. If I refuse to let her go, might not that cause her to openly defy me?"

Yes, this danger does exist, but I'm counting on your daughter's probable ambivalence, and her love for you and your values. After all, if she wanted to keep this a secret from you she could easily have done it. She may well want you to say "No." She may be as frightened as you.

One final piece of advice: If letters and phone calls prove unsatisfactory, do consider a quick trip to visit your daughter at school. It may be the most important journey you'll ever take.

Other sources of help: The Citizens Freedom Foundation, an organization that provides information on cults and support to families. Write c/o P.O. Box 113, Kensington, Maryland 20795. A good, basic primer on cults is Cults and Kids: A Study of Coercion. This book is available free by writing The Boys Town Center, Boys Town, Nebraska 68010.

Satanic Cults

A young person involved in a Satanic cult needs help immediately. Those particularly vulnerable to recruitment are the rebels, the alienated, the unsure, and the emotionally unstable.

Q: Our 18-year-old daughter, Barbi, is playing with fire. Her mother and I recently learned from Carol, her younger sister, that she's been attending meetings of a satanic cult. She's always been rebellious, but this is too much. Apparently she prays to the devil, sacrifices animals on an altar, and what else we don't know. Carol says not to worry, that Barbi is just "looking for excitement," that she'll get over it. What do you say?

A: My colleagues in adolescent psychiatry around the country are concerned that satanic cults are becoming more active in their efforts to recruit vulnerable teens: the rebels, the alienated, the unsure, the emotionally unstable.

Satanic cults are based on devil worship. They glorify sex, violence, and pleasures of the flesh. They are certainly much more dangerous than cults that preach "peace and love," although even some of these cults do horrible damage by entrapping young people and robbing them of their identity and free will.

In my own clinical experience it is relatively rare for a young girl to be drawn to Satanism.

Most of the adolescent recruits are boys, many of them drug users or psychologically disturbed. Don't fall for Carol's reassurances. Barbi needs your help.

Now.

Dead Rock Stars

Q: My daughter, Robin, is 17. The other night a couple of her girlfriends came to the house to listen to tapes. I was surprised to hear the unmistakable sounds of Jimmy Hendrix, one of my old favorites. As we talked, I learned that the girls also favored another deceased rock star, Lynrd Skynrd. Why this preoccupation with the past and with dead artists? Is it a trend?

A: Teens, to some extent, have always been preoccupied with themes of early death and young hopes dashed. It fulfills a certain tragic view that adolescents sometimes have of themselves. If you're old enough, for example, you might recall a popular song from the '50s, "Teen Angel," — same theme, an earlier era.

The idealization of dead rock stars serves the same purpose, but may also include an element of protest. Why? Today's rock music, unlike the '60s, is not the music of protest. So, if a teenager is looking to the music world for symbols of protest, she'll have to go back several years. Hence the resurrection of old heroes.

But you can carry the analysis too far. Your daughter and her friends may not be preoccupied with death or protest at all. Maybe they have a broad based, healthy respect for many artists and sub-types of rock 'n roll. Talk to them. It should be fun. You may even find yourself reminiscing a bit ... "Teen Angel, can you hear me?"

Interest in dead rock stars may, on the one hand, symbolize a teen's preoccupation with themes of early death, young hopes dashed, and social protest. On the other hand, teens may simply like the beat. It does go on, you know.

Money and Allowance

Miss Moneybags

Q: About a year ago, my husband inherited some money from a relative. It was not a great fortune, but enough to make us much better off than our neighbors and friends. We think it's been a blessing, but our daughter Heather, 17, hates it. She says that her friends have dropped her and that they call her names like "stuck-up" and "Miss Moneybags." It's ruining her senior year. What can we do?

A: Your blessing has become Heather's curse. Why? It has made her feel different. I suggest you start by examining your own reactions to the inheritance. Has it changed your values?

Too much interest, or too little interest, in money can be a sign of conflict. Some parents are better at talking about sex with teenagers than they are at talking about money.

Your lifestyle? Heather may also be reacting against these factors. Remember that late adolescence is a time of high-minded idealism. Your money may have become the handy target of Heather's own role with her friends. Is she unwittingly playing into their hands by, for example, outdressing them? Perhaps Heather protests too much. She may have been bitten by the money bug herself and is conflicted about it; therefore, she may secretly need her friends to dislike that part of her that she herself dislikes.

There are many possibilities. Money is often overlooked as an important psychological influence in child development. Yes, it should be a blessing. But it means different things to different people. Help Heather take an audit of what it means to her.

My Son, the Gambler

Something to wager on: most adult compulsive gamblers get started during their adolescence.

Q: My 17-year-old son, Davidson, gambles. He plays poker with his buddies two or three times per week and has now branched off into wagering on football games. Is this a phase or is he in danger of becoming an incurable adult gambler?

A: Most compulsive adult gamblers get an early start: they pick up the cards and the dice in their adolescence. Why? Identification with a gambling parent or other important adults is a prominent cause. Also, the act of gambling with its risk-taking and excitement plays right into the teenage appetite for action, especially if a youngster is not finding much happiness in other parts of his life. This may be the key for Davidson: make sure that he has plenty of opportunity for success in school and with friends. Finally, he may be attracted to the money, equating it with manliness or self-esteem. If so, the solution may be an honest-to-goodness part-time job.

While many teenagers gamble from time to time, Davidson seems to be stepping onto the fast track. You are wise to be concerned. Your best bet: help him find some action on the positive side of life.

Psychiatric and Behavioral Problems

Adjustment Reaction of Adolescence

Q: We call him Mr. Rebellion. Our Martin, 17, has just been kicked out of school because of refusing to do any work and talking back to his teachers. At home it's the same. He says he wants to be "free" and wants us to "leave him alone." A psychiatrist says that Martin has an adjustment reaction and needs therapy. Is this serious?

A: Adjustment reactions are among the least serious psychiatric disorders. Basically, they describe normative conflicts (such as an adolescent's need for independence and autonomy, and other everyday stress reactions) that have reached exaggerated proportions. The diagnosis rules out other, more serious, problems such as depression or anxiety disorders, and even conduct disorders, where behavior problems have become a more fixed feature of a youngster's personality.

So there is good news among the bad. While adjustment reactions do not always indicate the need for therapy, your son's psychiatrist has recommended it. So let's be sure Martin gets it. Tincture of time, in his case, may be a medication that is too little and too late.

Adjustment reactions are among the least serious psychiatric disorders: exaggerated responses to everyday garden variety crisis. Sometimes no therapy is required. Sometimes it is.

Manic-Depressive Illness

Q: Tim, our 17-year-old son, has experienced severe mood swings for about the last two years. Recently we took him to see a psychiatrist who says that Tim is manic depressive. What is it? Can it be cured?

A: Manic depressive illness, also called bipolar illness, is one of the most dramatic and most treatable psychiatric diseases. Sufferers like Tim experience extreme mood swings. Manic or euphoric highs, characterized by frenzied activity, grandiose schemes, sleepless nights, global self-confidence, rapid speech, and racing thoughts are followed by crushing lows that are punctuated by apathy, sudden crying spells, despair, and even suicide.

Manic-depressive illness can and does occur among late adolescents. The disease is dramatic, but so is the cure.

305

Sounds like Tim has exhibited this classic pattern of alternating ups and downs. Some people, however, may suffer only the recurrent mania or the cyclic depression.

Current research points to a defect in brain cell chemicals as the cause of this baffling illness. There is also strong evidence of genetic transmission: the condition does tend to run in families.

The best news, however, is that most cases can be well controlled by the use of lithium carbonate, a natural metallic salt similar to sodium chloride, otherwise known as common table salt.

Lithium can prevent about 80% of manic attacks and also reduce the severity of depressive bouts. Like all medication, it does have some side effects. Tim, therefore, will have to be monitored closely by his psychiatrist. He will probably continue on the drug for several years, perhaps for the rest of his life. Thanks to lithium and other medication and supportive psychotherapy, however, thousands of people, like Tim, are now leading normal lives.

Cognitive Therapy

A relatively new form of talking therapy that attempts to teach the patient that her bad feelings are the result of drawing erroneous conclusions from life events. Cognitive therapy is especially effective in the treatment of depression.

Q: Last week we took our 17-year-old, Jo Ann, to a psychiatrist because she's depressed. The doctor is planning to use something called cognitive therapy. What is it? Will it work?

A: Cognitive therapy is a newer form of talking therapy that emphasizes the patient's need to understand that her pattern of negative thinking and pessimistic expectations leads her to feel discouraged and depressed. By comparison, psychoanalysis focuses on the unconscious and early childhood experiences, while behavioral therapy, based on learning theory, focuses on stimulus and response.

In cognitive therapy, the therapist attempts to teach the patient that his bad feelings are the result of his drawing erroneous conclusions from life events, e.g., "If other kids tease me, I must be bad; therefore I have good reason to be depressed."

Cognitive therapy has proven to be quite effective, especially in the treatment of depression.

But, remember, any therapeutic approach is only as good as the person using it. In other words, techniques are what you use until the doctor arrives.

Depressed Parent, Depressed Child?

Q: My husband has been treated twice for depression. We have three children, 17, 15, and 3½. Are they at risk?

A: Research recently reported in the *Archives of General Psychiatry* strongly suggests that children of parents who suffer from major depression are at increased risk for developing mental disorders.

These children, for example, were found to suffer depression at twice the anticipated rate.

Interestingly, these youngsters, when they do become depressed, develop the illness much earlier (12 to 13) than depressed children of non-depressed parents (16 to 17).

The answer to the question "Why?" remains to be uncovered. Undoubtedly there are both genetic and environmental factors.

You can use this information constructively. If any of your children develop behavioral or emotional symptoms, it would be wise to seek early consultation. It is far easier to treat these conditions in the early phase of the illness. And the best news of all is that treatment works.

Children of parents who have suffered depression are at increased risk for depression themselves.

Family Therapy?

Q: We recently took our 17-year-old son, Justin, to a psychiatrist because he was feeling depressed and his grades were slipping badly. The psychiatrist evaluated Justin, then recommended family therapy. We don't understand. What does family therapy have to do with our son's depression?

A: That's an excellent question for Justin's psychiatrist. As his parents, you ought to ask several questions: What is the specific diagnosis? How is it that Justin has this problem now? What is the treatment plan? Why family therapy instead of individual or group therapy? Will medication be used? If so, why? What are the chances for successful treatment following this plan? How will Justin, and you, know if the treatment is working? How will you know when it can be terminated? How much will it cost?

Family therapy may well be the treatment of choice in this case, but I can't be absolutely sure with only your letter to go on. I can say that most adolescent psychiatrists tend to use more family therapy for early than for late adolescents. Be careful, therefore, that the psychiatrist is not so enamored with family therapy that all his patients receive it automatically.

Family therapy can be an effective and powerful treatment, but if it is recommended, make sure that the therapist explains specifically why it is indicated in your case. In the hands of some practitioners, family therapy is more a general philosophy than a specific treatment approach. More therapeutic procrustean beds we don't need.

Family therapy, in the hands of some practitioners, is less a specific treatment than a general philosophy. Justin needs a specific treatment with specific goals for his specific problems. If family therapy is the bottom-line answer to your questions, then go for it. If you're not sure, then seek a second opinion.

Son Refuses Divorce Therapy

Older adolescents whose developmental thrust is to leave the family may find it difficult to accept a family-oriented therapy for the pain of separation and divorce. Nevertheless, it can be very helpful to them. Ask them to give it a shot, and to give it an open mind for at least five sessions.

Q: I am the soon-to-be divorced mother of three children, ages 11, 14, and 17. It's been rough and I have recently seen a therapist who recommends counseling for all four of us. All of us agree except John, the oldest. "I have no problems with the divorce," he says, "you go." What should we do? Go without John? Not go at all in hopes that he'll feel pressured to join us?

A: While it is possible, of course, that John is less affected by the divorce than the rest of you, and not really in need of counseling for his own sake, he may simply be denying his hurt. I suggest that, as he is the oldest sibling, you appeal to his sense of obligation to the family as a whole. The therapy, after all, is to help you heal as a unit. John is an integral part of the unit. If he does not participate, he could, in essence, be left behind emotionally by the rest of you.

If John balks, insist that he attend five sessions and keep an open mind. After the five sessions, it's up to him: start walking or keep talking.

Bulimia

Bulimia, an eating disorder manifested by eating binges followed by forced purges using vomiting and/or laxatives, is not uncommon among late adolescent girls. Unlike the anorexic, whose severe weight loss is apparent, the bulimic may go undetected for years. Treatment can be difficult.

Q: Our 19-year-old daughter, Susan, is away at college. Yesterday she called to tell us that she's been seeing a doctor because of bulimia. She said not to worry, but of course, we are doing just that. Is it serious?

A: Bulimia, literally translated, means "ox hunger." It is a symptom that mostly strikes young women. If Susan fits into the classic pattern, she periodically goes on eating binges, stuffing herself with all sorts of food, only to purge herself immediately by forced vomiting or laxatives.

Bulimia is tricky. Most of these girls tend to maintain a fairly constant and normal weight. Anorexics, on the other hand, are self-starvation victims; their goal is profound weight loss. Therefore, the bulimic may go undetected for a long period of time while the anorexic, even if she hides her weight loss well, will eventually be discovered.

Bulimia is not uncommon. One researcher found that 10% of coeds at a private college regularly practiced self-induced vomiting and 3% used laxatives.

What causes bulimia? We are not certain at this point. Yet we do know that many of these young ladies do suffer from depression and other interpersonal problems.

Treatment involving psychotherapy and antidepressant medication can be difficult unless the patient really wants to rid herself of the problem. Sometimes a period of hospitalization is needed in order to control the environment and conduct intensive therapy.

Although bulimia itself is not as life-threatening as anorexia, it can cause serious physical problems, and the underlying psychological problems can be very serious. In fact, suicide is the most common cause of death among bulimics.

I'm not telling you this to alarm you, but I want you to be informed. I'm impressed that Susan has volunteered the information to you. That's a healthy sign. Why not get her permission now to consult with her doctor for more information?

Girl Gambler?

Q: Jenny, our 17-year-old, loves to gamble. She'll make bets on almost anything: sports and weather, even how many cars will pass the house in an hour. At first it was cute, but now we're worried. Last night two of her girlfriends came over and demanded that Jenny repay each of them over $100 that she borrowed — to gamble. Does she have a problem? What should we do?

Compulsive gambling is recognized as a disease. Although rarely diagnosed in adolescence, it often has its beginnings in the teen years.

A: Although compulsive gambling is rarely diagnosed in adolescence, it often has its beginning in the teen years. And, as you probably know, males are much more often affected, about 10:1.

Still, I am concerned about Jenny. Among the questions I would ask are 1) To what extent has the rest of her life (school, social, etc.) been damaged by gambling? 2) Does she habitually seek action and excitement? 3) Is there a family history of addiction of any kind? 4) Can she control her wagering?

Compulsive gambling is recognized as a disease by the American Psychiatric Association.

A psychiatrist would be able to apply the specific criteria in Jenny's case, if she would agree to an interview. Sounds to me as if you should urge her to do it.

Teen Suicide

Each year 5,000 teenagers take their own lives. In addition, over 500,000 adolescents make sub-lethal suicide attempts. Among the major risk factors: 1) family history of depression and/or suicide, 2) lack of previous treatment, 3) the presence of firearms in the home, 4) drug and alcohol abuse, and 5) a previous attempt.

Q: Our youngest, C.J., is 17. Last night she said she learned in a psychology class that 1 in every 7 teenagers has attempted suicide. Sounds incredible. Is she correct?

A: A recent survey of 11,000 eighth and tenth graders suggest that C.J. may be correct. The study, funded by the U.S. Department of Health and Human Services found that 18% of the girls and 11% of the boys admitted that they had attempted suicide.

Although the validity of the survey is only as good as the honesty and accuracy of the respondents (e.g., if a teenager thinks 10 aspirins will kill her, she'll call her ingestion a suicide attempt), we do know that the number of actual teen suicides has indeed been on the rise.

But, why quibble about research design and statistical interpretation? Let's take C.J., and all adolescents, seriously when they come to us with this kind of information.

Ask, therefore, why C.J. is bringing this information to you at this time. Probably nothing to be alarmed about, but better be alert.

Wrist Slashing

Although wrist slashing is more often a dramatic gesture than a method of suicide, the teenager needs help: a psychiatric evaluation, positive attention, and love.

Q: My niece, 18, has superficially slashed her wrists at least twice. There was a lot of blood, but on neither occasion did she need to go to the hospital. Her parents are taking a very breezy attitude about it. They say she just wants attention. I think she may be suicidal. What do you think?

A: I would certainly take it more seriously. Your niece's current suicide potential would have to be evaluated on the spot by a psychiatrist. As you may know, suicide is the second leading cause of death among adolescents. Each year about 5,000 teenagers take their own lives. Yet there are probably over 500,000 suicide attempts or gestures each year. Distinguishing serious suicidal risk from less dangerous attention-getting is a tough job.

But what about wrist slashing? Frightening, yes, but not actually a very common method of suicide. Wrist slashing is usually a dramatic gesture on the part of the troubled youngster. Some kids, in fact, make a habit or fetish of cutting themselves — never with full-blown suicidal intention but rather to watch themselves bleed, to feel pain, or to unconsciously signal a cry for help. Other youngsters, however, lead up to a bona fide suicide attempt after several sub-lethal rehearsals. Thus, there's real danger in assuming that your niece is not potentially suicidal just because she has failed at it twice. In fact, a great many teenagers who ultimately succeed in taking their own lives made one or more gestures before the real thing.

Please don't fault the parents for their nonchalant attitude. They may be scared or confused. They may feel guilty and they may be attempting to deny their guilt or shame beneath their seeming unconcern. They need your understanding and compassion. Your niece could use a psychiatric evaluation, some attention on the positive side of life, and lots of love.

Handguns and Teen Suicide

Q: My sister-in-law's son, 17, shot and killed himself last week. He used his father's gun to do it. You can imagine the agony and guilt that the family is feeling. The boy never gave any hints of being depressed but his parents are anguished. They think they should have known. They curse themselves for the gun. Any comments?

Most teenagers who kill themselves give little or no warning, but be aware of risk factors such as a family history of depression and/or suicide, and the presence of firearms in the home.

A: The survivors of suicide have a tough road to travel. For their son it's over, for them it's something they have to live with for the rest of their lives.

Guilt is a normal reaction and so is anger. Yes, they will second-guess themselves, but they should be told that most teenagers who kill themselves give little or no warning. That's why they succeed at it. Major risk factors include:

1) lack of previous mental health treatment,
2) diagnosis of major depression in retrospect,
3) family history of depression and/or suicide, and
4) the presence of firearms in the home.

Another high risk factor, reported in recent studies, is alcohol and drug abuse.

Recent studies, by the way, also demonstrate that the availability of firearms in the homes of suicide completers is much greater than that in a comparable group of high-risk adolescents.

I add this last bit of information not to add to the guilt of the grieving parents, but as a warning to other mothers, fathers — and teenagers too.

Teen Hotlines

Involved and caring people are to be applauded for their work on teen suicide hotlines. Hotlines are given high marks by callers; problems connected with them are solvable.

Q: Our 18-year-old son has been a volunteer at a teen suicide hotline for the past two years. He's learned a lot, we're proud of him, and our local hotline does good work. How successful are they around the country?

A: Some studies have been conducted into the issue. Generally, hotlines are given high marks by callers (girls use them and like them more than boys), and there may be a slight decrease in suicide in those communities that have hotlines.

There are, however, several problems:

1) The hotlines tend not to be used by those teens at greatest risk (boys).

2) Callers, although helped momentarily, tend not to follow advice for later appointments. (One Cleveland hotline, however, has a good compliance record. Its staffers make appointments for callers rather than merely suggesting the procedure.)

3) Some hotlines, utilizing inexperienced and poorly trained staff, too often provide poor or inappropriate advice.

The problems, I believe, are surmountable. I applaud your son and others like him for getting involved — and caring.

Teen Drug Users and Suicide Attempts

Abstinence and sobriety are important to preventing a repeat suicide attempt. Removing alcohol and guns from the house will help.

Q: My niece, Debby, is 17. She was recently admitted to a hospital after a suicide attempt. While she was hospitalized, her parents learned that she has a serious drug problem. She's back home now, but I'm worried. What are the chances she'll try it again? Should her parents remove the booze from the house? Should her Dad remove his gun? Please help.

A: Teen drug users are much more likely than non-users to attempt suicide. Berman and Schwartz in the March, 1990 edition of the *American Journal of* Diseases of Children surveyed 298 recovering adolescent substance abusers. Thirty percent of them admitted to a suicide attempt, a rate three times greater than the comparison group.

Therefore, Debby's vulnerability to a repeat attempt is certainly related to her success in maintaining abstinence and sobriety. There are, of course, other factors too, such as her overall psychological status and family issues.

Yes, I believe the booze should be removed from the house, at least in the early stages of Debby's recovery.

The gun? Get rid of it.

Remember: Most teenagers who do end up killing themselves have made a previous unsuccessful attempt. Let's do everything we can to stack the odds in Debby's favor.

Drugs and Alcohol

Teen Drug Scene

Q: We have two teenagers, 17 and 16. What drugs are teenagers using most these days?

A: Keep in mind that polls on teen drug abuse can vary from year to year and from one region of the country to another. Accessibility, cost, and fads are some of the differential factors.

Here's a comparison of the top 10 drugs ever used by teenagers ages 12 to 17, according to the National Institute of Drug Abuse (NIDA) polls taken in 1987 and 1989:

The teen drug scene shifts over time, and varies somewhat from one region of the country to another. Accessibility, cost, and current fads are among the differential factors. Alcohol and cigarettes, however, continue to consistently lead the list.

		1987	**1989**
1.	Alcohol	57%	50%
2.	Cigarettes	45%	42%
3.	Marijuana	24%	17%
4.	Smokeless tobacco	—	15%
5.	Inhalants	9%	9%
6.	Stimulants (not including cocaine)	6%	4%
7.	Pain killers	6%	4%
8.	Cocaine, crack	5%	4%
9.	Tranquilizers	5%	2%
10.	Sedatives	4%	2%
11.	Hallucinogens	0.5%	1%

Why Does He Drink?

Q: My son Allan, 17, just entered a rehabilitation center to cure his drinking problem. When he was 8 his best friend died. When he was 10 his cousin was killed on a motor bike. The next year his father and I got divorced. At 15, he was placed in detention for vandalism. Now it's alcohol. With all these problems, no wonder he drinks. Does he have a chance?

Teen drinkers, like adult alcoholics, can come up with dozens of rationalizations for why they drink. Finding out why is not really so important. Getting them into treatment is.

A: Sure he does. He's lucky. He's in treatment. Yes, there's plenty of hope. I suggest, however, that you (and Allan) let go of the past. Focus instead on the present. All alcoholics and drug addicts, given the chance, can come up with dozens of rationalizations for their substance abuse. Your own preoccupation with Allan's past tragedies only fuels his excuses and may encourage him to feel sorry for himself.

Start fresh. Allan is sober today. Make today the first day of the rest of his life. A guiding principle of Alcoholics Anonymous is "one day at a time." It works.

Cocaine and Crack

Cocaine and its inexpensive derivative, crack, make headlines for a good reason. They are increasingly accessible and affordable to teens. Are they becoming a fad among teens? Just ask your adolescent.

Q: I'm 29. I have a 17-year-old niece, Sherry, who's a senior in a Midwest high school. I must admit I did some pot in school and even tried LSD. Thank goodness Sherry doesn't use drugs, but I was surprised when she told me that kids don't do much pot or acid these days. Apparently, they prefer cocaine and crack. Comments?

A: Most studies confirm that teen use of marijuana and hallucinogens (such as LSD) is down somewhat, but these substances are still widely available.

A recent survey by the National Institute on Drug Abuse found that 85% of high school seniors said it is "easy" to obtain marijuana, and 26% reported is is "easy" to obtain LSD. The major change since you were in high school is the availability of cocaine, or its derivative, crack. In 1987 only 38% of seniors believed it was easily obtainable. Today 55% of current high school seniors believe it is easily obtainable.

Cocaine, therefore, makes today's headlines for good reason. But let's not forget about the continuing threat of other substances, including alcohol.

Psychological Aspects of Common Medical Problems

The use of anabolic steroids to increase muscle mass has trickled down from professional and college age athletes to teenagers, for whom it is even more dangerous.

Steroid Abuse

Q: My son, 17, is on the high school wrestling team. He says several of the athletes at his school are using steroids to increase their strength. I know it's dangerous. How widespread is this problem?

A: A recent report in the *Journal of the American Medical Association* sheds some light on this phenomenon. Over three thousand twelfth-grade males, from 46 private and public high schools across the nation, were surveyed. The investigators learned that 6.6% of the students either currently use, or have used, anabolic-androgenic steroids.

Applying these results to the entire population of U.S. male high school students suggests that between 250,000 and 500,000 boys have used, or are currently using, these drugs.

Yes, steroids are dangerous. I suggest you talk to your son's principal about them.

Premenstrual Syndrome

Q: My 18-year-old daughter, Cindy, is a high school senior. Every month like clockwork she develops symptoms two weeks before her menstrual period: abdominal swelling, irritation, even crying jags. The symptoms stop as soon as her period starts. Could this be psychological?

A: Some of Cindy's symptoms are certainly psychological, but we don't really know for sure what causes Premenstrual Syndrome or PMS. The cause (or causes) may well be a combination of hormonal and other factors.

There are several forms of treatment available, including hormone therapy, vitamin B6, special diets, exercise, diuretic medications, mild pain relievers and muscle relaxants, as well as counseling and support groups. Some work for some women, some for others.

My advice? Don't rush Cindy off to a psychiatrist. Start with her gynecologist for a thorough evaluation. And don't suggest to Cindy that it's all in her head. If later she needs a psychiatric evaluation, it would be to treat part of the problem — the emotional part.

Although many of the symptoms of PMS are psychological, that's not to suggest that it's all in your head. The causes are probably a mix of hormonal and other factors, including emotional ones.

Psychological Growth and Development

Identity Formation: The Fourth Task

The fourth and final task of adolescent development: Who am I? Where am I going? Few 17- or 18-year-olds have all the answers, but the answers will all fall into place sooner or later. Some adults, of course, never complete this task. They journey through life as adolescents in adult bodies, forever in search of themselves.

Q: Abby, our 17-year-old, is all messed up. She says she doesn't know who she is anymore. She says she's trying to "find herself." One day she's going to quit high school, the next she's planning on two Ph.D. degrees. Actually my husband and I were expecting something like this; we went through it too when we were young adults. We worked it out, but we were older. Should we be concerned about Abby's problems?

A: Concerned? Of course. But there's probably no need for excessive worry. You suggest that Abby's "identity crisis" is coming at an early age. Seventeen is about par for the course these days, especially if Abby is a high school senior. The beginning of an adult identity is, in fact, the last true task of adolescent development. Abby is leaving her childhood self behind and is suddenly faced with questions that previously she didn't even know existed. Who am I? Where am I going? For what purpose? With whom? etc. It can be a painful process for some youngsters, but it can be an inspirational process too.

So, let yourselves be sounding boards for Abby. Take her seriously, but don't let her do anything foolish, like quitting school. Any important and far-reaching decision made in the throes of a red-hot identity crisis will probably be regretted next week (or even tomorrow). So, safeguard the foundation while Abby is busy rearranging some of her psychological furniture. And don't expect Abby to solve these dilemmas immediately. Many adults never fully complete the final task of adolescent development. They journey through life in search of themselves.

My Son, the Philosopher

A holdover from middle adolescence. Preoccupation with philosophical and abstract concepts is not unusual for the late adolescent.

Q: My 17-year-old son, David, has become a real armchair philosopher. He's forever trying to "engage" me in "meaningful conversations": What is life? What is time? etc. What's happening?

A: David has reached a new plateau of psychological development. Piaget called this stage "formal operations." Child psychiatrists often refer to it as "abstract thinking." This skill is usually acquired at age 16 to 18. Before this time, teenagers' thinking is relatively concrete: things are what they appear to be.

David's new-found intellectual skills allow him to be reflective and to philosophize. For the first time in his life he is able to think about thought, to reason about reason, and to engage in a host of other wonderful mind games. It's as though he's discovered a new toy. He'll want to practice with it as much as possible.

Your son will probably begin to confront family values and moral dilemmas by asking thought-provoking questions. You see, up to this time such issues have been relatively simple for him. Things have been either good or bad, right or wrong, black or white. Now, David will be able to examine all the various shades of gray. It's one more step on his journey to adulthood.

Yes, these "meaningful conversations" can test a parent's patience. Hang in there. Humor him, if necessary.

Opposes Parents' Beliefs

Q: Our 17-year-old son, Frank, is a closet conservative. He's always spouting right-wing slogans around the house. He knows this bothers my husband and me — we're both quite liberal in our beliefs. The funny thing, though, is that Frank seems to be very liberal in the presence of his friends. My husband calls him a hypocrite. I say he's confused. What's going on?

A: Frank, when all the political chits are counted, is mostly a 17-year-old boy. He's trying to work out his beliefs. It will take time.

At this point, he's confronting the beliefs of his childhood as represented by his parents. Yet he must live in the world of his peers as well. He's caught on the horns of a developmental dilemma. With time, he'll hopefully combine the best of both worlds into his very own political belief system.

Just when you thought she was settling down, your teenager is again challenging your beliefs. Only now she's conceptual and more sophisticated. Give some intellectual slack. Don't take it personally. Listen. You may learn something.

He Wants to Change Religions

Q: We are a fairly religious family. My husband and I have raised our children with a firm belief in the church. Imagine our shock, therefore, when our 19-year-old son, Dennis, announced that he won't go to church with us anymore, and that he plans to change religions. My husband and I are sick at heart

Avoid attacking a late teen's newly found religion. Instead, listen to him, try to empathize, don't threaten, but do stand up for your own beliefs.

about it. Dennis refuses to talk with our pastor. He's rebellious. What can we do? Where have we gone wrong?

A: You're going wrong if you fall into the trap of taking this personally. Dennis is not rebelling against you. I also doubt that he's rebelling against your religion. What is he rebelling against? Dennis is probably rebelling against the remains of his childhood and some of the beliefs that he once, as a child, took for granted.

This kind of rebellion is not unusual among late adolescents as they strive, sometimes painfully, to define themselves as adults.

The best response is to listen to your son. Try to empathize with his crisis of conscience. Yes, you should stand up for your own beliefs, but don't clobber him with them. Don't threaten. And, by all means, don't criticize your son's newly found religion. Such an attack could boomerang on you.

Remember that most young people emerge from these crises as stronger and more mature individuals. If Dennis is like the majority, he'll ultimately become even more committed to his religion — your religion.

The Six Stages of Prejudice

Prejudice is the ugly product of self-loathing individuals. Unable to accept their own limitations, they project them onto other people or groups. Teens are vulnerable to prejudice because they are so uncomfortable with themselves. At the first sign, nip it in the bud.

Q: My 17-year-old son, John, recently joined an out-of-school club. He won't say much about it, but I've been picking up little tidbits of information that I don't like. For example, blacks and other minority boys are not allowed to join. And lately John has been telling a lot of ethnic and racial jokes. My husband and I are worried. Is our son becoming prejudiced?

A: Prejudice is a pattern of hostility against a group or its individual members. Does John fit the definition? You're concerned that he may be on the road to bigotry. You are a perceptive parent.

First, let's look at this matter from a developmental perspective. Youngsters, like John, often begin to confront the important issues of the world during their late adolescent years. It can be exciting — and confusing too. Their newly developed ability to use abstract thinking allows them, for the first time in their lives, to consider the nuances, the shades of gray, in the world. Up to this time things have been more neatly packaged: good or bad, right or wrong. Dealing with the nuances, however, can be painful; it takes a lot more soul searching and head work. This is why some teenagers band together in groups that do their thinking for them.

John may be seeking a kind of refuge for his exhausted conscience. It doesn't make him a bigot. He may be more of a fellow traveler at this point. But, yes, there is some danger. He could become overwhelmed by the peer pressure of his "club." He could be led beyond 1) private thoughts and 2) jokes and racial slurs into more serious stages of prejudice which have been described in Gordon Allport's classic study, 3) avoidance of certain groups, 4) active discrimination, 5) physical attack, and 6) organized opposition to an entire group.

The road to out-and-out bigotry starts with the first step. While most people tend to restrict their prejudice to one stage, it is true that intense activity at one stage makes transition to the next stage much easier. Try to understand John's need for the "club." Talk with him. Help him sort out his crisis of conscience and to be comfortable with himself; secure individuals who can accept their own feelings do not become prejudiced. With your sensitivity he can be spared the rest of the journey into the last, bitter stages of prejudice.

The "I'm-18-and-You-Can't-Stop-Me" Syndrome

Q: We have a problem. For several years we've been putting money into a savings account in our son's name. The money was to be used for his education. Our son has just turned 18 and insists that the money is legally his and that he plans to buy a home computer that costs $4,000. He knows nothing about computers. We're sure he'll forget all about it in a week. Help!

A: This situation is not uncommon. In fact, I call it the "I'm-18-and-you-can't-stop-me" syndrome.

A youngster's eighteenth birthday is a momentous event in our society. It represents, of course, a passage into adulthood. Many youngsters feel a need to put their new manhood or womanhood to a test. That's why you hear a lot of bravado from some of them, such as: "I'm moving out of the house and you can't stop me."

The youngsters who make the most noise are generally the ones who are less sure of themselves. Beneath their cries of independence they are afraid of giving up the easy joys of

Talk about your rites of passage. Your teenager may now test your limits with a brand new battle cry: "I'm 18 and you can't stop me." Should you still exert parental influence? Yes, but in a new way.

childhood. They want the privileges of adulthood, but they are not yet ready for the responsibilities of adult life.

On the other hand, your son might just want to get your attention. He's 18 and he wants to be darn sure that you know it! He wants to feel something new and to be treated differently.

In other words, the computer may be just a smoke screen. Don't get too wrapped up in all the hardware and software. Don't fall into the trap of telling your son, "Just because you're 18, it doesn't mean that you have mature judgement." Such pronouncements, of course, will only make him more resolute for the computer: now he's got to buy it just to show you that he can do it.

Try to avoid getting caught in an argument. Instead, give your son a dose of the adult-like respect that he craves. Listen to him. Talk it over with him. I'm not suggesting that you give in to him, especially if the money is vital for his educational needs. And I'm not suggesting that your parental obligations end with your son's eighteenth birthday. They don't. Your son will continue to need you as a parent, but the way in which he needs you is changing. He wants you to get that message. The computer is probably much less important to him than you think.

My Daughter Wants to "Find Herself!"

Yes, they now have to find themselves but you still have an obligation to protect them from foolish mistakes. Your job is not over yet.

Q: My 17-year-old daughter, Donna, is scheduled to enter a prestigious Eastern university in the fall. Imagine my shock when she came up to me last week and told me that she's decided not to go to college this year at all. Instead, she plans to take a year off for travel in the Southwest in order to "find herself." I tried to laugh it off at first, but she's serious. What should I do?

A: Hang in there. Donna has come face to face with an age-old dilemma: to grow up or not to grow up. Her "timeout" from life to "find" herself is just one way of postponing leaving behind the carefree years of adolescence for the more responsible and accountable years of adulthood.

Donna is also toying with a new-found intellectual tool: the ability to use abstract thinking. Like most late adolescents she is using this new skill to ask, for the first time in her life, such esoteric questions as "Who am I?" and "Where am I going?" Donna either does not have the answer to these questions (how many 17-year-olds do?) or she feels that she is just following a road map that has been designed by Mom. She desperately wants to be her own person. As one 17-year-old boy put it to me once: "I don't want to be stamped from my parents' cookie cutter."

I would urge you to explore these issues with Donna. Listen to her and try to understand. Yet I would also urge you not to give in to her sabbatical next year. She can "find" herself at Amherst as well as Albuquerque, Auburn as well as Aspen. Personally, I've seen too many bright youngsters fall by the wayside. What starts as a timeout, too often becomes a drop out. And I have yet to have such a youngster come back to me after a year away and announce that they have "found" themselves. Most of them are still in New Mexico or Colorado — still looking.

Join the Army?

Q: My nephew George, 18, barely made it through high school. He's been fired from his first two jobs because he can't take orders, and he thinks he knows it all. Now he stays out late at night and sleeps until noon. His parents are supporting him until he "finds himself." I say hogwash. He needs a kick in the you-know-what. I think he ought to join the army. What do you think?

Mom and Dad become part of the problem by underwriting their son's lack of discipline and responsibility. The military might help him, if he willingly volunteers.

A: I'm not so sure. My own experience as a navy flight surgeon was that young men who had behavior problems in their prior civilian life simply transferred those same problems to the military. Many of them ended up in the brig or at captain's mast. Many were discharged under less than honorable conditions. In short, they failed yet again.

On the other hand, there is some evidence that the military can have a beneficial effect on young men like George. Researchers at the University of California report that troubled youths who entered the armed forces were more likely to avoid problems after 18 than those who did not. The study, conducted over 30 years, is reported by Emmy Werner in her book, *Against the Odds*.

The key is George. If he is volunteered against his will, the plan is likely to backfire.

A kick in the behind? Yes, Mom and Dad, by underwriting George's lack of discipline and responsibility, are unwittingly becoming part of the problem.

Family Hero

A child can feel a great burden when parents want him to be a more perfect extension of themselves. In this situation, he needs someone to talk with and spend time with who accepts him for what he is.

Q: It's not fair. My brother and his wife have set their 17-year-old, Elliott, up to be a hero or something. He can do no wrong, get it? They worship him. Of course, he is a great kid: top grades, excellent behavior and everything, but still, I worry about him. Last night he confided to me that he thinks he's a "phony." He seems depressed to me, but he's afraid to tell his parents. He doesn't want to disappoint them.

A: You're absolutely right. We don't do children any favors when we project onto them our own needs for them to be more perfect extensions of ourselves. That's the dynamic behind a lot of hero-making.

Elliott is now saddled with a lot of Mom's and Dad's psychological baggage. He's carrying their banner for them and he won't let it touch the ground — even at the expense of his own mental health.

This obviously could be dangerous. The healthiest sign I see is that Elliott can at least let his defenses down with you.

I would urge you strongly to keep open your own channels of communications with your nephew. He needs you. Spend time with him. Accept him for who he is, not what he accomplishes. Ideally, I'd also like to see you talk to Elliott's parents about this, but I'm not sure how they'd react. Use your own judgement.

Is Our Teenager Too Good?

It used to be said "show me a normal teenager and I'll show you a neurotic adult." Not true. Many (one out of three) youngsters coast through adolescence with a minimum of turmoil and come out just fine on the other side — adulthood. But they still need acceptance for who they are, not what they do.

Q: I guess I should count my blessings. My 17-year-old daughter, Jamie, is wonderful. She's well-behaved, considerate, does well at school, isn't interested in drugs, and has beautiful friends. Is this too good to be true?

A: Count your blessings. Jamie could be the real thing: a happy, well-adjusted teenager. While the problem kids seem to get most of the attention, there are lots of youngsters like Jamie in our world.

It used to be the common wisdom, by the way, for psychiatrists to say that "show me a normal teenager and I'll show you a neurotic adult." The theory was that adolescent rebellion was normal and necessary — a safety valve for sexual and aggressive drives. If the drives did not get expressed, the theory went, they had to be forcibly repressed, only to leak out in later years in the form of a neurotic symptom. So much for theory.

Our experience today is that about a third of all teenagers resemble Jamie: solid, happy, non-rebellious kids. And guess what? The great majority of them grow up to be solid, happy, non-rebellious adults.

He Wants to Leave Home

Q: Our 19-year-old son, Tom, has been living at home for the past year following his high school graduation. He works at a local department store. We've given him a lot of freedom and we were surprised when he told us last week that he plans to move into his own apartment — so he can be free. We're not against the apartment, but it seems foolish. He has everything here that he needs and it's a lot cheaper. Any comments?

Independence is a state of mind, not a matter of where you live.

A: Tom is struggling with one of the tasks of adolescent development: autonomy and independence from parents. He may be making a mistake, though, of equating geographical independence with psychological independence. You see, independence is a state of the mind, not a matter of where you hang your hat.

For example, I know of 19- and 20-year-olds who live hundreds of miles away from parents, but who are still as dependent on Mom and Dad as they were at puberty: they rely on their parents for tuition, spending money, and, even more crucially, for the important decisions in their lives.

On the other hand, I know of young people who still live under the parental roof, but who are well on the road to psychological independence: they contribute financially to the household, and more importantly, they are beginning to make up their own minds about life choices.

Your situation, and Tom's, is getting more common all the time. In fact, since 1969 the number of young people remaining at home has increased 25 percent. The reasons are largely due to financial considerations and the fact that young people are marrying at a later age.

Empty Nest

Q: Our Mandy, 17, is a high school senior and our only child. She plans to go to college next year and I miss her already. Are parents of only children more prone to the Empty Nest Syndrome? I'm trying to hide my feelings from Mandy.

Should I?

Your job as a parent is to ultimately work yourself out of a job. So enjoy it while you can, and be sure you have other interests and sources of self-esteem; for leave you, they certainly must.

A: Generally, parents who are most prone to feelings of profound loss when their last child moves out of the home are those who have put all their eggs into the parenting basket, so to speak. It's important for mothers and fathers to make marriage their top priority, and to have other sources of interest and self-esteem, such as work, hobbies, and friends.

Yes, I have found that parents who have only one child tend to be somewhat more vulnerable, especially if they have not prepared in advance.

What to do now? Don't try to hide your feelings. I bet Mandy is aware of them anyway. She herself probably has some ambivalence about going off to college. It's worse for all of you if the subject of leaving has to be swept under the family carpet. Talking will help all three of you.

Fathers and the Empty Nest

Fathers may become disappointed and depressed when they realize they've not spent as much time as they wanted with their youngster — and he's left the nest.

Q: I knew I'd be sad when our last child, 18-year-old Greg, went off to college. I kind of prepared myself for it. What I wasn't prepared for was my husband's reaction. He's really taking it hard. He's smoking more and seems preoccupied most of the time. He really wasn't as close to Greg as I was. That's what has me perplexed.

A: Surprise. Fathers often have more trouble adjusting to the empty nest than mothers.

Researchers at the University of Minnesota have studied this phenomenon. They found that fathers suffer more stress when faced with the empty nest — maybe because they have not spent as much time with the kids as Mom. Generally, fathers are wrapped up in jobs and career pursuits during a youngster's early formative years. They tell themselves, however, that they'll make it up to the kids later. When later finally arrives, it may be too late. Hence, their disappointment and depression. Obviously, there's a lesson here for all fathers.

The Re-Feathered Nest Syndrome

The young adult who leaves, only to return, is a recent phenomenon. It calls for careful readjustment on all sides.

Q: I hate to admit it, but my husband and I were actually disappointed when our youngest daughter, Julie, 20, came back home to live with us after being in college for two years. We were just starting to enjoy a second honeymoon. Now we're back to nagging her about cleaning her room and coming home on time. It's like the teenage years all over again. Please help.

My husband and I thought we were finished with the parenting business. How can we get out of it this time around?

A: You can't. You never cease being a parent. But what should change is the manner in which Julie needs you as parents. Just when she had seemingly passed from an adolescent phase into an early adult phase, you find yourselves immersed in adolescent conflicts again. Why?

Sometimes a young person and her parents have not resolved the issues of adolescence. Julie's return, in that case, would have important unconscious psychological causes. Sometimes parental nagging is a thinly disguised effort to convince a youngster that she could do better elsewhere.

You may not be able to control Julie's behavior at this point, but you can control your own. Be straight with Julie about your resentment — she's picking up the unspoken cues anyway. Then, tell Julie that it's not in her interest or yours to relive her adolescence. Ask her to join you in drawing up a plan that will work for all of you.

Siblings

When Sis Becomes a Substitute Mom

Q: I think we've got a double problem on our hands. Please help. We have an 18-year-old daughter, Jewel, and a 4-year-old son, Jackson. Jewel has always been something of a substitute mother to Jackson. It seemed a natural role for her and we're all comfortable with it. I never took advantage of Jewel in this position, and I was always clear with Jackson that I was his mother and that I was in charge. The problem is this: Jewel has just entered college and Sonny is absolutely destroyed. He cries for her and has to call her every day. Jewel, of course, feels very badly too. She goes to college in our city and lives in a dorm. She comes home every weekend, and has even offered to move back home. Something tells me it's not a good idea. Should I let her move back in?

Older adolescents often become de facto substitute parents to very young siblings, either by parental design or personal choice. Not a good idea.

A: No. Not now, at least. For her part, Jewel must deal with the important developmental issue of leaving home and carving out her own identity. Be careful that her surface motivation to return home (i.e., to help Sonny) doesn't cover up some homesickness or separation anxiety of her own.

Sonny, on the other hand, has obviously invested much more importance in Jewel than anyone apparently intended. Unfortunately, you don't always realize this sort of thing until a separation occurs. Sonny clearly needs some help. By the way, I like the phone calls and I'd favor occasional visits, but not every weekend. Both Jewel and Jackson have some separating to do. There may be some temporary anguish involved, but in the long run they'll both be better off for it. You and your husband can help both of your children by being strong, sensitive, and supportive. Project confidence. We want them to perceive that everything's going to be alright.

School

The Senior Who's Suddenly Flunking

Strange things happen. The outwardly confident senior may collapse in a pile of self-doubt. The A student may suddenly flunk English. Beneath the bravado — fear.

Q: Our daughter, Lucy, has always been a good student. In fact, she's been accepted to three colleges already. Doctor, we don't understand what's happening. She's 17 and in the last semester of her senior year, and suddenly she's failing several courses. What's happening?

A: Lucy may be scared of growing up. Sudden academic nose dives are not uncommon among last-semester seniors who unconsciously fear giving up their adolescence for the uncertainties of young adulthood. Failure in the classroom obviously may postpone graduation and symbolically, therefore, may perpetuate the easy dependency of teenagedom. Youngsters who are shy, dependent on parents, and unsure of themselves are most prone to this particular form of senioritis. But appearances can be deceiving. Sometimes the least obvious boy or girl (the outwardly confident and gregarious type) may fall victim to this problem, because beneath their exterior bravados beat frightened hearts; their outward behavior is just a defense against very strong dependency needs and lack of sufficient identity formation.

One further word of caution. A common cause of sudden and unexplained radical change in behavior is, of course, drug abuse. I don't wish to alarm you, but you should also keep this possibility in mind.

At any rate, Lucy needs your loving understanding. Try to open communication with her. First help her to express her feelings. The facts will follow. Consultation with a psychiatrist who specializes in treating adolescents may be necessary if your own efforts do not get quick results. After all, we'd all like to see Lucy receive that diploma, on schedule, in June.

Let Her Quit School?

Q: Doni, our daughter, just turned 18. Imagine my shock when she told us she was quitting school. Imagine my shock when my husband said, "Go ahead, it's your life."

I say this is horrible. She's due to graduate from high school in one more semester. OK, so she's not doing too well. At least she'd have her diploma. Without it, where will she be?

Doctor, I'm desperate. What do you suggest?

A: Doni's ultimatum should not be taken at face value. Her announcement may have been less a statement of intent and more a question, i.e., "Now that I'm 18, how much freedom do I have — how much will you let me have?"

Doni and Dad were eyeball to eyeball and, unfortunately, Dad blinked first. Of course I realize that he may rationalize his actions by saying that since Doni is 18, she is old enough to make her own decisions. But he's focusing on the narrow legal aspects of her argument — and ignoring the broader psychological aspects. Doni is asking who's in charge. I think it should still be Mom and Dad in this case. Dad should have listened, empathized with her feelings, and then let her know that although she certainly should enjoy more freedom and responsibility now, he expects her to finish high school.

The newly 18-year-old marginal high school student may feel compelled to exert her new adult privileges in ways that are ultimately self-defeating, such as quitting school. Remain a parent. Exert your influence.

Intelligence vs Motivation

Q: My brother always bragged about his son's intelligence. He claims that Kevin, 17, has an IQ of 140. "So why did he fail two courses last year?" I ask. "Why doesn't he plan to go to college. What's all that intelligence worth to him if he doesn't use it?"

Our son, Marvin Jr., is 17 too. He's a pretty average guy, but he works like a dog in school. He's on the honor roll. He's going to college next year.

Doesn't this story prove that motivation is more important than intelligence any day?

A: Not quite. But you make a powerful point. I've met a lot of Kevins in my professional life: the classic unmotivated youngster with tremendous potential that sadly never gets used. On the other hand, I've also been impressed by boys and girls who

Which is best? Both, naturally. But if I had to choose, I'll take the teen with average intelligence who's motivated to work hard over the naturally gifted youngster who is intellectually lazy — any day.

make the most of average ability through sheer determination and hard work. It's my guess that there are more of them in positions of leadership in this world than there are geniuses.

But, of course, the ideal combination is superior intelligence plus strong motivation. Such youngsters are blessed, but remember, nobody's perfect.

College Application Jitters

How many college applications? Five. My formula: one long-shot, one sure-thing, three maybes but probables.

Q: Katie, our 17-year-old high school senior, is driving us nuts with college applications. She wants to apply to a dozen schools, and moreover, she insists on visiting each of them. This is our first experience with college application. Is she being extreme?

A: Yes. And I wonder why. Is she insecure about her chances of being accepted anywhere, or is she unsure about herself and just what she really wants to do?

In my opinion, five applications should be the limit. This, of course, requires some homework with resource books and catalogs. It should also include talks with Katie's high school counselor and with friends.

I suggest one "long shot" application and one "sure thing." The other three applications could go to schools that fit into the "maybe but probable" categories.

Visits? They're fun. But they're expensive. And they're not always necessary at this point. Katie could wait and then visit the schools that accept her, unless she's able to make some visits easily and without breaking the family bank.

Rejected by College of Choice

Guard against it by helping your youngster to be realistic in her choice of applications. But if the axe falls, listen and absorb her feelings before you launch into a pep talk.

Q: It arrived in the mail yesterday. A thin envelope. The letter read: "Regret to inform you ... difficult decision ... not an indication of your ability ... best wishes," and our Brenda, 18, was crushed. She had been turned down cold by the college of her dreams. We had, of course, warned her about the competition, but she wouldn't listen. Now she's so upset she doesn't want to accept her back-up choice, which, by the way, is a very respectable in-state college. What can we do?

A: First, try to get in touch with your own feelings. In such circumstances it is only natural that parents feel rejected too.

Then, before you give a pep talk and extol the virtues of State College, listen to Brenda. Help her get her feelings out and work them through. If State College requires a quick response to ensure her place in next year's freshman class, by all means mail the check. Explain to Brenda that she has to keep her options open.

Brenda, of course, is not alone. Thousands of highly qualified students get rejected by prestigious colleges and universities. Yes, you can remind her of this fact, but right now she's overwhelmed by feelings. Absorb the feelings first; the facts will help later.

Written on Bathroom Walls

Q: I'm 38, male, and a high school teacher. I've observed, of course, that today's teens are a lot different from the way we were back in the late '60s. My students (17- and 18-year-old seniors) are much more interested in getting good grades and getting into the colleges of their choice. But how about this observation as an index of change: I think the graffiti in the boys bathrooms in public school says it all — it's 95% sex, and almost never do I see a political slogan. Has teen graffiti ever been studied?

Are the political aspirations of our teens still written on bathroom walls? Not these days.

A: Graffiti and just about everything else, it seems, has been studied by students of human behavior. However, I don't know of any recent research — other than your own.

Your observations, of course, are right on the mark. Today's teens, as a group, are not rebelling against the system, they're trying to become a part of it. Even those rebels who attempt to express themselves in graffiti, for example, are hard pressed for slogans and symbols. That's why you'll find some terribly outdated "peace symbols" and references to Vietnam-era issues.

But, remember, these things go in cycles. So keep watching those bathroom walls. You may be able to discern the next wave of protest.

Freshman Fears

Q: Our oldest daughter, Francine, is an 18-year-old college freshman. We thought she'd get homesick, but her adjustment has been good, except for one thing. She's always worrying about making friends. All I ever fretted about in college was grades. Is she typical of today's college student?

Today's freshmen fear most of the same things we did: academic failure, making friends, being homesick, and gaining weight.

A: Not according to the findings of a recent Stanley Kaplan poll. The top fears of college freshman are: 1) academic failure,

74%, 2) making new friends, 9%, 3) being homesick, 8%, 4) roommate troubles, 5%, and 5) gaining weight, 4%.

While friends are important, Francine may be misplacing her priorities. Academic success should not take a back seat to anything. If her grades are not up to par, I suggest that she pay a visit to a college counselor. If her "friend fears" are preoccupying her, she could also use some help.

College Stress

The transition from high school to college has always been stressful, but recent studies suggest it is a bit tougher today than it used to be.

Q: Our Mary, 18, is a college freshman. She was a B+ student in high school, but is struggling to make C's now. She's very uptight about it: excessive worry, trouble sleeping, frequent headaches. She refuses to see a counselor, and we're four hours away from her. What can we do?

A: A recent UCLA survey confirms that today's college students are stressing out in record numbers. Over 300,000 students at 585 colleges responded to the interviewers. Slightly over 10% reported frequent depression, compared with just over 8% in 1987.

I'm concerned about Mary. The transition from high school to college can be very stressful and there's no shame in her struggle, but her refusal to get help is a danger sign. I urge you to pay her a visit. Reassure her. Listen to her. Then, walk her over to the school's Counseling Service.

A "Homesick" College Freshman

Separation anxiety revisited. The cure? It's to be found on campus, not back home. This is what college counseling services are made for.

Q: Our 18-year-old son, Andrew, went away to college several weeks ago. Since then he's been home every weekend. He complains that college is boring and he looks very sad. He calls home often during the week and only seems to get excited about family news or news about his old high school. We think he's homesick. What should we do?

A: Homesickness is not uncommon among college freshmen. It sort of goes with the territory. I wonder if Andrew has ever spent much time away from home. Youngsters for whom college is really their first true experience away from home are especially vulnerable. Also, if Andrew has typically reacted to separations from you and your husband by feeling lost, depressed, or apprehensive, you can almost bet that his initial adjustment to college life may well be tough; he may be suffering from a dose of separation anxiety.

There are some college students, on the other hand, who are not really homesick, in the classic sense, but may appear to be on the surface. These young people do not fear the separation from their families and familiar surroundings, but they are frightened of their new world. You might say that they are "college sick." They feel shy and self-conscious, socially unsure, and academically incapable. They've separated from the old world of home and high school, but have not yet landed safely in a new developmental haven.

Into which camp does Andrew fall? You'll only know by talking it over with him. I would also urge you to gently, but firmly, discourage his weekend visits. Whether he's homesick or college sick, the cure is to be found on campus, not back at home. And finally, please don't forget the college counselors. They help youngsters like Andrew all the time. The first few weeks of college can be crucial for guys like Andrew. Let's get him all the help we can.

Choose Dad's Career?

Q: My 18-year-old grandson, George, is a college freshman. He's planning to be a lawyer, but I'm afraid it's only to make his lawyer father happy. In fact, George told me last summer that he'd rather be a teacher. Should I talk to his father?

A: I don't think so. Not now. Instead, remain available to George as a neutral, non-judgmental confidant. He'll need you as a sounding board as he irons out the wrinkles of his identity crisis — a normal milestone in development. Many youngsters begin a career path based on identification with a parent. It's a starting point, but not usually a trustworthy anchor. Many such youngsters change their minds eventually, since, ultimately, they have to own these choices themselves.

Let's be honest. Most of us would love to see our kids follow our own career paths. Such decisions through the mechanism of identification, however, are often notoriously short-lived.

Lost Bedroom

Q: Carlton, our 18-year-old, just came home for his first weekend trip from college. We forgot to tell him that we had given his room to his 14-year-old brother. I can understand some disappointment, but you'd think we had stuck a knife in his ribs. He was so enraged. What goes?

A: What goes may well be Carlton's place in the family. A teenager's bedroom is less a place than a state of mind. It

Where does he fit in the family now? Should you make new, more lenient rules? A time of growth and readjustment for all.

symbolizes many things: independence, privacy, belonging, and self-identity.

Yes, Carlton should not have been so threatened by the loss of his room. But his overreaction tells me that he's still very much tied to his identity as a member of your family, and this is not a bad thing at all.

And, yes, your forgetting to discuss the issue before you reassigned Carlton's room was a regrettable error. Carlton's room is his special link to the past and present. Make sure he understands that you're not trying to get rid of him — that he now has a new and special place in the family.

Thanksgiving College Vacation

Parents have developmental stages, too. It's a change to be a parent to a young adult rather than a teenager. You can appeal to his new maturity while still maintaining reasonable house rules.

Q: Our 18-year-old son is a college freshman. His Thanksgiving vacation will be his first visit home since he went away to school. He's giving hints in his letters that he expects our old rules to go out the window, e.g., he can stay out late as he wants at college and seems to think he'll do the same at home when he returns. We're reasonable, but it is still our house and we feel that there must be some rules. What would you advise?

A: The first Thanksgiving vacation from college is an important, and sometimes momentous, event. In going away to school, your son not only left his childhood behind in a geographical sense, but he also, at least partially, left it behind in a psychological sense. Young people who are more uncertain about their growth, however, generally face more problems on their return because they tend to overreact: in order to reassure themselves that they are no longer the high school teenager that formerly inhabited your home, they may press your limits (and your tolerance) to the wall. Perhaps your son fits into this category.

You may be able to help him by beating him to the punch! In your next letter you might acknowledge your pride in him, and speculate about how some things will be different for all of you when he returns home at Thanksgiving. Tell him that you recognize that the old house rules no longer apply because he's more grown-up and responsible. Suggest that he talk it over with you and your husband on his return. You want to hear his ideas about curfew, etc.

Yes, there will be a curfew. It is unreasonable for a college student to expect carte blanche at home just because he may have it on campus. As a matter of fact, most young people do not expect it at home. They realize that parents still worry about them at night and that family rules, while hopefully more flexible, still exist.

The key is to handle the matter with sensitivity for the fact that your son has entered a new stage of psychological development (young adulthood), and that he's probably uncertain about his new-found maturity. Try to appeal to this maturity while, at the same time, maintaining reasonable house rules. Give him some slack, but not at the expense of your own sleepless nights.

Your son's Thanksgiving vacation, you see, also marks a new developmental stage for you and your husband. You must become the parents of your son's young adult life, leaving the parents of his teenage years behind. Happy Thanksgiving to all three of you!

Sexual Development

Teenage Pregnancy

Q: Our 17-year-old daughter, Leslie, is six months pregnant. Just when my husband and I were getting over the shock, she's dropped another bomb on us: she plans to have the baby and to raise it. We were sure she'd go along with an adoption, but her new plan is madness. How can we talk sense to her?

A: Teenage pregnancy is a national epidemic. Recent figures indicate a rate of 1,500,000 teenage pregnancies every year in this country.

In fact, the Alan Guttmacher Institute estimates that 1 out of every 10 adolescent girls will have given birth by the time they turn 18, if present trends continue. For Leslie and your family, the epidemic, sadly, has struck home.

Be patient. Leslie must be overwhelmed by conflicting emotions. She'll need lots of love and understanding from you if she's to sort them out.

Why does she want to keep the baby? Some girls do it out of guilt; they feel they can undo the mistake of getting pregnant by becoming a good mother. Other girls, understandably, are repulsed by abortion and even by "giving away" their baby in adoption. Still other girls, seeking revenge, may wear their pregnancy as a red flag in order to get back at Mom and Dad. Perhaps Leslie fits into still another category: the girl who aspires to instant adulthood through maternity. These girls are

Another one of those chilling epidemics you've heard about. It has been estimated that 1 out of 10 adolescent girls will give birth before she reaches 18. The usual result? Two babies in search of a mother.

often experiencing problems in adolescence; by becoming a mother they hope to achieve instant adulthood. Still other girls fall victim to what may be called "Baby Chic"; they are trapped into a fad at their school of having babies. There are a number of other possibilities. Listen. Learn.

Abortion Issue Divides Family

The most divisive social issue of our day. Compromise is very difficult when basic moral, religious, and humanistic values are involved. Just as the battle over abortion rights can divide our society, it can rupture your family — if you let it.

Q: My husband and I are strongly pro-life, anti-abortion. Our daughters, Martha, 17, and Mary, 18, share our values in almost everything except abortion. Both of them recently marched in a pro-choice demonstration. Whenever we try to talk about it, we end up in a messy argument. Neither side can compromise. In fact, Mary, who is away at college, is refusing to come home for her next vacation. I wish I could say it's not worth it, but I can't give up my principles and neither can my husband. Abortion is killing my family.

A: The four of you are allowing the issue of abortion rights to destroy your family. Just as this matter is the single most divisive issue currently facing our nation, it is eating away at the fabric of your own family.

To maintain your family's integrity you'll all need to agree to disagree. Back off. Why let a single issue paralyze the family? There are so many things that bind you together.

I suggest a cooling-off period for all parties. Why not declare abortion rights temporarily off-limits as a topic of conversation? In this way, each of you can maintain your beliefs, and even participate actively in your cause if you choose.

Compromise on this issue is exceedingly difficult. The experts can't seem to do it. So, don't expect it around your own kitchen table. But do try to refrain from personal attack and moralizing. Preserve love, understanding, respect, and communication. That's what will keep your family together when all else seems to be coming apart.

Secondary Virginity?

Can a once sexually active teenager swear off sex until he or she is more ready for it? Absolutely. But they'll need your understanding and guidance.

Q: My 17-year-old daughter, Tracy, recently confided to me that she had a very unhappy sexual relationship with her boyfriend and that now she has decided not to have sex anymore until she's ready for it. I really respect her for this, but is it possible for her to avoid sex?

A: Yes. The notion that once a teenage girl loses her virginity she can't say no is little more than wishful thinking on the part of sexually insecure adolescent boys.

I'd urge you to stay in touch, though, with Tracy. What happened in her relationship? I also respect her choice of abstinence, but I'd want to be sure that she's not repressing some worries and conflicts.

By the way, so-called secondary virginity is not limited to girls. Boys ensnared in the dilemma need the same kind of understanding and guidance.

Cross-Dressing

Q: Darryl, our 17-year-old son, has gone bonkers over the movie *Tootsie*. He thinks that the best way to really appreciate women is to do exactly what Dustin Hoffman did: dress up like a woman and temporarily adopt the feminine role. Last Saturday I caught him putting on some of my make-up. I laughed it off, but yesterday I found a brassiere and panties hidden in one of his drawers. What should I do?

A: I advise you to take this seriously, but not to overreact.

Darryl, as a 17-year-old, is prone to intellectualize his personal conflicts. Hence, any problems that he might have about his own sexual identity may be expressed in global metaphors or in terms of classic movies, like Tootsie.

By all means have a good talk with Darryl. Keep it gentle, understanding — and focused. Be sure to keep the focus not on Dustin, but on Darryl.

If your son persists, or you believe that he has simply taken his cross-dressing underground, by all means seek a consultation with a psychiatrist who specializes in adolescent psychiatry. One tip: habitual cross-dressing accompanied by sexual fantasies, masturbation, or other sexually oriented behavior, especially in a youngster who is struggling with issues of sexual orientation or development, is a strong indicator for psychiatric evaluation.

While Darryl may see himself as *Tootsie II*, we're talking real-life lore, not the movies. I'm concerned.

Many teenage boys experiment innocently with cross-dressing, but when a sexually conflicted late adolescent's habitual cross-dressing is accompanied by sexual fantasies, masturbation, or other sexualized behavior, it is a strong indication for a psychiatric evaluation.

Sexually Transmitted Diseases (STD)

Q: I'm a high school teacher. It's amazing how even my seniors are so naive about gonorrhea and other sexually transmitted diseases. It it a matter of denial? Comments?

About one in four sexually active teenagers will pick up a case of STD before they pick up their high school diplomas.

A: Look at it this way. About one in four sexually active teenagers will pick up a case of STD before they pick up their high school diplomas. In fact, the Center of Disease Control estimates that 2.5 million adolescents contract one of the sexually transmitted diseases each year.

Although you mention gonorrhea, the most common STD among teenagers is now human papilloma virus (HPV). It is very contagious and affects as many as 30% of sexually active adolescents in some areas of the country.

Yes, denial (the it-can't-happen-to-me syndrome) is an ever-present mechanism among teenagers. So is simple lack of information.

So, keep on hitting them with the facts, and remind them that STD can and does happen to youngsters just like them.

My Daughter Has AIDS

While I hate to end this book on a down note, I've concluded with a courageous note from the mother of a 19-year-old girl who contracted AIDS from a one-night fling. Why? AIDS, although among the most deadly matters addressed in these pages, is as preventable, if not more so, than some of the garden variety conflicts of everyday life you've discovered in these chapters. Terri's mother writes to warn other parents and teenagers that "AIDS happens." So get informed, get involved, get in charge. Now more than ever.

Q: AIDS used to be something I read about. It happened in other people's families. Not anymore. My 19-year-old daughter, Terri, has AIDS.

I couldn't believe it when our family doctor broke the news. Terri is a good kid. No drugs. Oh sure, I knew she was sexually active. She wasn't promiscuous, though, and besides, I had met all her boyfriends and they had seemed nice and safe and clean-cut.

Well, it was one of those clean-cut boys who infected my daughter. Terri says that they had sex only once. She has since learned that he is bisexual.

Our family was almost destroyed, but we're starting to bounce back now. Terri herself has a positive outlook and that's why I'm writing to you. We want other girls to know that AIDS *happens*.

A: Yes, AIDS does happen. Although the heterosexual transmission of HIV and the threat to women are often minimized (and sometimes dismissed almost entirely), we know that 4% of all adolescent AIDS cases (1987-1989) were contracted heterosexually.

Thank you for your courageous letter.

Quiz

Let's see how well you're doing at working yourself out of a job. That's right. Your youngster is 17 or older now — just about ready to leave the nest. But this last stage of adolescence is still very important from a developmental standpoint. There are still some finishing touches to be applied. So, try this final quiz and study any questions that you miss. You're almost at the finish line. Don't let up.

1. Your daughter, 18, is a high school senior. She's always been an excellent student (As and Bs) but suddenly her grades are falling. What are the most likely causes? (select all that apply):
    A. She is in love
    B. Drugs
    C. She's unconsciously fearful of the future

2. Your son, 17, has announced that instead of going away to college next year, he's decided to take a year off to "find himself." How should you respond?
    A. Let him go. He's obviously not ready for college
    B. He's just a little uncertain about things. He'll get over it. Insist that he goes to college
    C. Hear him out. Try to understand. Help him, but don't back down: he should go to college as planned

3. Cults are successful in recruiting some late adolescents for the following reasons (select all that apply):
    A. Family atmosphere
    B. Acceptance
    C. Easy answers to complex questions
    D. Physical coercion during recruitment

4. True or False? The adolescent who flaunts his "freedom" when he reaches his eighteenth birthday is very often the one who is most unsure of himself.

5. Late adolescence is normally characterized by? (Select all that apply):
    A. Idealism
    B. Conflict with parents
    C. Search for identity

6. Your son, 17, has been having problems. A psychiatrist has recommended psychotherapy. You should be able to get answers to which of the following questions? (Select all that apply):
    A. What is the diagnosis?
    B. What did he say about his father?
    C. About how long will it take?
    D. How much will it cost?

7. True or False? Most teenagers who commit suicide have made at least one previous unsuccessful attempt.

8. Adolescents are usually attracted to gambling for which of the following reasons? (Select all that apply):
    A. To make money
    B. Risk-taking
    C. Identification with a parent who gambles
    D. Action

9. The late adolescent who is insecure about himself and confused about the world may tend to project his worries onto other people rather than deal with his own problems. This can lead to prejudice. Rearrange the following six steps of prejudice in the order they usually appear:
    A. Avoidance of certain groups
    B. Jokes and racial or ethnic slurs
    C. Organized opposition
    D. Private thoughts
    E. Personal discrimination
    F. Physical attack

10. The incidence of teenage girls giving birth is:
    A. 1%
    B. 5%
    C. 10%
    D. 20%

11. True or False? It is so important for late adolescents to become independent that they should always be encouraged to leave home soon after graduating from high school.

12. A 19-year-old girl who suffers from bulimia would exhibit which of the following signs or symptoms? (Select all that apply):
    A. Binge eating
    B. Weight gain
    C. Weight loss
    D. Self-induced vomiting

13. According to recent research, who usually suffers most when the last child leaves home?
    A. Mothers
    B. Fathers
    C. Grandparents

14. The last major task of adolescent development is:
    A. Independence
    B. Conscience formation
    C. Identity formation
    D. Sexual maturity

15. Your 18-year-old son has just called home, saying that he hates college. He wants to quit. You recall that he's always had a tough time leaving home (i.e., he cried for days when he went to sleep away at camp at age 9, etc.). What should you do?
    A. Tell him to come home for a few days to talk it over
    B. Give him a pep talk. He's a man now. He can handle it
    C. Go to his college for a visit and/or recommend that he sees a counselor

Correct Answers

1) A, B, C; 2) C; 3) A, B, C; 4) True; 5) A, C; 6) A, C, D; 7) True; 8) B, C, D; 9) D, B, A, E, F, C; 10) C; 11) False; 12) A, D; 13) B; 14) C; 15) C

Index

Order Form

Title	Price	Quantity	Total
What To Do Until the Grownup Arrives	US $ 22.50		
1] White Knuckles and Wishful Thinking	22.50		
2] Self-Management in Organizations	19.95		
3] Seven Steps to Peak Performance	12.95		
4] Understanding and Treating Mental Illness	14.95		
5] Crisis: The Journal of Crisis Counseling and Suicide Prevention	39.00		
Subtotal			
Tax: Residents of WA and NY please add 8% sales tax			
Postage & Handling: $3.50 for first item, + 1.00 for each additional one			

Discounts of 20% apply for orders of ten items or more

Hogrefe & Huber Publishers • Seattle Office • Box 2487 • Kirkland, WA 98083
Phone [800] 228-3749

☐ Check enclosed   [ ] Please put me on your mailing list
☐ Credit Card   [ ] Visa   [ ] Mastercard   [ ] AMEX

Card Name_____
Signature_____ Card Number_____
Street Address_____
City_____ State_____ Zip_____ Phone_____

1] A practical guide to preventing relapse in alcoholism and other addictions, written by George DuWors, a clinician in the Los Angeles area with 20 years experience in this field. [1992, 288 pages, hardcover].

2] A guidebook for employee and manager survival in an era of mergers, buyouts, and uncertainty in the workplace. Focuses on how to clarify and maintain one's basic values while being highly productive in stressful environments, when the values of the larger organization are often not equal to one's own. Written by three consultants to major industries who also teach industrial psychology at the University of Quebec. [1993, 250 pages, hardcover].

3] A spiral-bound manual for applying important psychological principles to achieving success in athletic endeavors. Written by Dr Richard Suinn, an advisor the US Olympic Team, and chairman of the psychology department at Colorado St University. [1987, 64 pages, softbound].

4] This is the first book produced by the Canadian Psychiatric Association, and it describes the most important mental illnesses, and our currently best known approaches to dealing with them. It was written by a team of specialists headed by Dr Cleghon of the Clarke Institute in Toronto. [1991, 250 pages, softbound].

5] A new journal for crisis center directors and staff, as well as a wide variety of counselors and researchers. It focuses on new techniques, experiences from diverse environments, suicide prevention, and clear explanations of new research results. Features regular columns on crisis center management, suicide in the elderly, crisis hot lines, jail suicide, and legal/regulatory issues. [Quarterly, 48 pages per issue].